SPEAKING OF GOD

The Eerdmans Ekklesia Series

Editors

Michael L. Budde
Stephen E. Fowl

The Eerdmans Ekklesia Series explores matters of Christianity and discipleship across a wide expanse of disciplines, church traditions, and issues of current and historical concern.

The series is published in cooperation with the Ekklesia Project, a network of persons for whom "being a Christian" is seen to be the primary identity and allegiance for believers — superseding and ordering the claims on offer by the modern state, market, racial and ethnic groups, and other social forces. The Ekklesia Project emphasizes the importance of the church as a distinctive community in the world, called to carry into contemporary society the priorities and practices of Jesus Christ as conveyed in the Gospels.

The Ekklesia Series will draw from the broad spectrum of the Christian world — Protestantism of many traditions, Roman Catholicism, Anabaptism, Orthodoxy — in exploring critical issues in theology, history, social and political theory, biblical studies, and world affairs. The Series editors are Stephen E. Fowl, Professor and Chair, Department of Theology at Loyola College in Baltimore; and Michael L. Budde, Professor of Political Science and Catholic Studies and Chair, Department of Political Science, at DePaul University in Chicago.

Additional information about the Ekklesia Project, including submission guidelines for the Eerdmans Ekklesia book series, may be found at www.ekklesiaproject.org.

SPEAKING OF GOD

Theology, Language, and Truth

D. Stephen Long

WILLIAM B. EERDMANS PUBLISHING COMPANY
GRAND RAPIDS, MICHIGAN / CAMBRIDGE, U.K.

© 2009 D. Stephen Long

Published 2009 by
Wm. B. Eerdmans Publishing Co.
2140 Oak Industrial Drive N.E., Grand Rapids, Michigan 49505 /
P.O. Box 163, Cambridge CB3 9PU U.K.

Printed in the United States of America

15 14 13 12 11 10 09   7 6 5 4 3 2 1

Library of Congress Cataloging-in-Publication Data

Long, D. Stephen, 1960-
Speaking of God: theology, language, and truth / D. Stephen Long.
    p.   cm. — (Eerdmans Ekklesia series)
Includes bibliographical references.
ISBN 978-0-8028-4572-6 (pbk.: alk. paper)
1. Philosophical theology. 2. Truth — Religious aspects — Christianity.
3. Truth. 4. Language and languages.   I. Title.

BT40.L585 2009

230.01 — dc22

2008048957

www.eerdmans.com

Contents

v

CONTENTS

Preface

This work attempts to address questions of truth, their relationship to theology, and their political significance. It develops more fully one of the final sections of an earlier work, *The Divine Economy,* which was called "Speaking of God." I hope it also provides the doctrinal assumptions behind my earlier *The Goodness of God.* This work also assumes those earlier works. They are the only answer to the question that many readers might have in reading this work, that is, *what does this account of truth look like in practice, in everyday life?*

Early on, I decided that to pursue questions of truth in theology well would require listening to what the philosophers were saying about truth and language. Cristina Lafonte, professor of philosophy at Northwestern University, gave me permission to sit in on her doctoral seminar on truth, for which I remain grateful. I learned a great deal, but clearly not enough; what the philosophers are saying about truth is voluminous and contested. A scholar could dedicate her or his entire work to pursuing these philosophical questions, and I make no pretense to expertise on those matters. Charles Taylor, Board of Trustees Professor of Law and Philosophy at Northwestern, also kindly consented to let me sit in on his course entitled "After Epistemology." He also graciously gave me permission to quote from his unpublished manuscript on that theme in this work. I am grateful for the help these philosophers were willing to give to a theologian. Of course neither Professor Taylor nor Professor Lafonte can be held accountable for the philosophical errors the present work undoubtedly commits, nor be responsible for the claims it makes.

Although I offer a critique of fallibilism in the final chapter of this work, let me reassure the reader that I make no claims for infallibility in what is presented here. I hope that even my errors might contribute to a conversation that will invite theologians and philosophers more boldly to speak of God in and outside the university, and in and outside the church, while at the same time letting that boldness be the very source of a liberality that offers gracious hospitality for those not convinced. We find ourselves at the end of a modernity and postsecularity where all too easily held epistemological assumptions either cordoned speaking of God off to an ineffable realm or reduced speaking of God to speaking about ourselves. The justification for this was often moral. Liberalism and/or humanism seemed to require it. We no longer need to be bound by those assumptions. For the sake of a truthful politics we *must* no longer be bound to them. The historicist claim that language is always contextual led to improper conclusions about the limits of theological knowledge and the end of metaphysics. These conclusions became dogmas in too much modern theology, which is why the conversation needs to be expanded. My aim in this work is to contribute to the broadening of the theological conversation.

I owe many debts for the help I received with this work. Garrett-Evangelical Theological Seminary provided me with a yearlong sabbatical without which the research for this work would not have been possible. James K. A. Smith and John Wright made important criticisms that saved me from further errors. Stanley Hauerwas used an early version of it in a doctoral seminar at Duke Divinity School and offered wise counsel on how to restructure it. Jeff Conklin-Miller's critical evaluation from that seminar was most helpful. A number of graduate students from Garrett-Evangelical agreed to gather for lunch at my home during the summer of 2007 and discuss this work. I am grateful to Cynthia Anderson, Rusty Brian, Andrew Brubaker Kaethler, Jimmy Cooper, Jeremiah Gibbs, Andrew Guffey, Geoff Holsclaw, Jason Knott, Chanon Ross, and Eric Speece for not only reading part or all of the manuscript and presenting insightful critiques, but also for enjoying table fellowship during my final days at Garrett-Evangelical, where I was privileged to teach such fine students. Jimmy Cooper consistently challenges me to draw more fully on Scripture in writing and teaching. I appreciate the counsel. I also have responded to him that this entire work is, in one sense, nothing but a commentary on John 14:6. I'm not sure he is convinced. My colleagues George Kalantzis and Brent Waters at Garrett-Evangelical were important conversation partners throughout the long process of working on this manuscript. Finally, I am grateful to Stephen Fowl and Michael Budde, editors of the Eerdmans Ekklesia Series, for their help in seeing this manuscript into publication.

Chapter 1, part 4, "Analogia entis," was published earlier as "The Way of Aquinas," *Studies in Christian Ethics* (SAGE publications) 19, no. 3 (December 2006): 339-57.

Introduction

Truth, like goodness, is inescapable. Life would be impossible without its ever-present reality in language, thought, and action. Practical knowledge demands its foundational work, but theoretical knowledge consistently falters and falls short before it. Truth is inescapable, but explaining what it is escapes us again and again. It seems straightforward; as Aristotle put it, "To say of what is that it is, and of what is not that it is not, is true. To say of what is that it is not, or of what is not that it is, is false." Would that it were so simple. A host of questions immediately arise. What do we mean by 'say'? What is 'is'? What is its negation? How does what we say relate to what is? Theological knowledge of truth requires wading through philosophical and theological debates on language, ontology, and God that manifest how much more complex it is than any simple definition could acknowledge. Faced with the task of setting forth the theoretical account of truth's practical inescapability can easily lead us to the posture of Pilate where, throwing up our hands, we ask without expecting an answer, "What is truth?" even when its reality stands right before us.

If truth is inescapable, why do philosophers and theologians make it so difficult to understand? Perhaps it is not the theologians and philosophers who do this, but truth itself. Truth is inescapable because we exist within it; it does not exist within us. We cannot master it like a tool or turn it into an instrument to use at our discretion. We cannot stand outside of it and reduce it to a few succinct propositions. Therefore truth's inescapability does not mean anyone has an immediate awareness of it. Nor does it deny the noetic effects of sin, even 'total depravity.' In fact, it makes our falsity and evil all the more damnable. Unlike truth and goodness, they are unnecessary. They do not have to be, and yet they are. We can be without falsity and evil, but we cannot be without truth and goodness.

Much of contemporary theology and philosophy manufactures borders to prevent us from explaining what everyone knows: truth, like goodness, is inescapable. This occurs for good reasons. We are suspicious of anyone who claims unvarnished access to truth and fearful of the political consequences such truth claims produce. Nevertheless, we should not be tempted to abandon a genuine inquiry about this everyday reality, especially the 'metaphysical' question, "What is truth?" just because philosophical attempts to render our practical knowledge that truth is inescapable so often fail or we fear its political consequences. Nor should it prevent us from considering theological answers; for the inevitable failure of philosophy to render truth fully comprehensible is not in the end its failure, but its promise. It is an opening for something unmanageable, the reception of truth as a gift more so than an accomplishment.

This gift does not diminish philosophy; it strengthens it. It does not reduce philosophy to theology, nor divide them into equivocal disciplines that must then be correlated or placed in a dialectical relation. The 'excess' found in theology's exorbitant claims completes philosophy and makes it necessary. The paradigm for their relationship is the incarnation. This is what Pilate refuses to see and therefore dismisses with a question for which he expects no answer. His question is not a genuine inquiry after truth. But every worshiping Christian takes a different posture before Jesus. He or she tacitly or expressly believes the incarnation is true, and this requires a philosophical inquiry. We must pursue the question, what is this truth we find ourselves already acknowledging every time we worship? Because of this, theology needs philosophy. It needs to elaborate the reason assumed in this basic confession. Worshiping Christians tacitly or expressly acknowledge that truth is the Incarnate One, which also means philosophy needs theology. Truth is not a product of human reasoning, yet human reasoning presumes truth. It comes as a gift.

The incarnation is true. Truth is the incarnation. These basic theological propositions offer insight into how we speak of God, relate faith and reason, pursue theology within a common and publicly accessible language, and can recover truth, even the truth of politics, which are the themes of the five chapters of this work. These propositions are not abstract, speculative ideals. They only make explicit the consensus found in

2

the common act of Christian worship. In that sense, this work is a 'phenomenology' of sorts, beginning with, and growing out of a social location that is both particular and universal at the same time. Every Sunday (and throughout the week as well) people universally gather at a specific location and hear someone exclaim, "The Word of God!" or "The body and blood of Christ!" and seldom does anyone fall down laughing. This is an odd phenomenon that could elicit various and sundry explanations. It could be a sign of moral and intellectual failure on the part of those who participate. Perhaps they do not yet know that such claims cannot constitute genuine knowledge? Yet the people who participate in these activities seldom throw up their hands, interrupt the goings-on and protest, "You are violating the epistemological limits that constitute proper human knowledge," or, "You are using language improperly," or, "What method of verification do you have to prove these claims?" Instead, they appear untroubled that the language used might not accomplish its purpose of truthful speech about God. What renders this action intelligible, even if some participating in it would fail to acknowledge it in speech, is the transcendental reality of the incarnation.

These phenomena implicitly make claims about Jesus that must be, and have been, made explicit in Christian doctrine, primarily in the doctrine of the incarnation. This doctrine is no second order claim. It is present in, and to, the primary act which generates it. Without it, Christian worship becomes unintelligible. First and foremost the truly human Jesus is worshiped as God. Christian worship makes little sense if someone denies this claim embedded in these phenomena. In fact, without the dogma of the incarnation worship would be impossible and lead to such an inarticulate speech about God that Christianity could not be sustained. Nevertheless, neither the human voice nor bread and wine themselves are mistaken for God's word and presence. God is not a creature. Hans Urs von Balthasar understood well this relationship between the incarnation and our language of God when he wrote, "A God who would be expressed to the end in finite words (and deeds!) would no longer be God but an idol. But a God who did not wish to give himself away to this extreme end, but withheld a piece of himself from us and for himself would also no longer be our God: here too he would be an idol."[1] Theology succeeds when it ob-

---

1. Balthasar, *Theo-Logic II: The Truth of God*, trans. Adrian Walker (San Franciso: Ignatius, 2004), p. 279.

serves the logic of the incarnation where God gives himself fully in finite words and deeds and still confesses God cannot be exhaustively expressed in finite words and deeds.

A second claim, then, is that even though the man Jesus is God, humanity is not divinity. This is consistent with the Chalcedonian definition set forth by the church fathers, which was already explicit in the church's worship. It remains the only way to express adequately these phenomena without attributing a moral or intellectual failure to those who participate in them.

Given these phenomena, what might they teach us about language, truth, and speech about God? For one, as Denys Turner puts it, they assume the possibility of "logical inference across incommensurables." Much as when we see Jesus we worship God, we likewise see bread and wine, hear a human voice, and find in them God's presence. While simultaneously acknowledging that creatures are 'incommensurable' to God, we logically infer divinity from humanity without confusing the two. Does this imply a 'metaphysics of presence' that, according to many postmoderns, has come to an end? If that term means 'the coincidence of being and meaning,' then Christian theologians are hard-pressed to deny they perpetuate such a metaphysics. The risen Jesus, whose body no longer knows limitations of space and time, is a 'transcendental signified.' He is the 'ground' that ensures the coincident of being and meaning in the signs of Scripture and sacrament. As Kevin Hart states it, "Like other signs, Christ is both signifier and signified, body and soul. But Christ is also unlike other signs for here the signified — God — is perfectly expressed in the signifier. He is at once inside and outside the sign system; since Christ is God, what He signifies is signified in and of itself; He is what Derrida calls a 'transcendental signified.'"[2] Although Hart makes this confession, he also counsels Christian theologians to adopt Derrida's deconstruction as a set of practices that remedies a theology of metaphysics. Why heed this counsel? If Christ is the 'metaphysics of presence,' why should theologians join in the postmodern angst about it?

Does the logic of the incarnation entail metaphysics? This depends on what we mean by 'metaphysics,' and like all terms its meaning will be found in its use. Philosophers and theologians have diverse, overlapping,

---

2. Kevin Hart, *The Trespass of the Sign: Deconstruction, Theology and Philosophy* (New York: Fordham University Press, 2000), p. 8.

and conflicting uses for the term 'metaphysics.' The analytic philosopher Tarski, accused by others of still doing 'metaphysics,' warned that the term had become nothing but 'philosophical invective.' His own semantic theory of truth eschewed metaphysics, but he never claimed that theory could meet every philosophical need related to truth. In particular, he suggested, it could not meet 'aesthetic' or perhaps 'religious' needs.[3] For these we still need metaphysics, which could mean 'a general theory of objects (ontology),' or the opposite of empiricism.[4] On the contrary, Kevin Hart finds 'metaphysics' to be the problem within much of the tradition of Christian theology for it inevitably thinks and speaks of God in terms of 'cause,' 'ground,' or 'source' and leads to ontotheology. Deconstruction assists theology in 'overcoming' metaphysics, but it does so by recognizing that metaphysics cannot be overcome. Hart claims, "The very question 'What is beyond metaphysics' repeats the instituting question of philosophy, 'What is . . . ?,' and so the question turns out to manifest the problem."[5] We cannot finally overcome or move beyond metaphysics, but we can use deconstruction within metaphysics to "disable the totalization of a text by metaphysics."[6] For Hart, the error of metaphysics is that it totalizes texts within a philosophical account of origin, ground, and source. He points in the direction of a non-metaphysical theology similar to Barth's, but finally finds even Barth insufficient and opts for a mystical, negative theology in order to avoid the totalizing claims of metaphysics that inevitably lead to ontotheology.

Merold Westphal, like Hart, worries that too much of theology remains caught within the ontotheology Heidegger identified.[7] Heidegger famously critiqued ontotheology where God is understood as the causa sui — the self-caused cause who is the origin of all being. "Before the causa sui," Heidegger wrote, "man can neither fall to his knees in awe nor can he play music and dance before this god."[8] Heidegger and Westphal play the

3. Tarski, "The Semantic Conception of Truth," *Philosophy and Phenomenological Research* 4 (1944): 370.

4. Tarski, "The Semantic Conception of Truth," p. 365.

5. Hart, *Trespass of the Sign*, p. 231.

6. Hart, *Trespass of the Sign*, p. 230.

7. Kant first used the term 'ontotheology' to explain proofs for the existence of God grounded in being and thus also in 'pure reason.' He did not mean the term to be pejorative. See Kevin Hart, *Postmodernism: A Beginner's Guide* (Oxford: Oneworld, 2004), p. 164.

8. Merold Westphal, *Overcoming Ontotheology: Toward a Postmodern Christian Faith*

god of the philosophers against the God of the Holy Scriptures. They both follow in a tradition of what has become known as the 'dehellenizing' of the Christian tradition. Westphal identifies this tradition with Luther, Pascal, Kierkegaard, and Barth.[9] The so-called 'end of metaphysics' and its correlative 'overcoming ontotheology' is linked with this theological tradition of 'dehellenization.' It tends to juxtapose philosophy against theology, a putative static and totalizing Greek thought against a dynamic, open Hebrew thought. This has led to a separation between reason and faith such that faith needs to give no 'grounds,' no 'reasons' for its existence. Dividing reason and faith tends toward 'fideism.' Thus, the 'end of metaphysics,' 'overcoming theology,' 'dehellenization,' and 'fideism' share a conceptual family resemblance. Like all families, the resemblances here are exceedingly complex and cannot be nicely sorted out.

The arguments in this work assume with Hart and Westphal that ontotheology is a theological problem. But contra them, it makes no effort to 'overcome ontotheology' by deconstructing, or bringing to an end, metaphysics. It does not endorse dehellenizing the gospel because no such problem of hellenization exists in the first place. In his preface to *The Spirit of Early Christian Thought*, Robert Louis Wilken takes on the 'dehellenization' thesis that preoccupied so much of twentieth-century theology. He writes,

> The notion that the development of early Christian thought represented a hellenization of Christianity has outlived its usefulness. The time has come to bid a fond farewell to the ideas of Adolf von Harnack, the nineteenth-century historian of dogma whose thinking has influenced the interpretation of early Christian thought for more than a century. It will become clear in the course of this book that a more apt expression would be the Christianization of Hellenism, though that phrase does not capture the originality of Christian thought nor the debt owed to Jewish ways of thinking and to the Jewish Bible.[10]

(New York: Fordham University Press, 2001) p. 2. Heidegger, *Identity and Difference*, trans. Joan Stambaugh (New York: Harper & Row, 1969), p. 72.

9. Westphal, *Overcoming Ontotheology*, p. 18.

10. Robert Louis Wilken, *The Spirit of Early Christian Thought* (New Haven: Yale University Press, 2003), p. xvi.

Wilken then makes a compelling case for how Christ becomes the theologic that undergirds even 'metaphysical' claims by the church fathers. Here metaphysics is understood less as a 'totalizing' endeavor that captures divinity within human philosophical concepts and more of a recognition of the porosity between philosophy and theology.

Likewise Janet Soskice demonstrates how the so-called metaphysical 'attributes' of God that so many modern theologians have questioned — existence, simplicity, perfection, limitlessness (infinity), eternity, immutability, and impassibility — are less indebted to a Greek metaphysics and more explications of the giving of the divine name in Holy Scripture. That the giving of the name found resonance in Greek metaphysics was not something which Christians should fear, but something for which they should rejoice. Philosophy confirms Scripture, but it does so in an odd way. It does so by recognizing the limitations of what philosophy can achieve and thus philosophy only confirms Scripture when it remains open to the porosity between reason and faith. This means that these 'names' signify less a hellenization and more a recognition that what Scripture and Christian tradition teaches can be affirmed by human wisdom. This is a position that both Catholics and Anabaptists share. John Paul II made this claim in *Fides et Ratio* and John Howard Yoder stated something quite similar when he said that the Christian witness works "with the grain of the universe."[11]

In contrast to Hart and Westphal, Matthew Levering claims that the "renewal of the theology of the triune God requires that theologians reject the alleged opposition between scriptural modes and metaphysical modes of reflection without conflating the two modes."[12] Levering follows Giles Hibbert (and Thomas Aquinas) in finding metaphysics to be an enquiry that, beginning with creatures, moves beyond them. Metaphysics is that discipline that allows words to signify such that they are "able to point beyond themselves beyond the sphere and context of their own immediate origin."[13] Here metaphysics may not be able to provide proper verification or falsification as some analytic philosophy deems necessary for a statement to have a meaning; metaphysics is not preoccupied with questions of epistemic justification, but it is not so much a 'totalizing' discourse as one

---

11. For a compelling argument that brings John Paul II and John Howard Yoder together, see Stanley Hauerwas's *With the Grain of the Universe* (Grand Rapids: Brazos, 2001).

12. Matthew Levering, *Scripture and Metaphysics: Aquinas and the Renewal of Trinitarian Theology* (Oxford: Blackwell, 2004), p. 2.

13. Levering, *Scripture and Metaphysics*, p. 5.

always forestalling any closure of limiting the meaning of a sign to its context — including the sign that is the human creature. For this reason, metaphysics fosters a genuine humanism. Thomas Guarino issues a similar call for theologians to recover this kind of a metaphysics.[14]

The philosopher William Desmond recognizes that the 'end of metaphysics' is less a discovery than the invention of a secular program. Desmond questions whether we are 'postmetaphysical' and asks,

> Is it evident that we know what metaphysics is? . . . What space is there that post-metaphysical thinking might occupy, since all thinking, whether it attends to it or not, whether it knows or acknowledges it as such, is informed by basic presuppositions about, and orientations toward, the meaning of what is 'to be'? If this is so, to be postmetaphysical is to make a metaphysical claim, in the sense that some such basic presuppositions and orientations inform this claim too.[15]

But like Hart, Desmond avoids any metaphysics of totalization where everything slavishly serves 'Being' or where it authorizes an absolute, immanent politics. In fact, this is what he fears occurs in much putatively 'postmetaphysical' thought on both the 'totalitarian left' and the 'capitalist right.'[16] But metaphysics, he suggests, is 'beyond servility and sovereignty.' Desmond points in an important direction that will be assumed and examined throughout this work. Metaphysics implies a politics and vice versa; it is neither an other worldly nor ideal discourse.

Desmond critiques Nietzsche's proclamation of the end of metaphysics as little more than a criticism of a 'cartoon version' of Platonism where metaphysics supposedly "deserts the world here for the beyond world."[17] This offers another use of metaphysics where it becomes the

---

14. Thomas Guarino, *Foundations of Systematic Theology* (New York: T&T Clark, 2005).

15. William Desmond, "Neither Servility nor Sovereignty: Between Metaphysics and Politics," in *Theology and the Political: The New Debate,* ed. Creston Davis, John Milbank, and Slavoj Žižek (Durham, N.C.: Duke University Press, 2005), pp. 153-54.

16. William Desmond, "Neither Servility nor Sovereignty," p. 171.

17. This caricature of metaphysics and its supposed end has a political consequence: "The loss of the beyond of metaphysics, as going with the immanent absolutization of the political, tends to the loss of the wisdom of the immanent that is the genuine art of the political, a wisdom that lives by its worldly discernment of the relative." Desmond, "Neither Servility nor Sovereignty," pp. 155, 158.

'mirror of nature' such that what is in the ideal mirror is the real that supposedly grounds the 'signs' that appear in nature. In contrast to this, Desmond argues, the 'meta' in metaphysics can mean both 'in the midst' as well as 'beyond.' It works in the middle, in the inevitable porosity within a supposed secure immanence. Metaphysics is the beyond that only works in the middle, opening up a secularized immanence to an excess it cannot contain.

What is metaphysics? In this brief overview we find at least five answers, or five uses, for the term. First, metaphysics is a philosophical invective used against an imprecise use of language, which speaks of being or beings for which there can be neither verification nor falsification (metaphysics 1). Second, metaphysics is a totalizing discourse that presents Being as origin, cause, and goal and thinks everything within its structure (metaphysics 2). Third, metaphysics is the inevitable opening of a sign that exceeds its context (metaphysics 3). Fourth, metaphysics is the beyond that interrupts immanence 'in the middle' (metaphysics 4). Fifth, metaphysics is a beyond that secures the presence of any sign such that the sign is unnecessary. It is an objective, universal validation where a sign corresponds to a reality such that the reality could be known without the sign. In fact, the reality secures the sign and not vice versa (metaphysics 5). (Metaphysics 5 is the 'cartoon Platonism' post-metaphysical philosophy critiques and which can still be found in some post-Tridentine Catholic versions of the 'analogia entis.' Metaphysics 3 and 4 are also versions of the 'analogia entis.')

One need not choose among these options; in fact, they are not different options for thinking about metaphysics. They overlap in complex ways. For instance, metaphysics 1 is itself a form of metaphysics — nominalism. Yet the nominalism of metaphysics 1 shares a similar form to the realism in metaphysics 5. Both offer a complete picture as to how knowledge and truth function. The latter secures language to an objective and universal metaphysical ground. The former still assumes that if we were to have the truth of language it would look like this, but we do not have it. Thus it reduces both to a thoroughgoing immanence. Metaphysics 3 and 4 are quite different from 1 and 2, but strikingly similar to each other. They do not stand in opposition to metaphysics 2 even though it presents itself as 'postmetaphysical.' Deconstruction may be a metaphysics that critiques metaphysics 1 and 5 while finding an ally in metaphysics 3 and 4 inasmuch as it does not demand a thoroughgoing immanence that rejects truth. The point is not to choose among these but to recognize the inevitability of metaphysics and work within its proper scope recognizing the pitfalls into which either an unqualified endorsement of metaphysics or its facile rejection easily leads, the chief three being that we divide faith from reason, reject ontotheology and thereby falsely assume we have rejected metaphysics, or find no relationship between the god of the philosophers and the God of Holy Scripture and wrongly think theology can proceed without philosophy.

Karl Barth's theology could easily lead us to think we can do theology without metaphysics or philosophy. In fact, he wrote, "The great temptation and danger consists in this, that the theologian will actually become what he seems to be — a philosopher."[18] In this sense, Barth's take on metaphysics only construes it as a version of metaphysics 1 or possibly metaphysics 2. It is an invective or a threat. His critique of the Roman Catholic 'analogia entis' 'deconstructs' any philosophy of being that seeks to subordinate the logic of the incarnation to its own totalizing logic. Contemporary currents within Roman Catholic and evangelical theology draw deeply on metaphysics 5. They suggest that without a prior commitment to metaphysical objectivism we cannot think or speak adequately of the logic of the incarnation. Some truth exists in both positions. Barth's position has its proper place against some but not all Catholic versions of the relationship between theology and philosophy, especially post-Tridentine exaggerations as to what reason could accomplish.[19] The Catholic position seeks to secure the importance of truth against the constructivism set forth in much modern epistemology. Either position may have a salutary use, but neither is sufficient by itself.

Nevertheless, metaphysics 5 represents a greater threat to a proper relationship between faith and reason than Barth's critique of metaphysics, for it assumes a political or social world known without the incarnation. As Barth recognized in Harnack and Henri de Lubac in neoscholasticism, this seemingly generous position has negative political consequences. It contributed to liberal Protestantism's accommodation to Germany's aggressive war policy in World War I and Roman Catholic accommodation

18. Cited in Andrew Moore's *Realism and Christian Faith: God, Grammar, and Meaning* (Cambridge: Cambridge University Press, 2003), p. v.

19. Yet Barth was also well aware that Catholic theology, and in particular Aquinas, did not posit a nature outside of grace, and this still led him to oppose the 'analogia entis.'

to Vichy France. These are lessons that should make us take note.[20] On the one hand, this work is deeply influenced by Barth. His claim that "revelation conditions all things without itself being conditioned" is the most reasonable explication of the logic of the incarnation in contemporary theology. He taught us to be suspicious of a philosophical ground for theology because it rendered God's own speech superfluous to what we know by means other than revelation.[21] By 'revelation' he meant the manifestation of God's full presence in Jesus of Nazareth. George Hunsinger rightly states that Barth presents "one of the most fully elaborated Chalcedonian Christologies ever to have appeared in Christian doctrine."[22] On the other hand, the reasonableness of Barth's claim must be affirmed by human wisdom even in its 'secular' form. Thus this work is also indebted to Hans Urs von Balthasar's claim that "without philosophy there can be no theology." This work proceeds then under what could appear to be a contradiction. It affirms Barth's recognition that philosophy represents "the greatest temptation and danger" to the theologian and Balthasar's recognition that theology cannot proceed without philosophy. How can it affirm both?

The difference between Barth and Balthasar should not be overstated or understated. Balthasar also wrote, "Christology gives an account of an event that cannot be made subject to any universal law but that subjects all other laws (regulating the relationship between God and the creature, that is) to its own uniqueness." Thus he rejected any method where "philosophical laws devised beforehand" were then applied "as presuppositions to Christology."[23] Nevertheless, Barth's 'Nein' remains a bulwark against any

20. This is not to suggest that an orthodox Christology guarantees a proper moral or political response. That could not be defended; too many counterexamples are readily available. It only calls into question the assumption that for the sake of political or moral relevance we must be willing to revise basic and exclusive Christological themes.

21. Nicholas Wolterstorff challenges whether Barth truly allows for God to speak and he offers an interesting critique of the ways Barth fails to allow for a proper divine discourse. However, Wolterstorff's argument is theistic, not Christological, and thus he defends divine discourse outside the dogma of the incarnation by making God a member of the community of speakers, which leads one to wonder what the incarnation does which God did not already do? See Wolterstorff, *Divine Discourse: Philosophical Reflections on the Claim that God Speaks* (Cambridge: Cambridge University Press, 1995).

22. George Hunsinger, "Karl Barth's Christology: Its Basic Chalcedonian Character," in *The Cambridge Companion to Karl Barth,* ed. John Webster (Cambridge: Cambridge University Press, 2000), p. 129.

23. Balthasar, *Theo-Logic II: The Truth of God,* p. 311.

easy reconciliation between his Christological starting point and a Catholic 'analogia entis' even properly understood.[24] How can Balthasar suggest both positions? Can Barth and Balthasar be reconciled? Attempts at answers to these questions unfold in the following chapters by way of a discussion of the relation between faith and reason, theology and philosophy, the divine name(s) and metaphysics, and truth and the incarnation. It also assumes the correctness of two claims John Paul II made in *Fides et Ratio,* which must be kept together. First, human wisdom properly ordered will confirm Scripture and tradition. Second, a "dangerous discord" between faith and reason emerged at the end of the Middle Ages that continues into modernity. Both sides of John Paul II's teaching must be remembered. If we remember both sides, we will see that both Balthasar and Barth recognized what John Paul II set forth. I think the interplay between Barth and Balthasar remains one of the most fruitful for theology and the future of a unified church. It will be a shame if we train a generation of theologians, laity, pastors, and priests who cannot enter into that conversation.

Also essential to the argument in this work is Wittgenstein's private language argument. It helps us understand philosophical reason. In so doing it reminds us that all '. . . logy,' including theology, cannot be a private language. Theology proceeds using the same sign system as philosophy. Thus it cannot, nor should it be tempted to try to, escape philosophy. Reason is only 'conveyed' through language and thus it is always found in the particularity that language inevitably is (a metaphysical claim to be sure). As Andrew Moore persuasively argues, "Rationality is exemplified in particular practices of human conduct; there are family resemblances between them but no universal core feature that can be abstracted from those diverse practices and used as a neutral canon of rationality across all disciplines of art, skill and intellect."[25] But what is the inevitable particularity of language? How does it give us a more robust insight into 'rationality'? This will be a very different account of rationality than modernity's 'classical foundationalism.' It assumes true knowledge must be self-evident or incorrigibly designated by the empirical representation of a sign to an object or a valid inference from one of these two. This is a method of verification preoccupied with epistemic justification. It gives the conditions that some modern philosophers thought were necessary for language to have

24. I am indebted to Jason Knott for continually pointing this out to me.
25. Moore, *Realism and Christian Faith,* p. 126.

meaning. If this is what language must be in order to be true knowledge, then theology and metaphysics can only be 'fideistic' from the beginning, for they can never pass this epistemic test. But if so, then the game is rigged in advance.

William Abraham helps move us beyond this rigged game. Rather than beginning with epistemic justification through some method and then proceeding to state what is, theologians and philosophers are obliged first to tell us what is and then explain how it might be justified, recognizing that the ability or inability to justify does not logically entail that we do not know what is. This is Abraham's "platitude" that "particularism is to be preferred over methodism." As he puts it, "The default position is not that we know nothing until we can show that we can know something, but that we know far more than we are able to show that we know. This is the great merit of particularism."[26]

The emphasis on a methodism demanding high doctrines of epistemic justification produced an unwarranted charge of 'fideism' in much of modern theology and a theological neglect for boldly stating what is. 'Fideism' primarily emerges as a criticism after classical foundationalism. If Moore and Abraham are correct about rationality, then 'fideism' may be a near impossibility (which makes it all the stranger that Moore refers to his own method as 'dialectical fideism').[27] Classical foundationalist accounts of rationality produce fideism because they claim to know what can be justified and what cannot with a dogmatic certainty. But they do produce a fideism where some theologians deny epistemic content to faith.

---

26. Abraham, *Crossing the Threshold of Divine Revelation* (Grand Rapids: Eerdmans, 2006), p. 33. Although his work is ambiguous in its relationship to justified belief, Abraham would seem to follow Linda Zagzebski and others in claiming that knowledge is much more than justified belief. Zagzebski wrote, "Virtually all philosophers now and in the past have agreed that knowledge is more than true belief." Zagzebski, *Virtues of the Mind* (Cambridge: Cambridge University Press, 1996), p. 301. Abraham's work also resonates with Zagzebski's work when she treats "intellectual virtue" as a concept "deeper" than the "justifiability of a belief." The latter becomes derivative of the former and thus "normative epistemology" becomes a "branch of ethics." Zagzebski, *Virtues of the Mind*, pp. 2, xv. If we replace Zagzebski's intellectual virtues with the theological virtues, especially the virtue of faith, do we get Abraham's position? Zagzebski writes, "The nature of wisdom may be elusive, but it is clear that whatever it is, wisdom is an epistemic value qualitatively different from the piling up of beliefs that have the property of justification, warrant or certainty. . . . Wisdom . . . is a matter of grasping the whole of reality." *Virtues of the Mind*, p. 50.

27. Moore, *Realism and Christian Faith*, p. 133.

Faith and reason become distinguished from each other, policed by a rigid barricade that divides them. Such an account of reason and fideism are but two sides of the same coin, much as metaphysics 1 and 5 are. We only need fear fideism when we assume language traps us like a fly in a bottle, in an immanent, historical context of signification that can never exceed itself. This is the basis for the rejection of metaphysics in metaphysics 1 and the fear of language in metaphysics 5. It is also the tacit assumption in much of modern theology. In fact, it functions as an enthymeme.

Much of modern theology has become too predictable. It begins with the criticism that traditional language about God refused to recognize the sociology of our knowledge, and therefore worked without attention to its historical context. Then it claims that we now (usually thanks to Feuerbach) recognize our speaking about God is always limited by its socio-historical context. Because no one can speak of God from some ahistorical vantage point, all speaking of God is restricted by its historical and social situation. So the syllogism goes like this:

1. No neutral, universal standpoint exists from which anyone can speak of God.
2. All speaking of God emerges from a particular social location.
3. Therefore, all language of God is limited to its historical context.

Of course the third point does not follow from the first two, which can both be affirmed without the epistemological claim of 3. It is only a logical consequence with the hidden or assumed premise that we know a priori what the limits to language are. The enthymeme is that language traps us in a historical situation like a fly in a bottle. This is a metaphysical claim because it tells us what 'is'; it gives us an ontology without acknowledging it as such. It is an ontology unwarranted from the assumed premises. Theology opens up these premises to something other than the third claim.

The first two points affirm what we learn from the incarnation. They witness to the importance of the Creator-creature distinction in Christian theology; humanity is not divinity. As creatures we are timeful, historical beings who neither can nor should desire to escape that historicity. We have no neutral, universal ahistorical vantage point from which we can speak of God. If this is true, it calls into question metaphysics 5. But to move from this claim to then assert that all speaking of God is *limited* to its historical and social location as metaphysics 1 suggests is to deny the incarnation; for it also states that the eternal is found in the historical, the infinite in the finite. The incarnation tells us that Jesus, the socio-historical person, is God even though divinity is not humanity. If the incarnation is true, then the 'postmodern' recognition that no one has an ahistorical location for her or his rationality does not need to trap us within some immanent historical existence because God has assumed that existence into God's own being.

If we are to move beyond the less salutary effects of the historical contextualization of theology, it will require attention to the incarnation for our ontology, epistemology, and philosophy of language. In Christ, God assumed human nature, which includes, as the fathers and councils teach, human reason and will, the very 'stuff' that makes philosophy possible. To deny a relationship between philosophy and theology, including a relationship between the god of the philosophers and the God of Scripture, is to be 'Nestorian' in our theology. They remain too distinct, whether the distinction results in an emphasis on a 'pure' faith as the basis for a 'pure' reason (fideism) or a 'pure' reason as the presupposition for a 'pure' faith (religion within the limits of foundationalist reason alone). Likewise, to collapse reason into faith (fideism once again), or faith into reason (rationalism once again), is a species of 'Apollinarianism.' Both Christological errors have the same consequence: they cordon reason and faith off into separate areas to protect one from the other. The theological and political results are disastrous.

Modern theology finds itself swinging between two equally unpalatable poles. Either God is turned into some kind of mythical creature who begins to resemble us: God suffers, God changes, creation affects God, God is finite. Or God becomes an ineffable sublime about whom nothing can be reasonably said, so that any speech is just as good as any other. Both these tendencies emerge once theological language is assumed to be trapped within its historical context, for then our only options are to conceive of God in terms of a univocal account of language where God must now take on the same features as humanity if God is to be useful for us. God must suffer as we suffer if God is to love. God must change as we change if God is to redeem us. God must be affected by the world if God is to be engaged with it. Some modern theologians even construe God as finite or bodily. They follow the dehellenizing method such that they lose the divine names altogether. The names used for God prior to the nineteenth century — names such as Impassible, Eternal,

Immutable, the First Truth, Ens Perfectissimum — are construed to be mistaken — a result of the importation of a false Greek metaphysics, and must now be reconceived. Ironically, the result is a re-paganizing (helle-nizing) of God. Making God like us is a tendency that occurs across the theological spectrum, from staunchly Lutheran theologies that begin with the assumption that the cross must show us all things about God, to process and openness theologies to more popular forms of theology found in evangelical and liberal Protestant preaching. All of this is pri-marily a re-mythologizing of theology that sets itself against the Jewish and Christian tradition of the divine names, which first demythologized 'god.' But this re-conception of God's names is a re-mythologizing that assumes our language signifies God just as it is. As Karl Barth and Henri de Lubac taught us, the end result is that modern theology adopts Feuer-bach's projectionist account of language.

The other tendency in modern theology is no more palatable. It as-sumes God is so ineffable that no language is adequate to name God. Be-cause we know a priori that our language is always limited to its historical context, we also know it cannot signify God. Whereas the first option as-sumes our language univocally designates God just as it is, the second as-sumes our language is thoroughly equivocal and could never be used to in-tend a reference such as 'God.' This has two consequences for how we then proceed. On the one hand, it renders speaking about God irrational. Any name is just as adequate as any other, for all our names for God have the ex-act same function in their language-use; they are all metaphors that help us name what cannot be named for the sake of ourselves.[28] Our language never truly intends its reference. At most it speaks about us, our needs or our situation. This is why so much modern theology is sociology and psy-chology with a smattering of religious piety. On the other hand, we turn revelation into a propositional, epistemological category. No one can know the ineffable God, but we have propositions that bear little to no connection to socio-historical realities of language. These propositions can be identi-fied and used as names for God, primarily by insiders who possess a kind of private language. The prior tendency assumes that every use of language to speak about God is just as good as any other and no judgment can be made among the various uses. We lose the ability to discriminate theology's rea-

28. As Andrew Moore persuasively demonstrates, this can be as true of theistic real-ists as it is of non-realist constructivists. See *Realism and Christian Faith*.

sonableness. The latter tendency assumes that the language we use must have a precision to it, including a foundation in metaphysical objectivism whereby terms designate things in a one to one correspondence or theologians cannot truly mean what we say. Both tendencies possess a hermeneutics of critical suspicion. The first use their account of language to call into suspicion anyone who thinks he or she can truly intend to speak of God. The second call into suspicion any who refuse to accept its metaphysical foundation, even if they use identical language of God. It is not enough to affirm the creeds if you do not have a metaphysical objectivism to ensure the truth of your speech.

A second and related consequence to the dogmatic claim to know the limits of language in speaking about God is that theology, like much of modern philosophy, becomes mired in epistemology. Because we assume we know the a priori limits to what our language can do, we also assume we know the limits of that to which it refers. Language is a creaturely, historical reality. It shifts and changes. If we tie reference to its modes of signifying too tightly then we will assume that the object to which language refers shifts and changes with it. We become trapped in a synchrony of existence because our language can only designate things limited by its particular, temporal modes of signifying. One tradition of the linguistic turn tends to trap us within this designative function of language. It finds metaphysics and theology misleading us because they are not attentive to how language signifies. Once we become attentive to language, then questions of truth, God, goodness, beauty, and being lose their mysterious character and we realize that the questions only emerged because we let our language mislead us. This designative tradition posited 'verificationism' as the necessary means by which we can determine whether what we say has any meaning at all. In the process, it treated metaphysics with contempt and walked away from its questions, wrongly assuming that once we recognize such questions cannot be given meaning through verificationism they would disappear. But now this tradition itself has been called into question. It has been historicized and we recognize that far from escaping metaphysics, it worked within a metaphysics known as nominalism. It did not lead us to the 'end of metaphysics.' If anything, we are at the end of a secularism that tried to train us to refuse to ask metaphysical questions, which was more like an ideological program than a genuine search for wisdom.

A third consequence follows from modern theology's captivation with epistemology and a designative understanding of language that eschews metaphysics: theology becomes primarily about power rather than truth. Because speaking about God cannot escape its historical context and truly intend its reference, we must then treat with suspicion every claim to true speech of God. It must be unmasked as a disguised power play and countered by some alternative language that will include those the 'dominant' or traditional language was meant to exclude. Because we have no reasonable way to adjudicate theological differences, we can only construe them as assertions of power to be countered with protests, which will in turn be countered with protests. Protest becomes an end in itself. The logical result of this subordination of truth to power is a solipsism where each person is finally an individual who has the right to speak about God however she or he feels against any common judgments that some form of speaking is better than others.

This leads us to the fourth consequence of these predictable tendencies in modern theology. Faith and reason are rent asunder and we supposedly must choose between them. This is even found in the unfortunate nomenclature, which we use for contemporary theology. We have 'confessional' or 'church' theology and 'natural' or 'public' theology. These divisions are mistaken and bear the marks of the four consequences noted above. Although I will use these terms from time to time throughout this work, their use will be primarily an effort to undo these divisions.

These divisions have dire political consequences for the relationship between religion and politics in the modern world. First, religion is policed by a 'universal,' 'natural,' or 'public' reason to a 'private' or 'non-public' status. Then we are surprised when religion does not keep to its place. Second, religious people adopt this private posture and try to embody their religion in the only place allowed — a private, fideistic space with no public accountability. This leads to the superficial analysis that people are primarily killing each other in the name of God. 'God' may be used to execute violence, but it is a symptom of something much more profound than so-called 'sectarian' violence. Once theology is reduced to a solipsistic activity, either at the personal or communal level, then it has neither public accessibility nor accountability. Each individual or each cultural context can speak (and speaking always includes acting as well) without any need to be accountable to communities other than that of the insider's language because the only other alternative is a putatively universal, neutral, and 'public' reason that demands faith's subordination. This is something to which people of faith cannot submit.

The following work seeks to explore and assess these tendencies in modern theology. Notice I refer to them as 'tendencies.' They are not the entirety of modern theology; they cannot be. The tendencies toward a pure reason or a pure faith are impossible to actualize; faith and reason are too unruly to remain in their policed domains. As William Desmond puts it,

> We can plot a border between territories and insist that faith and reason only travel to the other's country under proper visa. Then they will enter illegally, without certification or passport. There are no univocal borders in mind and spirit which bar trespass or illegal entry; there is a porosity more elemental than all passports and academic policing. . . . Where is the pure faith relative to which thought is excluded? Where is there pure reason that entirely excludes all trust?[29]

So even if the policed division between faith and reason has to be endured, it will not succeed. Faith and reason eventually come to their true end.

The following work also brings into conversation various theologians' discontent with the policing between faith and reason that occurred in the modern era. The first step in the argument sets the context for the discussion. Why are these theologians discontent with modern theology? The first chapter begins with an analysis of the political problem the tendency toward fideism produces, especially how it depends upon and perpetuates an account of language where speaking of God is explicitly or implicitly primarily speaking about ourselves. It suggests four ills modern theology produces that contribute to dire political consequences. Chapters Two through Five then respond to those modern ills. Chapter Two constitutes a second step in the argument, which invites the reader into a complicated conversation as to why these theologians are discontent with modernity and what theological remedies they suggest. Barth found Feuerbach's projectionist account of theological language to be a logical consequence of a faulty Christology, the Lutheran 'communicatio idiomatum.' He also found a similar problem in the Roman Catholic analogia entis. It 'captured' God within a totalizing metaphysics. Barth's reaction against projectionist God language and metaphysics led him to emphasize God as 'totaliter aliter.' This could tend toward fideism. Denys Turner suggests Barth's response repeats rather than critiques Feuerbach and loses the im-

29. William Desmond, *Is There a Sabbatical for Thought? Between Religion and Philosophy* (New York: Fordham University Press, 2005), pp. 98-99.

portance of reason. He offers a different remedy to the ills of contemporary theology that tends toward a recovery of a neoscholastic rationalism. Barth and Turner provide the parameters within which modern theology's discontents work; they represent tendencies toward fideism or a return to neoscholastic rationalism. To take their work in either of these directions would be disastrous. The last thing we need in the life of the church is to repeat the sixteenth century.

The third step in the argument develops the constructive responses of modern theology's discontents, especially how they provide a different account of faith and reason. Chapters Three and Four develop this; they constitute the constructive proposal in this work. Chapter Three assesses the role of Aquinas's five ways toward God's existence and the tradition of the divine names. Insufficient attention has been given in modern theology to the dramatic interruption that the giving of the divine name is in Exodus 3. We tend to focus on the exodus itself for it fits with our contemporary emphases on emancipatory discourses. But we neglect that the exodus only works in the context of the giving of this name. The tradition of dehellenization downplayed this gift for fear that it led to a static or abstract metaphysics. Now that the end of metaphysics has come to an end, we can once again receive the theological importance of this name.

To receive the name requires a constructive theological rendering of language. The philosophy of Wittgenstein and the theology of Aquinas provide the basis for this constructive response. The fourth chapter draws on them as well as Charles Taylor's account of an 'expressivist' linguistic turn that not only has a place for speaking of God in modernity, but assumes it. This is contrasted with a 'designative' linguistic turn that assumes a methodological nominalism that makes speaking of God irrational.

The last step, in Chapter Five, brings truth and language into conversation with politics. Modernity offers significant gains in terms of political freedoms, but it often does so by excluding truth and faith. Inevitably these exclusions have come back to haunt it and challenge those gains. How can we maintain these gains and have a politics that subordinates power to truth rather than vice versa? How can we show that faith is itself already political without losing the virtues of generosity and liberality toward neighbors and enemies who do not share these theological commitments? We can speak the truth about God without apology and at the same time cultivate those virtues because of the Truth that speaks.

CHAPTER 1

Speaking of God in Modernity

Few contemporary theologians find themselves content with something called modernity since the announcement of postmodernity's birth. In fact, being 'discontent' with modernity is something of a cottage industry. Who defends it today? Nearly every theologian now knows and affirms the problem with modernity. Modernity assumed that although 'God' and the 'natural' order cannot be trusted, and in fact should be doubted as the foundation for politics, ethics, economics, and social relations, there is nonetheless something within us, within our interiority, that can still be trusted to provide such a foundation. It is a subjectivity grounded in will, which makes possible a secure form of knowledge free of deception — "I think, therefore I am." But 'think' here is not coherence with a rational world; it is an assertion of power. The emphasis is on the 'I.' I assert this doubt, and this is the one thing that cannot be doubted. Therefore I never need to be taken in by anything that came before me, by anyone's imposition of a god, or of his or her interpretation of truth or goodness. I can always call such putative foundations into question for the sake of something new, the 'modo' or 'just now' that is almost here, although it never quite arrives.

Modernity emphasizes and commands the will's freedom to call everything into question. 'Critique' and reason become synonymous. This results in the bifurcation of the human person between two realms, mind and body, where mind participates in the realm of freedom that can be asserted against body, against nature. It also sets forth a moral obligation where I must call into question everything that came before me for the sake of the new, even when this moral obligation is exactly what came before me. Modernity, then, is the illusion of difference under an unrecognizable sameness. While few defend it, many seem to emphasize 'diversity,' even the difference of the postmodern from the modern, and thereby repeat it.

If modernity is defined by the strategy to secure humanity against God and/or nature's arbitrariness through a foundational subjectivity where nearly all of human activity, including politics, economics, and religion, is founded upon the will, then postmodernity is the effort to remove that last vestige of a secure center for human activity (a metaphysics of presence). It recognizes what modernity is without claiming to move beyond it. We know the 'game,' even when we cannot get out of it. In one sense, the postmodern does nothing more than produce a disposition of discontent toward the modern. We recognize it, laugh at it, and then perpetuate it. To be 'discontent' with modernity is to be modern; it is to wait on the next thing, possibly the postmodern, that will emancipate us from the present.

Postmodernity intensifies the modern assertion of will until it (hopefully) exhausts itself. When theologians seek to be relevant to the 'postmodern' as the next historical stage after the modern, they once again repeat it and keep us trapped in its immanent eschatology, awaiting a 'modo' that we know cannot and must not arrive. The emphasis in this work on the transcendental predicates of being, especially truth, does not seek to be relevant to anything modern or postmodern. It does not seek to be a 'political' strategy at all. It seeks to be about truth, the truth of how we speak about God and how that influences metaphysics and politics; both of which are practical concerns. I begin by drawing upon theologians' discontent with modernity only to the extent that they help us diagnose why it has become controversial to say something as simple as "this work is about the truth of God," which makes nearly every reader and even the author bristle and ask, "Who are you to claim to know the truth about God?" But what else would one expect from a theologian? Why should anyone expect us to do something other than tell the truth about God? In this work I will tell the truth about God and how it might relate to something other than the well-worn ruts of a modernist politics.

Discontentment with modernity can be one more form of it when we allow it to raise the question of 'relevance'; for modern-cum-postmodern discontent always finds the question of 'relevance' to be the pressing question. How can we be relevant to . . . ? What defines modern theology is a preoccupation with a dialectical question: how do we negotiate between identity and relevance? But there is another form of discontent which asserts that the difficulty with modern theology is not this identity/relevance dialectic, but its utter redundancy. Everything theology does has been handed over to other disciplines — history, the social sciences, psychology, managerial studies ('leadership'), and so on. Here we have two forms of modern discontent. The first asserts relevance to the modern, calls into question Christian identity, but still seeks to salvage identity within this dialectical tension. The second asserts a different problematic. Theology is always already too relevant; it is redundant.[1] If redundancy characterizes the discontentment with modernity, then the question of relevance merely exacerbates the problem that gives rise to the discontent in the first place. How did we get into this situation?

Theologians who find discontentment with modernity because of theology's redundancy help us identify four ills with modern theology that contribute to this situation. They do not all explicitly identify them as ills, nor do they identically name them, but four ills can be distilled from their work that unnecessarily trouble modern speech and knowledge of God. The first is a false alternative between a pure faith and a pure reason. It leads to an improper either/or — either 'rationalism' grounded in a pure nature or 'fideism' solely grounded in the church's self-description. This false alternative has political consequences. Second is a projectionist account of theological language. It relates to the problem of fideism, for if our language about God is nothing but language about ourselves, then we have no public accountability for it. The third ill is ontotheology. Much

---

1. These two problematics could be identified with a revisionist versus postliberal or postmodern divide in contemporary theology. I appreciate those such as Paul DeHart who challenge this division, trying to break down the dividing wall of hostility. Yet the very terms of that challenge, as well as its execution, miss this significant difference. For instance, DeHart frames his critique of Lindbeck and retrieval of Frei in terms of the first problematic when he writes, "Even though the deeper issues [between revisionists and postliberals] remained stubbornly elusive, the opposition obviously had something to do with how theology balanced the twin demands for faithfulness and change, and with the role in striking this balance of modern thought-forms uncommitted or even potentially hostile to Christian claims." *The Trial of the Witnesses: The Rise and Decline of Postliberal Theology* (Oxford: Blackwell, 2006) p. xiii. Although there is much to learn from DeHart's interesting critique, it frames the conversation in terms of this problematic and finally doesn't help us discern the "stubbornly elusive" division between the forms of modern discontent in contemporary theology.

like projectionism, it also traps 'God' within a philosophical immanence and denies our language or knowledge can escape it. The fourth is related to this third ill; it is Barth's critique of the Roman Catholic 'analogia entis,' a critique that anticipated much of the concern about ontotheology. The four ills are fideism, projectionism, ontotheology, and a deficient metaphysical understanding of the 'analogia entis.' Before we can offer a theological therapy to these modern ills, they require a diagnosis.

1. Fideism

'Fideism' only emerges as a problem, as an invective that can be used against others, once reason and faith are rendered asunder. If there is no 'rationalism' there can be no 'fideism,' for the accusation of 'fideism' only makes sense when someone assumes pure domains of reason and faith. Once this occurs, faith is usually considered private and juxtaposed with something more public and universal, a 'pure reason.' Because modern theology's discontents call into question such a reason they also call into question 'fideism.' This is not to deny the real problem 'fideism' produces in modernity. In fact, the tendency toward fideism is a serious political problem. A putative 'public' reason seeks to force people of faith into an arational space where they can have their faith in private. Some religious people accept that 'invitation' and act accordingly, refusing to be policed by a putative universal reason. Fundamentalism, as Žižek noted, is less persons seeking dogmatic certainty in a time of ever changing flux, and more persons asserting the freedom to violate the dogmatic certainties that so define our times.[2] Before discussing how they do this and why it produces negative political consequences, we should clarify what fideism is. It has four major features. First, it is faith in something without any public accessibility or responsibility for it. Second, fideism has a peculiar relation to language: it claims a private language for which, by definition, it can have no public accountability. Third, fideism misconstrues the relationship between faith and reason. It either divides them into discrete entities and allows no traffic between them, or it reduces one into the other. Finally, it re-

---

2. Žižek, *The Fragile Absolute* (London: Verso, 2000), p. 132. Žižek's point has primarily to do with resurgent nationalist fundamentalisms, but I think the point also helps us understand religious fundamentalism and its odd relationship to nationalism.

fuses to acknowledge that politics, religion, or morality can be anything other than power. Here is where the 'projectionist' account of language (the second modern ill) and fideism (the first ill) coalesce. If the language of faith is nothing but the assertion of our own will to power, it can have no public accessibility. Likewise if we have no public accessibility for our languages and practices, then the only way to adjudicate differences is through force, power, and coercion. This is why fideism can be a serious political problem.

We see 'fideism'[3] among those persons and religious movements who cling to a faith devoid of all reason and allow it to guide their actions without any rational accountability to the consequences of their actions. From Islamic terrorists to Mormon cults and Christian fundamentalists, a convergence between fideism and politics is emerging in these post-secular times. By 'post-secular times' I mean that cultural period, which I believe is upon us, that recognizes that the hold of 'secularity' (modernity's twin) has run its course, even if we do not recognize exactly what that means. The great philosophers of secularity, Freud, Marx, and Nietzsche, all thought that theology would have run its course by these times in which we live. Yet for better or worse, they were wrong. 'God' did not disappear; 'God' returned with a vengeance. What are we to make of this? Some fear it; they view it as a barbarization that loses the gains of the Western Enlightenment where God was reduced to a private preference in a nonpublic realm that could do no harm in the public sphere. Some seem so puzzled by it that they simply do not know what to do. Some exploit it for their own gain. Others celebrate and affirm it. Some fear it is a return to frightening medieval times before the temple of reason subdued faith. But all these responses are woefully mistaken. The fideism that characterizes these post-secular times is much less a fearful return to some premodern medieval religious 'worldview' and more the result of a lingering division between faith and reason produced and policed in the modern cultural period.

3. As I stated previously, 'fideism' does not *actually* exist, for one of the conditions for its actual existence is impossible — a private language. No one can sustain 'fideism' because no one can sustain the kind of impermeable cultural membrane necessary for a private language. Fideism is, therefore, more a tendency and virtual reality than an actually existent one. This does not mean that the political consequences of a virtual fideism are not real. Evil is the privation of good; it has no actual existence. But it still kills. Whenever I use the term 'fideism' in this work I mean it as this tendency and virtual reality.

In an important editorial shortly after the attack on the World Trade Center in 2001, the philosopher Samuel Fleischacker wrote,

> It is commonly said that Osama bin Laden represents a medieval worldview. If only! What is most dangerous about his brand of radical Islam derives from something peculiarly modern in it. In Islam, as well as Judaism and Christianity, the Middle Ages saw the highest development of the notion that faith and reason can go together. For medieval philosophers, faith could enhance one's understanding of the secular world, and secular understanding could deepen faith. The existence and nature of God, for instance, could be ascertained by reason. A great deal of morality could also be determined without faith, and this view of morality — as largely independent of faith — was, later, to be of great importance to the development of liberal politics. One consequence of this viewpoint was a moral constraint on the interpretation of revealed texts. Many medieval thinkers held that if the holy scriptures — of any faith — seem to contradict what reason tells us God must be like, then the scriptures need to be reinterpreted. God has given us scriptures, but God has also given us reason; so reason can serve as a guide to what the scriptures mean. Thus, if God can have no bodily parts, then references to 'God's hand' must be metaphorical. Similarly, if a good God, to whom each human being is precious, could not possibly desire the death of many innocent human beings, then we cannot accept the apparent meaning of passages in scriptures that approve of mass killing.[4]

I find Fleischacker to be basically correct, and he wisely acknowledges that how we read Scripture will determine the relation between faith and reason. Unlike the moderns, the medievals refused to separate faith and reason. In fact, faith was a kind of reason, and this gave them an ability to interpret Scripture without seizing on one single text and using it for immoral means. It allowed for the importance of allegorical reading. No pure faith demanded contradicting God's goodness. But we have become accustomed to faith and reason's division, and we have come to see how dangerous this is both in Islam and on the Christian left and right, as each

---

4. *The Guardian*, October 2001. Nicholas Wolterstorff makes a similar claim as to how one should interpret God's speech in his *Divine Discourse* (Cambridge: Cambridge University Press, 1995), pp. 204-6.

is tempted to engage politics based on a faith that knows only power and nothing of reason.

But I also wonder whether Fleischacker is correct that modern liberal politics is grounded more in the medieval tradition of faith and reason's mutual enhancement than the modern split between them. Here I think he may himself divide faith from reason and allow a pure reason to police faith. Of course, we should not read an editorial as we would a carefully argued philosophical position, but Fleischacker's intriguing suggestion gives us a good place to begin to think about how not only faith and reason, but also how faith and politics "can go together." He first tells us that "the Middle Ages saw the highest development of the notion that faith and reason can go together," but then proceeds to set them against each other by suggesting that morality and politics can be known by a reason that is "without faith," and that this was an important medieval influence on modern, liberal politics.[5] Does this not assume a 'pure' reason as well as a division between faith and reason that contradicts his earlier statement that for the medievals, faith and reason go together? For Fleischacker, justice is a political virtue grounded in something like a pure reason.

Fleischacker's editorial is all the more intriguing because he is not known for setting the modern era against the medieval and finding the latter preferable to the former. He is no anti-modernist. His *A Short History of Distributive Justice* argues that modern calls for 'social justice' of-

---

5. De Lubac's work on pre-critical interpretation is important at just this point. He makes the point that the two orderings found in Origen and others gave two different accounts of how faith, morality, and politics would relate. When biblical interpretation is ordered in terms of the literal, then moral, then allegorical, the moral and political will not need faith for its intelligibility. When literal-allegorical-moral orders the reading, then the moral and political will be read in terms of the faith. De Lubac writes, "In the first instance, Origen draws diverse 'moralities' from the sacred text. It is possible for them to have nothing specially Christian, even before one reads in them any allusion to the Mystery of Christ. . . . In the first case, he gives us, in general, a series of speculations on the soul, its faculties, its virtues etc. . . . In the second case, he expounds an asceticism and a mysticism that has a Christological, ecclesial, and sacramental complexion. Founded as it is on dogma, it is a veritable history of the spiritual life. In this second case, Origen's exegesis, connected in its entirety to 'the soul of the believer,' to 'the soul of the one who is faithful,' and to 'the ecclesiastical soul,' of 'the soul that is in the Church, is thus wholly Christian, in its content no less than it its form, in its end results no less than its deeply rooted foundations." *Medieval Exegesis, Volume 1: The Four Senses of Scripture* (Grand Rapids: Eerdmans, 1998), p. 147.

ten have a "nostalgia for premodern attitudes toward the poor" that are unwarranted. By 'social justice' most people mean distributive justice, which "calls on the state to guarantee that property is distributed throughout society so that everyone is supplied with a certain level of material means."[6] This is neither an ancient nor a medieval understanding of justice, but emerges with the transition to capitalism. Therefore those who think capitalism represents some kind of 'wrong turn' where social justice no longer matters fail to recognize that a distribution of goods according to need rather than merit reflects the transition from an Aristotelian to a modern (Kantian and Smithian) economics. Capitalism invented 'social justice,' if by that term one means distributive justice. It is a virtue arising from the tradition of the natural law, which also gave rise to modern political orders.[7]

Fleischacker finds precedence for liberal politics in the tradition of the 'natural law,' where justice as a virtue was understood as distinct from "the virtues that take one into the presence of God."[8] Both Aquinas and Vitoria stand in the natural law tradition, where justice can be known apart from the theological virtues. Kant and Rawls develop this virtue of justice as "independent of the other virtues," and this provides the basis for modern liberal political structures.

> Long after Aquinas and Vitoria, this view of justice as independent of other virtues shows up in Immanuel Kant's claims that duties of justice, unlike other moral duties, are not concerned with the intentions of those who must keep them, and in John Rawls's conception of justice and politics as abstracting from differences over religion, culture, or other comprehensive views about how to live.[9]

6. Samuel Fleischacker, *A Short History of Distributive Justice* (Cambridge, Mass.: Harvard University Press, 2004), pp. 3-4. In Roman Catholic social teaching 'social justice' is not 'distributive justice,' but 'contributive justice.' It states that everyone has a duty to contribute to the common good and therefore for anyone to give a wage that denies someone the means to fulfill this duty is unjust.

7. For a similar account of a modern political theology grounded in the natural law but with more opposition between Christian faith and political reason see Mark Lilla's *The Stillborn God* (New York: Alfred A. Knopf, 2007).

8. Fleischacker, *A Short History of Distributive Justice*, p. 11. Here his argument follows closely that of John Rawls.

9. Fleischacker, *A Short History of Distributive Justice*, p. 12.

Fleischacker's narrative about social justice is compelling and persuasive.[10] Social justice is a 'modern' virtue that depends upon the kind of disinterestedness capitalism invents. That disinterestedness separates justice from the other virtues, especially the theological ones, and treats justice as a matter of reason alone, of reason universally recognizable and grounded in a natural law known without any determination by faith, which is a theological virtue.

This is persuasive as an understanding of 'social justice'; what is less persuasive is that Fleischacker reads this back into Aquinas. His work does not fit so cleanly into Fleischacker's "short history" because the natural and supernatural virtues, as well as reason and faith, cannot be so easily divided for him. But nor does this seem to fit well Fleischacker's intriguing claim that the kind of fideism present in Osama bin Laden has a peculiarly modern character to it. I hope to offer a different reading of Aquinas in this work; one that recognizes the rightness of Fleischacker's claim — medievals refused to separate faith and reason, and with that they refused to separate the natural and supernatural virtues. This refusal is a rejection both of reducing faith to reason and reason to faith. They could refuse this because faith and reason are not discrete entities one can either collapse into, or set against, each other.

Setting reason as a discrete entity over and against faith is one of the components of political liberalism. Once this occurs, then theologies of correlation emerge where faith and reason are first separated and then have to be 'correlated,' but it always assumes they remain two distinct things. How can we avoid this bifurcation of faith and reason, this "dangerous discord"? How can we speak of God such that we avoid reducing reason to faith or setting them over and against each only to be correlated at a later date?

---

10. He made a similar argument in his *On Adam Smith's Wealth of Nations: A Philosophical Companion* (Princeton: Princeton University Press, 2004.) Here we find something akin to Rawls's political liberalism as the basis for Smith's market exchanges: "For markets to provide information and distribute goods efficiently, the agents exchanging must be rationally pursuing some interest, rather than following rules of ritual or taboo, and mutually disinterested — uninterested in the projects of the people with whom they are exchanging. But they do not need to be *self*-interested. They may care about their families and friends, their religious communities, or any of a variety of political and social projects. It is just important that these commitments not significantly affect who they buy from or sell to, or at what price they buy or sell" (p. 100).

Recognizing that no private language exists, that language always bears within it a public accessibility, and that this is as true for people of faith as for those who claim to cling to a reason devoid of faith, is the best counter to modernity's fideism, for it challenges it without drawing upon the putatively universal, neutral reason that produces fideism. Public accessibility is not the same as universal, objective criteria or what political liberalism intends by its 'public reason,' which is so often uncritically accepted by 'public theology.' It de-politicizes faith by removing it from political reasoning about justice, wrongly assuming that the latter can be purified from faith — the theological and natural virtues have no bearing upon each other. This is the condition for fideism.

When reason is wrongly identified with universal criteria or 'public reason,' it will be abstracted from language and turned into its own 'temple' that demands that faith be blind and private. A temple to reason that is putatively universal reduces all other reasons, even the reasons of faith, to the status of private, or nonpublic, as John Rawls's defense of political liberalism demands. For Rawls, the church's faith is a priori "non-public reason."[11] Public reason is grounded in a conception of justice that bears no relationship to theological virtues. At best, it does not necessarily contradict them. This does not avoid the problem of fideism; it repeats it. It makes any public speaking of God almost impossible, for it is permitted only in a 'nonpublic' space (whatever that might be). It is forced into a private language that must first translate itself into something putatively more universal for it to have a reasonable politics. Only persons who already assume 'faith' and 'reason' can be correlated with 'nonpublic' and 'public' can accept such a version of political liberalism. If people of faith are to be welcomed into liberal politics as something other than irrational fideists, then it will have to discover a different conception of rationality and a different understanding of the relationship between faith and reason: one that opens up space for reasons of faith. Political liberalism produces fideism by forcing faith into a private sphere, policing it with a putatively universal public reason where matters of justice are rendered irreconcilable with matters of faith.

John Paul II and John Rawls greatly differ in their understanding of this division between reason and faith. John Rawls recognizes it as the con-

11. John Rawls, *Political Liberalism* (New York: Columbia University Press, 1996), p. lvii.

dition for political liberalism. John Paul II warns against it and refers to it as a "dangerous discord," which needs remedy. He writes,

> Although St. Albert the Great and St. Thomas insisted on the existence of a close link between theology and philosophy, even so they were the first learned men to admit the necessary autonomy that philosophy and the sciences needed, so that each should depend upon arguments belonging to their own sphere. Yet from the end of the Middle Ages the legitimate distinction between these two areas of knowledge gradually developed into a dangerous discord.[12]

The relationship between theology and philosophy bears great similarity to that between faith and reason as well as between the theological and natural virtues. Whereas John Paul II acknowledges an 'autonomy' of philosophy, he denies this autonomy should be so distinct that it produces a discord. Faith still informs the natural virtues, as do hope and charity. The same historical developments John Paul II identifies as a "dangerous discord," John Rawls narrates as the condition for the emergence of political liberalism out of the Reformation's dismantling of medieval Christianity. Rawls finds medieval Christianity's synthesis between faith and reason preventing the emergence of the "free faith" that is necessary for political liberalism.[13] If this is correct, then John Paul II's worries about fideism are warranted. It is not the church that propagates fideism, it is political liberalism, at least as set forth by Rawls. It seeks to keep 'faith' limited to a 'confessional' language that cannot exceed its boundaries. Yet faith seeks a reason that must exceed such boundaries. Faith requires a form of metaphysical reasoning (metaphysics 3).

If we are to avoid fideism, we will need to recover a theological metaphysics. Much to our detriment, the modern secular university offers philosophical courses in truth, moral goodness, beauty, knowledge, and a host of other subjects, but seldom God. This is to our detriment because the intellectual quest seems inescapably to raise the question of God, and most of those who ask the question only find a receptive hearing outside, or on the margins of, university intellectual life. We were taught not to

12. *Restoring Faith in Reason: A New Translation of the Encyclical Letter Faith and Reason of John Paul II Together with a Commentary and Discussion,* ed. Laurence Paul Hemming and Susan Frank Parsons (London, SCM, 2002), p. 75.

13. See Rawls, *Political Liberalism,* pp. xxv-xxvii.

speak about God in public; it was thought to be too divisive. But this refusal to think and speak about God within the pursuit of reason, knowledge, and wisdom leaves people open to fideism. To avoid fideism, theology must not shy away from a 'metaphysical' reason. Yet what is the status of 'reason'? How shall we think, speak, and write theology so that it is a rational endeavor? This requires theologians to overcome their fear of metaphysics. Giles Hibbert recognizes that "metaphysical realization" is simply the use of words "being able to point beyond themselves, beyond the sphere and context of their own immediate origin."[14] Metaphysics uses language to say something about that which cannot be merely indicated by pointing.

Faith and reason, although different, are not distinct. They represent overlapping epistemic sources, which mutually reinforce each other insofar as neither is viewed as cut off from the other. Faith and reason are not incommensurable epistemic sources; neither are they completely translatable one into another. To think that they must be either incommensurable or utterly translatable will also produce fideism. Faith and reason are both epistemic; they are sources of knowledge. They both presume, and seek after the same end, truth. Yet neither can be 'pure.' The quest for a 'pure' faith or a 'pure' reason polices out too much of ordinary life; it is a dangerous quest.

Since the 'linguistic turn' we now know that we can have neither faith nor reason separate from language, and language is never 'pure' unless it is so abstracted from everyday life that it accomplishes nothing.[15] Faith and reason take up language differently, even though they can only be expressed in a common language. This was one of Brunner's important insights in his famous dispute with Karl Barth over 'natural' theology. Revelation assumes the human capacity for words *(Wortmachtigkeit)*.[16] Barth misunderstood this point as a human capacity for revelation *(Offenbarungsmachtigkeit)*.[17] Yet Barth also acknowledged that in revelation we are not given a different language than the one we already speak. Barth simply

14. Cited in Matthew Levering's *Scripture and Metaphysics: Aquinas and the Renewal of Trinitarian Theology* (Oxford: Blackwell, 2004), p. 5.

15. Which 'linguistic turn' is an important question. The answer to it will be made clearer in later sections of this work.

16. Emil Brunner and Karl Barth, *Natural Theology,* trans. Peter Fraenkel (Eugene, Ore.: Wipf and Stock, 2002), p. 23.

17. See John Baillie's introduction to Brunner and Barth, *Natural Theology,* p. 9.

insisted that this 'how' of revelation must never be confused with the 'what.'[18] The similarities here between Barth and Aquinas's distinction between the 'modus significandi'/'res' significata are significant, even if Barth constantly accused Brunner of 'Thomism.' Because faith and reason are only possible in language, and neither has a private language distinct from the other, they cannot be separated. Their differences are not so much the modes of signifying they present, but what they claim those modes can signify. Theology, grounded in faith, claims that the same modes of signifying that reason uses can exceed the language used and give knowledge of God, because it always is a gift from God given in language.

This is controversial within modern epistemologies, for some are a priori convinced that finite language cannot signify 'God.' Theo-logy is always a performative contradiction. Because 'God' transcends the phenomenal order, language cannot give us knowledge of God, even if God can be thought. Kant suggested something like this when he wrote,

> If we were to flatter ourselves so much as to claim that we know the *modum noumenon,* then we would have to be in community with God so as to participate immediately in the divine ideas, which are the authors of all things in themselves. To expect this in the present life is the business of mystics and theosophists.[19]

Kant claimed to know a priori that this was impossible. But how could he know that? He offers one possibility for knowledge of God. We know because of what we know about pure reason that we cannot know God.

Many modern theologians agree with Kant. They too critique reason to make room for a theology grounded solely on 'faith.' This makes for a second reasonable possibility where only faith 'knows' God. This possibility remains confined to a modern epistemology. 'God' as an object of rational inquiry is rejected in favor of a faith that knows no reason. Both positions affirm that finite language a priori cannot adequately signify God. Both deny a real participation of our language in communion with God. But this overlooks an important third possibility — in the performative contradiction that theo-logy always is we discover the reasonableness of

---

18. Brunner and Barth, *Natural Theology,* p. 126.

19. Kant's *Lectures on Philosophical Theology.* Quoted in Kevin Hart, *The Trespass of the Sign: Deconstruction, Theology, and Philosophy* (New York: Fordham University Press, 2000), p. 209.

reason's failure in speaking well of God. But the 'how' is not confused with the 'what.' We recognize that our mode of signifying cannot alone account for what is signified, but we do not conclude that this means it cannot be so. Then we find ourselves open to something more, but never less, than reason. One does not need faith in order to understand the first part of this claim — reason alone fails in obtaining 'God.' We have ample evidence of this in the limited persuasiveness of the proofs for God's existence. But one needs faith to 'see' the second part of the claim. Reason's failure becomes a reasonable demonstration of God's existence; for it allows us to receive what philosophy desires but can never achieve — knowledge of God.

In this third possibility, reason can never be 'pure' and abstracted from Scripture, tradition, conciliar decrees. Reason devoid of tradition was the illusion of the Enlightenment; only a few reactionaries still cling to that old illusion. Theological rationality has no meaning within the context of the Enlightenment's pure reason; this has been amply demonstrated and politically enforced within modern, secular universities. But pure reason now seems as quaint an idea as the development of a universal, value free language. This renders the division between 'confessional' and 'natural' theology not only porous, but also mistaken. We can only be asked to choose one rather than the other when we think they offer two distinct domains. At his best, Barth's 'Nein' was to this distinction. For that reason he refused even the refusal *(Ablehnung)* of natural theology.[20] He simply didn't play.

20. I think it significant that his exchange with Brunner was called "Nein" and not "Ablehnung." As Barth put it, "For 'natural theology' does not exist as an entity capable of becoming a separate subject within what I consider to be real theology — not even for the sake of being rejected." Brunner and Barth, *Natural Theology*, p. 75. Barth does not say no to natural theology. He says no to its very possibility. It cannot be and thus it cannot even be rejected. Had Barth left the matter there it would have been better; for he then would not have to be so exercised that 'natural theology' posed a serious problem in the first place. He contradicts this early refusal of natural theology when he then uses it as an actually existing category in order to critique Brunner. T. F. Torrance sheds light on this when he tells us of his last conversation with Barth. It was the dualism of faith and reason, revelation and reason, that Barth found problematic in natural theology, or, as Torrance put it, the distinction in Aquinas between the One God who can be known by reason and the Triune God who can be known only by faith. Barth concurred that this was the difficulty and affirmed Torrance's more integrative natural theology. See T. F. Torrance, *Space, Time, and Resurrection* (Edinburgh: T&T Clark, 1998). Of course, as I hope to show throughout this work, this is a caricatured reading of Aquinas and the faith/reason dichotomy in the Middle Ages. But it is one that has a certain plausibility with post-Tridentine readings of Scholasticism and its energetic recovery in the early twentieth century by Catholics to fight against modernity.

By maintaining a sharp distinction between faith and reason, the 'dangerous discord' that emerged in the later Middle Ages, was brought into modernity. It is dangerous because faith without reason subordinates truth to power.[21] Something is held to be true simply because some political authority asserts it to be so, whether that political authority be the magisterium, an emperor, a priest, 'the people,' 'the church,' an individual invested with a right to read and interpret the Bible him or herself, or a 'culture.' This produces a form of fideism where human authority *alone* makes truth; it has no other foundation than human making. Such a fideism flourishes in the context of historicism, especially when it claims to be post-metaphysical.

Likewise separating 'natural theology' from confession produces a second form of fideism, which renders truth and power asunder. It assumes our truth claims have an innocence to them unrelated to power or to any cultural or communal politics; religion proceeds through reason alone. Then truth and rationality become non- or super-human activities. Truth has no foundation in human making. Truth exists solely in God, or in some divine-like perspective such as a metaphysical realm independent from everyday, concrete, material existence. Or truth becomes nothing but a superfluous assertion as some disquotational theories of truth suggest. Here rationality is grounded in a putatively universal and self-evident reading of 'nature' whether we mean by that term God's creation, physical processes, a thing's essence, or a pure reason unalloyed with sensibility, desire, faith, or power. It flourishes when we assume metaphysics without history (metaphysics 5). But this form of fideism — rationalism as fideism — also, in the end, subordinates truth to power. It fails to acknowledge that its account of pure reason must be politically guarded against any incursions from a tradition-embodied rationality and its attendant politics. The common element in both kinds of fideism is the subordination of truth to power, and this is truly — as Samuel Fleischacker noted — the modern problem of religion and politics. Theologians cannot work through modernity without addressing, and calling into question, this subordination. The task before

---

21. This form of fideism corresponds roughly to that noted by John Paul II in *Fides et Ratio* when he notes that fideism is characterized by a "disdain for classical philosophy" and by those who "distrust every proposition that claims any absoluteness or universality and prefer to suppose that truth is arrived at by general agreement and not derived from the intellect's exposure to objective reality." *Fides et Ratio*, p. 95. Here truth is subordinated to political power or "general agreement."

us, both with respect to faith and reason, is to discover how to subordinate power to truth while avoiding both forms of fideism.

The theological task of working through modernity is at the same time the task of working through this divorce between faith and reason. Both Wittgenstein and Aquinas are helpful guides in this because of their understanding of language. Because fideism emerges when language about God is nothing but language about ourselves, we need something more than a 'projectionist' account of language in order to provide a remedy to the ills of modern theology. If theological language is nothing but projection, fideism will be inevitable.

2. Projectionist Theological Language

Philip Quinn notes that two 'defeater' arguments for theism are the problem of evil and the projectionist account of God language one finds in Feuerbach, Freud, and Durkheim.[22] For Quinn, an "intellectually sophisticated adult theist in our culture" will know these two arguments and be able to counter them in order to hold a rational faith. I don't know if 'defeater arguments' necessarily require counter arguments for the faith to be defended. This may be too rationalistic. Few of us came to faith because of rational proofs for God. Faith often arises from less 'noble' means such as Augustine's hearing God speak through a child who says, 'take and read.'

This is not to deny the legitimacy of Quinn's point; for we must not confuse two things: first, how faith emerges and second, how faith is sustained. Neither can do so without reason. Nevertheless, the speed at which 'our culture' now moves makes me suspicious against speaking in terms of a generic 'adult theist' who may or may not find arguments for and against God compelling and who must be answered. For instance, Graham Ward finds Feuerbach's secular "attempts to exorcise religion's presence" by way of 'anthropology' to have failed in our post-secular times.[23] That a 'sophisticated adult theist' would find Feuerbach persuasive is certainly no longer self-evident. Perhaps he or she should find William Desmond's philosophical expose of such a secular program more compelling, and thus walk away

22. Linda Zagzebski, ed., *Rational Faith: Catholic Responses to Reformed Epistemology* (Notre Dame, Ind.: University of Notre Dame Press, 1993), p. 35.

23. Graham Ward, *True Religion* (London: Blackwell, 2003), p. vii.

from it. Nevertheless, whether or not Feuerbach's projectionist account of God-language remains culturally persuasive, it continues to hold a central place, odd as this reality may be, among contemporary theologians. Alasdair MacIntyre noted in 1968 that "nothing has been more startling than to note how much contemporary Christian theology is trying to perform Feuerbach's work all over again."[24] The process has not yet subsided.

The place for 'God' became determined in Western thought not only by Feuerbach's philosophy, but by those discourses his philosophy made possible: critical social analysis, psychoanalysis, and the nihilistic quest to create new divinities who will serve better our cultural needs. Marxist social analysis, the Nietzschian quest for the creation of new gods, and Freudian psychoanalysis too thoroughly define the space within which 'God' can function even in theologies that are supposed to be developed within non-European 'contexts.' 'God' either functions as political alienation by the marginalized proletariat (Marxism), as the search for the development of new rituals of humanity's own will to power and self-assertion (Nietzsche), or as a thetic stage in the symbolic development of human subjectivity (Freudianism). Each of these discourses assumes that when we say 'God,' we are actually saying something else — either something sinister that masks our political interests or something 'symbolic' about our own powers. Marx, Nietzsche, and Freud, following Feuerbach's lead, politicize theology such that 'God' becomes a projection of our capacities and/or desires. As Regina Schwartz recognizes, the 'secular Freud' could only find a place for 'God' as "a projection of infantile wishes for a protective father."[25] In so doing, the truth of theology is subordinated to a politics based solely on the assertion of power. This subordination of theological truth to politics does not make politics theological; it makes theology political, for the standard by which theology is measured is politics defined as human self-assertion. It emerged because modern theology was preoccupied with making our speech of God relevant to modern philosophical and cultural forms.

24. Cited in Tracey Rowland's *Culture and the Thomist Tradition* (London: Routledge, 2003), p. 93. The quote is found in MacIntyre's *Marxism and Christianity* (Notre Dame, Ind.: University of Notre Dame Press, 1984), p. 142.

25. Regina Schwartz, "Freud's God," in *Postsecular Philosophy*, ed. Philip Blond (London: Routledge, 1998), p. 282. As Schwartz goes on to argue, the 'secular Freud' is not the only Freud. There is another Freud who has a much more interesting place for God. My critique would not be relevant against that other Freud.

Modern theology's discontents avoid the problems of projectionism because of their different analysis of theology's basic problem in modernity. Theology certainly has a problematic existence in the modern era, but how this problem gets diagnosed will lead to different approaches to language about God. For most the problem is relevance. How can we speak of God such that our speech is relevant to the philosophical and cultural forms within which we now live? As previously noted, this also produces a kind of discontent, but one that remains thoroughly modern. It cannot avoid Feuerbach because in speaking about God, it requires that we must do so in terms that make our speech univocal with our own context. For modern theology's discontents the problem is not relevance, but redundancy. This is why theologians who misdiagnose the problem as 'relevance' fail to recognize theology's proper dilemma. If the problem is redundancy, then misdiagnosing it as 'relevance' will be disastrous. For then the remedy to theology's thoroughgoing marginalization will be to seek to secure its meaning by making it relevant via some acceptable modern discipline. But if the problem is redundancy, then theology is always already acceptable via some modern discipline because everything that theology does can now be done in another discipline, an anthropological one, without loss. The work of theology has been 'outsourced.' Neil MacDonald calls this the 'metatheological dilemma' and he shows how this is the dilemma that animates Karl Barth's theology.

Karl Barth, Stanley Hauerwas, Henri de Lubac, John Milbank, and Catherine Pickstock all develop a version of this theological problematic. The question they put to theology is less what it is, and more what it is not. In an age when *everything* and *anything,* just as well as *nothing,* counts as proper speaking of God, how might we recognize something as not theological or as inadequately theological? For once theology has been so thoroughly correlated to modernity via every newly developed discipline it produces, then theology becomes nothing but anthropology. As Milbank put it, it is "turned into the oracular voice of some finite idol, such as historical scholarship, humanist psychology, or transcendental philosophy."[26] If the modern theological problematic is redundancy not relevance, then emphasizing relevance only accentuates its redundancy.

Although Barth, de Lubac, Milbank, and Pickstock recognize a common problem, their means of addressing this problem differ. They all rec-

---

26. John Milbank, *Theology and Social Theory* (London: Blackwell, 1990), p. 1.

ognize theology produced the problem internally, but they offer different genealogical developments. Barth traced the origins of the problem back to the Lutheran tradition and its understanding of faith and Christology where the divine and human became confused.[27] Balthasar makes a similar claim. The logical result of this tradition was Feuerbach. De Lubac traces the origin of the problem to a rigorous Aristotelianism in late Scholastic Thomism, particularly in Cajetan and Suarez, where the natural and supernatural become utterly divided. In an attempt to protect the supernatural, theologians so emphasized transcendence that the supernatural was removed from history.[28] Milbank and Pickstock give a slightly different genealogical rendering. For them, Duns Scotus's univocity of being produces an ontotheology where metaphysics and theology become divided and the latter subordinated to the former. They are more concerned with modern theology's third ill than this second one. Their response is not a 'Barthian' eschewal of metaphysics in favor of a 'pure' theology, or a modern 'updating' of metaphysics through the social sciences as one sees in some liberation theologies. Instead, they seek to show how metaphysics is inevitable even in these modern disciplines and how this provides the possibility of a theological engagement that does not begin on the terms only set forth by such modern disciplines.

These different genealogies result in different remedies for theology's redundancy. Barth seeks to solve it by refusing to mediate theology through any discourse outside the content of an autonomous theological project based on 'the strange new world in the Bible.' His is a thoroughgoing Reformed response. De Lubac addresses it by developing a natural theology within a supernatural orientation, drawing on the work of Aquinas. His is a very Roman Catholic response, and one that draws on Vatican I's two-source theory of truth.[29] Milbank and Pickstock also look to Thomas Aquinas to address the difficulty of theology's redundancy, but they do so via an Anglican mediating theology that seeks to be ecumenical.

27. This is not to suggest Barth rejected the Lutheran tradition in toto. That is obviously false. George Hunsinger develops the positive debts Barth incurred from Lutheranism in his "What Karl Barth Learned from Martin Luther," in *Disruptive Grace* (Grand Rapids: Eerdmans, 2000), pp. 279-305.

28. De Lubac would find an ally in Wolterstorff's critique of the Barthian understanding of God as *ganz anders*.

29. As will be shown in the next chapter, Denys Turner takes this Catholic position even further than did de Lubac.

Milbank does not so much reject Feuerbach as he recognizes the truth in what he saw and how that truth can be developed in terms of orthodox Christian theology rather than modernity's a-theology. We must work through modern theology and not repeat it either by accommodating it or by trying to reject and overcome it for the sake of something new. This means seeing the truth in Feuerbach, which is found in the very being of the church. It is always only a receptive being. As de Lubac put it, the Eucharist makes the church when the church makes the Eucharist. The church receives its being as a gift as when it receives the Scriptures as God's Word, but the receptive being of the church is an activity and not a passivity — the Eucharist only makes the church as the church makes the Eucharist, the received Word makes the church as the church actively receives the Word. This images the relationship between the First and Second Person of the Trinity, which the Fourth Lateran Council sets forth (as Balthasar understood it) as "the eternal Father gives his entire Godhead, without holding anything back, to his Son (that is, the Father does not merely give the Son some divine essence, distinct from, and excluding, the Father's Person), yet without losing his Godhead in this act of self-surrender."[30] The Son's receptivity of his Person from the Father includes the generative act that is the Father without the Son being the Father. It is an active receptivity and is the most plausible theological case for the filioque. This active receptivity is also the freedom in which, through the Holy Spirit, creation comes into existence and exercises its own agency. The exercise of this agency will also be a receptivity.

Theology then is anthropology, but only when anthropology is Christology as Rahner noted. Feuerbach is not wrong but woefully inadequate. Victor Preller also recognized some truth in Feuerbach's position. He affirmed with Feuerbach, "all theology has become anthropology," and Preller immediately adds, "all anthropology has become Christology." Without this move, which is indebted to Rahner, his previous affirmation would trap us in the immanence of a limited human language à la Feuerbach. But with this move, as Turner emphasizes, inferences from humanity to divinity can be made as something other than assertions of human power. Because theology is anthropology, a 'natural' theology is possible. However, because modernity reduces theology to

30. Balthasar, *Theo-Logic III: The Spirit of Truth,* trans. Graham Harrison (San Francisco: Ignatius, 2005), p. 225.

anthropology, natural theology in the modern context is more danger-ous than ever before.[31]

Feuerbach's projectionist account of theological language is danger-ous because it is to some extent unavoidable. Henri de Lubac recognizes this when he begins *The Discovery of God* by posing a question, which is the question of God in the modern era. He asks, "Was Moses right, or Xenophanes? Did God make man in his image, or is it not rather man who has made God in his?"[32] This question recognizes that we still have the lan-guage of 'God' in modernity; the concept is still with us and therefore needs to be taken into account. Why do we still speak of God even now when so many thought such language would disappear? De Lubac offers two possibilities; we speak of God because we are made in God's image and thus the concept of God haunts us because the reality of God haunts us. Or we speak of God because we make God in our image for the sake of ourselves and thus the concept of God haunts us because of our inability to make sense of our reality on its own terms.

De Lubac never simply rejected Feuerbach. In *The Drama of Atheist Hu-manism,* a work published six years earlier than *The Discovery of God,* he of-fers a genealogy of modernity where Feuerbach's influence gives rise not to a rigid rationalism, but a new metaphysical 'rapture.' De Lubac traces Feuer-bach's basic thesis through Nietzsche into Dostoevsky, who represents its an-tidote. This thesis assumes a 'divinity' without God because God's attributes remain without God's proper name. All that was meant by 'God' can now be better served by attributing it to humanity. In fact, it is the only means to pre-serve humanism. "The inference is," de Lubac stated, "that in order not to sac-rifice love to 'God,' we must sacrifice 'God' to love."[33] We are presented with an unpalatable either/or. Since a genuine humanism will bear the 'attributes' we once ascribed to God, it requires choosing who is the genuine subject here. Can this preserve humanism? De Lubac thinks not. He writes, "We are prov-ing by experience that 'where there is not God, there is no man either.'"[34]

---

31. For a brief discussion of this see David Bentley Hart's *The Doors of the Sea* (Grand Rapids: Eerdmans, 2005). Hart notes that our modern conception of nature relies upon "metaphysical fideisms" where we see it as brute, inert matter (pp. 45-46). Without first con-verting such an account of nature, it would be unusable for theology.

32. Henri de Lubac, *The Discovery of God* (Grand Rapids: Eerdmans, 2002), p. 5.

33. Henri de Lubac, *The Drama of Atheist Humanism,* trans. Edith M. Riley (New York: Meridian, 1963) p. 11.

34. De Lubac, *The Drama of Atheist Humanism,* p. 31.

Read one way this could lend itself to the very problem in theology Barth identified. 'God' becomes instrumentalized for the sake of something other than God. We need God because only God can preserve a genuine humanism. This is always the temptation to an improper 'analogia entis' where God and being, or God and nature, culture, civilization, morality, or humanism become necessary for each other such that we think we know the latter without the mediation of Christ and then we 'index' our knowledge of God to what we know without God. Feuerbach's divinity without God was the logical conclusion as Barth pointed out. It made theology redundant because theology always depended upon, and was mediated by, what we knew without knowing or receiving God's name.

Barth recognized the disastrous political consequences that followed this seemingly generous position, seemingly generous because it appears 'liberal.' That is to say it has the virtue of being open to other modes of discourse not linked to the priority of Christ and thus putatively open to the other. Yet Barth recognized that this theological position had the exact reverse political consequence. This was why he opposed it in his own teacher, Adolf von Harnack. He thought we could know the true, good, and beautiful through a 'critical historical reason' outside of faith. It could then function as an external condition for faith reasonableness. Barth placed such knowledge in question. It confronted a 'crisis' where such knowledge will always escape us because revelation 'negates' and then 'reconstitutes' these transcendentals on a 'higher plane.'[35] Barth does not dismiss the transcendentals as if we were at the end of metaphysics. In fact, his position begins similar to that of Aquinas. Revelation first calls into question our presumed natural knowledge of them. We begin with 'remotio' or negation because, in contrast to Harnack, we have no univocal access to them through a critical reason alone. Then they are reconstituted on a 'higher plane.' This too bears a similarity to Aquinas's 'via eminentiae.' But for Barth a dialectic determines the relationship between the reconstituted essence of these transcendentals and their creaturely existence. For that reason we can never know them, nor can we expect them to do much work in theology. Negation takes precedence over the 'via eminentiae,' which is the opposite of Aquinas's approach to language and knowledge about God. This has Christological implications. If we acknowledge, as Aquinas did

---

35. Hunsinger, "The Harnack/Barth Correspondence: A Paraphrase with Comments," in *Disruptive Grace*, p. 329.

and I think we must, that the true and good are identical with God, then if they are permanently in crisis with creaturely reality we can never adequately affirm the hypostatic union. This would work against Barth's best insight, the heart of his theology.[36] Dialectic cannot render the Chalcedonian logic intelligible. Instead it requires a constant revision of everything that came before, for it is always placed in crisis. The burden of a Reformed 'semper reformanda' and modernity's 'modo' enter into an unholy alliance. Will it not have an inevitably anti-humanist result? God and humanity remain in competition.

De Lubac's theological defense of humanism may appear to offer an instrumentalization of God for the preservation of humanism, but that would be an unfortunate reading. Just as Barth recognized that Harnack's privileging of modes of discourse outside the priority of Christ led to constraining God in a conservative politics that preserved unjust power relations, so de Lubac recognized the same dynamic in neoscholastic doctrines of pure nature. This led (or at least did not prevent) Garigou-Lagrange and other neoscholastics from supporting Vichy France through a doctrine of pure nature.[37] When de Lubac tells us that an authentic humanism requires God and man, we should not read his claim as if we know what humanism is and then call upon God to support it. It is best read as a Christological claim. Because we confess that God and humanity are found in one Person, we do not a priori know the limits of the truth and goodness present in everyday life, even in something as ordinary as our language.

Barth and de Lubac offered different responses to a common 'problem of theology' in modernity. Barth thought that too much of modern theology, including the liberal Protestant tradition and the Roman Catholic understanding of the 'analogia entis,' simply made the option that God is made in our image the more compelling one. For this reason Barth found an odd ally in the philosophical work of Ludwig Feuerbach. Barth thought that he "penetrated the contemporary theological situation"

---

36. Whether Barth moved from this dialectic to an account of analogy that better develops the Chalcedonian logic as Balthasar stated, or remains within it as Bruce MacCormack seems to suggest, may still be the most important debate in Barth studies.

37. See Joseph A. Komonchak, "Theology and Culture at Mid-Century: The Example of Henri De Lubac," *Theological Studies* 51 (1990): 601. For an excellent discussion of this see Bryan C. Hollon's *Henri de Lubac and the Politics of Spiritual Exegesis* (Eugene, Ore.: Cascade, forthcoming).

better than any other philosopher.[38] For Barth, Feuerbach accomplished this by bringing to completion a trend that began with Luther where theology speaks primarily of God 'for us' and not of God 'in himself.' This move already made theology a predicate of anthropology. It raises the key question in modern theology, "whether and in what measure religion, revelation and the relation of God can be interpreted as a predicate of man."[39] Barth thought that Protestant, especially Lutheran, theology accomplished Feuerbach's task for three reasons. First, it separated faith from its object and turned faith into a hypostasis of its own 'within us.' Faith became an existential orientation that said more about anthropology than it said about God. In separating faith from its object, Barth tacitly acknowledges that faith became unmoored from reason. Once this occurs, faith needs no rational mediation and can be whatever anyone wants it to be, for it is only an 'existential' orientation; it has no object. It is like a private language, which because it has no public accessibility cannot be true or false. This leads to the modern problem of theology's redundancy. Whatever my existence finds meaningful becomes 'faith' for me, and this is beyond rational judgment. It is also, of course, solipsistic and philosophically indefensible.

Second, the peculiar Lutheran teaching on the 'communicatio idiomatum' claimed the divine predicates "really belong to the humanity of Jesus and in abstracto." Barth thought this was a fateful turning away from the Reformed 'Finitum non capax infinitum.'[40] Luther went beyond the assumption that Christ's two natures are predicated of the 'concretum' of his Person to the grander claim that the predicates can be abstracted from each nature and applied to the other. This not only leads to that emphasis in modern theology on God's passibility, it also cannot avoid Feuerbach's theological problematic, and logically concludes in the death of God. For if divinity is humanity, then it can suffer and die. We lose the importance of the divine names such as simplicity, impassibility, and immutability.

38. Barth, "Introductory Essay," in Feuerbach, *The Essence of Christianity* (New York: Harper, 1957) p. x.

39. Barth, "Introductory Essay," p. xx.

40. Barth puts this differently and much better in the *Church Dogmatics*. He says, "we do not say *finitum* but *homo peccator non capax.* . . ." Karl Barth, *Church Dogmatics* I.1, trans. G. W. Bromiley (Edinburgh: T&T Clark, 1986), p. 218. He then qualifies this claim when he writes, "we must now make the positive statement that in faith men have real experience of the Word of God and no *finitum non capax infiniti*, no *peccator non capax verbi divini* can now prevent us from taking this standpoint seriously with all that it involves."

Both Barth and Balthasar thought Luther set forth a faulty incarnational logic. Because Luther spoke and wrote of the properties of the divine and human nature formally and thus directly attributed one to the other without developing the significant 'concretion' of the one Person who unites the two natures, modern theology began to speak of God as if God were human, and of humanity as if it were God. Luther's modernizing of Christology leads to Feuerbach. Barth asked, "Was it mere impudence that L. Feuerbach usually liked to appeal to Luther for his theory of the identity of divine with human essence, and therefore of God's becoming man which is really the manifestation of man become God?"[41] Barth, like Balthasar, finds in the peculiar rendering of the Lutheran 'communicatio idiomatum' the "distinctive modern transition from theology to a speculative anthropology."[42]

Just as Barth and de Lubac identified a similar modern theological problem in an anthropology that perdured outside of Christology (as if such would be possible, as if 'internal' or 'external' discourses could even make sense), so did Balthasar. Like Barth, he traced it to a Lutheran doctrine of the 'communicatio idiomatum.' Balthasar also found Luther's interpretation of the 'admirabile commercium' between God and humanity problematic. In fact, it "tore open abysses that no theological or ecumenical soft-pedaling has managed to close."[43] Luther produced a 'dialectical theology' based on a contradiction between God and humanity where the humanity of Christ plays no positive role. In turn, faith as justification becomes utterly devoid of the gift of the Spirit to work in us sanctification. Von Balthasar states that the problem in Luther is that "the communication of idioms always takes place only from nature to nature and the identical Person of the Son does not effect the mediation between them."[44] This,

41. Karl Barth, *Church Dogmatics* IV.2, trans. G. W. Bromiley (Edinburgh: T&T Clark, 1985), p. 83.

42. Barth, *Church Dogmatics* IV.2. Barth writes, "Luther and the older Lutherans did in fact compromise — at a most crucial point — the irreversibility of the relationship between God and man, long before the message of the Church was similarly affected by a very secular human self-understanding which drew its nourishment from a very different quarter. Their successors necessarily find themselves embarrassed and defenceless in face of this secular humanism, and if modern Protestant theology could and has become essentially anthropology, this was not so much due to external pressures as to its own internal entanglement."

43. Balthasar, *Theo-Logic II: Truth of God*, trans. Adrian Walker (San Francisco: Ignatius, 2004), p. 345, n. 74.

44. Balthasar, *Theo-Logic II*, p. 341.

coupled with Luther's theology of a 'naked God' behind the revealed God in Christ, tears open the abyss that ultimately gives pure negativity (which would be the devil) too great a role in theology. Moreover, it does not account for the importance of Christ's obedience as the Second Person of the Trinity, which is not to be understood as 'in abstracto' but 'in concreto.' Once Christ's obedience is discounted, so is that of the believer. 'Faith' and 'grace' become purely passive existential orientations, which is also Barth's first account of modern theology's move toward Feuerbach. Two of modern theology's great discontents — Karl Barth and Hans Urs von Balthasar — both trace its problems to developments within Luther's Christology. Barth then gave this a socio-political reading that is lacking in Balthasar as Barth's third reason why Protestant theology leads to Feuerbach suggests.

For Barth the third move in modern theology toward Feuerbach occurred when modern theologians avoided the concrete, material problems of the working class by establishing hypostases such as the 'value' of private property and turning them into idols. 'God' became associated with those hypostases; when they were deconstructed for the sake of sensuous, material existence, so was God. But, Barth asks, "Could the church, earlier than Marx, have said and shown in her practice, that the very knowledge of God inherently and powerfully involves and engenders a liberation from all hypostases and idols?"[45] Here and elsewhere Barth engages philosophical and cultural movements in the modern era by subjecting them to an intriguing theological critique. However, this is also why Barth was suspicious of metaphysics. It leads to hypostases that become idols. Did Barth concede too much to Marx as he possibly did to Feuerbach?

Barth never simply dismisses Feuerbach's theological problematic. He doesn't counter the claim that theology is anthropology by positing some privileged private theological language that knows how to speak well of God without doing it as human creatures. Instead, Barth argues that theology must avoid hypostatizing false notions of God through separating faith from its object, misunderstanding the incarnation, and failing to attack the idols of Christianity's own making. He concludes, "The church will recover from the sting of Feuerbach's question only when her ethics is fundamentally separated from the worship of old and new hypostases and ideologies. Only then will men again accept the church's word that her

---

45. Barth, "Introductory Essay," p. xxvi.

God is not merely an illusion."[46] Feuerbach is not merely the church's enemy; he also helps it observe the first commandment given to Moses.

Like Barth, de Lubac recognizes that the modern theological problematic is the problem of immanence, although as we shall see they take significantly different twists on why 'immanence' is a problem. De Lubac also sees the development of this immanence, which is the problem of the secular, not as a conspiracy against Christianity, but a deformation from within it. However, while Barth often traces the problem no farther back than Schleiermacher, or perhaps Luther, de Lubac finds the emergence of the secular in the late medieval period.[47] The problem of immanence resulted from a desire "to protect the supernatural from any contamination" with the result that "people had exiled it altogether." This produces a significant difference in Barth and de Lubac's diagnosis of the problem of the secular. For Barth, the 'wall of secularity' has been violated and God's transcendence reduced to immanence. For de Lubac, God has been removed from the immanent structures of creaturely existence. For Barth, God's transcendence has been reduced to immanence. For de Lubac, God's immanence has been rejected for a pure transcendence.

They also differ in finding the problem to arise from different Christological errors. For Barth, the problem emerges from a hyper-Cyrillian Christology of Lutheranism, which results in the blurring of the boundary between divinity and humanity. Although de Lubac does not

---

46. Barth, "Introductory Essay," p. xxvii.

47. Both in *Corpus Mysticum* and *Medieval Exegesis, Volume 1*, de Lubac traces the problem back to early developments in scholasticism, particularly in Anselm, where 'faith seeking reason' was given a new determination. It was less the investigation of a mystery and more a dialectical rational procedure. De Lubac traces a shift, albeit not an opposition, in the interpretation of Scripture to the "dialectic" that emerged with the "new questions" that were being asked by the dialecticians in the eleventh century which worked against the more allegorical model of Augustinianism. What is this dialectical model? According to those of a more Augustinian persuasion the dialecticians "presumed to submit the mysteries of God himself or his action in the world to the laws which rule the nature of things." *Medieval Exegesis, Volume 1*, pp. 62-63. It was a new conception of 'faith seeking reason.' In *Medieval Exegesis* De Lubac does state that we should not read the dialecticians versus the allegorists too sharply or see in this division a division between reason/authority or fideists/free thinkers. Yet in *Corpus Mysticum* he sets Augustine and Anselm in sharp relief. Anselm's 'fides quaerens intellectum' was not only an "innovation, we might also say [it was] a revolution." See *Corpus Mysticum: The Eucharist and the Church in the Middle Ages*, trans. Gemma Simmonds, C.J., with Richard Price and Christopher Stephens (Notre Dame, Ind.: University of Notre Dame Press, 2006) p. 237.

trace the problem to Christology per se, he finds the problem of immanence present less in a blurring of the boundary between divinity and humanity and more in securing that boundary by emphasizing a pure nature without any supernatural orientation — in a kind of extreme Nestorianism. For Barth the error is a confusion of humanity and divinity and the remedy is reasserting God's transcendence. For de Lubac the error is the unbridgeable distinction between humanity and divinity and the remedy is God's immanence. But these two errors and remedies are not necessarily opposed, for both errors lead naturally to thinking that Xenophanes or Feuerbach teach us best how to speak of God. In both readings of the problem of modern theology, the result is the same: we read God's nature off of a human nature that does not first appear in the concretion of the one Person of Christ. We have a kind of Chalcedonian logic, for we still have the two natures. But we lose what matters most, the hypostatic union. The result is the same: to speak of God becomes nothing more than a predication of human action whether it be Barth's concern that Protestant theology cannot avoid Feuerbachian projectionism, or de Lubac's concern that trends in Scholastic Catholic theology made human nature so secure in itself that it failed to avoid the age-old problem raised by Xenophanes. We can understand what people mean by using the term 'God' simply by explaining the natural causal mechanisms that produce the illusion. God is a predicate of humanity. The political consequence is that the actual becomes the rational without any necessary mediation of faith or a role for the church.

Since both Feuerbach and Xenophanes identify this problematic use of God-language, the former in the modern era, the latter in the ancient one, they are both of invaluable help to theologians discontented with modern modes of speaking of God. However, as von Balthasar states in his *Theo-Logic,* all that Xenophanes (and by implication Feuerbach) can actually accomplish is a negative theology, and no theologians who repeat this negative theology (including Philo, Clement of Alexandria, the Cappadocians, Kierkegaard, and Eric Przywara) can "appeal to biblical revelation to support their claims." Why? Negative theology requires an analogy that can only stress the 'dissimilarity' between God and creatures. Von Balthasar states, "It is hard to see how such an understanding of analogy can sustain a Christology."[48] Von Balthasar even suggests that negative

48. Balthasar, *Theo-Logic II,* p. 94.

theology is "the strongest bastion against Christianity."[49] This is because it assumes that negation is prior to affirmation and eminence in speaking about God. We cannot know who God is, and even when we say that we know what God is not and not what God is as Aquinas did, this no longer emerges out of a 'via eminentiae' whereby the 'not' tacitly assumes the 'more' God is. Even that is negated. Then we know a priori that no one can know anything of God, and the door is open to turn God either into something familiar, something useful for us or into a sublimity that cannot be represented. These are the twin errors of 'mythology' and a negative 'metaphysics.'

'God' becomes problematic in the modern era because this concept can so readily be understood as nothing but a predication of humanity explained on secular terms, whether that predicate is historical, sociological, or biological. Much of contemporary theology, especially what is often called 'contextual' theology or theology preoccupied with 'culture,' simply accepts this and seeks to reinvent Christianity on Feuerbachian grounds, abstracting Christianity from questions of truth.[50] Such theology primarily raises questions of power — who gets to speak about God? whose interests are served by speaking about God in this way? — and this is an undeniable gain in theology in that it makes it more open to critical analysis. However, such questions are often asked in order to avoid questions of the truth of our speech about God, assuming every such claim to truth is a disguised power play. They trump ontology with epistemology. The question 'What is truth?' is less a question and more an answer in the guise of a question. Truth is a human construction for the sake of power. As (the early) Nietzsche put it, "Truths are illusions which we have forgotten are illusions; they are metaphors that have become worn out and have been drained of sensuous force, coins which have lost their embossing and are now considered as metal and no longer as coins."[51] Nietzsche himself could not remain with this account

---

49. Balthasar, *Theo-Logic II*, p. 45.

50. For a defense of this claim see my "Fetishisizing Feuerbach's God: Contextual Theology as the End of Modernity," *Pro Ecclesia* (Fall 2003). See also my *Theology and Culture* (Eugene, Ore.: Cascade, 2007) for a brief discussion of the positive and negative roles 'culture' plays in modern theology. This work is an attempt to supplement the inevitable role culture plays in theology with the inevitable role metaphysics also has, especially truth.

51. For an excellent discussion of Nietzsche on truth see Paul Griffiths's *Lying: An Augustinian Theology of Duplicity* (Grand Rapids: Brazos, 2004) p. 214. Griffiths notes how Nietzsche agrees with the "Kantian claim that the nature of human beings and their relation

of truth, but some theologians do. If truth has this status, then the only question that can be put to theological claims is, Whose interest is being served? In other words, whose power sets forth truth as something other than a metaphor? This question inevitably accomplishes little else than proving Feuerbach's atheology to be the unstated 'truth' even among the theologians. It also perpetuates modern theology's third ill — ontotheology.

3. Ontotheology

The problem of 'Feuerbach' is not just Feuerbach, but rather a long tradition of thinking about God which Heidegger named 'ontotheology.' What is 'ontotheology'? It is when theology becomes so defined by a specific metaphysics that our speech about God fails because we make God an item in the world. When we say 'God' we primarily speak in terms of being and causality such that God becomes nothing more than a necessary concept that traces a cause back to its origin. We are indebted to Kant for pointing this out to us. It was an invaluable service. His critique of ontotheology in the *Critique of Pure Reason* examined "the arguments of speculative reason in proof of the existence of a supreme being" such as God as 'ens realissimum.' From such an argument, he stated, "it by no means follows that the concept of a limited being which does not have the highest reality is for that reason incompatible with absolute necessity."[52] Heidegger developed the notion of ontotheology as the effort to speak or think of God primarily in terms of being. It turns God into the 'causa sui,' before whom we can neither pray nor sing and dance. 'Ontotheology' can also designate the so-called 'metaphysical attributes' of God as existence, simplicity, perfection, immutability, infinity, and unity.[53]

---

to the world make the utterance of nonmetaphorical truth an impossibility" (p. 217). The result is that lying as a sinful act as Augustine set it forth becomes an impossibility.

52. Kant, *Critique of Pure Reason,* trans. Norman Kemp Smith (New York: St. Martin's Press, 1965), p. 498. Kevin Hart notes that 'ontotheology' was a term "first used by Kant to denote the attempt to think God through pure reason." Hart, *Postmodernism: A Beginner's Guide* (London: Oneworld, 2004), p. 164.

53. Merold Westphal states that "it is a mistake to identify the God of ontotheology simply as 'the omnipotent, omniscient, and benevolent God" as does Hent de Vries or as "the God who divinely, eternally precontains all things in a mind so immense that all creation is but a supplemental *imago dei,* a simulacrum of the Infinite and Eternal, which means Infinitely and Eternally the Same" as does Caputo. See Westphal, *Overcoming Ontotheology* (New York: Fordham University Press, 2001), p. 5.

Therefore some theologians in an effort to overcome ontotheology remove these 'attributes' from proper speech of God. This, however, is a mistake. For these 'attributes' are not metaphysical attributes known through pure reason alone, which would make them ontotheological, but they stand in the tradition of the divine names.[54] While few of them go so far as to overcome the tradition of the divine names, nearly every one of the theologians discontent with modern theology also expresses discontent with something like ontotheology. We think we are speaking about God, but are truly only speaking about one more 'limited being.' Ontotheology results in linguistic confusion in our speech about God.

Both de Lubac and Preller find one of the key pieces in the development of linguistic confusion to be Cajetan's 'radical error of interpretation' of Aquinas. De Lubac denies that we can speak well of God by speaking in terms of any chain of being. "God is not the first link in the chain of being," he writes; then he argues that anyone who speaks of God in this manner produces 'ontologism.'[55] Preller traces a similar error to the development of a "so-called analogy of proper proportionality" which begins with the claim "God is the 'cause of the world'" and assumes we know what this means such that we can then "predicate certain 'perfections' of God in a mode appropriate to the 'cause' of the world."[56] This involves a bad circular reasoning because our ordinary use of the term 'cause' cannot make sense of creation out of nothing. This is not what we usually mean when we say x caused y. Thus this (neo)Thomistic interpretation must also argue that we are using the term 'cause' in a way that applies only to God, which of course assumes such a use would have some meaning for us even though it is a thoroughly equivocal use of the term. When pressed as to what this use signifies, the Thomist would reply, "A being who does not need to be made or created in the way in which the world does and who is able to create out of nothing as God has."[57] For Preller, this response is unhelpful. Having attempted to tie our language of God to the language of causality, we must then so thoroughly equivocate on the language of causality that our language about God fails. It either becomes another means

54. This point, which draws on the work of Janet Soskice, will be developed more thoroughly below.

55. De Lubac, *Discovery of God*, pp. 38, 39, n. 7.

56. Victor Preller, *Divine Science and the Science of God: A Reformulation of Thomas Aquinas* (Princeton: Princeton University Press, 1967), p. 19.

57. Preller, *Divine Science and the Science of God*, p. 21.

of expressing causality, which would be inappropriate to God or it becomes so equivocal to our ordinary use of language that the term no longer bears any meaning.

Preller does not use the term 'ontotheology' to explain this mistaken
Thomistic interpretation, but his criticism of the analogy of proper proportionality seems quite similar to what is commonly referred to as ontotheology, which also seems to be the target when Turner describes how
speaking about God cannot be tied to causality. He wrote, "the bringing
about of anything 'out of nothing' cannot be any kind of causal process such
that any kind of causal law governs it, for it is not in any sense a 'process.'"[58]

Turner wisely questions how readily the label of ontotheology can
be applied to contemporary theologians or the theological tradition. He
notes that Aquinas does say, "esse is 'predicable in common' of both God
and creatures: of creatures as created esse; of God as esse's Creator." And
then asks, "Is this 'ontotheology'?"[59] To which we should answer no because the 'esse' that is 'predicable in common' between God and creatures
is not a genus greater than God alone. But what theologian would assume
that 'being' was ever that kind of genus? Should we speak of God without
being and affirm the end of metaphysics because of the problem of
ontotheology? Ontotheology emerges as a problem when being and causality are tied together, not only when we predicate being of God and
creatures; the latter is unavoidable even though it must be done in such a
way that the use of the term 'being' is neither univocal nor equivocal,
which is what analogy seeks to accomplish. It is inevitable because we
must say God Is.

Turner is correct that we need not follow Heidegger so closely that
we refuse ever to use God and being in the same sentence. We must speak
about God in terms of being for this is given to us as the divine name. To
do otherwise is to assume that God cannot be expressed in language. We
need not agree with Derrida that this name makes God a mortal. The revelation of God's name is not the beginning of ontotheology. As Kevin Hart
notes, God 'dies' in Derrida because "God is unable to reveal himself in
language." For Derrida, the giving of the divine name in Exodus is the
source of God's death. He writes,

58. Denys Turner, *Faith, Reason, and the Existence of God* (Cambridge: Cambridge
University Press, 2004), p. 252.
59. Turner, *Faith, Reason, and the Existence of God*, p. 183.

The *I am,* being experienced only as an *I am present,* itself presupposes the relationship with presence in general, with being as presence. The appearing of the *I* to itself in the *I am* is thus originally a relation with its own possible disappearance. Therefore *I am* originally means *I am mortal. I am immortal* is an impossible proposition. We can even go further: as a linguistic statement 'I am he who am' is the admission of a mortal.[60]

'I am immortal' is the Christological proposition that can only make sense through bodily resurrection. What kind of language would we need to say this? Derrida appears to have only a univocal account of being in the above passage. He knows of only one way 'I am' could be uttered — what it 'originally means.' Aquinas's analogical language will be able to take into account what Derrida fears and nevertheless avoid its 'ontotheological' consequence. God pronounces 'I am' without being univocally determined by the space and time of that utterance. God pronounces it also by becoming flesh in that space and time and taking it into God's own being.

Stanley Hauerwas also finds a problem of modern theology to be its perceived limitation in the relationship between subject matter and language. He too correlates this kind of modern theology with Feuerbach. For instance, he finds Reinhold Niebuhr's pragmatic test of truth for Christianity akin to ontotheology, which inevitably leads back to Feuerbach. Its truth depends on the "ability to provide provocative accounts of the human condition. Accordingly Niebuhr's theology seems to be a perfect exemplification of Ludwig Feuerbach's argument that theology, in spite of its pretentious presumption that its subject matter is God, is in fact but a disguised way to talk about humanity."[61] Hauerwas suggests that theology should be about God; it should speak about God and not settle for an anthropological reductionism — but that is no easy task, for the only way for us to speak about God is as humans speak, in the modes of discourse humans alone know. If that is acknowledged, how can Feuerbach be avoided? Feuerbach is not avoided by assuming some privileged language that bears no relation to our ordinary use of terms at all.

Nicholas Wolterstorff appears to offer an alternative to Feuerbachian

60. Hart, *Trespass of the Sign,* p. 287.
61. Hauerwas, *With the Grain of the Universe: The Church's Witness and Natural Theology* (Grand Rapids: Brazos, 2001), p. 115.

projection. He presents a reasonable argument for God's speech in human speech. In fact, he makes a stronger claim for God's speech than did Barth, whom Wolterstorff finds incapable of adequately defending God's speech. For Barth, human speech only witnesses to God.[62] For this reason Wolterstorff rightly challenges the notion of God's otherness in Barthian theology which can lead to a transcendence bordering on Kantianism. He states, "The conviction that God speaks and that we can interpret that speech presupposes that God is not *ganz anders.*"[63] Barth's critique of Feuerbach tempted him to turn God into an ineffable other who never gave himself over to human hands — as occurs in Mary's yes to the incarnation and its continual 'handing over' in the preaching of the Word and the making of the Eucharist. But Wolterstorff does not develop God's speech with any Christological basis. Instead he asks, "Could God fit into the texture of moral rights and duties in the way necessary for speaking?"[64] He answers yes. Notice his question is not Christological. It does not ask if God can assume humanity and via the one Person Jesus assume such a texture; there is no concretion of Christ's Person as the site for such speech. Instead it asks if God in his divinity can accomplish this. If we answer yes to this question, we reproduce several of the ills afflicting modern theology. First, we assume a univocity of speech where our language attains its end without conversion in and through Christ. God becomes a 'member' of the community of language users without an adequate role for the incarnation. Second, this tempts us to repeat Feuerbach, disallowing us to distinguish speaking of God from speaking about ourselves. Succumbing to such a temptation fails to honor the divine name, whose grammar is found in the rule 'Deus non est genere' (God is not in a genus). Affirming this without the Barthian 'totaliter aliter' will help us avoid the ills Barth himself so ably identified.

At its best, Duns Scotus's doctrine of univocity sought to avoid the kind of equivocation in our language that God as 'totaliter aliter' implies. He also sought to avoid fideism. As Allen Wolter notes, the impetus of Scotus's work opposes the assumption that God's will alone makes moral

---

62. Wolterstorff, *Divine Discourse*, p. 64. For this reason he thinks Barth's account of Scripture is only "presentational" and not "authorial." Kevin Vanhoozer develops the significance of this difference, and its difference from post-liberal theology, in his *Drama of Doctrine* (Louisville: Westminster/John Knox, 2005).

63. Wolterstorff, *Divine Discourse*, p. 225.

64. Wolterstorff, *Divine Discourse*, p. 95.

truth and thus moral truth is not open to natural reason.[65] Scotus works against such a fideistic take on both the good and the true. In so doing he emphasizes our 'natural endowments' in both their moral and intellectual employment; sometimes this borders on Pelagianism. This follows from his development of the doctrine of pure nature. He writes, "I say that God can be loved above all not only by charity, but also by one's natural endowments, at least in the state in which nature was instituted."[66] That God can be 'loved' by natural endowments could be replaced by 'known' and one would have Scotus's doctrine of univocity. He emphasizes what our natural endowments can achieve in order to avoid the kind of equivocation that emerges from the analogy of proper proportionality. But this too has its price, for it assumes that speech about God is so similar to what our natural, ordinary language accomplishes that it tempts us to neglect any distinction between the linguistic use of being with respect to God and with respect to us.

How can we avoid speaking of God such that on the one hand our speech is so equivocal with ordinary language that it is meaningless and God becomes 'completely other,' and on the other it is so tied in to our everyday, ordinary language that speaking of God is finally nothing but speaking about us? (Aquinas and Wittgenstein will help us avoid both these errors.) The first error produces theology that makes God the sublime other about which nothing can be reasonably said; this is the metaphysical temptation deconstruction helps us avoid (metaphysics 2). The second leads to Feuerbach where everything anybody says about God has the same truth value, and speech about God becomes mythological. Both errors are found in contemporary theology; its discontents seek to avoid both.

4. Analogia Entis

Feuerbach's atheology makes sense against the backdrop of the metaphysical tradition of ontotheology. It leads to his projectionist understanding of language about God. Karl Barth thought this was also the problem of the

---

65. See A. B. Wolter, "Introduction" to *Duns Scotus on the Will and Morality*, trans. William A. Frank (Washington, D.C.: Catholic University of America Press, 1997), p. 3.

66. *Duns Scotus on the Will and Morality*, p. 286.

'analogia entis.' It was why he found Catholicism and liberal Protestantism to be similar in form. How is Feuerbach to be opposed? He cannot be so by simply adopting some fideistic position that asserts we have a language to speak about God not subject to the criticism that it will be like all other language, a form of human predication. Instead, as both Barth and de Lubac recognized, Feuerbach (as well as Xenophanes) cannot be 'refuted,' but in de Lubac's terms 'absorbed' or in Milbank's terms 'outnarrated.' Or to put it in the terms of Thomas Aquinas, when it comes to our mode of signifying, it is undoubtedly true that our speaking of God is a form of human predication. But this does not entail that the same is true of the thing signified. Thomas Aquinas's theology is important in the modern era not because it refutes Feuerbach, but because it absorbs the truth of Feuerbach's atheology without supporting the immanent humanism it entails.

De Lubac's *Mystery of the Supernatural,* his *Augustinianism and Modern Theology,* and Milbank's *Theology and Social Theory* are all attempts to respond to the dominance of a secular reason that assumes a dogmatic knowledge of what can reasonably be said, or not said, about God. It culminates in a secular humanism, confining the human creature to its own immanent plane of being, which may not be able to sustain the humanism it seeks. For how can we be human if we cannot speak well of truth, goodness, or beauty? How can they be sustained only through immanence? Neither of them sets secular reason up as an idol to be either refuted or emulated by theology. They do not 'overcome' it with a more powerful version of rationality because that would be merely repeating rather than refuting secular reason. De Lubac began *The Mystery of the Supernatural* recognizing the problem of immanence (which is the problem of secular reason) and stating, "I realize that the only way to 'refute' it is by absorption."[67] His work never counters secular reason with a new, secure theological rationality impervious to the challenges of secular reason. Instead he accomplishes two things. First he traces the history of the rise of the problem of immanence and in so doing he shows how it is not a problem outside theology but within it. Second, he 'absorbs' it by showing how this 'problem' can be viewed under a different aspect.

The problem of immanence results from the sharp distinction between nature and supernature in late Scholastic theology. It produced a "being sufficient to himself and wishing to be so" as well as a "natural mo-

---

67. De Lubac, *Mystery of the Supernatural* (New York: Herder and Herder, 1967), p. xii.

rality pure and simple."[68] But far from presenting to us a concrete, material, empirical creature, we arrive at a 'hypothetical' one that "has no kind of relationship of love with God, and at a 'beatitude' which the creature requires and which God owes him." De Lubac thought this was the heresy of Baianism or Pelagianism, which he takes up at length in his *Augustinianism and Modern Theology*.

This heresy was one of two contrasting trajectories that led to a similar denial of the proper natural activity of humanity. One was Jansenism, which refused to countenance the possibility that God could have left creation in a purely natural state. The other was Baianism that allowed for such a purely natural state. Both were forms of Augustinianism. Baianism sought to purify Augustinianism from scholastic mutations that merged it with Aristotle and verged on naturalizing grace. It 'freed' grace from this Aristotelian influence to such a degree that nature became a 'pure' realm with its own autonomous activity. But this was condemned as simply a form of Pelagianism where nature was sufficient to itself, which is ironically an Aristotelian position. The result, wrote de Lubac, was that Baianism "transfers God's attributes to man" because human nature qua nature can achieve its end without grace.[69]

The trajectory toward Feuerbach is found not only in Luther, but in this earlier version of Augustinianism. It produced deleterious consequences not only in understanding grace, but also with respect to reason: "human nature without being open to grace in the sense understood by authentic Christianity, since its end remains proportionate to its demand as a creature, does not possess that interiority without the existence of which there can be no connection with philosophy, since for its natural operation an intrusion from outside is required."[70] The role of revelation then becomes completely 'external.' It does not connect with any natural desire or rationality, but completes a nature, which was already sufficient unto itself in the first place. In other words, reason is confined to pure nature; it does not exceed this limit unless revelation adds something to it that it would never seek on its own. Thus Baius rules out any 'natural' image of God in man.[71] Jansenism, like Baianism, also posits a 'contest' between grace and

---

68. De Lubac *Mystery of the Supernatural*, p. 61.

69. De Lubac, *Augustinianism and Modern Theology*, trans. Lancelot Sheppard (New York: Crossroad, 2000), p. 6.

70. De Lubac, *Augustinianism and Modern Theology*, p. 6.

71. De Lubac, *Augustinianism and Modern Theology*, p. 22.

nature, but from the completely opposite perspective. It loses nature altogether. Both lose the Augustinian insight that the relationship between grace and nature is to be one of union and not competition.[72]

After de Lubac traces the problem of the rise of pure nature and the subsequent policing of the supernatural to a transcendent (one could say noumenal) realm, he then offers a different take on the problem of immanence without venturing into any fideistic proper object for theology. An 'object,' for instance, projected by human predication, viewed through a secular reason poses a problem for theology. But the same object viewed as theology's formal object becomes just as intelligible without requiring us to see anything that we could not see before. We need neither a different set of eyes than Feuerbach had, nor some private theological language, but only to see the things he rightly saw and those he said under a different formal object. The 'illumination' that comes is not some special privileged epistemology, but a way of recognizing a depth to our everyday natural vision that need not conflict with that vision.

Perhaps one way to think of this is with the help of Wittgenstein's image of a man inclined on a hill. Given that 'object' we do not know if he is sliding down or climbing forward. Only as we see him under the form of climbing up or sliding down does that object gain intelligibility. If we know that he told us he planned to climb a hill with Jill today, we will be able to see one thing. If we discovered rain had made the hill impossible to climb, we might see something else. Of course we seldom, if ever, simply 'see' something as a solitary, timeless 'thing.' We always see it as a 'formal object,' to use Thomas's words. As John O'Callaghan has explained, an 'object' for Thomas is not a 'thing.' "Thus 'objecta' are not things (res) simply. They are things taken as either moving a power to act or terminating the act of a power."[73] We do not see only a form or an object. We see an object under the form of what allows us to render it intelligible. For Thomas, the form and the object are not two different things that can finally be divided; if that were the case we would have a mind-world problem like empiricism produces. We would only really know the 'form' under which we know. It would be purely epistemological. For Aquinas, however, form allows for a likeness between the knower and known without "attributing characteris-

---

72. De Lubac, *Augustinianism and Modern Theology*, p. 68.

73. John P. O'Callaghan, *Thomist Realism and the Linguistic Turn: Toward a More Perfect Form of Existence* (Notre Dame, Ind.: University of Notre Dame Press, 2003), p. 206.

tics of the mode of knowing to the thing known."[74] This does not deny that
we contribute to the knowledge of an object through our cognitive activity,
but it denies that cognitive activity occurs in some internal mental realm
cut off from the world.

This makes sense of an overarching theme in de Lubac's work: his
emphasis on the Thomistic claim that "man, as God's image, is fitted to enter into communion with him, in liberty of mind and initiative of love."[75]
We must first accept something like the mind-world problem before we
can see 'god' simply as an image of man. The nouvelle théologie, through
the influence of Thomas, denies this problem. The idea of 'God' is not a
concept produced in an internal mental realm that we project upon the
world because we need a 'scheme' in order to make sense of 'content.'
Knowledge does not take place through this kind of internal activity. Only
because humanity already participates in the image of God can this form
render intelligible the objects in the world. This image is a transcendental.
De Lubac writes, "God, Moses says, made man in his image. . . . And so one
cannot say that this knowledge, at its root, is a human acquisition. It is an
'image,' an 'imprint,' a 'seal.' It is the mark of God upon us. We do not construct it; we do not borrow it from elsewhere; it is in us, for all our misery;
it is our very selves — more even than ourselves. It comes before the operation of will and intellect, presupposed by consciousness itself, and our
initiative goes for nothing."[76] It is our First Truth, without which all our
speaking would be unintelligible. However, although this knowledge is not
a 'human acquisition,' this does not imply a form of fideism. As de Lubac
puts it, "That does not mean the suppression of our natural activity of
mind; it indicates the prime condition and guarantee of its validity."[77] The
supernatural makes possible the natural. De Lubac goes so far as to suggest
"there is something sacred in our humble reason."[78]

This entails a strong doctrine of participation. The connatural and supernatural cooperates with the natural; it depends on the connatural, which
in turn depends on the supernatural. Without the exercise of the will and intellect, there is no attaining a connatural end. Without the faith-infused ex-

---

74. O'Callaghan, *Thomist Realism and the Linguistic Turn*, p. 223.

75. This is a quote from Chenu, with which de Lubac begins the *Mystery of the Supernatural*, p. xiii.

76. De Lubac, *The Discovery of God*, pp. 6-7.

77. De Lubac, *The Discovery of God*, p. 7.

78. De Lubac, *The Discovery of God*, p. 11.

ercise of our connatural activity, our supernatural end could not be attained. But will and intellect are not just 'there'; they are not brute faculties we can know separate from their connatural and supernatural end; instead it is in the light of such an end that we now see these natural powers.[79]

John Milbank critiques de Lubac's revisions of the *surnaturel* in *The Mystery of the Supernatural*. He finds the latter to be too much an accommodation to Pius XII's criticisms in *Humani Generis*. In responding to those criticisms, de Lubac moves his theology more in a Barthian direction where nature is supposedly defined as a 'negative lack' rather than the 'natural desire for the supernatural.' Milbank acknowledges de Lubac's 'admiration' for Barth, but he argues we must choose between them. He writes, "Von Balthasar's critique of Barth, however which develops the insights of de Lubac and of Przywara, marks the crucial meeting and parting of the ways in all Western twentieth-century theology. No pure Barthianism has survived this encounter, even among insightful Protestants."[80] If Milbank told us what a 'pure Barthianism' was, more sense might be made of his critique. Pure Barthianism includes a "baroque contrast of nature with grace, and of reason with revelation," and a failure "to reckon either with the *analogia entis* or the *surnaturel* as governing both philosophy and theology according to a logic rooted in a non-idolatrous understanding of the Creator-creature divide."[81] In other words, Milbank finds in Barth a doctrine of pure nature that allows for a division between reason and revelation that makes God so utterly transcendent that 'nature' is abandoned to its own resource. Although Balthasar's critique first sets forth this parting of the ways between Barth and de Lubac, Balthasar also later succumbs to Barthianism through his tendency to "shift the call of the supernatural towards a full identity with historically received grace, instead of seeing it as at once paradoxically 'prehistorical' and yet entirely oriented toward sa-

---

79. For a helpful discussion of what is meant by 'participation' here and how it differs from Neoplatonism see Rudi A. te Velde's *Participation and Substantiality in Thomas Aquinas* (Leiden: Brill, 1995). Te Velde shows how Aquinas merged a Platonic metaphysics of participation without assuming the good is merely an extrinsic feature of creatures or that creatures were necessarily emanated from God with an Aristotelian substantialist metaphysics that affirmed creatures were intrinsically good but not divine for the good in itself is identical with God.

80. John Milbank, *The Suspended Middle: Henri de Lubac and the Debate Concerning the Supernatural* (Grand Rapids: Eerdmans, 2005), p. 65.

81. John Milbank, *The Suspended Middle*, p. 64.

cred history."[82] How is the 'call of the supernatural' to be understood as 'prehistorical'? To what does it call prior to history?

Rather than positing 'pure' positions that require decisions for or against,[83] we might question why de Lubac saw similarities with Barth. De Lubac's position does not radically differ from Barth's doctrine of creation, especially his two key principles: "creation as the external basis of the covenant" and "the covenant as the internal basis of creation." Regarding the former, Barth writes, "The creature is not self-existent. . . . The creature is no more its own goal and purpose than it is its own ground and beginning. . . . The creature's right and meaning and goal and purpose and dignity lie — only — in the fact that God as the Creator has turned toward it with His purpose."[84] The supernatural makes the natural possible. Regarding the latter, Barth insists that the purpose to which creation points is God's free love. For Barth, love characterizes God's freedom; it is not a freedom to be other than the love that is the Triune God. This is the 'covenant' toward which creation points. Although how creatures receive grace remains unclear in Barth, they do not seem simply to possess a non-repugnance that makes grace extrinsic. Barth writes, "The fact that the covenant is the goal of creation is not something which is added later to the reality of the creature, as though the history of creation might equally have been succeeded by any other history. It already characterizes creation itself and as such, and therefore the being and existence of the creature. The covenant whose history had still to commence was the covenant which, as the goal appointed for creation and the creature, made creation necessary and possible, and determined and limited the creature."[85]

Nevertheless, Barth and de Lubac differ on the role of immanence in theology. For Barth, the problem is a theological reduction of God to immanent forces. For de Lubac, the problem is that immanence no longer bears a natural form or image of God. Von Balthasar developed this difference in his critique of Barth. Barth refuses a proper role for human action in the sphere of grace. Grace was only a divine and never a creaturely activ-

---

82. John Milbank, *The Suspended Middle*, p. 66.

83. See John Milbank, *The Suspended Middle*, p. 73. I find Milbank reading Balthasar as too favorable to the Lutheran 'sub contrario,' which he thoroughly critiques in his *Theo-Logic*.

84. Karl Barth, *Church Dogmatics* III.1, trans. G. W. Bromiley (Edinburgh: T&T Clark, 1958), p. 95.

85. Barth, *Church Dogmatics* III.1, p. 231.

ity. It was always transcendent, and never immanent.[86] Thus Balthasar found Protestant doctrine confining human activity to nature alone; it assumed the very doctrine of pure nature it identified as the problem with Catholicism. "We now learn that the proper place for the true activity and cooperation of the creature is the realm of nature or creation, while the realm of grace is reserved for God's activity alone. While there is a real 'mediation' in the order of nature, this is ruled out in the order of grace."[87] For Balthasar this will not do. Moreover he finds it inconsistent within Barth's own theology because Barth adopts an account of secondary causality that "unfolds along the lines of Thomism" even though Barth and Thomas start theology in very different places.

Balthasar finds in Barth a contradiction which, when he thinks it through, requires that human activity be more than confined to the realm of nature. This contradiction is based on two of Barth's admissions. First, the "creature in its creatureliness and autonomy is a secondary cause." Second, "true freedom must be interpreted in terms of the economy of grace." If both these are true, then Balthasar states, "only one conclusion is possible." This one conclusion, "contrary to Protestant doctrine," is that "the causality of the creature achieves its true character and its fullest maturity in the order of grace."[88] Thus Catholics hold forth the "possibility of reigning with God in grace, faith, obedience, prayer and, above all, in petitionary prayer," which is a possibility Balthasar thinks Barth tacitly acknowledges but refuses to honor in his doctrine of the church. This tacit acknowledgment allows Balthasar to refuse to dismiss Barth as a fideist, but without it fideism is unavoidable. For Barth "faith awakens man to an action that is proper to him. This action not only lies within the scope of his created nature, it actually corresponds to the highest natural determination of his creatureliness."[89] The model for this is the incarnation, which for Balthasar is also the basis for the 'analogia entis.' A proper reading of the Catholic 'analogia entis' where "nature is the presupposition for grace," would make

---

86. Is this a problem with Barth or with Reformed theology per se? Does it labor under the burden that God is never fully present to us, not even in the sacrament, and thus theology and worship always takes place under a critique and relativism of all that has occurred? Must everything always be re-formed?

87. Hans Urs von Balthasar, *The Theology of Karl Barth*, trans. Edward T. Oakes, S.J. (San Francisco: Ignatius, 1992), pp. 52, 132.

88. Balthasar, *The Theology of Karl Barth*, p. 135.

89. Balthasar, *The Theology of Karl Barth*, p. 140.

the best sense of Barth's own theology.[90] When Barth thinks through his Reformed account of nature and grace, he will recognize that an emphasis on human activity in the order of grace is not laying hands on God, as he fears the 'analogia entis' does, but grace's proper work. This, in turn, will allow a more properly 'secular' politics, economics, and ethics that neither eschews the Lordship of Christ nor renders nature atheological.

This difference is why Barth would not have gone as far as de Lubac when he wrote, "That is why, strictly speaking, no other revelation of God is absolutely necessary: that 'natural revelation' suffices, quite apart from any supernatural intervention."[91] And I certainly think he would be suspicious of Milbank's extension of de Lubac's idea when he states, "There is no gratuity in addition to the gratuity of creation," but the differences among the three theologians here are slighter than they may appear.[92] What might these claims mean?

Neither Barth, de Lubac, nor Milbank present a 'natural' theology where nature is self-interpreting apart from Christology. They both put forth the orthodox claim that the doctrine of creation does not come before Christology, otherwise we would altogether lose the doctrine of the Trinity. Instead, as Balthasar puts it, "The world [creation, nature] cannot have any locus but within the distinction between the [Triune] Hypostases (there is nothing outside God)."[93] If this were taken seriously, it would deconstruct the logic of internal/external discourses over which so much debate in modern theology rages.[94] The logic of Christianity must presume

90. Balthasar, *The Theology of Karl Barth,* p. 165.

91. De Lubac, *The Discovery of God,* p. 12.

92. At least Milbank suggests this is "closer" to his own position than it is de Lubac's. *Theology and Social Theory* (Oxford: Blackwell, 1990), p. 221.

93. Hans Urs von Balthasar, *Theo-Drama: Theological Dramatic Theory, IV: The Action,* trans. Graham Harrison (San Francisco: Ignatius, 1994), p. 333.

94. For instance, Paul DeHart helpfully challenges postliberalism's account of intratextuality. But then he uses a sharp internal/external distinction in order to defend a liberal revisionist theology that requires correlation to discourses 'external' to Christianity. If we have an adequate account of the Trinity as Balthasar does here, correlation would not be possible. See DeHart, *The Trial of the Witnesses,* p. 253. This causes DeHart to claim that the doctrine of the Trinity somehow gives us more space for external discourses and correlation as a critique of Christianity's 'internal' discourse than would clinging to the incarnation alone. H. Richard Niebuhr's 'logos asarkos' tempers Barth's 'Christomonism' and it is the former in Frei's work that he finds worth salvaging after having announced the dismantling of postliberalism. DeHart writes, "Niebuhr does not wish to see the inexhaustible universal-

that any discussion of creation, nature, or the world can only come after Trinity and Christology and therefore ecclesiology.[95] They are the most universally accessible 'categories' Christianity contains.

Barth feared that Thomas Aquinas and Roman Catholicism divided 'nature' and Christology, philosophy and theology, or reason and faith such that they offered two sets of distinct norms. He inadequately read Aquinas. It was impossible for him to conceive nature in these terms because Jesus is the Second Person of the Trinity, who is the Wisdom in which, through which, and toward which all creation exists.[96] Christ is the Image of God and all creation is made in and toward that Image. This means that all true desire is ultimately on its way toward its end, for this end is also the source and way of that desire.

Barth's understanding of Thomas was not, however, only this caricatured one. He recognized Brunner's presentation of it was wrong, even "sadly distorted." Brunner wrongly read Catholic natural theology as "a self-sufficient rational system detachable from the *theologia revelata* and capable of serving it for a solid foundation."[97] Barth even acknowledged that the Reformers' opposition to this caricature of natural theology was because "they faced the very questionable pelagianizing formulations of the later Nominalism," and not the genius of Thomism. Barth then states something that is surprising given that he always associated neo-Protestantism

---

ity of Christ's being in and for all humanity simply 'contained within' the canonically witnessed historical and personal particularity of his incarnation as he thinks Barth does." *Trial of the Witnesses*, p. 262. Discussions of the 'logos asarkos' are exceedingly complex. But they seem to function here as that element of the divine that is not present in the 'personal particularity' of Jesus. How does this maintain the Chalcedonian logic or the 'unsubstitutable identity' of Jesus that Hans Frei's work rightly identified?

95. Milbank seemed to acknowledge this in *Theology and Social Theory,* but his later work appears to be moving slightly away from it. He distances himself from James K. A. Smith's reading of Radical Orthodoxy by noting that "Smith stresses just a little more the centrality of specific doctrine and the institutional church." Smith, *Introducing Radical Orthodoxy* (Grand Rapids: Baker Academic, 2004), p. 18. Does the church still play a central role in mediating Christ in Milbank's work or is Christ's typological figuration in all creation sufficient? The latter can give Milbank the universality and 'Christian Enlightenment' he defends without the emphasis on postmodern particularity. See Milbank, "Materialism and Transcendence," in *Theology and the Political: The New Debate,* ed. Creston Davis, John Milbank, and Slavoj Žižek (Durham, N.C.: Duke University Press, 2005).

96. Of course he got this from St. Paul; see 1 Cor. 8:4-6, Col. 1:15-17, as well as John 1:1-4.

97. Brunner and Barth, *Natural Theology,* p. 95.

with Thomism, regularly accused interlocutors such as Brunner of it, and called Schleiermacher's theology a "secularized Thomism."[98] Nevertheless, he stated, "[The Reformers] did not know — or knew only superficially — the superior systematic method and harmony with which St. Thomas Aquinas had developed the principle: *Gratia non tollit sed praesupposit et perficit naturam* — *Santa Maria sopra Minerva*, to let the *genius loci* speak once more!"[99] Given that Barth understood this, why then did he continue to accuse neo-Protestant theologians of 'Thomism' and reject the 'analogia entis'? For Barth, Thomism still remained the problem because of how it handled the question of the knowledge of God. The Reformers did not see how the problem of justification and the knowledge of God were related because Thomism had not yet been recovered. When it was, it only exacerbated the problem the Reformers addressed — that we are justified by faith alone and by nothing that we contribute. Thomism found a preparatory "pre-Christian core of truth" that it then correlated within a framework of analogy whereby the human creature cooperates with grace. It denied the Calvinist principle that the finite has no capacity for the infinite. In so doing, the 'preparatory' and pre-Christian philosophy 'coordinated' with grace "becomes the framework and secret law of the latter."[100] Barth did not deny that Thomism sought to maintain the priority of Christology over nature, but it failed by mediating theology at all with a non or pre-Christian philosophy. This does push in the direction of a 'pure' Barthianism, against which Milbank rightly warns.

Nevertheless, Barth was not completely wrong in finding this error in Thomism and Catholic theology. Post-Tridentine Catholic accounts of the relationship between nature and grace, as well as philosophy and theology, often separate them too finely and give a privilege to 'nature' understood either outside Christology or one that inadequately points to Christ as creation's true end. Then theology is correlated to an autonomous nature. We learn this from de Lubac. If postliberal (Protestant) theology is tempted to eschew metaphysics for biblical narrative and a kind of historicism, Roman Catholic theology is often tempted to divide metaphysics from theology too thoroughly and make the former the foundation for the latter.

Some contemporary Catholic theologians use the work of Aquinas

98. Brunner and Barth, *Natural Theology*, p. 101.
99. Brunner and Barth, *Natural Theology*, p. 101.
100. Brunner and Barth, *Natural Theology*, p. 102.

to differentiate their understanding of the relation between nature (or reason) and grace (or faith) so that philosophy and theology remain two distinct sources with little interaction between them, or even such that philosophy becomes the foundation upon which theology then builds. Catholicism begins with nature rather than grace in thinking about philosophy, morals, economics, and politics. This supposedly gives an advantage over Protestantism because it provides Catholics criteria external to the Christian tradition by which it makes alliances across traditional boundaries. Such alliances are thought to be impossible if we cannot begin with a common understanding of being or nature.[101] What confuses Protestants about this position is how *traditionally* Roman Catholic it is, at least traditional since the Counter-Reformation, when Catholicism defined itself against Protestantism. In other words, traditional Catholic thought is superior to Protestant thought because it has a higher view of natural reason that does not depend upon traditional Catholic thought. This produces the odd consequence that 'nature' rather than 'faith' divides Catholics and Protestants. We can agree on basic doctrinal matters, but still not find unity because Protestants have an insufficient ground for those doctrinal matters in nature. Thomas Aquinas is the theologian used to ground faith in nature in order to demonstrate Catholicism's superiority. Unfortunately, he becomes a 'wedge' theologian dividing what does not need to be divided.

If Catholicism sets forth knowledge and speech of God in terms of an 'analogia entis' that prioritizes nature over faith, then as Barth reminded us, no alliance can be made between Protestant and Catholic theology. The only reason I see for remaining Protestant is precisely the reason Karl Barth named in his 1932 preface to the *Church Dogmatics* when he wrote,

> I can see no third alternative between that exploitation of the *analogia entis* which is legitimate only on the basis of Roman Catholicism, between the greatness and misery of a so-called natural knowledge of God in the sense of the Vaticanum, and a Protestant theology which draws from its own source, which stands on its own feet, and which is finally liberated from this secular misery. Hence I have no option but to say No at this point. I regard the *analogia entis* as the invention of

101. For some the term 'catholic' then becomes determined by a universality dissociated from any Catholic dogmatic claims as if the term had nothing to do with communion with the bishop of Rome or the teaching office of the church.

the Antichrist, and I believe that because of it it is impossible ever to become a Roman Catholic, all other reasons for not doing so being to my mind short-sighted and trivial.[102]

Barth thought Catholicism proceeded by a formal analogy which began with nature or being and then had to read the faith within it. This leads to a Catholic legitimation of secularism because politics and economics became grounded in a nature not construed under the Lordship of Christ. Politics, economics, and ethics proceed on the basis of a nature understood outside the realm of Christ.

Barth saw the 'analogia entis' not merely as a material matter — one peculiar dogma — that easily could be otherwise in Roman Catholic thought. If it were just a material dogma, it would not be church dividing for then all of Catholicism would not depend upon it. But it was more than this; it functioned as a formal principle affecting the entirety of Catholicism.[103] Nature (or being) rendered intelligible Christology, and thus Catholicism 'laid hands' on God and made him conform to our standards. The problem with the 'analogia entis' is a Christological problem. Whenever Catholic theologians can claim to begin with nature rather than grace, or when they find the category of natural reason more universal than that of faith, they are making tacit claims about Christ's two natures; claims that betray Christian orthodoxy. Humanity and divinity are set in opposition to each other such that one is had without the other. Rather than discovering both in the concrete Person of Christ, we already know 'nature' and use it to understand divinity. Barth found this version of an 'analogia entis' in Thomism, but here he was wrong. Thomas never set nature and Christology in opposition, although some post-Tridentine Catholicism, neoscholasticism, and important contemporary Catholic theology does.[104]

Much of Roman Catholic and Protestant theology discontent with modern theology sought a way beyond the either-or Barth laid out in his 1932 preface to the *Church Dogmatics*. Both sides show how Barth misrepresented the 'analogia entis' and thus it need not be a church-dividing is-

102. Karl Barth, *Church Dogmatics* I.1, trans. G. W. Bromiley (Edinburgh: T&T Clark, 1975), p. xiii.

103. Balthasar, *The Theology of Karl Barth*, p. 52.

104. As Barth rightly noted, this was (and is) the dominant motif in liberal Protestantism as well.

sue. We need not choose between nature or being and Christology.[105] But the version of the 'analogia entis' Barth critiqued has returned among significant Catholic thinkers working today, even though they make unlikely allies. We see it in a moral theologian like Jean Porter, as well as in the theology of Romanus Cessario and in the Catholic philosopher Linda Zagzebski. It can also be found in a nuanced and qualified way in the work of Denys Turner.[106] All suggest an account of nature or reason that bears a striking resemblance to the "greatness and misery of a so-called natural knowledge of God in the sense of the Vaticanum." For it requires that we choose, as Porter seems to suggest, between starting with nature or Christology, especially when theology engages politics and economics. It assumes that if we start with the latter we have limited the universal scope of our work and cannot have an adequate doctrine of nature. Then we will not be able to have conversation outside our tradition.[107]

105. I think here not only of the work of Balthasar and de Lubac that was already mentioned, but also David Schindler, Fergus Kerr, David Burrell, Gustavo Gutiérrez, Victor Preller, George Lindbeck, Stanley Hauerwas, Eugene Rogers, Joseph Incandela, and Robert Barron, as well as those influenced by them and especially their interpretation of Aquinas.

106. If it were not for the fact that Turner so greatly distances his work from Barth, the nouvelle théologie, and John Milbank, it might be read as something other than what Barth protested against. Here I think the problem is less with Turner's interesting development of Vatican I's 'analogia entis,' and more with his interpretation of those from whom he distances his work.

107. I will draw primarily on Porter's early work in *The Recovery of Virtue* (Louisville: Westminster/John Knox, 1990), p. 202. I recognize that she has moved away from the account of the 'natural' in her recent works. However, I still do not see where the theology she adopts has any more place for Christology or Trinity than this earlier work. Her "theological account of the natural law" still lacks a substantive engagement with theology and thus it is hard to countenance it as a Thomistic theory. See Jean Porter, *Nature as Reason: A Thomistic Theory of the Natural Law* (Grand Rapids: Eerdmans, 2005), p. 5. It does not need any doctrines beyond 'creation,' which seems to stand on its own without Christology or Trinity. Aquinas does not allow for that. He thinks both these doctrines are necessary to understand creation properly. In fact, Porter states that for Thomas, "the natural law represents the rational creature's way of attaining the final end that is proportionate to its nature — which is also to say, union with God, considered as the first principle and final end of all created existence" (*Nature as Reason*, p. 321). If I understand what she is attributing to Thomas here, it would seem to make him out to be Pelagian. She seems to suggest that via the natural law the creature can attain its true end "proportionate to its nature," which is "union with God." Porter also affirms Vatican I's 'duplex ordo cognitionis.' She writes, "The existence of God can also be established through rational reflection — or that, at least, is a long-standing and officially sanctioned view among Catholic theologians, and one which I share." Revelation

For Porter, Thomas provides ethics with the "motif of the goodness of the natural, broadly understood."[108] This allows for criteria 'external' to the Christian tradition by which moral action can be assessed.[109] Porter argues that such an account of the goodness of nature can bring together diverse theological ethicists like Outka, Gustafson, Grisez, Finnis, and possibly even O'Donovan into a "unified moral theory." But because Stanley Hauerwas begins theological ethics with Jesus Christ, his work cannot participate in this unification. His work is "characterized by an uncompromising denial" of the need for an "interpretation of the Christian moral tradition" that includes "some criteria that are external to that tradition."[110] Such an approach unnecessarily constrains moral options. For Porter, Aquinas provides a more thorough understanding of moral action because his Christology does not limit his moral teaching.

This criticism suggests that because Hauerwas begins Christian ethics with Jesus, he cannot have an adequate account of nature, and therefore he does not begin where Aquinas begins. This difference between Porter and Hauerwas, as set forth by Porter, reflects a traditional Catholic/Protestant division that runs from the Council of Trent to at least Vatican II. As Leo XIII set forth in his encyclical *On the Restoration of Christian Philosophy According to the Mind of St. Thomas Aquinas*, the 'wedge' theologian between Catholics and Protestants on the role of nature is Thomas Aquinas. In that encyclical Leo never intended to separate Christian doctrine from philosophy; in fact his call for the recovery of Aquinas as the

---

then "confirms and supplements what we knew or thought we knew about God, it also indicates the proper significance of God's existence for us, in the process transforming even those elements that could be independently established" (*Nature as Reason*, p. 328). I find this too Tridentine and wonder if it is the reason why there is so little place for Christology in her theology of the natural law. Here I find agreement with Martin Rhonheimer, who wrote, "The Christological perspective is indispensable" for Thomas's account of the natural law. He also stated that this perspective is "absent from Porter's book." See Martin Rhonheimer, "Review Article: Jean Porter, *Nature as Reason*," *Studies in Christian Ethics* 19:2: 377. In her response to Rhonheimer, Porter emphasizes that her understanding of the natural law is grounded in "human nature itself" and works with an Aristotelian notion of "natural perfection," but other than these comments she does not respond to Rhonheimer's question whether she can sustain the indispensable Christology in Aquinas's natural law. I hope her future work will explain how Christology relates to the natural law.

108. Porter, *Recovery of Virtue*, p. 27.
109. Porter, *Recovery of Virtue*, p. 28.
110. Porter, *Recovery of Virtue*, p. 28.

philosopher of reason stated that human reason "shows us the truth about the Church instituted by Christ."[111] But Leonine Thomism became the impetus for an understanding of Aquinas that made him the defender of natural reason against modern skepticism.[112]

Porter develops a similar Catholic theme when she states, "Aquinas's theory of morality is grounded in a theory of the human good that gives content to the fundamental norms of love of neighbor and nonmalificence and provides criteria by which to evaluate the goodness both of actions and states of character."[113] This means that, unlike Hauerwas's Christ-centered ethics, Aquinas provides criteria that can be used to assess moral actions of those outside the Christian tradition without presuming the Christian tradition in such an assessment.[114] Porter proceeds to offer us this more unified theory of morality through a "reconstruction of the more strictly philosophical components of [Aquinas'] theory" that brackets out its "more properly theological components."[115] For Porter, Aquinas's philosophy can be distinguished from his theology.

Tempting reasons exist for beginning with natural reason alone. If we begin theology with Christology how will we be able to make common cause with those outside our tradition? In a world where sectarian differences seem to issue forth in violent political contests and where fideism is on the rise, finding common ground outside our traditions would be a pressing political matter. This concern also animates Denys Turner's defense of Vatican I's claim for a natural knowledge of the existence of God, which he calls "my Thomas of rational proof."[116] He defends it for two reasons. The first is that it provides the Western Christian tradition with an

111. Encyclical of Leo XIII, in St. Thomas Aquinas, *Summa Theologia* (Westminster, Md.: Christian Classics, 1948), p. xi. Throughout this work references to the *Summa* will take the form ST followed by the part, question, and article. This edition (Benzinger Brothers) will be assumed unless explicit reference is made to the Pegis edition, *Summa Theologia* (New York: Random House, 1945). All references to the Latin come from *St. Thomas Aquinatis Opera Omnia* (Stuttgart-Bad Cannstatt: Fromann-Holzboog, 1988).

112. Fergus Kerr, *After Aquinas: Versions of Thomism* (Oxford: Blackwell, 2002), pp. 17-19, 37-39.

113. Porter, *Recovery of Virtue*, p. 31.

114. Hauerwas is more than willing to assess human actions outside the Christian tradition, but he does so based on the Christian faith.

115. Porter, *Recovery of Virtue*, p. 32.

116. Turner does not read Aquinas as an Augustinian, but as an alternative to that tradition, a tradition which of course Protestantism draws upon.

alternative to Augustinianism. He states his second reason as, "I want to be able to talk and debate without prejudice with Jews and Muslims about God."[117] Vatican I's recognition of a natural demonstration for the existence of God allows for this kind of interfaith conversation rather than the fideism of Barthianism, Radical Orthodoxy, or the nouvelle théologie.

Likewise, Linda Zagzebski assumes that much of modern Reformed epistemology is a species of fideism that doesn't take adequately into account natural reason. A version of the 'analogia entis' separates her Catholic epistemology from a Reformed one.[118] The difference is not so much that one has an account of 'natural reason' and the other does not, but that it provides the 'foundation' upon which Catholic theology must then build. Thus Zagzebski writes,

> A deep respect for natural theology is, of course, an important part of the Catholic tradition, and the efficacy of natural reason in obtaining religious knowledge has been forcefully and repeatedly stated in official documents of the Catholic Church. Furthermore, Catholic scholarship long accepted the idea that revealed theology rests on natural theology, which is to say, the work of philosophers, and the preeminent philosophy was that of Thomas Aquinas.[119]

Is this Catholic teaching? Does revealed theology rest on natural theology? If it is, Barth did not caricature the 'analogia entis.' In seeking to avoid fideism, Zagzebski restates Barth's understanding of the formal principle in Catholicism. But this distinguishes faith from nature so thoroughly that it gives little space for faith to influence the 'natural' realm.

In his essay, "The Twofold Order of Knowledge," Romanus Cessario does the same. He makes the same formal claim as Porter, Turner, and Zagzebski, but with different material implications. Whereas for them the

117. Denys Turner, *Reason, Faith, and the Existence of God* (Cambridge: Cambridge University Press, 2004), pp. xi-xii.
118. David Schindler from the Catholic side, and James McClendon from the Protestant-Anabaptist side both offer an interesting alternative to Reformed epistemology that does not begin with this sharp nature-grace distinction. See Schindler's *Heart of the World, Center of the Church: Communo Ecclesiology, Liberalism and Liberation* (Grand Rapids: Eerdmans, 1996), p. 152; and McClendon and James M. Smith's *Convictions: Defusing Religious Relativism* (Valley Forge, Pa.: Trinity, 1994).
119. Zagzebski, *Rational Faith: Catholic Responses to Reformed Epistemology* (Notre Dame, Ind.: University of Notre Dame Press, 1993), p. 3.

'analogia entis' provides the means for alliances across confessional boundaries, for Cessario it provides the means by which we can be assured that some of Catholicism's more controversial teachings are not fideistic but grounded in the way the world really is. He states, "Realist philosophy and metaphysics provide an absolutely indispensable foundation for the appropriation of sacred truth and in the development of both systematic and moral theology."[120] Once again natural reason provides the foundation upon which both moral and systematic theology can build. In fact, Cessario suggests that we would not be able to make sense of the incarnation if we did not follow this analogy of being.

> Often it is proposed that the fall has so undermined the epistemic reliability of human reason as to vitiate the capacity to know absolutely. It is thought that one may somehow 'bracket' the issue of metaphysical objectivity and then continue to use reason within theological discourse as though truth and logic were sufficiently addressed merely by pointing to the data of revelation and subsequently interpreting it according to any given categories whatsoever. . . . Frankly, what is it that the Second Person of the Trinity assumed if not human nature? And if human nature is unintelligible in its own right, what possible sense can be given to the doctrine of the incarnation of the Word? If being is unintelligible, then the revelation of God — who is perfect being — will be perfectly unintelligible.[121]

In other words, we know human nature objectively and universally without the illumination of revelation. Because we know it, we can know Christ as God. Cessario provides the most unreformed statement of a Catholic 'analogia entis' as a formal principle upon which all else depends. Metaphysical objectivism (metaphysics 5) allows us to understand Jesus and not vice versa. We know Jesus primarily because of what we know outside of him, to which he conforms.

Contemporary Catholic theology sets forth moral theology (Porter), knowledge of God (Turner), epistemology (Zagzebski), and even doctrine (Cessario) based on what we first know via natural reason. For some this provides the possibility of moral and political action that makes common

120. Paul Griffiths and Reinhard Hütter, *Reason and the Reasons of Faith* (London: T&T Clark, 2005), p. 328.
121. Griffiths and Hütter, *Reason and the Reasons of Faith*, p. 330.

alliances outside of the Catholic tradition without assuming that tradition. (Of course the shape of those political alliances will vastly differ among Catholic theologians.) For others it means that a moral teaching such as Catholicism's prohibition against artificial contraception is not a peculiar Catholic practice of faith, but a universal norm of reason based on metaphysical objectivism. Although the material uses differ, all these positions assume the same formal principle of an 'analogia entis.'

This version of an analogia entis leads Protestant theologians to be suspicious that certain teachings in Roman Catholic moral theology have more to do with clinging to claims about nature outside of the faith than they do with the unity of the faith we should share in Jesus. The tenacity by which Catholic moral theology clings to its denial of artificial contraception in its official teachings, as well as the denial of the ordination of women, may have more to do with Catholic theology's concern to maintain this 'analogia entis' than with finding unity in Christ. However, even those Catholic moral theologies that would advocate the overturning of these teachings, such as some proportionalists do, do so more because of a debate internal to the Roman Catholic 'analogia entis' than any attempt to move beyond it.[122]

What Porter, Turner, Zagzebski, and Cessario share in common is an attachment to Aquinas as the philosopher of nature. But is this the way of Aquinas? For instance, does he offer us rational proofs for the existence of God independent of faith? Or is it the case, as Joseph Incandela notes (and we will discuss below), that for Thomas the five ways should be read within the way Christ is and therefore natural reason cannot escape Christology. If this reading of Aquinas is correct, it challenges Barth's reading of the 'analogia entis.' Because Barth was wrong, the work of Porter, Turner, Zagzebski, and Cessario would have to be qualified — at least inasmuch as they draw upon Aquinas to ground theology and ethics in something other than Christology. If Barth were correct, their work stands unqualified, but any possible unification of Protestant and Catholic theology would remain jeopardized. This would be a strange conclusion to a theological position that seeks to make alliances outside of its own tradition.

Barth's reason to remain Protestant is not the best way to construe

---

122. As I argued in *The Goodness of God,* I think John Paul II's *Veritatis Splendor* was an excellent articulation of a Roman Catholic moral theology that did not bring Jesus into the overarching system of the 'analogia entis.' I also think that is true of his *Fides et Ratio.*

'nature' within the 'analogia entis.' There is no 'nature' outside Christology; as Balthasar noted, it is (theo)logically impossible to assert such a space. Likewise, de Lubac rightly opposed the more narrow Aristotelianism he found invading late Scholasticism through the work of Thomists such as Cajetan. For de Lubac, Cajetan and Suarez are the source of a theological deformation more so than Scotus, who plays that role in Milbank's work. Cajetan sought to refute Scotus on Thomistic grounds.[123] He, along with a number of Thomist theologians, thought that Scotus's distinction between innate appetite and elicited desire created a theological problem. As de Lubac tells the story, Scotus held "in all essentials the same desire for the vision of God as held by St. Thomas," which is a natural desire to see God. However, what kind of 'desire' is such a natural desire for something supernatural? Is it innate or is it elicited? If it is innate, how can it be oriented to the supernatural? If it is elicited, how can it be natural? Scotus insisted on its innateness, using the analogy of a 'weight of nature.' Certain Thomist theologians thought this lost the transcendent spiritual element of the vision of God. In opposition to Scotus, they insisted on the vision as an 'elicited appetite.' But, argues de Lubac, this is a thorough change within Thomist teaching: "With St. Thomas, the elicited act of desire was clearly the sign of a genuine natural desire, that is, of an appetite of nature even when this latter was not mentioned by name; for this reason alone, St. Thomas could argue from it as he often did. On the basis of a natural desire that can be observed he sets out to show reflexively what could be called the ontological appetite of intellectual substance, practically identical with its finality. To reduce his thought to the clumsy affirmation of an 'elicited appetite' without deep roots in the nature of the soul is to deprive his thought of all its significance."[124] But such, argues de Lubac, occurred. The vision became only an elicited appetite and nature became 'pure,' devoid of desire for that which lay beyond it. This leads not only to a deformation within theology, but a loss in philosophy as well. It becomes a self-enclosed, autonomous sphere.

This also led to a faulty bifurcation of the creature's ends — one which was natural and immanent, the other which was supernatural and

---

123. De Lubac, *Augustinianism and Modern Theology*, p. 113.

124. De Lubac, *Augustinianism and Modern Theology*, p. 125. For an important defense of the notion of an 'elicited desire' in Thomism that qualifies de Lubac's claims here see Reinhard Hütter's "Desiderium Naturale Visionis Dei — Est autem du; lex hominis beatitude sive felicitas," *Nova et Vetera* 5:1 (Winter 2007): 85.

transcendent — a demarcation based on the Aristotelian principle that "every being must find its end, corresponding to its natural appetite and natural power within the limitations of its own nature. The case of the soul has to be included as a whole in the more general case of the natural being."[125] In order to protect the transcendent, supernatural order, these Thomists removed it altogether from natural, everyday desire. "With Francis Suarez [the new doctrine of pure nature] took a gigantic step forward. . . . Suarez starts from the idea that man, being a natural being, must normally have an end within the limits of his nature, since according to a principle of Aristotle all natural beings must have an end proportionate to them."[126] This differs from the traditional teaching found in Aquinas and Scotus as well as Soto, Bellarmine, and Toletus that the human creature's true end is 'natural with respect to appetite, supernatural with respect to attainment.' It produces a new Thomist school — "Henceforth there was a Thomist trend, there was a Thomist school to maintain in opposition to St. Thomas, that rational nature is an enclosed whole in which active tendencies and capacities rigorously correspond."[127] This Thomistic school makes possible a modern 'natural theology' where nature no longer needs to be rendered intelligible in terms of its desire for friendship with God. This resulted from Thomists' adhering to an Aristotelianism more rigidly than Thomas himself ever did, and it produced a 'naturalization' or 'materialization' of the soul. It is this type of Aristotelianism to which Barth, following Calvin, rightly objects. Barth writes, "The weakness and folly of all philosophical talk about the 'supreme good' is that in it man is restricted to himself."[128] But Barth seems to think most if not all philosophy presumes this limitation. This lends support to the charge Radical Orthodoxy brings against Barth that in rejecting philosophy he merely keeps in place its autonomy.[129]

125. De Lubac, *Augustinianism and Modern Theology*, p. 205.

126. De Lubac, *Augustinianism and Modern Theology*, pp. 157-58.

127. De Lubac, *Augustinianism and Modern Theology*, p. 168.

128. Barth, *Church Dogmatics* I.1, p. 221.

129. I have already alluded to the fact that I don't find this completely convincing. Barth wrote sustained critical analyses of a host of philosophers. However, as the above quote notes, Barth could be dismissive in his criticisms of philosophy, but this should not mislead readers to think he refused to engage philosophy. James K. A. Smith has a helpful discussion of Milbank's criticism of Barth. See his *Introducing Radical Orthodoxy: Mapping a Post-Secular Theology* (Grand Rapids: Baker Academic, 2004), pp. 154-55. See also Joseph L. Mangina, "Mediating Theologies: Karl Barth Between Radical Orthodoxy and Neo-Orthodoxy," *Scottish Journal of Theology* 56:4 (2003).

Similar to de Lubac, Barth does acknowledge the problem of modern theology as an immanence trapped within its own epistemological limits. Whereas de Lubac identified the problem with this immanence as removing God from 'nature' and policing him in a transcendent, supernatural sphere, Barth identified it as capturing God within an immanence that 'naturalized' knowledge of God without God's self-gift. This is the reason Barth categorically rejects the 'analogia entis'; he wrongly thinks it only functions as he feared much of philosophy functions — it holds us captive within a metaphysics that prevents us from hearing or speaking well of God. Barth called this problem the "anthropologizing of theology."[130] He was not thoroughly mistaken in his criticisms of the 'analogia entis' and his fear of metaphysics. De Lubac himself recognized the validity of something like Barth's critique. In *Augustinianism and Modern Theology* he defines a version of Thomism, which is identical to the kind of Thomism Barth rejected. Like de Lubac, Barth located the decisive historical movement leading into the modern theological problematic in "sixteenth-century Roman Catholicism."[131] Unlike de Lubac, Barth thought these sixteenth-century Scholastics faithfully developed Thomas's central ideas. Barth associated Catholic ecclesiology with the anthropologizing of theology. It is an "alien dogmatics" because "their presupposition is that the being of the Church, Jesus Christ, is no longer the free Lord of its existence, but that He is incorporated into the existence of the Church and is thus ultimately restricted and conditioned by certain concrete forms of the human understanding of His revelation and of the faith which grasps it."[132] For Barth this means that grace becomes nature, which is the theological problem of the 'analogia entis.'[133] But isn't the fact that Jesus is 'incorporated' into the church essential to the Scripture? What does it mean when it and the tradition refer to the church as the body of Christ? Indeed we must always make sure that Christ is the head and the church the body, but it is his body that we are. Why can Barth not affirm this?[134]

Does Barth unwittingly repeat the sixteenth-century Scholastics he identifies as the problem when he, like Cajetan, seeks to protect grace from nature? Perhaps Barth is more inclined to do this in *The Doctrine of the*

130. Barth, *Church Dogmatics* I.1, p. 20.
131. Barth, *Church Dogmatics* I.1, p. 34.
132. Barth, *Church Dogmatics* I.1, p. 40.
133. Barth, *Church Dogmatics* I.1, p. 41.
134. This becomes particularly acute in his account of the sacraments.

Word of God in the early part of his *Church Dogmatics,* but is it a tremendous misunderstanding to think Barth removes grace from nature and thereby legitimates a neutral, secular space? He does explicitly state, "There is no genuinely profane speech."[135] Yet he also insists, unlike de Lubac and Thomas, that "There is a way from Christology to anthropology, but there is no way from anthropology to Christology."[136] Here he does seem merely to turn Feuerbach on his head, repeating the modern theological problematic he himself identified. If, as Barth insists throughout the *Dogmatics,* it is the 'unio' of the two natures that makes theological speech possible, then this would be a mistaken notion. Anthropology is always already *theologically* significant, although it does not have the resources in itself to recognize those signs. We need not fear a natural desire that transcends itself and can only be attained supernaturally.

The more significant difference among Barth, Milbank, and the nouvelle théologie has less to do with the relationship between grace and nature, or between theology and philosophy, and more to do with grace and freedom. Here is where Barth tempts us toward modernity, and it plays itself out in his ecclesiology. Barth worries that Catholic theology always absorbs Christology into ecclesiology. To counter this he upholds the freedom of God against any claim by the church to be able to make Christ present. This is also why he opposes the 'analogia entis.' If we say, "God was able and had to reveal himself to us," then Barth insists that it is "not on the ground of an 'analogia entis' already visible to us beforehand, of an affinity and aptitude for God's revelation . . . as if God were utterly bound to it."[137] But how does this fit with his later emphasis on God's freedom not as an absolute freedom over and against God's ordained power, but rather as the freedom to love? How does this not sneak into his theology what he otherwise recognizes as a problem — the nominalist distinction between God's absolute and ordained power? References such as these can easily lead one to read Barth as a nominalist who severs God's absolute and ordained power such that we never quite know who God is and we get that modern problematic of a 'deus absconditus.'[138] This is akin to Kant's 'po-

135. Barth, *Church Dogmatics* I.1, p. 47.

136. Barth, *Church Dogmatics* I.1, p. 131.

137. Karl Barth, *Church Dogmatics* I.2, trans. G. W. Bromiley (Edinburgh: T&T Clark, 1963), p. 37.

138. Kevin Hart recognizes that "modernity was haunted by the deus absconditus." *Postmodernism: A Beginner's Guide* (Oxford: Oneworld, 2006), p. 11.

licing' of God, and is why some philosophers who seek to defend the liberal tradition find Barth attractive as we shall see in our concluding chapter. God's 'wholly otherness' removes God from any specific politics. But it is not the whole of Barth; his equal insistence that God's freedom is the freedom to love denies this nominalism and does 'tie' God to God's ordained power. God can give himself over to Mary to be born as the Chalcedonian Definition sets forth. Moreover, we should not forget that it was Barth more so than de Lubac or Balthasar who actually developed a significant theological politics.

Barth and de Lubac identify a similar challenge confronting modern theology where it is nothing but a predicate of anthropology. This similar challenge, however, works itself out into two different theological politics. For de Lubac, God is removed from nature and politics is given over to a secular analysis based on reason alone. For Barth, God is reduced to a secular politics and it can accomplish everything needful for a theological politics on its own. MacDonald puts Barth's 'metatheological dilemma,' which he received from Overbeck, this way: "If the content of the Bible was not qualitatively different from history, psychology, anthropology — nontheology — then theology was a non-subject; and everything hitherto studied in the theology faculty or department ought to be transferred to the departments of history, psychology, anthropology, etc." Barth responds to the Enlightenment's 'metatheological dilemma' by drawing on the Reformed tradition's emphasis on 'sola scriptura.'[139] The "strange new world of the Bible," with its "sui generis historicality" avoids the Enlightenment's policing of God, which Immanuel Kant's *Religion within the Limits of Reason Alone* initiated.[140] Barth does not develop this strange new world by playing revelation against reason; nor does he accept Kant's strictures that human reason contains an innate measure against which revelation is assessed.[141] MacDonald summarizes Barth's position nicely: "Barth's conclusion did not imply that revelation was opposed to reason, or that revelation was contrary to reason; rather reason as it pertained to revelation originated in revelation."[142] This too is a Christological claim and one fitting with Balthasar's understanding of the 'analogia entis.'

139. Neil B. MacDonald, *Karl Barth and the Strange New World within the Bible* (Waynesboro, Ga.: Paternoster Press, 2000), p. 74.

140. MacDonald, *Karl Barth and the Strange New World within the Bible*, pp. 110-12.

141. MacDonald, *Karl Barth and the Strange New World within the Bible*, pp. 115-19.

142. MacDonald, *Karl Barth and the Strange New World within the Bible*, p. 116.

Is de Lubac's response to the problem of modern theology that radically different from Barth's? Any answer to that question must be yes and no. Yes in that, like Aquinas, de Lubac moves from anthropology to theology. No in that by so doing he never leaves Christology behind. De Lubac developed his response more from the perspective of a 'natural' theology by drawing on the work of Thomas Aquinas, especially his prohibition against any easy division between the natural and supernatural. The heart of de Lubac's position was thinking through Aquinas's claim, "Every intellect naturally desires a vision of the divine substance."[143] This natural desire for a supernatural vision excluded a natural theology grounded on pure reason or pure nature. At the same time it refused a fideism that responded to the Xenophanes/Feuerbach/Overbeck problematic by marking out some unique privileged terrain upon which an autonomous theology worked. But the natural was not self-interpreting and thus de Lubac's position does not fall into the policing of theology by Kant's restrictions on reason and revelation. A natural desire for a supernatural vision is not an innate measurement to which theology (and God) must conform. The natural becomes more natural when seized by a supernatural vision. Thus de Lubac writes, "That is why, if I fail to achieve this which is my end, it may be said that I have failed in everything."[144]

For de Lubac, understanding how to speak well of God brought Augustine and Aquinas together — he did not invent this, but found it in how Aquinas refused separating a 'natural' and 'confessional' theology by drawing upon Augustine. Thomas wrote in *De Spiritualibus:* "Augustine spoke of human nature not as it is considered in natural being, but as it is ordered to beatitude."[145] Thus de Lubac found in Aquinas the way to absorb philosophy into theology without sacrificing the truth in either. He writes, "Aquinas was not satisfied with establishing his first point that Greek man could in the strictest sense adapt himself to Christianity; he wanted to prove positively that 'Christianity was necessary for him' because 'only it could guarantee his ideal and let him fully realize it.'"[146] This did not mean everything in Greek philosophy was to be counted as true; it meant that humans had a natural desire that could finally not be satisfied with philos-

---

143. Aquinas, *Summa Contra Gentiles*, book 3, chap. 57, quoted in de Lubac, *Mystery of the Supernatural*, p. 11.

144. De Lubac, *Mystery of the Supernatural*, p. 73.

145. De Lubac, *Mystery of the Supernatural*, p. 29.

146. De Lubac, *Mystery of the Supernatural*, p. 32.

ophy alone. It is precisely philosophy's constant failure to achieve its aspirations that makes it invaluable to theology. Thus de Lubac quotes Balthasar, "Supernatural reality only crowns and completes human efforts because it first of all turns them upside down."[147] But this is also why the doctrine of immanence was so dangerous; it could lead philosophers to be content with no longer asking questions such as the question of truth or being — why is there something rather than nothing? Because they could not answer these questions, they turned them into issues of language alone and walked away from them. Secular reason became content to ask for something much less than metaphysics, let alone theology. And much of modern theology, de Lubac thought, assisted in this process by allowing a realm of pure nature, or a reason free from the desire to know beyond itself. The result was that the texts from Augustine and Aquinas on humanity's final end and beatitude were "systematically brought down to a natural plane and their whole meaning thus perverted. They will no longer be taken to be anything but affirmations of a purely natural philosophy."[148] It is Augustine who shows Aquinas what 'esse naturali' is, and it is never purely natural; it is only intelligible when 'ordinatur ad beatitudinem.' Theology can mediate 'nature,' including all the disciplines that present it to us, and not become intratextual, correlationist, accommodationist, or relevant only when nature is recognized within the context of its supernatural ordering toward beatitude. Here theology will no longer be redundant by simply giving us knowledge we can always secure from other disciplines, but nor does it strive for an autonomous theology with its own proper subject matter.

This first chapter examined four modern theological ills that keep us from properly speaking of God: fideism, projectionism, ontotheology, and a post-Tridentine version of the 'analogia entis.' These ills are related. Fideism emerges as the detritus from a presumed reason putatively grounded in a pure nature, a nature metaphysically objective and accessible to anyone with or without faith, a nature that bears no theological significance. Only when we first assume such a reason and make it the basis for politics, does 'fideism' arise as a possibility for persons of faith or as a critique of theological positions. This presumed metaphysically objective reason also makes possible a modern 'natural theology' where nature be-

147. De Lubac, *Mystery of the Supernatural*, p. 37.
148. De Lubac, *Mystery of the Supernatural*, p. 48.

comes the basis for what we can know of God independent from faith. Faith loses any epistemic status and must either present itself as 'fideistic' or legitimate itself through a metaphysical objectivism (metaphysics 5). Strong post-Tridentine versions of the 'analogia entis,' supposedly grounded in such a metaphysical objectivism, tend to make what we can know of nature independent from faith as the necessary foundation for faith. But in the end we wind up turning theology into nothing but speech about ourselves, our own nature, and mistake it for God, thinking that our being qua being gives us epistemic access to God. Indeed we reproduce ontotheology, speaking of a God before whom we do not pray, sing, nor dance. This god is not the God we proclaim in Word and sacrament when we say, "The Word of God," or, "The body of Christ."

Identifying these four ills is not the same as remedying them, but it does begin the therapeutic process. The next step in the process is to develop more fully ways of thinking about the relationship between faith and reason that might resist the pull of these modern maladies.

CHAPTER 2

Faith and Reason

This chapter responds to the fideism that divides faith from reason and asks us to choose between them. It does not give a single remedy for this modern theological ill, but sets forth a range between a Barthianism that verges on fideism on the one hand, and a neoscholastic rationalism on the other. Any theologian discontent with modernity could not concede that reason proceeds without faith or faith without reason. For this reason, the role of philosophy within theology requires a new emphasis. But notice this is the role of philosophy *within* theology. To emphasize philosophy for its own sake, or to set it forth as the necessary precondition for theology, as neoscholastic rationalism is wont to do, simply repeats the faith/reason distinction that brings speaking of God under suspicion in the modern era. The move into modernity from late Scholasticism is less a move out of one epoch into another and more an intensification of the latter. Faith and reason were first placed in a "dangerous discord" in the late Middle Ages, before one could police the other in modernity. But without faith, reason and philosophy lose their proper telos. Philosophy should be the love of wisdom that prompts persons to use reason in a quest for truth, goodness, and beauty. It uses what is 'natural' to creatures for this quest — thought, language, culture, desire, vision, senses, passions, etc. Some philosophers and theologians, including the First Vatican Council, suggested that these natural sources could even prove God's existence. The attempt to use these sources alone to speak of God is called 'natural theology.' Natural theology is a branch of the philosophical discipline of metaphysics.

Theology is the quest to speak well of, and to know, God. It also uses what is natural to creatures for this quest — thought, language, culture, desire, vision, senses, passions, etc. But it assumes these sources also open up to something that is more than natural, the 'supernatural.' Theological virtues, especially faith, along with beatitudes, gifts of the Holy Spirit, sacraments, and the church's confessions take up what is natural and lead it into the Divine Life so that knowledge of God is possible. Sometimes this is called or even dismissed as 'confessional theology.' Given that both a 'natural' and a 'confessional' theology inevitably use the same sources, the only ones we have as creatures, to speak of God, to differentiate them from each other creates unnecessary problems. When are we doing 'natural' and when 'confessional' theology? Every natural account of God will be some form of confession and every confession can only be done through natural means. Philosophy and theology have distinct tasks, but those tasks cannot be delineated solely in terms of nature and supernature or reason and faith. Knowledge of God is not first and foremost an epistemological issue but an ontological one. The inevitability of metaphysics challenges any such sharp division of labor.

If philosophy closes itself off into an immanent space and refuses an opening toward something more, then it loses its proper quest and becomes little more than an activity of policing against anything that could exceed the space it claims to know so intimately. Then we can agree with Barth that "the great temptation and danger consists in this, that the theologian will actually become what he seems to be — a philosopher." When philosophy opens itself to something more, it finds its proper quest not so much by what it can accomplish without assistance, but by that which it can receive given its own limitations. Because all speech, reason, and knowledge of God can only come through means 'natural' to creatures, we can also agree with Balthasar that "without philosophy there can be no theology." We must not choose between them. Yet only God knows God's self. Creatures cannot know God unless they somehow participate in God's self-knowledge. They can do this only because God participates in that which is not God, which is creaturely or 'natural' being. God does this in the incarnation. Knowledge of God, therefore, is an ontological matter because being is Christologically determined.

1. Modern Theology's Discontents

Barth and Balthasar represent theological traditions within Protestantism and Catholicism that identify and remedy modern theological ills. However, they did not repristinate some premodern era. To be discontent with modernity is not to abandon it, but to seek the good in it without adopting its ills. Balthasar's *Razing the Bastion* is hardly an anti-modern treatise; nor is Barth's *Church Dogmatics*. In fact, Bruce McCormack may be correct that Barth's theology is deeply modern in both its understanding of authority and its epistemology.[1] Barth's early epistemology was neo-Kantian such that it placed "knowledge of God outside the realm of cognitive activity. In the strictest sense, there is no such thing as knowledge of God (Gotteserkenntnis). There is only experience of God (Gotteserlebnis)."[2] *If* Barth's theology tends toward fideism it may be due to the lingering effects of Barth's appreciation for modernity, especially for a neo-Kantian epistemology. 'God' becomes an ineffable sublime who cannot be known and thus functions primarily as critique. This is why some theologians who seek to defend political liberalism find this version of Barthianism compelling. It in effect depoliticizes 'God,' rendering theology innocuous in some nonpublic space. But there is much more to Barth than this. The centrality of the hypostatic union in his *Dogmatics* resists any neo-Kantian or Kantian epistemology from totalizing the role for God within it. The incarnation is the Christian metaphysics. It is what makes Barth's theology inevitably 'metaphysical,' at least in terms of metaphysics 3 and 4, even if he did not acknowledge it as such.[3]

1. McCormack states, "Barth shared with the Enlightenment a self-consciousness which was critically disposed towards traditional authorities. . . . And the standpoint from which he subjected traditional authorities to critical scrutiny . . . would itself have been impossible without building upon the conception of human freedom and autonomy already present in the Enlightenment." *Karl Barth's Critically Realistic Dialectical Theology: Its Genesis and Development, 1909-1936* (Oxford: Oxford University Press, 1997), p. 27.

2. McCormack, *Karl Barth's Critically Realistic Dialectical Theology*, p. 75. McCormack finds Barth moving from the neo-Kantian 'constructivist' epistemology of these early years to a Kantian approach that allows for an 'intuition' of the 'unintuitable God' in Romans 2; see p. 226. But this 'intuition' of the 'unintuitable' God only occurs within the 'diastasis' motif that McCormack finds consistent throughout Barth's work. It only occurs 'sub specie mortis.' See p. 253.

3. McCormack finds a 'conclusive argument' against Balthasar's interpretation of Barth's dogmatics in terms of 'dialectic' or 'analogy' to be "Barth's adoption of the ancient

In Christian theology, the incarnation is where God's eternity and creation's temporality meet. What is the relationship between God and creation? Any answer to this question must be given in Christological terms. In fact, Christians claim the answer is given before we even know how to ask the proper question. By meditating upon this gift, we learn which questions are reasonable and which are utterly speculative and useless. Because the incarnation provides the answer for the question as to how God and creation relate, it also provides the answer for how we must think about the relationship between faith and reason. Barth taught this with his Chalcedonian logic, but it can also be found in the work of John Paul II.

John Paul II sought to reinstate truth as the transcendental mystery it is by relating reason and faith through the logic of the incarnation. One of his later encyclicals, *Fides et ratio,* examines the church's 'diakonia' of truth. It begins by citing his first encyclical, *Redemptor hominis,* in order to explain this 'ministry of truth.' He writes, "From the moment when, from within the Paschal Mystery, she [the church] received the ultimate truth about human life as a gift, she in her turn was made a pilgrim upon the highways of the world in order to preach that Jesus Christ is 'the way, and the truth, and the life.'"[4] The Paschal Mystery grounds the ministry of truth through a twofold task. The first task is to "share in the common struggle by which humanity seeks to attain to truth." This is the task of reason and it makes a place for humanism within the Christian tradition. The second task is the church "proclaiming the certainties that she knows, while conscious herself that every truth arrived at is just one stopping-place on the way to that fullness of truth which will be shown forth in the final revelation of God."[5] Here truth is a 'way'; it is something discovered through a journey. The connection between John Paul II's emphasis on

---

anhypostatic-enhypostatic model of Christology in May 1924 (together with his elaboration of a doctrine of the immanent Trinity) which provided the material conditions needed to set free the elaboration of the analogia fidei." *Karl Barth's Critically Realistic Dialectical Theology,* pp. 19-20. I find this puzzling because it is precisely Balthasar's claim that Przywara's 'analogia entis' can only be properly understood within a similar Christology. Barthians and Balthasarians often seem intent to distance themselves from each other unnecessarily.

4. *Restoring Faith in Reason: A New Translation of the Encyclical Letter Faith and Reason of John Paul II Together with a Commentary and Discussion,* ed. Laurence Paul Hemming and Susan Frank Parsons (London: SCM, 2002), p. 5.

5. *Restoring Faith in Reason,* p. 5.

truth as a 'way' or 'via' and that which Aquinas makes between the 'quinque viae,' or five ways, with Jesus' claim in John 14:6 to be the Way, Truth, and Life should not be lost on the reader. Aquinas's 'quinque viae,' or the five ways that became known as five proofs for God's existence, prepare the theological beginner for the 'way' that is Christ. The natural five ways gain flesh and richness through Christ as the way.[6] Truth, then, is not a proposition that relates language to the world. It emerges as one journeys on a way. For John Paul II, the journey has a twofold character. First, the church proclaims the truths given to it in and through the Paschal Mystery, but even these truths never exhaust the 'fullness of truth.' They are only 'stopping places' on the journey. Second, the church joins in a 'common struggle' with all of humanity to seek the truth. This is the philosophical task.

These two tasks interrelate. The certainties which the church has received as a gift require its participation in humanity's "common struggle" to attain truth. The human search for truth, which is philosophy's vocation, is not set in opposition to theology's reception of truth as a gift. What we struggle to understand by reason we also receive by faith. No dichotomy exists between the certainties of faith and the common struggle by human reason to attain truth. This will not make sense if we fail to realize how these two fit together — perhaps the best way to think of it would be that the truths humanity seeks by common reason (philosophy) and the certainties of faith can be placed over each other such that each illumines the other and renders it intelligible until the two ultimately become one, which is of course what the incarnation does in reverse. The concretion of the one Person illumines the natures of both divinity and humanity.

John Paul II makes explicit that the incarnation establishes the truth: "The Incarnation of the Son of God allows the expression of the perfect and complete whole which the mind of man desires but could never fashion for himself: the Eternal enters time, Who is Whole is concealed in the part, God takes on human face." If this is true, then it shatters the epistemological limits upon which much of modern theology rests. He continues, "This means that the truth expressed in the Revelation of Christ is circumscribed by no narrow limits of places or cultures. Instead, every man and woman has opened up to them, should they wish to embrace it,

6. The importance of Aquinas's five ways and Christ as the way will be more fully discussed below in Chapter Four.

the definitive statement which is to give sense to life."[7] The incarnation illumines both human reason and the gift of faith. It is an adequate presentation of truth, for it satisfies the natural desire the question of being (which would include questions of truth, goodness, and beauty) poses to humanity, and at the same time does so in a way that acknowledges that the reception of the gift which this truth is, a reception that entails obedience, is the most reasonable account of being we can give once we ask the question, "Why is there something rather than nothing?"

Faith seeks reason; reason assists faith. They mutually enrich each other. As John Paul II puts it, "Reason, in transcending the end to which it tended by its very nature, albeit unconsciously, was able to attain to the highest good and highest truth in the person of the incarnate Word."[8] Reason sets us on a quest, which is inevitably a quest for truth. The central means we have to pursue this quest well is language. The "incarnate Word" becomes the highest possible response to this quest, for "it" requires attentiveness both to language and nature. For John Paul II the incarnation does not negate the philosophical task, but intensifies it; it makes a search for the "natural basis" of our quest for God and truth necessary. This is the role of philosophy within theology. "The Word of God lays bare the final purpose of man and adds meaning to his actions upon earth. For this reason it exhorts philosophy to give itself to recovering the natural basis of that sense, which is part of the religious make up of each of us."[9]

Barthians are uneasy with this 'natural basis.' They hear in it a reference to an 'analogia entis'; yet Barth would agree with John Paul II that the incarnation establishes truth. If that is the case, then he too brings faith and reason together in ways that modern epistemology and politics often divide. By identfying ills in modern theology, Barth, Balthasar, and Henri de Lubac teach us how to negotiate it. We will need to examine not only these theologians, but also their heirs if we are to see a way through modernity while we remain within it. These theologians never adopted the modern compulsion to 'kill the fathers' by sacrificing the old for the sake of the new that was about to arrive. Nor did they simply repeat premodern Christian wisdom without engaging the important gains of modernity, even those of Feuerbach. Instead, as we have seen, they traced

7. *Restoring Faith in Reason*, p. 21.
8. *Restoring Faith in Reason*, p. 69.
9. *Restoring Faith in Reason*, p. 133.

the errors of projectionist accounts of language to errors internal to theology, especially Christology. Modernity and Christianity were never merely juxtaposed as opposite. The former was understood as a simulacrum of the latter, its virtual reality, which continues to need it for its own intelligibility. For this reason much of modernity was to be 'absorbed' rather than negated. To do this requires a philosophical investigation of the relationship between modernity and Christianity that would refuse any stark distinction between faith and reason, between a so-called 'confessional' and 'natural' theology. For instance, Stanley Hauerwas, long before his Gifford Lectures that defended Barth as a natural theologian, consistently argued against any division between natural and confessional theology. In his *Peaceable Kingdom,* he writes, "I find the traditional distinction between natural knowledge of God and revelation to be misleading. All knowledge of God is at once natural and revelatory." He learned this from Thomas Aquinas, Karl Barth, Victor Preller, and David Burrell. John Paul II reinforced this teaching. The work of Henri de Lubac, Hans Urs von Balthasar, and John Milbank both supplement and correct Hauerwas's point by showing that the distinction between natural knowledge of God and revelation is not that 'traditional'; the division between a purely natural theology and revealed theology can only occur after a doctrine of pure nature was first invented in the latter Middle Ages. Only then could we be confronted with the either/or of a purely natural or confessional theology — an either/or that leads to both types of fideism noted in the first chapter.

What I learned from the above theologians, and from the contemporary theological movements that draw upon them, is how to avoid the unpalatable either/or of fideism/rationalism; for while much of contemporary theology fluctuates between them — by beginning with a decision for 'fideism' or 'natural theology,' 'church' or 'public theology,' these theologians teach us how to avoid those distinctions altogether. Stanley Hauerwas's 'natural' theology, Victor Preller's Thomism, the *nouvelle théologie* of de Lubac and Balthasar, Karl Barth's ecclesial dogmatics and its development in the 'Yale School' of postliberal theology, Radical Orthodoxy, John Paul II, and even Denys Turner's theological defense of reason will provide the theological ideas that help resist these modern ills.[10] I rec-

---

10. 'Postliberal' may be a term that has outlived its usefulness, although I am not convinced by Paul DeHart's claim that it has been dismantled through his work and that of

ognize that many contemporary theologians will dismiss such a claim for they see many on this list as exemplars of fideism. Some on this list even make such accusations against others on it. In fact, they set themselves over and against the others, not always reading each other charitably. A gathering of persons representing these various theological positions could quickly degenerate into that charmingly narrated 'debate' on the poverty of Christ between Franciscans and Dominicans in Umberto Eco's *The Name of the Rose*. After a Dominican seeks to advance the argument by pulling off the beard of a Franciscan opponent, a young novice who observes the debate asks, "Are there no better arguments to prove or refute the poverty of Christ?"[11]

I am not putting these various theologians in conversation out of some irenic commitment to make them all get along, nor to invite the reader to join some theological school or movement. That is no part of the motivation for this work. I place these theologians together because they share a sensibility that any theology confined to the limited 'rationality' developed within modernity unnecessarily constrains the truthful speech about God. This makes them discontent with developments of theology within the logical space modernity provides, and since those spaces provide so much warrant for contemporary theology these theologians' work will be controversial to those committed to the modernist project. My hope is to broaden the contemporary theological conversation by asking readers to engage less with these theologians and/or the caricatures of them, and more with the philosophical and theological themes in their work. Perhaps the most important is that we can pursue the truth of God in continuity with those who came before us and find satisfying results. We need not be bound by the burden of always being modern or progressive.

Although these theologians have great differences, they share at least three similar themes. First, Kant's critique of pure reason in order to make room for faith is no friend to the theologian's cause. That theology must be correlated to Kant's pure reason or take its place via an arational fideism is

---

Kathryn Tanner. But DeHart does help us name it as a 'vague mood.' I find this preferable to thinking of it as a well thought-out school. It fits with my own understanding of it as a theological 'discontent' with modernity. I find the way he characterizes this vague mood helpful. DeHart, *The Trial of the Witnesses: The Rise and Decline of Postliberal Theology* (London: Blackwell, 2006), pp. 43-46.

11. Umberto Eco, *The Name of the Rose*, trans. William Weaver (San Diego: Harcourt, Brace & Company, 1980), p. 345.

a confinement from which theology has now been liberated. All of these theologians oppose fideism without falling prey to an illusory pure reason; speaking of God can be a rational activity. But what is meant by 'reason' will have to be broader than much of what counts for 'reason' in the modern era, especially as defined by classical foundationalism. But they also refuse to limit reason to the designative tradition of the linguistic turn. Most of them turn to Thomas Aquinas (and some to Wittgenstein as well) for a version of theology that brings faith and reason together. This is an alternative to three options modernity bequeaths us: religion within the limits of reason alone; religion only based on faith; and religion correlating faith and reason as discrete internal versus external discourses. No theologian or theological movement noted above proceeds in speaking of God by adopting one of these three options.

Second, the confinement of reason in the modern era produced an unfaithful reduction of theology to anthropology that could not avoid the consequences of Feuerbach (and Xenophanes); talk of God is finally nothing but talk of humanity. They seek to deny these consequences without denying that theology is anthropology. Not only Victor Preller but also Hans Urs von Balthasar affirmed that "all theology remains anthropology for eternity,"[12] by drawing on Rahner's statement that "all anthropology has become Christology."[13] Theologians discontent with modernity, and those modern contextual theologians who are not, agree in some sense with Feuerbach's claim that "all theology is anthropology." But for modern theology's discontents that is only a Christological claim, whereas those less dissatisfied with modernity find in it an epistemological claim. This is the great divide in contemporary theology. It results in modern theology's discontents moving beyond epistemology and recovering ontology as well as a theological metaphysic.

The third common theme is related to this move out of epistemology for ontology; the discontented theologians seek to subordinate power to truth, whereas those less dissatisfied with modernity and/or postmodernity remain satisfied with the critical hermeneutical task that seeks to expose every truth claim, ad infinitum, for the power interest it masks. But

---

12. Hans Urs von Balthasar, *Theo-Logic: II: The Truth of God*, trans. Adrian Walker (San Francisco: Ignatius, 2004), p. 284.

13. Preller, *The Divine Science and the Science of God: A Reformulation of Thomas Aquinas* (Princeton: Princeton University Press, 1967), p. 260.

this task underwrites the nihilistic assumption that power and interest are more basic to created being than truth, goodness, or beauty. This is the ultimate concession to fideism, for it denies the rationality of God's good creation. Modern theology's discontents will have a place for the transcendental predicates of being — truth, goodness, beauty.

Differences exist among these various theological schools. None of them can finally stand without hearing from, and responding to, corrections from the others. Once again, the point of this exercise is not to convince someone to join up with some theological camp or movement, whether Barthianism, postliberalism, Radical Orthodoxy, etc. The point is less to write about these theologians and theological movements and instead to examine what it is that they write about. That is what is interesting in their work. Thus I am as much interested in sorting out the arguments by which these theologians see themselves differing, than building some easy consensus. This is no easy task. Barth thought Balthasar's theology 'laid hands' on God and subordinated theology to metaphysics. Balthasar thought Barth refused the necessary task of philosophical anthropology, denying an adequate development of natural understanding in favor of an overly determined pneumatological one. Interestingly, Balthasar thought philosophical anthropology was necessary because "theology is a linguistic event."[14] Hauerwas finds Radical Orthodoxy too Platonistic and missing the significant materiality of Christianity. It does not heed Wittgenstein's warnings against the "craving for generality." Milbank worries that Hauerwasianism may fetishize the particular, as does the nominalist tradition. Milbank thinks postliberalism mischaracterizes the problem, confronting modern theology as ecumenism when in fact it is secularism.[15] Yet neither Hauerwas nor Milbank have room for a natural theology purified of faith, for they do not think such is possible.

Turner, the nouvelle théologie, Radical Orthodoxy, Hauerwas, postliberal theology, Preller, and Barth all stand with John Paul II and recognize that a proper reading of Christ's two natures hypostatically united provides the means to relate faith and reason, theology and philosophy. It gives us the proper form in which to develop an adequate response to

---

14. Balthasar, *Theo-Logic III: The Spirit of Truth,* trans. Adrian Walker (San Francisco: Ignatius, 2005), p. 359.

15. John Milbank, *Being Reconciled: Ontology and Pardon* (London: Routledge, 2003), p. 112.

questions of being and truth as well as to the relationship between philosophy and theology. But how it does so differs among them. On the whole, we could place these theologians on a continuum where Turner represents the position closest to, and yet to the right of, John Paul II, which would allow philosophy an 'autonomous' task. At the left end would be Barth, who would never concede an autonomous role for philosophy and yet who, by failing to incorporate philosophy into theology, may have unintentionally conceded Turner's position and left room for a pure nature. The ends of the continuum may finally form a circle. Hauerwas, postliberalism, Preller's Thomism, Milbank, Pickstock and Radical Orthodoxy, the nouvelle théologie, and John Paul II would come between Barth and Turner in that order. But I think all of them still share something significant when it comes to what philosophy accomplishes, and they share this in part with the philosopher Wittgenstein — that is, they think that an essential part of the philosophical task is the ability to quit doing it when necessary and to receive something that is more (but not less) than the natural activity of our own cognitive faculties. Wittgenstein is the ultimate anti-Pelagian. Philosophy's failure to achieve what it seeks is part of its 'autonomous task' (which is therefore an infelicitous phrase). 'Gift' is philosophically reasonable, but gift does not put an end to philosophy; it establishes its possibility and necessity. It is not a 'given,' but a mission.

Remedies to the four ills plaguing modern theology cannot be singular. We do not need decisive either/ors, even if they are both/ands. Remedies will emerge in terms of a range of theological possibilities. That range exists between a trajectory toward fideism some find in Barth, and one toward neoscholasticism others find in Turner. By setting forth that range between a 'Barthian fideism' and a 'neoscholastic rationalism,' we will understand more fully the maladies before modern theology and possible remedies. The next two sections examine this range in an effort to avoid the fideism of modernity and at the same time refuse to counter it with a return to neoscholasticism.

2. Barthian Fideism?

Why do many theologians, especially Catholic ones, dismiss Barth as a fideist? They worry that he and the Reformed tradition, with its emphasis on total depravity, cannot give reason its proper theological due. In turn, theology becomes 'positivist.' Positivism sets forth an object for theology, such as faith, that is a pure given, to be received without the activity of human reasoning. Positivism assumes that certain facts are simply given and that language primarily functions as designative; we 'point' to these facts. They always remain extrinsic to our being. Theology begins and ends simply by collecting divinely given information.[16] It turns revelation into a privileged epistemological position, giving it the status of a private semantics. Turner, Milbank, and Kerr share this common suspicion; Barthianism entails positivism in theology. Turner finds that same positivism present in Milbank and the nouvelle théologie. John Paul II also expressed concern that modern theology, especially Protestant theology, trades in positivism and thereby neglects the proper role of philosophy and reason by avoiding metaphysical questions of being.[17]

Does Barth abandon the necessary task of reason (and metaphysics) to cling to 'faith' as a pure, extrinsic given? His dismissal of a kind of metaphysics in *Church Dogmatics* I.1, when he calls the 'analogia entis' the "Antichrist," could lend support to the worry that his theology trades in positivism and fideism, especially when he goes on to develop dogmatics as "the scientific self-examination of the Christian Church with respect to the content of its distinctive talk about God."[18] Is theology a "science" only because it examines the church's distinctive speech about God? What makes this speech "distinctive"? Is it a private language that can only be understood from the 'inside,' whether that inside be the solipsistic ego or the closed-off community? The language of worship is not a private language; nor does it function this way for Barth. The Word of God is in no sense a private language only available to an insider group. He writes, "Revelation would not be revelation if any man were in position to advance and to establish against others the claim that he specifically speaks of and from revelation."[19] Revelation only occurs in the languages all human creatures speak. Nevertheless Barth seems to be giving us a mere tautology: theology is the examination of the church's talk about its own speech. But because theology is this examination, we get the tautology that

16. Carl Henry's theology, with its insistence on the Bible as containing propositional truth, would be an example.

17. *Restoring Faith to Reason*, p. 143.

18. Karl Barth, *Church Dogmatics* I.1, trans. G. W. Bromiley (Edinburgh: T&T Clark, 1986), pp. xiii, 3.

19. *Church Dogmatics* I.1. p. 346.

theology is theology. Correlated with the assertion that 'self-examination' of our speech about God makes it 'scientific' leads to the fear of fideism. Such fideism, if it is Barthian, would express little to no discontent with modernity.

Whether Barth is sufficiently discontent with modernity can certainly be contested. Theologians disagree over the extent to which Barth and/or Barthianism developed theology based on the space to which Kant relegated it — either faith or reason. Milbank, Kerr, and Turner, although they differ with each other, all seem to agree that in the end Barthianism is misguided. They all read him as a Kantian who, in Turner's words, polarizes "history" and a "timeless 'ahistorical reason,'" because Barth assumes a "Kantian agnostic rational epistemology."[20] He denies any external or natural standpoint outside faith from which reason can work. We only know God by standing within the posited historical information God conveys. Of course, if Barth does this, then he contributes to fideism. For Turner (and for me as well but with different consequences), Barth's position is similar to the nouvelle théologie in that both allow for reason to play a role, "*but only* within and as presupposing the context of faith."[21] Turner wants something more; he affirms a role for reason independent of faith. His position approaches that of the neoscholastics, drawing on Vatican I and its connection to Tridentine Catholicism. Yet if faith and reason are two different forms of participating in the world that nevertheless overlap, then Turner's distinction would not seem to hold.

Fergus Kerr represents the position of the nouvelle théologie in Turner's work, and thus as he charges Barth so Turner charges Kerr with denying reason a sufficiently independent role in theology. Yet oddly enough Kerr agrees with Turner that Barth's theology does not give due place to reason. Like Turner, Kerr finds Barth problematic in that he "turns to revelation not reason." God's self-disclosure then functions epistemologically. Kerr states, "We need God to step in between our minds and the external word, indeed between our minds and themselves, to fill the gap, to guarantee that what seems to be really is."[22] We are still mired in epistemology and have not moved into ontology. Without recognizing that we

---

20. Turner, *Faith, Reason, and the Existence of God* (Cambridge: Cambridge University Press, 2004), p. 12.
21. Turner, *Faith, Reason, and the Existence of God*, p. 14.
22. Kerr, *After Aquinas* (London: Blackwell, 2002), p. 25.

always already participate in what is real and do not simply construct it, we will never have an adequate account of reason or truth. Is this an adequate reading of Barth?

Barth does argue that "awareness of creaturely existence" is certain only because of God's self-disclosure. This leads to a Reformed emphasis on election with Barth's important twist — the election is the election of Jesus Christ. That God freely chooses to enter into human existence is what makes our existence certain. He writes,

> It can know no fluctuation or doubt, because it does not depend upon any choice of the creature, but upon the choice of the Creator which is implicit in His self-disclosure, and in view of which the possibility that he and his fellow creatures might equally well not be is excluded from the very outset and definitively.[23]

In other words, human certainty is not grounded in epistemology. Our existence is not certain because we have an 'I' that can doubt and subject everything to criticism. But it is nevertheless certain; it is certain because God's election of the man Jesus entails election of "his fellow creatures." In this section of the *Dogmatics* Barth explicitly denies any dependence upon a Cartesian ego as giving us certain knowledge of our existence. Nowhere does he find intrinsic to human being a necessary existence secure from, and external to, the contingencies of history; nor does he set these in contrast to each other. The incarnation would not allow it. This makes it difficult to find Barth polarizing history and eternity in a Kantian sense and then invoke God to close the epistemological gap it opened up between the world and our mind. His criticism of Lessing and other philosophers for doing these very things renders this accusation implausible.

In the first volume of the *Church Dogmatics*, Barth finds an "intolerable distinction" in Lessing, Kant, Herder, Fichte, and Hegel "between the eternal content and the historical 'vehicle.'" He calls this the "nadir of the modern misunderstanding of the Bible."[24] He carries this criticism into his 'doctrine of reconciliation' when he argues that modern persons seek the historical distance of the so-called problem of eternity and history for the sake of their own self-secure power. We need Lessing's ditch, and the security it gives us, in order to protect ourselves from the radical dissolution of

---

23. Barth, *Church Dogmatics* III.1, p. 350.
24. Barth, *Church Dogmatics* I.1, p. 329.

our world that Jesus Christ's incarnation, crucifixion, and resurrection produce, a radical dissolution of any secure division between metaphysics and history. Speaking and repeating this 'problem' protects us against God's act. It assumes revelation is a 'fact' done back then, which we must make relevant now through our own activity. Our consciousness remains the dominant secure form of agency against that of God-made-flesh and our 'time' remains certain. We stand over and against Christ's time by assuming ours is most real and then we must mediate Christ's time to our own by making his relevant to ours through our conscious activity. But rather than allowing the question of the problem of time to stand as Lessing and the 'faith and history' debate posed it, Barth turns the question back on itself and asks, "How will it stand with us when we are alongside Jesus Christ and follow Him, when we are in His environment and time and space? Can the reconciliation of the world with God accomplished in Him consist in anything but the dissolution of the world?"[25] What does Barth mean by the 'dissolution of the world'? Is this where his dialectic does work 'sub contrario' such that the only way God redeems the world is by dissolving it? A more theologically palatable reading is to recognize that for Barth reconciliation precedes creation.

Barth never polarized history and eternity, for that would deny the central role the hypostatic union plays in his theology. The principle driving Barth's theological reflections is that Christ is 'very God' and 'very man.' "At no level can we have to do with God without having to do with this man."[26] He cannot think God without thinking the hypostatic union, which asserts the "direct unity of the Son of God with the man Jesus of Nazareth."[27] Everything hinges upon this 'unio.' The divine disclosure is so united to the material, locatable presence of Jesus of Nazareth that God cannot be thought without this form.[28] But how can we think this? To do so we must think that

---

25. Barth, *Church Dogmatics* IV.1, p. 293.

26. Barth, *Church Dogmatics* IV.2, p. 33.

27. Barth, *Church Dogmatics* IV.2, p. 51.

28. Barth, *Church Dogmatics* IV.1, p. 33. "But is it so inconceivable, does it need such a great imagination to realize, is it not the simplest thing in the world, that if the history of Jesus is the event of atonement, if the atonement is real and effective because God Himself became man to be the subject of this event, if this is not concealed but revealed, if it is the factor which calls us irresistibly to faith and obedience, then how can it be otherwise than that in this factor, and therefore in the history of Jesus, we have to do with the reality which underlies and precedes all other reality as the first and eternal Word of God, that in this history

reconciliation precedes creation, and that our time is not as real as God's 'time,' which is not bound by the same successiveness our time is.[29] Eternity is not known separate from the contingency of history.[30] Metaphysics does not abstract from history; nor does an awareness that knowledge is historically mediated put an end to metaphysics. (Those who interpret Barth in a 'Hegeling' direction deny the 'logos asarkos' and God's impassibility, collapse metaphysics into history, and develop Barth in a fideistic direction.) Barth's position here seems similar to claims made by John Milbank.

Milbank's relationship to Barthianism is more complex than that of Turner and Kerr. He recognizes that his own work, especially its 'Christological poetics', stands in the tradition of the nouvelle théologie, especially of Balthasar, whose "Christocentric emphasis" derives "immediately" from Barth. The similarity between Barth and Milbank is found in Milbank's claim, "Nothing can prove or establish the perfection of Jesus' human work, for if it is perfect, then the work must itself define the character of perfection."[31] And in *Being Reconciled,* Milbank states that Barth (and Hooker) are correct that "theology only expounds ecclesial law; dogmatics is 'Church Dogmatics', or 'The Laws of Ecclesiastical Polity.'"[32] But in *Truth in Aquinas* Milbank and Pickstock conclude that any "post-Kantian mediation" between Thomas and Barth fails "because the weak analogical resources of metaphysics which reason to God only as first cause are in fact the only terms in which *sacra doctrina* can receive and comprehend the revelation of God as he is in himself."[33] In other words, philosophy in the form of metaphysics is a necessary feature of theology. Revelation and natural theology (or metaphysics) are related such that the 'weak' account of analogy Aquinas offers is alone what allows for the reception of revelation. Metaphysics seems to make revelation possible, which would be a claim

we have actually to do with the ground and sphere, the atmosphere of the being of every man, whether they lived thousands of years before or after Jesus?"

29. Neil MacDonald develops this theme in his *Metaphysics and the God of Israel: Systematic Theology of the Old and New Testaments* (Grand Rapids: Baker Academic, 2006).

30. Turner, *Reason, Faith, and the Existence of God,* p. xi. Turner clearly finds this polarization misguided, although the Radical Orthodox theologians find a similar problem in Barth, which they remedy with a more Augustinian and Platonist reading of Thomism, largely inherited from the nouvelle théologie. Turner does not find this convincing in that it would not let him read Thomas as the theological rationalist he reads him to be.

31. Milbank, *The Word Made Strange* (London: Blackwell, 1997), p. 135.

32. Milbank, *Being Reconciled,* p. 109.

33. Milbank and Pickstock, *Truth in Aquinas* (London: Routledge, 2001), p. 26.

more in line with Denys Turner and Vatican I, although they differ in their qualification of this analogy as 'weak.' God's simplicity, a metaphysical claim known via reason, distances Aquinas from Barth and makes any mediation between them impossible. Thus they tell us,

> for Aquinas in an un-Barthian fashion, Scripture records the event of the augmentation of human intellect through a deepened participation in the divine simplicity. Thus, for Aquinas, it is less that metaphysics is abandoned by reflection on scripture, and much more that it is fulfilled in its intention, but beyond its own understanding of this intention. It is both suspended and subsumed.[34]

Is this a fair reading of Barth? Does he assume that Scripture abandons metaphysics by asserting its own independent epistemology? If so, then Barthianism would put forth an argument similar to the 'private language' argument Wittgenstein demolished. However, I do not think this adequately captures Barth's work. Even though he stood too firmly in a trajectory of the Protestant tradition that could treat philosophy (especially metaphysics) as the usurpation of sacred doctrine and perhaps remained unwittingly influenced by the hellenization thesis of his teacher, he nevertheless adopted and used much of that philosophy, especially as it was absorbed and converted within the Christian tradition. Moreover, Barth patiently identified how that usurpation occurred.

Milbank's criticism of Barth does not always engage Barth's works. To claim Barth neglects philosophy is to overlook his *Protestant Thought from Rousseau to Ritschl,* which is one of the more interesting theological engagements with philosophy in the twentieth century. Barth also gives us an intriguing account of 'metaphysics' in his "Man in the Eighteenth Century," which brings together history, philosophy, and theology and shows how philosophy became a 'mystery,' but without theology. This work bears great similarities to de Lubac's *Drama of Atheist Humanism,* which also argues that the humanistic 'temptation' that besets us is not one merely of 'rationalism,' but the promise of a 'rapture' grounded in a return to myth.[35] In Nietzsche, this 'myth' appears indistinguishable from mystery, but de Lubac argues they must be distinguished, for they are "two opposite types of sacredness." But he does not reject the category of myth altogether. Mystery

---

34. Milbank and Pickstock, *Truth in Aquinas,* p. 25.
35. De Lubac, *Drama of Atheist Humanism,* p. 45.

does not reject myth, but "takes over a part of it, filters it, purifies it, exorcises it, as it were. There is an authentic sacredness in the cosmos, for it is full of 'vestiges' of divinity."[36] This is where de Lubac differs from Barth. They both see this element of myth-as-mystery as characterizing modern rationality. It tempts us toward a pagan religiosity. But de Lubac thinks it can be 'exorcised' and 'purified.' Barth rejects it altogether for theology as a 'science' shorn of all myth. Perhaps it is Barth who is the rationalist?[37]

Yet, Barth also argues that the eighteenth-century Enlightenment was marked less by a 'rationalism' that needs to be overcome than by a return to 'mystery.'[38] Absolutism characterizes this 'return to mystery.' Barth narrates 'absolutism' as a 'program' that begins once 'man' recognizes Copernicus and Galileo were correct. Humanity is not the center of the universe. But the consequences of this recognition are counterintuitive. Rather than relativizing man, it accentuates his self-importance and power through the creation of "philosophical systems of rationalism, empiricism, and skepticism."[39] Barth traces this absolutist program through various persons, technologies, and movements: Columbus, the creation of atlases, the horrors of the slave trade, the new tourism, salons for tea and tobacco, presuppositionless science, the fateful division among "logic, observation, and mathematics" in the universities and technological inventions. Poli-

---

36. De Lubac, *Drama of Atheist Humanism*, p. 47.

37. For this reason I don't find Joseph Ratzinger's argument that both Barth and Schleiermacher return to a pagan account of myth that the early church rejected convincing. Ratzinger states that in Barth we find "the retreat from the truth of reason into a realm of mere piety, mere faith, mere revelation; a retreat that in reality bears a fatal resemblance, whether by design or by accident and whether the fact is admitted or not, to the ancient religion's retreat before the logos, to the flight from truth to beautiful custom, from nature to politics." Joseph Cardinal Ratzinger, *Introduction to Christianity* (San Francisco: Ignatius, 2000), p. 139. In opposition to this "retreat from the logos," Christianity must engage the "god of the philosophers." But Ratzinger also notes that there must be a "transformation of the god of the philosophers" because of their two overarching themes: first, they are basically 'self-centered' ("thought contemplating itself,") and second, they are grounded in 'pure thought.' Ratzinger, *Introduction to Christianity*, pp. 147-48. Both of these are transformed by seeing God fundamentally as Love, as relationship, as Triune. Barth did not have a sufficient account of the god of the philosophers, but he understood with Ratzinger that reason must be transformed by God as Triune. More so than any other theologian in the early twentieth century, he recognized this.

38. Karl Barth, *Protestant Thought from Rousseau to Ritschl* (Salem, N.H.: Ayer, 1971), p. 13.

39. Barth, *Protestant Thought from Rousseau to Ritschl*, pp. 15-16.

tically, this results in the destruction of the nobility and a "territorializa-
tion" of politics in the "unitary state." "War," then, "becomes a latent principle" in all politics.[40]

From this history, Barth makes two metaphysical claims. The first
has to do with the effect this history has on anthropology. "And so man too
grew in this space in the sense that he unmistakably became more and
more master of his existence."[41] Barth tacitly recognized that "man" as the
"master of his existence" is the true end of metaphysics, a technological
end that we are now fated to repeat endlessly, even if Foucault announced
this man's death. The second metaphysical claim has to do with the politics
and theology that both underwrite and sustain this anthropology. He discusses this by examining the Declaration of Independence of the United
States, which he calls "Calvinism gone to seed," and that of France, which
is "Catholicism gone to seed." He states, "Both of them show that those
who drew them up imagine that they were standing before an ultimate reality, and indeed before a reality beyond which no man would ever see.
Face to face with the supreme Being, or self-evidently, man knows according to both documents that he has a right to life, liberty, property, and so
on."[42] Modern absolutist politics, both in monarchical and liberal democratic form, claim to see something like the end of history, to see reality as
it is and beyond which we will never be able to see. This 'ultimate reality'
may be confrontation with the 'supreme Being' or its own self-evident disclosure; it does not matter which it is, for the consequences are the same. It
supposedly traps us within a metaphysical closure that has no 'beyond.' It
is the myth that becomes the fate of 'modern man.'

Barth then analyzes "the inner and outer form imparted to life by
man as he lived at that time." Its outer form strives "to reduce everything to
an absolute form."[43] This takes many inner forms, but one of the most significant is what leads to Feuerbach: "Man knows that he is linked with, and
ultimately of the same substance as, the God significant for him in this

40. Barth, *Protestant Thought from Rousseau to Ritschl,* pp. 15-21.

41. Barth, *Protestant Thought from Rousseau to Ritschl,* p. 17.

42. Barth, *Protestant Thought from Rousseau to Ritschl,* pp. 27-29. Barth calls these
declarations a "unanimous confession of faith," which are "confined within the same vicious
circle" as the political absolutist.

43. Barth, *Protestant Thought from Rousseau to Ritschl,* pp. 32-33. Barth also notes that
the "right to free association" contributes to this absolutist program. That he recognizes this
should mollify those who find in him too voluntarist an ecclesiology.

double function. God is spirit, man is spirit too."[44] For Barth, this is what makes any 'natural theology' so dangerous. It trades on this univocity that links 'man' and 'God' under a more universal category. It cannot but perpetuate the myth.[45] Its relationship to ethics also produces problems. For it first tells us that "we must therefore allow Nature (and this is in our power) to tell us what is good." Barth then asks, "But has not man in fact asked himself and himself given the answer he apparently really wished to hear from some other source?" The result is a "strange vicious circle" that suggests a metaphysics similar to ontotheology — "that in virtue of the reality of his own existence he could vouch for God and in so doing for the possible existence of God. This may have been the secret of his inward attitude in outline."[46]

Clearly Barth engages philosophy critically, and does so perhaps more thoroughly than many if not most twentieth-century theologians. Clearly he gives attention to metaphysics. Theologians who suggest otherwise are wrong. But this may not be the heart of the criticism brought against Barth. It is that he has no way of moving from anthropology to God, or from philosophy to theology. He only has a critique of metaphysics. He can tell us how it misled us, but not how we need it. His theology is unidirectional; it only moves from faith to reason and has no place for a natural desire that finds itself fulfilled in faith despite its own intention. Two responses present themselves. First, it is not Barth who rejects such movement; it is 'Eighteenth-Century Man.' He traps us in a mythic-metaphysical-natural law closure where God, being, nature, and anthropology become univocal. Barth identifies metaphysics as metaphysics 2. But in tracing this history of being Barth also ruptures its immanence and makes possible for metaphysics to be something other than this. Second, it is Christology, and especially the incarnation, that allows him to do so, and it is Feuerbach who assists the theologian by both bringing this history to completion and at the same time fracturing it upon the rejected building stone. In explaining Feuerbach's position Barth acknowledges its similarity to Christian theology: "Theology itself in fact admits in Christology that God is entirely human. He is human — and this is the true Christ — in the consciousness of

44. Barth, *Protestant Thought from Rousseau to Ritschl*, p. 52.

45. If Mark Lilla's analysis in *The Stillborn God: Religion, Politics, and the Modern West* (New York: Knopf, 2007) is correct, then Barth's work here would have some vindication. It is no coincidence that they both begin with Rousseau.

46. Barth, *Protestant Thought from Rousseau to Ritschl*, pp. 53-54.

the species, in which we actually partake together of redemption, peace and fellowship."[47] Feuerbach, Barth concedes, has "radical Easter belief, the belief in the resurrection of the flesh" on his side. Here is a place where we can and must move from humanity to God, but we can only ever make this move Christologically. Barth acknowledges a logical inference from humanity to divinity without confusing God and humanity.

Metaphysics is an inescapable component of theology, even for Barth. Thus Milbank and Pickstock are both mistaken and correct in their reading of Barth. They are correct to see an absence of attentiveness in Barth's work to a positive account of metaphysics. His fear of repeating 'Eighteenth-Century Man' leads him to see metaphysics primarily as metaphysics 2 and prevents him from giving due agency to human creatures. But they are mistaken to see in Barth an attachment to Scripture that negates metaphysics. It is because of Barth's attachment to Scripture that he too reads it as the fulfillment of something like metaphysics, which he captures in his important proposition, "covenant is the internal basis of creation, creation is the external basis of the covenant." Hauerwas's defense of Barth as a metaphysician in *With the Grain of the Universe* seeks to answer concerns about Barth such as Milbank and Pickstock raise.[48]

---

47. Barth, *Protestant Thought from Rousseau to Ritschl*, p. 357.

48. A similar development of a Barthian metaphysics drawing on Scripture can be found in Neil MacDonald's *Metaphysics and the God of Israel*. MacDonald refuses to call this metaphysics 'natural theology' because he does not think Barth nor Scripture allow us to move from creation to God. We can think of creation without God, even though MacDonald denies the nominalist and voluntarist thesis that the world's utter contingency as an act of will means that God could have created various different worlds. Instead, he emphasizes that 'creator of heaven and earth' is a predicate of God, not creation. Thus, creation is grounded in divine self-determination. This makes his position compatible with Thomistic rationalism, without underwriting a 'natural theology.' The result of his metaphysics is that traditional 'attributes' such as eternity, which can be found from the Patristics through Calvin, are revaluated through the biblical insistence that God is active in history. MacDonald follows von Rad in focusing on God's revelation to Moses in Exodus 3 to be primarily one of exodus and liberation. Although I find much of his theology compelling, I think he fails to see how biblical the traditional metaphysics was as it is grounded in the giving of the divine name. As we will see in the next chapter, this is something von Rad failed to discern adequately with his focus on so-called 'dynamic' Hebrew thought. I do think there is a lurking hellenization thesis in MacDonald's biblical metaphysics when he tells us, "Patristic theology on the whole drew on the legacy of Greek metaphysics and defined God in terms of divine nature" (p. 231). This is the temptation Barth's work without a supplementation from metaphysics faces.

Stanley Hauerwas claims Barth is "the great 'natural theologian' of the Giffords." This may come as a surprise to Barth, whose response to such a claim would most likely be "Nein!" For Hauerwas, Barth is this even more so than William James or Reinhold Niebuhr, because Barth alone "rightly understood that natural theology is impossible abstracted from a full doctrine of God."[49] What could this mean? Hauerwas explains,

> I think that Barth, in spite of his disavowal of natural theology, provides the resources necessary for developing an adequate theological metaphysics, or, in other words, a natural theology. Of course, I assume that 'natural theology' simply names how Christian convictions work to describe all that is as God's good creation.[50]

The words "describe" and "creation" are key here. For Hauerwas, natural theology is less an explanation based on filling in some gaps in causal mechanisms through pure reason, and more a description of how the world 'naturally' is if what Christians claim is true. Christians call that 'creation.' But this is no fideism, for Wittgenstein's philosophy gives Hauerwas the resources for a 'natural' theology.

For Hauerwas, natural theology is "the nongodforsakenness of the world even under the condition of sin."[51] This is an interesting and odd interpretation of natural theology. De Lubac carefully traces the origins of natural theology in Scholasticism to a possible knowledge of God prior to the world under the condition of sin. At least in the latter Middle Ages, 'nature' in a 'natural' theology speculated on Adam's condition prior to the Fall. It is not yet the self-enclosed reality Barth traces in the eighteenth century. The term 'nature' underwent a decisive shift from the Scholastics to Rousseau. The Scholastics asked the following questions: Did Adam have a natural beatitude separate from grace? Was grace itself the condition of his creation? If so, was there anything outside of grace? How then could the fall and redemption have any dramatic import if all was always already grace? If there were nothing outside grace, then grace would be owed to the creature simply for being creature. Then nature is an empty category; everything is grace. The doctrine of pure nature developed in or-

---

49. Stanley Hauerwas, *With the Grain of the Universe: The Church's Witness and Natural Theology* (Grand Rapids: Brazos, 2001), pp. 9-10.

50. Hauerwas, *With the Grain of the Universe*, p. 142.

51. Hauerwas, *With the Grain of the Universe*, p. 20.

der to preserve grace's gratuity. A theology built on such a nature would not be a theology "under the conditions of sin," but a theology that speculated on the knowledge of God in a hypothetical situation — one where sin did not exist. This speculative knowledge developed out of a hypothetical distinction between God's absolute and ordained power.[52] Given that we know how God has ordered the world in and through Jesus Christ, what might it have been like if it were not ordered as such? For de Lubac problems arise when the hypothetical distinction becomes real.

Hauerwas and Barth offer a very different understanding of natural theology. It does not speculate about a state of nature without sin, but asks about the knowledge of God under the condition of sin, which is the only condition we know. It refuses to divide God's ordained and absolute power as did the speculative natural theology of the latter Middle Ages. For Barth and Hauerwas natural theology can only be rightly done in reverse as a kind of apophatic discipline. We begin with who God is and how God has ordered the creation in Christ and move back from there to 'nature.' Nature, for Hauerwas, then is not a neutral, inert substance, but is always already 'significant'; it points toward Christ. In fact, he critiques a tradition of thought beginning with Troeltsch and running through William James, Reinhold Niebuhr, and James Gustafson where nature is 'purposeless' and 'impersonal,' only given significance by our actions upon it. Hauerwas may not have explicitly developed the significance of 'nature' or creation as itself a sign, but this is presumed throughout his work. It is the reason for the title to the Gifford Lectures: *With the Grain of the Universe: The Church's Witness and Natural Theology.* This is why there can be no adequate demarcation of theology into 'natural' and 'confessional.'

Hauerwas, like de Lubac, recognizes what is right about the questions the theologians of 'pure nature' were asking, without repeating their answers. They asked the question, because we have been graced through God's gift in Christ, how are we to understand nature? Inasmuch as this was a hypothetical question, it caused few problems. Only when it became a real question through a sundering of God's absolute and ordained power did the question produce a strong doctrine of nature that lost its meaning in God's gracious gift. Hauerwas could not have recognized this without the work of Karl Barth. (Could de Lubac or Balthasar have done so as

52. As Neil MacDonald notes, it requires a God who could have created other possible worlds. See footnote 48 above.

well?) For this reason, Barth is the great natural theologian. He reminds us that abstracting the knowledge of God ('potentia absoluta') from how God makes himself known ('potentia ordinata') is the temptation behind every speculative natural theology.[53] Once this division gets made, then we will not know how to work with the grain of the universe; nature becomes a mystery to us, concealed by the very language we use to speak about it because we wrongly assume we have an unmediated awareness of 'nature.' We falsely think it is just there as inert stuff that is 'given' to us. We find it more 'certain' than anything else and seek to build our knowledge of God on its supposed certitude. Our knowledge of nature becomes fideistic, grounded in a superficial positivism. For this reason it is key to Hauerwas's work that revelation is not an epistemological category. No such privileged form of knowledge exists, either in the solipsism of an individual or of a community. He does not divide the logic, language, or rationality of theology off from philosophy, science, or other disciplines.[54] In fact, much like how in Barth's thought we at times find God more readily in a variety show done well than in church, so Hauerwas constantly finds God in the most unusual places, such as Iris Murdoch's novels.[55]

Hauerwas's defense of Barth against the charge of fideism finds an ally in Hans Urs von Balthasar. At the end of the third volume of his *Theo-Logic*, Balthasar takes up the relationship between the Spirit and creation, which is another version of the question of the relationship between grace and nature. Interestingly, Balthasar finds Barth's development of this per-

---

53. This is not the exact language Barth and Hauerwas use, but the point is the same. Hauerwas writes, "The idea that we might know God abstracted from how God makes himself known was the result of the loss of a Christian politics called church." *With the Grain of the Universe*, p. 16.

54. Hauerwas does engage the specifics of natural theology. For instance, he argues that the 'ontological argument' is less a deductive proof than an argument from analogy. "Anselm's argument does not make existence a predicate but reveals that existence itself is an analogical predicate." *With the Grain of the Universe*, p. 186.

55. Hauerwas concludes his Gifford Lectures recognizing that the Catholic Church, under the leadership of John Paul II, far from being 'fideistic,' finds itself "defending the activity of reasoning" against a secular culture that is itself increasingly antagonistic to reason because of its dogmatic certainty that appeals to truth are always disguised power plays. Hauerwas notes approvingly, "We find [John Paul II] honoring the good of philosophy as a discipline. Yet we also find him arguing that although the results of reasoning may be true, they 'acquire their true meaning only if they are set within the larger horizon of faith.'" *With the Grain of the Universe*, p. 236.

suasive because it gives an account of "being a creature" that is not something which is "suspect," but "excellent." Barth, suggests Balthasar, "can read the creation of a single salvation history from the development of nature up to mankind and from mankind up to Christ *(creatio continua),* in which nature is always oriented toward and surrounded by grace, and the creature's apportioned time is allotted to it from God's eternally triune time and history."[56] For Barth, then, nature is something of a retrospective, remainder concept. We only know it because we read backwards from Christ to the presupposition that he assumes in humanity to the presupposition it assumes in creation. This move in Barth clearly allows, and even requires, a strong role for philosophy as one of these presuppositions. But like 'sin' and 'evil' in Barth's theology, its role is understood only after the fullness of God's grace is first seen.

Is Barth then a fideist? He may have failed to provide a positive metaphysics and his work could border on nominalism when God's attributes were grounded in such a sovereign act of God's freedom that they bore no relation to what we do know of God's perfections.[57] His claim that we must only know God from Christ forgets the importance of the tradition of the divine names. We must know God's name before we can know Christ bears it. We know that because God gave it to Moses. Barth played fast and loose with those names, finding in them elements of Greek metaphysics rather than the scriptural witness, which Greek metaphysics intimated and which only Scripture confirmed. This misleads Barthian theologians and tempts some to turn God into a mythological figure, who must suffer as we do in order to love, or who must be timeful. Some (mis)read Barth as denying any 'logos asarkos.' But Barth's work is like a large city with so many places to visit that one can never claim to have mastered it simply sitting in one spot. Better readings of Barth are possible than some of these criticisms suggest. To dismiss it with one 'type,' like fideism, is the worst form of theological voluntarism. Theology is always richer and more complex than such types provide. For instance, Balthasar finds Barth's opposition to nominalism to be one of his important insights. Barth opposed any "strict" or "semi-nominalism" where we have a "description of the es-

56. Balthasar, *Theo-Logic III: The Spirit of Truth,* pp. 418-19.

57. I am indebted to Alasdair MacIntyre's account of this in his presentation "Rediscovering Tradition within Modernity" at the Lumen Christi Institute, University of Chicago, April 30, 2005.

sential properties of a *nuda essentia* [naked essence] of God that leaves the hypostases out of account."[58] Balthasar states, "One can accept this statement, which is correct, without having to accept Barth's refusal to acknowledge any natural knowledge of God."[59] Balthasar does not seem to find his own position and Barth's to have quite the dramatic either/or many find in them; it is less "the crucial meeting and parting of the ways in all Western twentieth-century theology" as it is an important convergence between Protestant and Catholic theology whereby Balthasar sees that Barth's position does not mean we must reject natural theology.[60] Theology is always 'in via.'

What, then, should theology expect from philosophy in order to avoid fideism? Shall we expect a rational 'proof' for the existence of God as Vatican I claimed? Is this the only antidote to modern fideism? If so, then is this rational 'proof' available to all reasonable persons as neoscholasticism asserts but never seems capable of providing? What is this proof? Why has it been so long forthcoming? Why is it that it is usually put forward only within the context of faith — as Vatican I explicitly stated? But should theology reject a natural knowledge of God? What could that even mean? How would such a rejection be possible? Who speaks, writes, thinks, prays, or worships God non-naturally? If Barth and Barthians do claim to reject such knowledge, then they embody the twentieth century's wrongheaded opposition to metaphysics.[61] It is the ongoing commitment to dialectics, and its development by Barthians, that poses the real problem. It can too easily lose Barth's opposition to nominalism and develop an irrational form of Reformed theology. So Christopher Schwöbel writes, "The absolute difference between God and the world is expressed with astounding dialectics when Barth says that the 'line of death' that separates what God

58. Balthasar, *Theo-Logic II*, p. 138, citing Barth, *Church Dogmatics* II.1, pp. 52-53.

59. Balthasar, *Theo-Logic II*, p. 138, n. 15.

60. Balthasar concludes this section in the *Theo-Logic* by stating, "We cannot follow Nominalism in elevating God's decrees as 'absolute' above the sense that they make, both in themselves and in their coherence with all the other divine decrees. Speculations about a *potentia absoluta* [absolute power] in God, dissociated from his *potentia ordinata* [ordained power] earn the theologians nothing but disgrace." *Theo-Logic II*, p. 147.

61. Bruce McCormack notes that Barth remains both a 'liberal' theologian and in continuity with modernity, and this is found in his Kantian epistemology and rejection of metaphysics: "There is no epistemological way that leads from the empirical world to the divine source. The metaphysical way taken by classical realism would remain forever closed to Barth." *Karl Barth's Critically Realistic Dialectical Theology*, p. 130.

is and does from human being and action cannot be transcended, but then goes on to say that it is also the 'life-line,' the end which is the beginning, the 'No' which is 'Yes.' No wonder Barth quotes Tertullian's credo quia absurdum in order to underline the paradoxical claim that the negation of life is also the affirmation."[62] Does Barth seek to join Derrida and espouse the gift of death? Can we have Barth's dialectic without a kind of nominalism, all too present in Reformed theology, that so clings to the doctrine of justification by faith that it makes it nearly impossible for human creatures to be holy, which is our great vocation?[63]

Barth only lends support to fideism when his work gets stuck in a dialectical form, when it makes it impossible for God to give himself away in human representation, or when we focus on the two natures as if they are not seen through the unity of the one Person. Dialectics only affirms the first part of Balthasar's acknowledgment of the relationship between language and the incarnation — "A God who would be expressed to the end in finite words (and deeds!) would no longer be God but an idol." This produces an emphasis on negation and destruction; it can too easily lead to a 'negative theology' alone. Then we will get fideism, for God cannot be known, but only thought where every thought, like every language, only works when placed under erasure. If we are to affirm the logic of the incarnation, then the second part of Balthasar's statement must also be affirmed — "But a God who did not wish to give himself away to this extreme end, but withheld a piece of himself from us and for himself would also no longer be our God: here too he would be an idol."[64] Of course, to argue that our own reason can get epistemic access to God without God drawing us into God's self-knowledge will lose the incarnation altogether and replace it with a self-sufficient human reason.

62. *The Cambridge Companion to Karl Barth,* ed. John Webster (Cambridge: Cambridge University Press, 2000), p. 21.

63. See Bruce McCormack's essay "What's at Stake in Current Debates Over Justification?" where he rejects the language of 'participation' because it owes too much to "ancient Greek ontologies of pure being"; defends a strong doctrine of justification by faith against Aquinas and any lingering Catholicism in Reformation theology; and tacitly defends a nominalism against any realism. In *Justification,* ed. Mark Husbands and Daniel J. Treier (Downers Grove: InterVarsity, 2004), pp. 86-91, 107, 110.

64. Balthasar, *Theo-Logic II,* p. 279.

3. Neoscholastic Rationalism?

If certain trajectories within Barthianism tend toward fideism or nominalism despite other, better trajectories, then Denys Turner's defense of Vatican I against Barth could tend toward its opposite, rationalism despite other better trajectories within it as well. Neither a fideistic nor a rationalistic theology would find itself discontent in modernity, and therefore both positions are tempted to repeat modernity's endless theological — and political — options, the first by drawing on faith without reason, and the second by equating reason with nature independent of faith. That I find both Barth's and Turner's work ill at ease in modernity suggests that these trajectories in their work lend themselves toward accommodation to modern sensibilities, but that such trajectories are not the best interpretations of them. This may be surprising with Turner's work because he distances it from most of those I am calling modern theology's discontents. Turner not only finds Barthianism to have an insufficient natural theology, he also finds the same to be the case for the nouvelle théologie and Radical Orthodoxy.[65] In other words, the charge Milbank levies against Barth is similar to the one Turner brings against these other theologians. Their reliance on an Augustinian doctrine of illumination, and their reading of Aquinas within that Augustinian light, worries Turner because it contaminates Thomistic rationalism with an unnecessary commitment to faith.

Turner defends the Vatican I decree "that there is a twofold order of knowledge, distinct not only as regards its source, but also as regards its object." This provides a context to converse across faith traditions as well as between philosophy and theology. It allows for good citizenship in a world marked by a religious and philosophical pluralism. His theological rationalism has the benefit of "talking and debating without prejudice with Jews and Muslims about God."[66] If we claim the existence of God is only rationally known within the context of faith, we will be less open to the good citizenship that interfaith conversation requires. But here I think Turner creates a problem that does not exist. Turner's argument misnames the modern problem between politics and religion. It assumes that we have either incommensurable faith communities or a universal reason indepen-

---

65. He does not offer us extensive readings of these various theological movements.
66. Turner, *Faith, Reason, and the Existence of God,* p. xi.

dent of faith. Turner's position pushes in the direction of reason as an independent criterion (classical foundationalism) rather than public accessibility (Wittgenstein). Wittgenstein's private language argument challenges this basic assumption and helps us avoid the inevitable production of fideism once faith gets policed by a universal reason.

Why would 'reason alone' outside the context of faith make room for such a conversation better than a reason within the context of faith, especially among the Abrahamic faiths? Is there a lingering Kantian cosmopolitanism seeking a pure reason devoid of faith commitments in such an assumption? Does Turner assume what James K. A. Smith has called "the logic of determination" as opposed to the "logic of the incarnation"? The logic of determination assumes a binary opposition where any conceptual 'determination' of God is always already a corruption and form of violence.[67] Smith finds the logic of determination resulting in a "kind of radical, negative theology for which to say anything specific is to act from a deep hubris, that, in the very act of confession corrupts the divine."[68] Smith contrasts this with the "logic of incarnation," which warrants speaking of God beyond the modern/postmodern assumption that every act of determinate speaking is a form of violence.

Turner's argument for a natural knowledge of God outside faith approaches Smith's logic of determination, for the God of which reason alone speaks is a God about whom finally nothing can be said. We are tempted by negative theology. Although Turner recognizes that "Thomas's economy of speech accompanies, and probably derives from, a fundamental confidence in theological language, a trust that our ordinary ways of talking about creation are fundamentally in order as ways of talking about God," he nevertheless concludes, "What else could speech be but that which, before God, fails?"[69] God cannot be represented in language. But can this make sense of what we do in worship? Turner comes close to Barthian dialectics. He affirms only Balthasar's first acknowledgment of the relationship between language and the incarnation in its dialectical mode. However, before concluding that Turner has adopted a modern

67. See James K. A. Smith, *Speech and Theology: Language and the Logic of Incarnation* (London: Routledge, 2002), pp. 127-33.

68. James K. A. Smith, *Introducing Radical Orthodoxy: Mapping a Post-Secular Theology* (Grand Rapids: Baker Academic, 2004), p. 58.

69. Turner, *Faith, Reason, and the Existence of God*, pp. 102-3. Turner does not discuss Thomas's claim that we have words 'proprie' for God.

logic of determination, we must attend with great care to how this claim differs from other theologians' discontent with modernity.

Every theologian must recognize that to some extent language finally fails in naming God. The question is, How does language fail? Does language fail in speaking well about God because we know the limits of what language can accomplish and it cannot signify the 'res' we call 'God'? Or does language fail in speaking well about God because we have no adequate mode of signifying even though we can still intend and speak of the 'res'? This is a crucial distinction. The first position assumes that any failure as to *how* our language works (the 'modus significandi') will also entail a failure of *what* it signifies (the 'res significata'). This is the danger modern epistemology coupled with a designative version of the linguistic turn poses for language about God. We already saw it in Derrida, when he asserts that the form of signifying God gives us in the divine name makes God a mortal. It assumes univocal identity between our modes of language and the objects to which they refer. The second assumes that the failure of the 'how' is not a failure of intending or understanding God, but of comprehending, and the two should not be confused. A lack of comprehension does not logically correlate to a failure to understand the 'what' that is signified.

Turner's theology approaches a logic of determination: "Insofar, then, as God is found in human language, within its characteristic rationality, God is found not, as Nietzsche thought, in the good order of 'grammar,' but in the disordered collapse of speech into paradox, oxymoron and the negation of the negation."[70] Turner comes perilously close to the logic of determination and therefore to giving us a negative theology akin to that of Derrida's; perilously close, but he does not finally arrive there because his 'reason alone' is based on the truth of Christological dogma. The 'reasons of faith' that allow for a demonstration of God's existence by 'reason alone' are found in the incarnation. It shows us that inference across incommensurables is possible. We can move from humanity to divinity. Much as human flesh makes knowledge of God possible, so does human language and reason. We would not know this without faith, yet by faith we recognize that a natural knowledge of God must be possible.

For Turner, then, Christian dogma entails a role for an autonomous use of reason, although not in the Kantian sense. The latter has a too limited understanding of what constitutes reason. Turner's argument assumes

---

70. Turner, *Faith, Reason, and the Existence of God*, p. 106.

an expanded notion of what we mean by 'reason' based on the doctrine of the incarnation. As he says, "These things are simply a matter of the 'logic' of the incarnation, at any rate of a Chalcedonian Christology."[71] He draws on Aquinas to make his argument: "For Thomas . . . it is precisely on account of the logic of incommensurability which obtains between them that inferences from the human to the divine *are* possible in the person of Jesus Christ."[72] The two natures of Christ do not compete on some equal logical plane; their incommensurability means it is not a logical contradiction to move from one to the other. So like Milbank and Pickstock, Turner follows Aquinas in moving from humanity to divinity. But how does Turner move from 'reasons of faith' to 'reason alone'? Is this a sleight of hand? He argues that this is not the "logical oddity" it appears to be.[73] But if Chalcedonian dogma is the basis for asserting reason alone can demonstrate God's existence, why then does Turner indict Milbank for arguing that Thomas's proofs for the existence of God presume an "explicitly theological presupposition"?[74] Doesn't Turner's argument also assume such a presupposition? What else is the 'logic of the incarnation'?

Sorting out the differences between Turner on the one hand and Barthianism, Radical Orthodoxy, and the nouvelle théologie on the other, is not easy. A Barthian such as Colin Gunton explicitly rejects any "two-source theory of truth," as did Barth himself. Radical Orthodoxy, drawing on the nouvelle théologie, certainly has no place for a doctrine of pure nature, if that is what this Vatican I decree entails. But why Turner sets his position over and against that of the nouvelle théologie is even more puzzling. De Lubac affirms the Vatican I decree as much as Turner. In his *The Discovery of God*, he was accused of neglecting Christology for a natural theology. He defends himself against this, stating, "How could I, or anyone, have abstracted entirely from all that the Christian revelation has definitely given us?"[75] Nevertheless, de Lubac adheres, as does Turner, to a clear distinction between faith and reason. He writes, "The mysteries of the faith remain inaccessible to rational investigation, while the authority and the laws of reason remain essentially unchanged in the believing intelligence," and he cites Vatican I's "twofold order of knowledge" for a defense

71. Turner, *Faith, Reason, and the Existence of God*, p. 220.
72. Turner, *Faith, Reason, and the Existence of God*, p. 219.
73. Turner, *Faith, Reason, and the Existence of God*, p. 5.
74. Turner, *Faith, Reason, and the Existence of God*, p. 201.
75. De Lubac, *At the Service of the Church* (San Francisco: Ignatius, 1992).

of his own development of natural theology, which assumes but does not require divine faith.[76] Moreover, in his reflections back over his work de Lubac confesses that he was "never completely at ease" outside of the specific terrain of natural theology.[77]

More similarities exist between de Lubac and Turner than perhaps any of the theologians and theological movements noted above, which makes it all the more surprising that Turner seeks to distance himself from the nouvelle théologie. The difference between them is so subtle that it might be missed altogether (and might be a difference without a distinction). Perhaps the difference can be seen in a statement Gilson made to de Lubac, "You are right to insist on the natural vocation of the intellect to a vision of God of which it is naturally incapable."[78] Natural theology is the intellect's "natural vocation." It is what de Lubac pursued. For de Lubac and Gilson (and I think for Aquinas as well) the pursuit could not be successful, but its very lack of success was a kind of argument in favor of natural theology. The question of God does not disappear, despite efforts to silence it. Yet nor does it ever receive a definitive answer. We know that we cannot know God fully by our unaided reason, yet we have a natural desire nevertheless to seek to know God. And how can we know that we do not know something fully without some tacit knowledge of the more up against which our knowledge fails?[79] Otherwise our inability to know God would not trouble us so. Either Turner seems to be saying something quite similar or he appears to argue that the natural vocation of the intellect is not only ordered toward the vision of God, but also able to attain it. If he says the latter, then he would differ from de Lubac, but this would also make Turner's position Pelagian. It entails a stronger version of Aristotelianism than most of the church's theologians countenanced — including Thomas and Scotus. Turner surely is not a Pelagian and so he cannot be saying that we not only have a natural vision for God, but resources in nature alone to find God.

76. De Lubac, *The Discovery of God* (Grand Rapids: Eerdmans, 1996), p. 218.
77. De Lubac, *At the Service of the Church*, p. 81.
78. De Lubac, *At the Service of the Church*, p. 123.
79. This is why for de Lubac 'remotio' or negation can only take place after the 'via eminentiae,' which, I shall argue below, is Aquinas's position as well. Kant recognized a similar account of our knowledge of God, but he used it to divide faith from reason and divided them with a nonporous boundary.

4. Faith and Its Reasons

Denys Turner finds a similar deficiency in Radical Orthodoxy, the nouvelle théologie, and Barthianism, which Vatican I could correct with its insistence that faith assumes the possibility of a rational proof for the existence of God. He advocates for a more substantive role for natural theology than one finds in these other theologies. He provides the basis for a kind of natural theology where reason's failure is a reasonable demonstration for God's existence. If this is correct, philosophy works *within* theology for him, but this is a conclusion he rejects. He recognizes that Barthianism and Vatican I "are at one in affirming the epistemic authority of faith over reason and the primacy of the historical events of salvation over the non-historical, timeless standpoint of nature." But he does not seem to find this similarity significant. It only suggests the "tautology that faith must exclude as false any standpoint which is defined or posited as 'natural' in some sense of 'natural' which a priori rivals faith as a 'standpoint.'"[80]

Has Turner underestimated the significance of this commonality between Barth and Vatican I and the presence in contemporary theology of just such an understanding of the 'natural' as a rival to faith? Has Western philosophy not developed a significant tradition that treats rationality grounded in nature qua nature as not only rivaling but also excluding faith a priori from reason?[81] Barth traces this understanding in *Protestant Thought from Rousseau to Ritschl*. Turner himself recognizes Kant did just this. The list of other significant thinkers who still play a significant role in theology and philosophy, and who do precisely this, is not inconsiderable. Hume, Rousseau, Feuerbach, Marx, Freud, Nietzsche, and Weber would have to be on that list. These modern fathers of the secular university continue to hold pride of place in disciplines such as economics, psychology, sociology, and philosophy as well as theology. Could Turner's acknowledgement that Barth and Vatican I, strange bedfellows indeed, share a common assumption "in affirming the epistemic authority of faith over reason" be a great deal more than a tautology? If not, what does he mean by an "*epistemic* authority of faith over reason"? If faith is a form of knowl-

80. Turner, *Faith, Reason, and the Existence of God*, p. 11.
81. Not only Mark Lilla's *A Stillborn God*, but also Charles Taylor's *A Secular Age* (Cambridge, Mass.: Belknap, 2007) traces just such an account of nature showing its thoroughgoing importance for Western politics.

edge having an authority over reason, how is reason separate from faith in Turner's work?

What concerns Turner is that faith becomes viewed as *the* epistemic authority and then we have another version of fideism, which is positivism. But the use of Wittgenstein's private language argument by Hauerwas, 'postliberal' theology, and some within Radical Orthodoxy makes fideism and positivism impossible. How someone who denies a private language could be described with the term 'fideism' is one of contemporary theology and philosophy's baffling ironies. Far from advocating fideism, theologians discontent with modernity provide a therapy for it.

Turner not only diagnoses fideism as a modern theological ill, he also offers us a reasoned, nuanced critique of 'ontotheology' in order to show why reason must work outside the domain of faith. On the one hand, he recognizes the indeterminate character of the charge of ontotheology when it is used to dismiss any theology that speaks of God in terms of being. Why should Heidegger be given the authority to police theology? On the other hand, he recognizes that thinking 'God' and 'creation' under a common genus such as 'being' does violate a proper Christian theology. This is to think God in terms of univocity. Like Milbank, Turner finds the doctrine of univocity problematic, and thus he too expresses concerns about Duns Scotus's theology. However, he also finds the radical Augustinianism of Henry of Ghent problematic because it trades on such an equivocation between God and creatures that no inference from creatures to God is possible. This inference is bypassed by an activity of the 'intellectus' that allows creatures to reason about God without the discursive activity of natural cognition. Here is where he makes an invaluable contribution to theology. His insistence upon this activity reminds us that the task of philosophy is a necessary feature of theology. He sides with Balthasar: "In order to be a serious theologian one must also, indeed, first, be a philosopher."[82] To short-circuit this task and appeal to an immediate participation of our mind in the Divine Mind through illumination without presupposing our natural discursive cognitive activity is the error Turner finds in the strong Augustinianism of Henry of Ghent, in much of Augustinian-Thomism, and especially in John Milbank. Milbank's theology, in its effort to avoid univocity and ontotheology, falls prey to this radical Augustinianism.

---

82. Hans Urs von Balthasar, *Theo-Logic I: The Truth of the Word,* trans. Adrian Walker (San Francisco: Ignatius, 2004), p. 8.

The Augustinian doctrine of illumination proposes that reason judges "by means of the 'unchangeable and true eternity of truth above my changing mind.'" This 'Platonic' reading of the function of reason can tempt us away from the natural, human activity of reason. For Turner, the genius of Thomas is to resist this version of a radical Augustinianism. Thus Turner reads Thomas more as a rationalist than do Milbank and Pickstock, who read him in terms of the Platonic-Augustinian tradition. In that tradition, Turner argues, "the mind (reason) judges by means of a light which is both in it and not of it."[83] This is a "source of knowing that exceeds the human, the point in the soul where it overlaps with that which is above it."[84] Turner questions what role is left for human reason within such a doctrine of illumination. Milbank (and by implication Barth) resembles Henry of Ghent, who presents a radical Augustinianism with no natural cognitive activity left to the human being. As Turner puts it, with Henry, the mind has no "created 'exemplar', no 'universal concept' — of its own making by which our human minds are illuminated. Hence the universals in the mind are not the product of our created rationality as such, being received in them from their source in the divine light itself."[85] Whether this is similar to the position Barth and Milbank put forward will be discussed below. It is far from anything set forth by de Lubac or Balthasar. Perhaps Preller could be seen to embody this kind of radical Augustinianism. He explains our knowledge of God as a "wholly other object of apprehension besides the world, an object which manifests itself in a novel way and creates a new and noncommunicable mode of intelligibility shared only by those to whom it has manifested itself," and suggests this is the reason there is no similarity between natural and religious language. He also reads Thomas in the 'light' of this Platonist-Augustinian inheritance.[86]

Scotus's doctrine of univocity offers a minimal Augustinianism

83. Turner, *Faith, Reason, and the Existence of God*, p. 81.
84. Turner, *Faith, Reason, and the Existence of God*, p. 83.
85. Turner, *Faith, Reason, and the Existence of God*, p. 84.
86. Preller, *Divine Science and the Science of God*, p. 198. Preller also reads Thomas primarily in terms of the Platonic-Augustinian tradition over and against Aristotelianism. Rudi A. te Velde's *Participation and Substantiality in Thomas Aquinas* (Leiden: Brill, 1995) offers an important explanation as to how Thomas could affirm a Platonic metaphysics of participation with an Aristotelian metaphysics of substance that allows for the natural, human work of conceptualizing (ratio) without neglecting the significance of creaturely participation in that which exceeds it.

against Henry of Ghent. It provides for more direct reference to God based on what we know about creatures. Scotus accomplishes this through his understanding that language about God can be univocal to language about creatures. If it is not, then Scotus worries that we could not make any inference from creatures to God.[87] This can easily lead to an ontotheology, as we have seen in Feuerbach, where talk of God is nothing but talk about creatures. But Scotists think the risk is inevitable if we are to do theology at all. As Richard Cross states, "An uncharitable account would be that Scotus's God is just a human person writ large. But it looks to me as though Scotus's account of religious language [univocity] is necessary for the intelligibility and viability of the whole theological project."[88] Why does the whole theological project require this? It alone allows for determinate truth conditions.[89] Here we see the alliance between Scotist theology and some versions of analytic philosophy. If theology is to be true, and if truth is a function of propositions, then the only way to claim speaking about God is true is through the doctrine of univocity. Thus Scotus states, "I designate that concept univocal which possesses sufficient unity in itself, so that to affirm and deny it of one and the same thing would be a contradiction."[90] Of course, theologians should be interested in discerning the truth of their speech about God; this is a necessary task if we are not to lapse into fideism. But truth does not need to be confined to "determinate truth conditions." This is a species of verificationism that Charles Taylor's 'expressive' theory of language successfully challenges. Turner likewise raises an important question about this need for univocity in order to de-

87. Richard Cross, *Duns Scotus* (Oxford: Oxford University Press, 2006), p. 36.

88. Richard Cross, *Duns Scotus*, p. 45.

89. Richard Cross, *Duns Scotus*, p. 36. Cross acknowledges that for Scotus "God and creatures fall under the extension of the concept *being*." But he denies that this makes Scotus's work "ontotheological" in any metaphysical sense. It is not because his 'univocity' is a semantic theory that has no "ontological commitments." It is a "vicious abstraction" that does not presume to attain the object of its referent. I don't understand how this fits with Cross's claim that if we are to have a true science of God, it must be a deductive syllogistic science where the middle term is univocal. How can it be both deductive and true while being merely semantic and an abstraction? See Cross, "Duns Scotus and Suárez at the Origins of Modernity," in ed. Wayne J. Hankey and Douglas Hedley, *Deconstructing Radical Orthodoxy: Postmodern Theology, Rhetoric and Truth* (Aldershot, England: Ashgate Press, 2005), pp. 71-72. For a fuller claim that Scotus's claims to univocity are semantic without metaphysical obligations see Cross, *Duns Scotus on God* (Aldershot, England: Ashgate Press, 2005), pp. 251-56.

90. Richard Cross, *Duns Scotus*, p. 37.

termine truth. "To say, as Scotus does, that 'univocity' of meaning is that possessed by such middle terms as are required for deductive validity is to beg the question: the determination of validity presupposes criteria for the determination of univocity, not the other way around."[91] In other words, as Turner goes on to argue, Scotus tests validity of inference by the requirements of univocity and univocity by validity of inference.

If Henry of Ghent's 'radical Augustinianism' leaves little to no room for natural cognitive powers, then Duns Scotus's 'minimal Augustinianism' concedes too much. Aquinas's theology avoids both errors. All three recognize a place for 'intellectus,' a form of knowledge which is a participation in the 'divine light of truth.' Thus all three work within an Augustinianism. God is the 'prima veritas' that is the condition for the knowledge of anything. Without our participation in this light, truth is not possible. Yet Turner finds all three theologians differing over the nature of this participation. Illumination in Henry of Ghent comes at the expense of natural reason. But for Scotus and Aquinas, illumination functions through the exercise of natural reason. Turner notes that "like Scotus and unlike Henry, for Thomas human reason is able to construct for itself, through its own natural powers, its own access to universal and necessary truths."[92] But Scotus and Aquinas still differ over the exercise of natural reason. Scotus is trapped in a natural capacity, which verges on Pelagianism. He remains too Aristotelian (an argument de Lubac also made). Whereas for Aquinas reason reaches to a conclusion that "lies beyond any which could stand in a relation of univocity to the created order."[93] Thus Turner admits what both de Lubac and Milbank stated, "the implications of Scotus's having diminished the scope of reason to a 'closed' circle of univocity are, in the terms of Heidegger, 'ontotheological' in effect, and in medieval terms, amount to a severing of reason from *intellectus*."[94]

Henry of Ghent privileges 'intellectus' over reason; Scotus does the opposite. Thomas holds them in their proper order, and in so doing he recognizes that we are "linguistic animals" and thus our rationality is discursive.[95] Turner thinks the Augustinian-Thomism of Radical Orthodoxy neglects this important point. Because 'intellectus' and reason, as well as illumination and discursive reasoning, are held together in any properly analogical speaking of

91. Turner, *Faith, Reason, and the Existence of God,* p. 128.
92. Turner, *Faith, Reason, and the Existence of God,* p. 87.
93. Turner, *Faith, Reason, and the Existence of God,* p. 87.
94. Turner, *Faith, Reason, and the Existence of God,* p. 87.
95. Turner, *Faith, Reason, and the Existence of God,* p. 92.

God, Turner is also suspicious of Barthianism. It simply reverses the direction of Feuerbach's ontotheological speech about God, leaving the basic structure intact. Barth's theism and Feuerbach's atheism possess the relationship "between an object and its image in a mirror: all the connections of thought are identical, but their relations are, as it were, horizontally reversed."[96] The alternative for Turner is that Christian theologians are obligated, for reasons of faith, to demonstrate God's existence by reason alone. But what they demonstrate is a "demonstrated unknowability: *Et hoc omnes dicunt Deum.*"[97]

Turner develops his position by drawing on the Scholastic material and formal aspects of the object and correlating them to the modern philosophical distinction in the theory of meaning between extension and intension. Meaning as extension names all the objects to which a proposition can be extended; meaning is in its extension. The standard example in philosophy is that the morning star is the evening star. Both are the planet Venus; what it is can be extended to what we call 'morning star' and 'evening star.' However, meaning as intension is not simply to what the proposition extends but also its intensional meaning and here 'morning star' is not the same as 'evening star.'[98] Turner translates Aquinas's formal/material distinction into these modern philosophical terms. What Aquinas means by 'God' in the first thirteen questions of the *Summa* has the same extension as what the philosophers mean, for this 'everyone calls God.' This is the case even if they have different intensions. Father, Son, and Holy Spirit is not intensionally equivalent to the Unmoved Mover even though they have the same extension. How then do we know that they are extensionally equivalent? Only faith lets us know this. Turner writes, "The descriptions of the philosopher and of the ordinary believer are, as I have put it, extensionally equivalent; but of course they do not mean the same thing. How, then, do we know that these 'Gods' are extensionally equivalent, are one and the same God? Only by faith: reason alone could not know that."[99]

Turner translates this distinction in meaning back into the Scholastics' formal/material distinction. Materially, the evening and morning star, like the Triune God and the Unmoved Mover, mean the same thing. They have the same extension. They differ by the formal descriptions used. Faith

96. Turner, *Faith, Reason, and the Existence of God*, p. 230.
97. Turner, *Faith, Reason, and the Existence of God*, p. 256.
98. Turner, *Faith, Reason, and the Existence of God*, p. 17.
99. Turner, *Faith, Reason, and the Existence of God*, pp. 19-20.

knows that the formal descriptions do not remove the material similarity, which can be explained through reason alone. What does this distinction accomplish? For Turner it not only makes conversation possible between Christian theology and the god of the philosophers by locating a common object, it also makes possible a philosophical refutation of the Christian God. Natural theology not only demonstrates God's existence, it also makes faith "vulnerable to philosophical refutation." He states, "Faith *is* logically vulnerable to philosophical, as also to empirical, refutation. For there are possibly true, if in fact false, states of affairs such that, if they were actually true, then Christian faith would be false."[100] Because meaning has the extension Turner suggests it has, he hands over the virtue of theological faith to the philosophers for critical investigation.

Would de Lubac, Barth, Preller, Hauerwas, or Milbank teach that faith can be philosophically and/or empirically falsifiable? The basic premise of de Lubac's *Discovery of God* suggests he would not find this troubling. Thinking of Barth conceding that role to philosophy does seem odd; he would probably consider it a capitulation to the 'analogia entis' that denies the sui generis character of theology's object. Likewise, reconciling this role for philosophy and empirical evidence to Preller's work seems more than difficult given his claim that knowledge of God is a "wholly other object of apprehension besides the world, an object which manifests itself in a novel way and creates a new and noncommunicable mode of intelligibility shared only by those to whom it has manifested itself." Yet persons influenced by, and faithful to, the work inaugurated by Barth and Preller are able to make an argument similar to Turner's.

Hans Frei, for instance, would certainly deny that God's existence or the church's teachings are empirically verifiable; yet he held forth the possibility that they could be empirically falsifiable. Frei wrote,

> there is no historical evidence that counts in favor of the claim that Jesus was resurrected. This is a good thing, because faith is not based on factual evidence. . . . On the other hand, I believe that, because it is more nearly fact-like than not, reliable historical evidence against the resurrection would tend to falsify it decisively, and that the forthcoming of such evidence is conceivable.[101]

---

100. Turner, *Faith, Reason, and the Existence of God,* pp. 19-20.
101. Frei, *Identity of Jesus Christ,* p. 45.

What would such evidence look like? We find Jesus' remains. Even though Preller sets his work against empiricism, he also allows "at least one straightforward and nonproblematic empirical referent," which he finds in "Jesus Christ was resurrected from the dead."[102] (Of course there may be good reasons to reject empiricism as a philosophy, as Preller does, without thereby rejecting a role for an empirical referent. Empiricism and an empirical referent are not the same.) But even this is of no use without the 'light of faith.' In an argument quite similar to Turner's, Preller argues for an inference from humanity to divinity. But contrary to Turner this logical inference occurs only within the illumination of faith. "In the act of faith one sees or knows the humanity of Christ and believes the divinity."[103]

Hauerwas's work is, in large part, a philosophical development, based on reason, for what would count as falsification of Christianity. In this sense, he always had a 'natural theology' in his work. He consistently asks, what would true or false Christianity look like? In his important essay "Reconciling the Practice of Reason: Casuistry in a Christian Context," he explicitly states that "theological ethics is different in kind" from other philosophical theories of ethics, but this does not therefore entail a rejection that Christianity could be philosophically or empirically falsifiable by those within or without the Christian faith.[104] For Hauerwas such falsification can occur only as a function of practical reason, which is akin to casuistry; as "the ongoing attempt of a community to understand itself through analogical comparison, such comparison requires the location of central paradigmatic examples."[105] Is there nothing outside the community that stabilizes this understanding? If we mean by 'outside' an independent criterion, which would be a neutrally observable reality universally accessible, then the answer must be no. If we mean by 'outside' a connection to reality every community potentially shares with other communities through its own discursive rationality and the consensus produced by action, then the answer has to be yes. Otherwise Hauerwas would have no reason to present this essay to philosophers at Rice University. Only when we are trapped in an a priori either/or of complete translatability or utter incommensurability would it be a performative contradiction for a Christian to defend the

102. Preller, *Divine Science and the Science of God*, p. 249.

103. Preller, *Divine Science and the Science of God*, p. 251.

104. Hauerwas, *Christian Existence Today: Essays on Church, World, and Living in Between* (Durham, N.C.: Labyrinth, 1988), p. 67.

105. Hauerwas, *Christian Existence Today*, p. 71.

specificities of a Christian practical reason before others, some of whom do not share the Christian's faith. George Lindbeck also makes allowances for a philosophical and empirical refutation of faith. He argues that the utterance "Jesus is Lord" in the mouth of a crusader cleaving the skull of an infidel falsifies the claim. So the question is not whether philosophy and/or empirical reality can falsify faith; rather, the question is which philosophy and/or empirical realities would falsify faith and how. As we shall see, Wittgenstein and Charles Taylor give us one response to this question, whereas Richard Rorty and Donald Davidson offer a very different one.

We must nevertheless be careful with any argument for verification and/or falsification. For as philosophers themselves remind us, the difficulty with the verification thesis is that it can be neither verified nor falsified. Moreover, accepting certain specific philosophical notions of verification or falsification forces theology into metaphysical affirmations we may not wish to make such as Rorty's nominalism. His call for a verification or falsification of theological and metaphysical claims proves Milbank and Pickstock right that we must exercise caution with such claims because there is a common trajectory from nominalism to empiricism and positivism.

5. Formal and Material Aspects of Faith and Reason

Turner's proposition has the merit of recognizing that we do have conversations across religious traditions and between philosophers and theologians and assume we are talking about a similar 'object.' Our speech about God assumes an extension of meaning such that when we write or speak 'God is . . .' we assume some form of agreement, even if we do not assume complete translatability. But the proposition 'God is . . .' in any Christian theology can only finally have an intensional meaning of 'God is Triune.' We do not think this is one way among others to name God; it is God's name. 'Yahweh' and 'Trinity' are not different names for a set larger than them designated 'God.' Their meaning cannot be extended without violating a basic theological rule of grammar: 'Deus non est genere.' Without denying that philosophy could refute the truth of theology, we must still ask if it can be done by privileging extension over intension. Can the language of God across traditions bear an extensional meaning like the morning and evening star can within a common language? Turner correlates extensional meaning with reason and intensional meaning with faith, and then correlates them both to the Scholastic formal/material distinction. But this does not work and it provides too rigid a distinction between faith and reason, both of which would have a formal and material dimension. This means that the Scholastic formal/material distinction may not be so easily translated into modern analytic philosophy's intension/extension distinction.

Faith has a formal and a material dimension. Formally, it is an openness to receive something that cannot fit within a rational system alone but is nevertheless necessary for its intelligibility. Faith and reason are not the same, but they are necessary for each other. Materially, it is the specific content that is to be received.[106] Faith, then, is a 'transcendental'; we cannot reason without it. But it is not a 'ground.' It does not provide certainty by which reason can work. It is not a first principle upon which a classic foundationalism could be built.

Thomas Aquinas helps us understand this. Aquinas begins his question on faith in the secunda secundae with the objection that "the object of faith is not the first Truth." This is because one would think that faith is something one must receive from others; the 'First Truth' is not proposed to us, but underlies all our speech and action. It is what makes reason possible; in that sense, it is transcendental. As Vivian Boland states, faith is central for Aquinas in all human knowing, "Such initial faith is required not just for religious teaching because, as Thomas reminds us, all human knowing begins with faith (and most of it, for most people, remains a matter of faith)."[107] But that faith is the 'First Truth' presents a dilemma. If it has this transcendental status that is always already present in human knowing, why would it need to be 'proposed' to us?[108] Aquinas follows Dionysius in answering why this is still necessary. He does this by explaining all 'cognitive habits.' They are composed of a 'material object' and a 'formal aspect.' The material objects are the things we know about God,

106. Bruce Marshall explains this well in his "Aquinas as Postliberal Theologian," *Thomist* 53:3 (1989): 371. He writes, "It is essential, Thomas argues, to distinguish from the outset two different ways in which God is the object of faith; he is both faith's material object and its formal object. Like any cognitive habit, faith not only knows various things, but knows them in a distinctive way. These are what Thomas speaks of as, respectively, the material and formal 'objects' of a given cognitive habit. So faith embraces both 'what is known, which is as it were the material object, and that through which it is known which is the formal object.'"

107. Vivian Boland, O.P., "Truth, Knowledge, and Communication: Thomas Aquinas on the Mystery of Teaching," *Studies in Christian Ethics* 19:3 (2006): 299.

108. ST II.

such as that God is, that God is Triune, that God is incarnate in Jesus. We do not know these naturally; they are proposed to us and must be received. Thus it would seem again that they cannot be about 'first truths,' for the First Truth is not something we affirm; it is something necessary even in order to affirm. However, the 'formal aspect' by which we know and assent to these material objects is the 'First Truth' because "the faith of which we are speaking does not assent to anything except because it is revealed by God."[109] God then becomes both the 'formal aspect' under which we can know the material objects of faith, and because God provides this 'formal aspect,' God is also 'in a way' the material object of the First Truth, for the formal aspect allows us to relate everything to God. Aquinas will make the same argument concerning charity; this is why faith and charity are theological virtues and why they always precede every other virtue and every act of knowing. For Aquinas, then, both with the virtue of faith and the virtue of justice, the formal and the material dimensions cannot be divided into autonomous spheres. This is why the extension/intension distinction does not work for him. The formal aspect of both faith and reason illumines the material aspect; it does not provide the possibility of two very different kinds of conversation.

Because the object of faith in both its material and formal aspect is the First Truth (God), Aquinas then asks whether it can be 'complex.' God is simple, yet the faiths of the church are propositions that have a complex discursive structure. How do we claim both constitute the virtue of faith? This is the question of the relationship between God and language, especially God and 'propositions.' Thomas's response to this dilemma is that "the thing known is in the knower according to the mode of the knower."[110] Faith here is a virtue that assumes a participation both in the thing known, the First Truth who is God, and the "mode of the knower." This is a discursive form of knowing that assumes judgment in terms of "composition and division." It allows us to acknowledge that all modes of signifying are contextual, while also allowing for a 'thing' to be signified that exceeds the context alone. This raises the question of metaphysics — how does language point beyond itself? It is why Thomas can absorb the insights of 'contextual' theology without becoming trapped in a modern epistemology. Thomas concludes:

109. ST II-II.1.1. resp. (Pegis edition).
110. ST II-II.1.2.

125

Accordingly, the object of faith may be considered in two ways. First as regards the thing itself which is believed (ex parte ipsius rei creditae), and thus the object of faith is something simple, namely, the thing itself about which we have faith (res ipsa de qua fides habetur); secondly, on the part of the believer, and in this respect the object of faith is something complex, such as a proposition.[111]

Thomas already explained this when he set forth "The Names of God" in the prima secunda in response to the question, "If affirmative propositions can be formed about God?" His answer assumes that true affirmative propositions always bring together predicates and subjects so that they can signify "the same thing in reality, and diverse things in idea." An example he gives is "man is an animal." Although the predicate differs in 'idea' from the subject, the reality to which it refers is the same. We do not assume that the complex proposition, "man is an animal" is composed of two different things which we can somehow divide from one another to allow us to have conversations about 'man' in one context and 'animal' in another. The subject and predicate differ only in 'idea.' The intellect is not confused by this, but knows that this proposition "signifies the identity of the thing by the composition itself." As true as this is for all true propositions, it is even more so for God.

> God, however, as considered in Himself, is altogether one and simple, yet our intellect knows Him according to diverse conceptions because it cannot see Him as He is in Himself. Nevertheless, although it understands Him under diverse conceptions, it yet knows that absolutely one and the same reality corresponds to its conceptions. Therefore, the plurality of predicate and subject represents the plurality of idea; and the intellect represents the unity by composition.[112]

Our language does not confuse us. Although we must use composite, creaturely means such as language and propositions to speak of God, we do not then assume that God is composite. We understand that composite creatures, which are all that language is, can signify a simple being like God, even when we are uncertain as to what 'simplicity' specifies. Language works; it accomplishes this task.

Faith as a virtue has both a material object and a formal aspect. The for-

111. ST II.
112. ST I.13 resp. (Pegis edition).

126

mal aspect allows us to predicate diverse things to a material 'object,' which can even be simple and thus contain no diversity. For Thomas this is possible because of how language functions. The 'modus significandi' provides the formal aspect under which we can predicate diversity in idea but still maintain the unity and simplicity of the 'res significata.' Therefore the virtue of faith is inextricably related to truth, reason, and language; for without these we would have no adequate account of how we know anything, let alone God.

Victor Preller developed the Scholastic formal/material distinction for a modern account of theological language without translating it into the modern extension/intension theories of meaning. He drew on Quine's critique of the extension/intension distinction by means of his distinction between transparent and opaque reference. His development offers some similar and different conclusions than Turner's.

Preller divides theology into two sciences. One is 'scientia divina' (divine knowledge), which is "a body of propositions resulting from philosophical reflection on the 'cognitions of God' available to man on the basis of the natural powers of reason alone." This is philosophical or natural theology. The other is 'scientia dei' (knowledge of God), which is a "dispositional state of the intellect called 'faith.'"[113] Unlike Turner, Preller does not pose as sharp a distinction between reason and faith; both are 'scientiae.' Preller's work sets forth a "reformulated Thomism" that relates these two more closely precisely by delineating the limits of 'scientia divina.' For Preller, meaningfully speaking of God is a question of intending to speak of an 'object' who in no way can be an 'object.' This is the "problem of reference to God," which is the problem of theology itself. Can we speak about God if we acknowledge that God is not an object that can be known solely on the basis of natural powers of reason as other objects are known?[114] Preller is much less worried than Turner about reading Aquinas's natural theology through the lens of dogmatic theology. He thinks that the unwillingness to do this contributed to the misreading of Aquinas by Cajetan and other Thomists who followed in his wake. They "analyzed" his so-called philosophical work "in total isolation from the distinctly dogmatic settings in which they occur." This led to three misinterpretations of Aquinas: that he is motivated by a "purely philosophical intention"; that the philosophical positions in Aquinas "are his own posi-

---

113. Preller, *Divine Science and the Science of God*, p. 3.
114. Preller, *Divine Science and the Science of God*, p. 4.

tions"; and that his philosophical statements are unchanged when "integrated into a theological framework."[115]

Preller does not deny Thomas does philosophy, but he denies any such thing as a pure philosophy in Thomas. For Preller, "Aquinas's sole intention in writing such works as the *Summa Theologia* is the articulation of theological truth."[116] All Aquinas's arguments are "from authority"; they are from Scripture, the saints, or the philosophers. The philosophical statements are either "external and probable evidence for truth of theological claims" or "conceptual material for the articulation of theological claims."[117] For this reason he finds both those who see in Thomas a consistent philosophy (Garrigou-Lagrange, Maritain) and those who find in him a "Christian philosophy" (Gilson) to be "radically mistaken."[118] Instead, "the purpose of 'natural theology' is not to convey information about God, but rather to empty the mind of any pretension of possessing concepts in terms of which to judge the nature of the 'final intelligibility' of reality."[119] Thus "only faith can recognize the referent of the proofs."[120] This would appear to differ markedly from Turner, but that depends on what is meant by faith here.

For Preller, much like for de Lubac, "man's mind is ordered to know that which it cannot discover" and this is a "frustrating fact."[121] This natural orientation to beatitude produces a natural quest for God that examines the world through reason alone, but this quest will always fail because the end of the quest exceeds the abilities of reason alone. Therefore Preller states, "To investigate, on the basis of reason alone, things which have to do with God, is to investigate the world and attribute it to an unknown source."[122] Here Preller and Turner recognize a similar role for reason in theology. For both of them, it succeeds precisely because it fails. Natural

---

115. Preller, *Divine Science and the Science of God*, p. 22.

116. Preller, *Divine Science and the Science of God*, p. 22.

117. Preller, *Divine Science and the Science of God*, pp. 23, 25.

118. Preller, *Divine Science and the Science of God*, p. 26.

119. Here Preller's account of what philosophy can do with respect to the knowledge of God is similar to that of Rudi te Velde's interpretation. Te Velde writes, "For Thomas the existence of an 'unmoved mover' is not simply a conclusion to be reached in the science of nature; it is that at which the science of nature confronts its limits and terminates." *Aquinas on God: The 'Divine Science' of the Summa Theologiae* (Burlington, Vt.: Ashgate, 2006), p. 60.

120. Preller, *Divine Science and the Science of God*, p. 32.

121. Preller, *Divine Science and the Science of God*, p. 29.

122. Preller, *Divine Science and the Science of God*, p. 32.

reason does not produce a proof of God's existence by identifying it with something in the creation; it accomplishes just the opposite. It is capable of recognizing that nothing in creation can be identified with God and yet creation itself is unintelligible without God.[123] This becomes a kind of negative proof for the existence of God. Where Turner and Preller differ is the significance of this conclusion. For Preller it is a temptation to trust too much in the accomplishment of natural reason alone without its necessary supplementation by faith. For Turner it is evidence as to what natural reason can accomplish independent of faith even though faith supports this accomplishment. What natural reason accomplishes for both theologians is similar; it primarily accomplishes a negative task by telling us what God is not, which is what Aquinas tells us that the philosopher can accomplish. But this can only finally make sense if we have a transcendental argument that acknowledges something more against which the metaphysical question of why something more than creation is necessary to render it intelligible. An extensional theory of meaning cannot adequately answer this question; this is why 'scientia dei' is necessary for reason.

Preller develops Aquinas's complex response to the philosopher's proposition that God exists by imagining a Barthian interlocutor. Imagine a "philosopher Brown" who "believes that God exists." Then imagine a "Barthian theologian" who asks, "Does philosopher Brown then believe that the Father of our Lord Jesus Christ exists?" What should be the Thomistic response? Preller gives us a 'yes' and 'no' answer.

> We might reply (in terms of referential transparency), "Yes! As for that being capable of rendering our experience of reality transparently intelligible [whom we know *in fact* to be the Father of our Lord Jesus Christ], Brown believes that he exists." In most properly *theological* contexts, however, the modus significandi of 'God' is of such overriding importance, that it would be much less misleading to reply (in terms of referential opacity), "No! Brown believes that 'A being capable of rendering our experience of reality transparently intelligible exists' is true: but he does not believe that 'The Father of our Lord Jesus Christ exists' is true."[124]

---

123. If MacDonald is correct in his interpretation of Barth, this is precisely what Barth denies. It is completely reasonable to think of creation without thinking or speaking of God.

124. Preller, *Divine Science and the Science of God*, p. 143.

If we adopt Preller's 'referential transparency'/'referential opacity' rather than Turner's extensional/intensional distinction, then the Barthian theologian is satisfied. Extension does not determine the truth of our speaking of God; the mode of signifying, which will be given in sacred doctrine, can never be bracketed out. We know by faith that the Triune God and that being which is not created but who renders our being intelligible are, in fact, the same 'res.' But theology is as concerned with the 'modus significandi' as the 'res significata' and therefore, in Barthian fashion, we also know that we are not literally speaking of the same God.

Notice how the significance of the 'modus significandi' in Preller, a mode which is produced by us in and through our natural, everyday language, assumes neither the univocity of Scotus nor the de-naturalization of reason in Henry of Ghent. By emphasizing this distinction instead of simply abiding by the modern philosopher's intensional/extensional theory of meaning, Preller is able to accomplish better what Turner seeks, but without some of the difficulties involved in the modern analytic distinction. A central place is preserved for the significance of our natural discursive powers without dissolving them into some mystical illumination where the 'modus' is not naturally produced by us or by rendering the 'modus' superfluous through assuming a univocity where we already know what the 'res' is irrespective of the 'modus significandi.' Yet 'extension' does not trump 'intension,' as it must do in much of analytic philosophy, in order for its logic to work in terms of bound variables and quantifiers. They can only distinguish meaning understood as extension.[125] For Preller, by implication, extension does not trump intension because language, which we produce, matters. It has a constitutive function. It does something.

Turner comes close to letting extension trump intension in signifying God. He knows that the god of philosopher Brown is the same as the Triune God before he asks Brown whether the mode of signifying matters. What do we do if Brown says, "No! You cannot signify this god through that mode." Do we then still say, "But we know by faith that the god to whom you reason is signified by that mode"? Can we say, "Our gods are

---

125. See Susan Langer's *Introduction to Symbolic Logic* (New York: Dover, 1937), pp. 131, 134, 284. She notes that the "class is the extension of the concept" and therefore symbolic logic finds it "advantageous" to treat meaning primarily in terms of extension. She states, "Meanings, or intensions, are irrelevant."

the same via an extensional theory of meaning, but we also know via an intensional theory of meaning that they are not the same, even if you do not know that"?

Preller's use of Thomas's 'modus significandi'/'res significata' distinction depends upon his formal/material distinction. Preller writes, "In Aquinas's terminology, the *id a quo imponitur nomen ad significandum* is the formal nature of the *id ad quod significandum nomen*."[126] The importance of signifying makes knowledge less passive; our significations make a contribution to the thing known. Preller denies that Thomas is an empiricist such that perception is primarily passive; instead the agent intellect contributes to our knowledge by allowing us to perceive objects through a 'conceptual system.' It is a mode of signifying, or using form to make sense of the 'material' elements of our experience. Preller states, "The forms by which we judge experience are not learned from experience but result from the natural tendency of the mind to use the 'first principles of the intellect.' . . . In this general claim I believe Aquinas is correct."[127]

Preller's reading of Aquinas bears many similarities to Kant's transcendental argument, except that these forms are not categories immanent to human experience; they are the eternal ideas in God, based on the divine processions and missions, in which we participate as creatures. Perception is not simple passive reception of these ideas. The active intellect contributes positively to our perception by its action in judging through composing and dividing. Like Wittgenstein (and Kant), Aquinas recognized we make a contribution both to knowledge and truth by our activity. This is also why the 'modus significandi' remains so important. It does not merely register the 'res significata'; it is a participation in it. Preller states,

> The way in which a word refers to its object (its modus significandi) depends upon the intention that a person has of the object. An intention may be defined as a conception of the intellect by means of which an object (in the broadest sense) is known or thought. . . . That which makes the intention the 'intention of the signified object' is that which makes the object *what it is*.[128]

126. Preller, *Divine Science and the Science of God*, p. 138.
127. Preller, *Divine Science and the Science of God*, p. 53.
128. Preller, *Divine Science and the Science of God*, p. 137.

Preller even states, "The modus significandi of a referential term may in certain contexts be more relevant to the determination of the truth of a belief statement than the actual nature of the res significata."[129]

This claim could easily be misunderstood in a Feuerbachian direction. It suggests that our mode of signifying, because it expresses the intention of the object and without such an intention an object cannot be known, actually *makes* the object "what it is." Is Preller (and Aquinas) then saying that we make God what God is through our mode of signifying? In one sense, no; for this act of making produces a 'nominal definition,' and no such thing is possible for God. But in another sense, with some important qualifications, we can say yes to this question. If this is how we know, and if we are to know God, then we must know God through the activity of the agent intellect. But this does not imply that the mode of signifying is only a subjective, relativistic intention. This must be understood within Aquinas's statement, "The intellect, informed by the species of a thing, forms within itself, by an act of understanding, a certain intention of the thing that is understood, which is the very notion that the definition signifies."[130] Although we produce the form by the agent intellect's act of judging through composing and dividing, it is not only our product. It is both informed by "the species of a thing" at the same time it is our intentional act, known through the mode of signifying we use. As we shall see, the best way to think of this is through Mary's yes. It becomes the paradigm for all theology, for all signifying 'God.'[131]

This makes knowledge of God exceedingly complex, for how can we have an intention that we produce through a form that has also been informed by the species of a thing when God is not a thing, not an object in the world that we can know as we know other created objects? This is why sacred doctrine is so essential for Aquinas and Preller. Preller finds Aquinas resolving our dilemma by a "radically different *modus significandi*" which comes from dogmatic theology and not a natural theology. The latter only lets us know that no 'modus significandi' can attain its 'object' when it is God, for no species of a thing can be grasped by the agent intellect and produce the requisite form. The transcendental terms we must use

129. Preller, *Divine Science and the Science of God*, p. 142.
130. Preller, *Divine Science and the Science of God*, p. 137.
131. This will be more fully developed in the last chapter. In some sense, this work builds to the point where this claim makes sense.

to speak about God, especially being itself, function 'metalinguistically.' They will always have a certain opacity for us because we are situated within them; we can never get outside of them and point to them, exhaust their meaning.[132] (Here is a key similarity between Aquinas and Wittgenstein.) Natural theology asserts the 'res significata' of God's existence without any means for a 'modus significandi,' which means that the most it can accomplish is that the proposition is not "necessarily irrational" even though we have no natural mode of signifying it.[133] Philosophy cannot distinguish among 'gods,' but must treat them all in terms of a class of a being who renders the world intelligible. But 'faith' is "not merely an extension of the natural powers of the intellect."[134] Reason alone has no adequate 'modus significandi,' even though it does accomplish the amazing feat of recognizing it has no such mode. The wisest of the pagan philosophers accomplished this. Yet if we are to have knowledge of God, we must still have a language, a mode of signifying, that allows us to 'locate' via our intentions the 'object' to which we refer. Otherwise we cannot intend to speak of God, and theology would be impossible or utter nonsense.

Theology remains a "linguistic problem," but for Preller and Aquinas the linguistic problem is remedied, albeit never solved, through sacred doctrine.[135] For Aquinas, "an intention is a *conceptio intellectus* on which is based a symbolic or mental *verbum*"; speech about God then only becomes intelligible through a 'principio supernaturalis,' which must be "God himself." If God does not speak, then the only language we have to speak of God is the natural language that only speaks of God when it recognizes it fails to do so. How could proclamation follow if this is all we have? The 'principio supernaturalis' is God's own Speech (the Word made flesh) within which we can participate and thus speak well of God.[136]

132. Preller, *Divine Science and the Science of God*, p. 153.

133. Preller, *Divine Science and the Science of God*, p. 173.

134. Preller, *Divine Science and the Science of God*, p. 181.

135. Preller, *Divine Science and the Science of God*, p. 183.

136. The difference here between Preller and Wolterstorff is significant. For Wolterstorff, God is as God a member of the community of speakers. For Preller, God's speech is always to be understood Christologically. Bruce Marshall recognizes the importance of this claim when he states, "The transcendental *prima veritas* has revealed himself, not simply in a concept or in isolated atomic propositions, but in a complex body of propositions. . . ." *Aquinas as Postliberal Theologian*, p. 383. Of course, the revelation is not so much "in a complex body of propositions," which are at best the formal object, as in a Person, who is the material object.

However, for Preller this is not an Augustinian doctrine of illumination where the First Truth illumines our mind immediately, which could easily tend toward fideism. We possess no adequate 'mode of signifying' to speak well of God because all our modes are, in fact, creaturely modes. What we do possess is the Christological dogma, a natural language that refers indirectly to God by way of Jesus' humanity, a creaturely mode of signifying. Jesus' humanity is the only sign that allows our language of God to attain its proper 'res.' This places limits on what language we can or cannot use in intending God, while at the same time it allows us to exceed those limits and speak of God. Here the humanity of Christ, a mode of signifying proper to us, is taken on good authority to be at the same time a mode of signifying of the Divine, even though that latter mode always remains a mystery to us.[137] Because Christ is the only proper mode of signifying God, natural theology does not intend the same object until it is brought within the orbit of faith. One must first believe in order to understand.

Eugene Rogers develops Preller's insights by recognizing the similarity between the function of sacred doctrine in Thomas and Barth's 'analogia fidei.' He states,

> Just because according to sacred doctrine human beings properly relate to all things by the God-bestowed disposition to believe God, the *scientia Dei* works the change in the soul through a formal rationale analogous to ones Aristotle accords other sciences. In that case Thomas calls the formal rationale 'faith.' And because in sacred doctrine we relate to all things by believing God, what we have here is a description of what Barth and others would call the *analogia fidei*. With that we have one way of stating the technical *theological* means by which Thomas engulfs Aristotle.[138]

Faith in Aquinas is an epistemic activity; it is that by which all things can be understood because it gives them form. The 'modus significandi' of dog-

---

137. This mode of signifying is God's own mode because of the isomorphism between the procession and mission of the Second Person. "All revelation, however, and thus all sacra doctrina, is an extension of the eternal procession of the Word: it is, in theological terminology, the temporal mission of the eternal Person." Preller, *Divine Science and the Science of God*, p. 232.

138. Rogers, *Thomas Aquinas and Karl Barth: Sacred Doctrine and the Natural Knowledge of God* (Notre Dame, Ind.: University of Notre Dame Press, 1995), p. 48.

matic theology, even when we are unaware of exactly how it works, nevertheless works such that it makes possible a knowledge *of* God that reaches its aim; God is the intended reference of theology, not the world either in its affirmation or negation. This does not deny a legitimate independence to other sciences. Faith adds less a material content to geology, physics, mathematics, evolutionary science, economics, etc., than the form within which they can be properly understood so that they are never closed off from the mystery that makes all creaturely being possible. But this should not be understood too lightly.

Reinhard Hütter and Paul Griffiths outline this relationship between faith and reason well. Some things, they suggest, are knowable by faith, some by reason, and some by both. Based on these levels of relationship between faith and reason, they offer three important conclusions. First, "faith will never become the only kind of reasoning that Christians use or need." Notice that faith is assumed to be a "kind of reasoning." This is how Aquinas understood it. But it is also the case that faith does not exhaust reasoning. Hütter and Griffiths's second conclusion is that the "deliverances of faith have, for Christians, certitude; they are irrefragably correct." This then leads to their important third conclusion: "once the disposition for faith becomes active, it transfigures and reframes every form of reasoning."[139] Faith not only seeks and presumes reason, it converts it. Every account of reason assumes something beyond it, some enabling condition that makes it possible but cannot be accounted for it within its own systematic aspirations. (Is this not analogous to Gödel's theorem?) Likewise faith can never be pure; it will always assume and use reason even as it transfigures it.

6. God Is . . . Triune

Turner finds the "Thomistic interpretation" of Preller, primarily developed by Fergus Kerr, "opposed" to his. Their difference focuses on whether the proposition 'God exists' for Aquinas is "radically different" when held on grounds of faith rather than that of a natural philosophy. Kerr makes this claim in his *After Aquinas*, referring to Preller for support, by stating that the proposition 'God exists' is "radically different" in Aquinas's teaching

---

139. Paul Griffiths and Reinhard Hütter, *Reason and the Reasons of Faith* (New York: Continuum, 2005), pp. 10, 12.

between the pagan who believes God exists and the Christian who believes because of faith. Preller writes,

> Even those propositions concerning God which philosophy investigates function quite differently as part of sacred doctrine. The proposition, 'God exists' for example takes on such utterly new significance for faith that Aquinas is willing to say that the pagans (who after all proved the truth of the proposition 'God exists') cannot be said to believe in God. The reason that Aquinas gives for this claim is rather complex. In the body of the article [ST II-II, 2, 2], he argues that the act of faith establishes a threefold relationship to God.[140]

In this intriguing statement Preller recognizes Aquinas acknowledged both that pagans "proved the truth of the proposition 'God exists'" and nevertheless they "cannot be said to believe in God." Pagans proved by reason that God exists, but this did not entail faith. This may be, oddly enough, consistent with Turner's position — the pagans prove 'God exists' by reason alone, which faith acknowledges as something possible for them to do, but they do so without faith. Thus, where Turner and Preller differ is whether this counts for true knowledge of God. The difference is that the pagans do not recognize the significance of what they prove.

Preller places this achievement within Aquinas's interpretation of Augustine's threefold account of faith, based on three different uses of the term 'to believe' — 'credere Deum' (believing that God exists), 'credere Deo' (believing what God says), 'credere in Deum' (faith of commitment). He interprets Aquinas's use of Augustine's threefold account as follows:

1. Credere Deum — "the intellect of the believer is related to God (or acknowledges him) by the very nature of the matter to which it assents"
2. Credere Deo — "The contents of faith share materially in common the mere fact that they pertain in some way to God. Formally speaking, however, they possess another and more profound character: they have been revealed by God. In giving assent to sacred doctrine, the believer submits to the teaching authority of God himself. . . . He adheres to God precisely as the *veritas prima* — the first truth — the highest and most authoritative object of the intellect."

140. Preller, *Divine Science and the Science of God*, p. 228.

3. Credere in Deum — "The will is also related to God in the act of faith in that the intellect is moved by the will to give its assent. . . . The will adheres to God as *summum bonum*."[141]

Once we recognize that faith is a theological virtue that contains these three aspects of belief, then the differences among Preller, Kerr, and Turner are not that stark. We do not need to choose among them, but work within them. Preller says the proposition 'God exists' "takes on new significance" because of the second and third aspects of faith. Kerr argues it is "radically different." Turner argues that what is known "in purely philosophical mode" can in fact be "one and the same God" with what is known by faith. All three positions might be reconciled when understood within the proper ordering that faith as a theological virtue provides for reason.

That God exists is the first aspect of faith. If philosophers, pagan, secular, or religious, produce an argument based on reason alone for God's existence, then such a proof could be consistent with the God of faith. We must not choose between them. Aristotle demonstrated that 'God' is that which measures and not what is measured. A nearly identical statement could easily be found on many pages in Karl Barth's *Church Dogmatics*. How do we account for this? We should not be surprised by it, for the God we know by faith is also the God of reason. Such knowledge goes "with the grain of the universe." Yet neither Aristotle nor any other philosopher demonstrates the doctrine of the Trinity or that of the incarnation, both of which are essential for the full knowledge of what it means to affirm that God exists. Therefore Preller's argument that the proposition 'God exists' takes on new significance within sacred doctrine and Kerr's claim that this new significance is even radically different from the same proposition when set forth by philosophy also makes sense. But this assumes an 'intensionalist' theory of meaning where the name matters in defining the concept. We do not have a number of objects — 'God of the philosopher,' 'God of the Christian,' 'God of . . .' — that can be placed under some over-arching concept — 'the God.' Turner would not need to reject this radical difference (as he seems to do at present) when he also argues that the proposition 'God exists' locates the same subject matter among the philosophers and theologians. This is only necessary if all that matters is extensionality.

141. Preller, *Divine Science and the Science of God*, p. 229.

The question of the relationship between faith and reason cannot ignore the various aspects involved in the virtue of faith, but it is the *virtue* of faith, which is under discussion. These three aspects are all aspects of the one virtue. But note how the question — 'what is the relationship between faith and reason?' — does not readily emerge from these three aspects because faith and reason are not considered to be two distinct things that must be brought together. Reason does not designate only the first aspect ('credere Deum'); it is not as if we move from reason in the first aspect to something called 'faith' in the second and third aspects. The intellect and will are involved in each aspect. It is true that the first aspect represents what philosophers like Plato and Aristotle achieved. They gave intellectual assent to the fact 'that God is.' But as Preller notes, whether this is 'faith' and a true 'reason' about God is ambiguous in Aquinas's work. Aquinas both affirms and denies that Aristotle 'can be said to believe that God exists.'[142] This is not because he is a dialectical thinker, but because of the analogy between God and the world these three aspects make possible. Aristotle can only finally know that there is a God in this first aspect, which says more about the world than it does about God; it tempts toward ontotheology. True faith, which would also require the will and the intellect to recognize its true end, and therefore entails true reason about God as well, needs the second and third aspects of the virtue of faith. Sacred doctrine does not operate outside the realm of reason, although it does not have the same limitations of reason that philosophy or natural theology would.

Natural theology is finally about creation, because what it can know by its unsupplemented reason is only what can be ascertained within creaturely existence alone, which will always be mired in negation. We discover that creation, although significant, is not self-interpreting; its meaning, if it has any, resides beyond it. We are tempted to reduce it to insignificance as occurs in the modern fact/value split. Creation has no meaning; it is brute fact, until we give it value. But if we are fortunate, metaphysics will continue to ask why there is something rather than nothing. The question itself points beyond the world trapped in its own immanence. Many ancient and modern philosophers recognized this. Clearly this question arises and is investigated apart from faith and sacred doctrine. Yet whether this is truly a reason that has God as its intention is similar to the question

---

142. Preller, *Divine Science and the Science of God*, p. 143.

whether the virtues philosophers discovered without the help of sacred doctrine are truly virtues. And of course, for Thomas, the answer is qualified. They are at best imperfect virtues.

Thomas's 'natural theology,' and its relationship to faith, is best understood analogously to his understanding of the natural virtues. Much like Thomas patiently develops the 'natural' virtues only to conclude that without the theological virtues they can only be virtues improperly considered, so Thomas acknowledges that the first aspect of faith cannot be the true knowledge of God, which is faith proper. It can at best be an imperfect virtue, for this is the role Thomas gives the natural virtues, those virtues acquired by natural means.

> It is therefore clear from what has been said that only the infused virtues are perfect, and deserve to be called virtues simply: since they direct man well to the ultimate end. But the other virtues, those, namely that are acquired, are virtues in a restricted sense, but not simply: for they direct man well in respect of the last end in some particular genus of action, but not in respect of the last end simply.[143]

Faith is such an infused virtue. It revises, corrects, and perfects what we might acquire by nature.

Aquinas moves far beyond Aristotle's claim that the actualization of any potential can be accomplished only through the natural, immanent activity within which that power resides, which is the Pelagian temptation. For a similar reason he rejects Aristotle's account of cognition. In a question that asks whether God knows or understands himself in the disputed questions on truth, Aquinas states the ancient philosophers' error in saying "simile, simili cognosci."[144] In this same question, Aquinas also notes that "verbo Deus" the finite intellect can be led to the end of its cognition, which is infinite.[145] As Thomas pushes Aristotle beyond any naturalization of the moral virtues through the odd notion of a 'theological virtue,' so he does the same with the intellectual virtues in their relationship to faith. Knowledge is incomplete without faith.

Aquinas quotes both St. Paul and St. Augustine to explain this. Paul writes in Romans 14:23, "All that is not of faith is sin." Augustine's gloss

143. ST I-II.65.2.
144. *Quaestio disputata de veritate*, in *S. Thomae Aquinatis Opera Omnia*, 2.2 co.
145. In *Quaestio disputata de veritate*, 2.2, ra 7.

states, "He that fails to acknowledge the truth, has no true virtue, even if his conduct is good."[146] Faith requires the truth of intellectual assent to the Triune God. But both Augustine and Aquinas acknowledge that even without faith, conduct has a kind of goodness and moral virtues have a kind of virtue. Imperfect virtue is still virtue; it is better to have imperfect virtue than to lack it altogether. Imperfect virtues have their place in God's good economy in that they can be ordered toward perfect virtues; they can be completed and in so doing become something they are not in themselves. Thomas explains this in his question "whether moral virtues can be without charity." By nature virtue can "dispose" us toward our end, but to attain it one "needs not only a virtue disposing him well to the end, but also those virtues which dispose him well to whatever is referred to the end: for the virtue which regards the end is the chief and moving principle in respect of those things that are referred to the end. Therefore it is necessary to have the moral virtues together with charity."[147] Each moral virtue disposes one to an end, but charity disposes all the moral virtues to one's true end. It gives the natural virtues their proper role: without it they are only imperfect virtues, with it they are made perfect. But charity also requires the proper disposition of the moral virtues. If I did not eat, sleep, speak, walk, live with others, etc. — everything that is entailed in the fact that "the world is all that is the case" — then I could not exercise the infused virtue of charity. But by themselves the moral virtues remain insufficient.

The first aspect of the virtue of faith, 'credere Deum,' which is known by reason without sacred doctrine, can be consistent with the virtue of faith once sacred doctrine properly orders it. That God is, and is one, is properly understood within the context that God is Triune. They are not opposed to each other. Christian tradition never suggested that once we receive God's threeness we then reject God's oneness. As the very structure of the prima pars of the *Summa* recognizes, 'de Deo uno' and 'de Deo trino' can never be set against each other unless something has gone wrong in theology (or someone has badly interpreted what a theologian such as Aquinas was doing). There is a place for this first aspect of faith which natural theology can possibly produce through reason alone within the whole virtue of faith, but never simply by itself. Therefore faith and reason cannot be correlated as if they inhabited different logical spaces, which need

146. ST I-II.65.2.
147. ST I-II.65.3 resp. 1.

140

to be brought into some kind of relationship. They do not represent competing internal and external or private and public domains. Nor do they compete within the same logical space. Faith is an *infused* virtue. Reason is an activity that virtue always requires; it is the human contribution God demands of us, even though it is made possible and completed only through the faith God gives us. Theological reasoning cannot be done outside the context of faith because there is no 'outside' to faith, even though reasoning can be done by natural means. Faith, like grace, will always assume these natural means.

Does natural theology speak well of God; is it truly theology, true knowledge of God? Thomas suggests it is not. He states, "Quod credere deum non convenit infidelibus sub ea ratione qua ponitur actus fidei, non enim credunt deum esse sub his conditionibus quas fides determinat. Et ideo nec vere deum credunt, quia, ut philosopus dicit, ix metaphys., 'in simplicibus defectus cognitionis est solum in non attingendo totaliter.'"[148] Thomas affirms Aristotle's account of knowledge in order to use it against Aristotle's claim to know God. What he knows of God, because it is defective, cannot be knowledge "at all."

The above quote from Thomas is intriguing for a number of reasons. First, the knowledge of God, which Thomas is concerned with here, is the first aspect of faith. It is 'credere Deum.' Second, just as in the prologue to question three in the prima pars of the *Summa,* Thomas seeks to discern what is 'fitting' to say of God. Third, Thomas is not concerned only with 'faith' as opposed to 'reason,' but his concern is with the reason by which faith acts. Finally, Thomas uses Aristotle's own notion of cognition against him. Because any defect in cognition of things prevents altogether understanding them, the defect in any knowledge of God that lacks the formal object and the will's movement, finally lacks true knowledge of God altogether. This does seem somewhat harsh, and one wonders why Thomas does not offer a more positive appraisal of Aristotle's knowledge of God. But the reason for this is clear: the form under which an object is known matters because knowledge is a conformity of the intellect to the object, and when it comes to faith, this is for Thomas a question of salvation itself.

---

148. "Unbelievers cannot be said *to believe in a God* as we understand it in relation to the act of faith. For they do not believe that God exists under the conditions that faith determines; and hence they do not truly believe in a God, since, as the Philosopher observes [*Metaphysics,* VIII, 10 (1051b 25)], *to know simple things defectively is not to know them at all.*" ST II-II.2.2 rep. 3 (Pegis).

What is meant here by 'form'? Remember that for Aquinas God is formless. But faith is the form that allows our knowledge to conform to its object; in that sense it is like all intellectual virtues. How can faith as a theological virtue that conforms to something without form also be similar to the form of intellectual virtue? Aquinas tries to explain this: "The wisdom which the Philosopher reckons as an intellectual virtue, considers Divine things so far as they are open to the research of human reason. Theological virtue, on the other hand, is about those same things so far as they surpass human reason."[149] Thomas appears to be arguing for (at least) two different positions, not easily reconciled. First, faith and intellectual virtue are distinguished because of their different formal objects, which are the incomprehensible and the comprehensible. Second, faith and intellectual virtue 'consider' the same 'thing' — 'Divine things' — but they consider the same thing from different aspects, one in the mode of what is accessible to human reason and the other in the mode of what surpasses it. Can these two positions be reconciled?

The complexity of, perhaps even contradiction within, Aquinas's position is contained in the very notion of a 'theological *virtue*.' Virtue is a natural human power, but a *theological* virtue exceeds natural human powers. How can these two terms be put together without resulting in a thoroughgoing contradiction? Aquinas makes matters even more complex when he puts them together under the notion of an 'end.' He states, "The theological virtues direct man to supernatural happiness in the same way as by the natural inclination man is directed to his connatural end." Just as the intellect and will direct the human creature to the connatural end of happiness, so they direct him or her as well to supernatural happiness. But this makes matters even more confusing, because Aquinas first argued that faith and natural reason differ in their formal object. Then he argues they consider the same 'thing' but in different modes. Now he argues they direct the human creature to different ends — one supernatural, one connatural — but do so "in the same way." Can this make sense?

The apparent disparity in Aquinas's position somewhat dissolves when we recognize the significance of what he means by a 'formal object.' It has less to do with an external object in the world that we can know through either natural or supernatural powers, and more to do with the mode by which we know. Aquinas does not have a mind-world distinction

149. ST I-II.62.2.

that needs some epistemological mechanism to mediate between them. Natural reason is not some secure means of knowledge that connects the mind to the world any more than faith is a secure means of knowledge that connects the mind to what is beyond the world. Instead, faith (a theological virtue) only works in and through nature — intellect and will (intellectual and moral virtues) to direct the human creature to a connatural and supernatural end, which is finally the same. Knowledge here does not require mediation between the mind and world to secure it against the acids of skepticism. Knowledge is always a participation in what is known, which is first and foremost a participation in everything that constitutes the world. For Aquinas the knower can never be abstracted from the world; she is part of the world.

Aquinas could have easily affirmed Wittgenstein's similar understanding in both the *Tractatus* and the *Investigations* that denied a secure place for the ego outside the world, and thus denied the possibility of a private language. Natural reason works only within the world; everything begins there. This we have in common with all earth's inhabitants. However, for Aquinas (whether this is true for Wittgenstein remains to be seen), the world has a depth to it, which can be known because all knowledge is always a participation in its First Truth, the truth that is its Creator. This gives the form to all knowledge, and thus knowing cannot escape faith. So Aquinas writes:

> Consequently in respect of both the above things [intellect and will] man needed to receive in addition something supernatural to direct him to a supernatural end. First, as regards the intellect, man receives certain supernatural principles which are held by means of a Divine light: these are the articles of faith, about which is faith. Secondly, the will is directed to this end, both as to the movement of intention, which tends to that end as something attainable, — and this pertains to hope, — and as to a spiritual union, whereby the will is, so to speak, transformed into that end — and this belongs to charity. For the appetite of a thing is moved and tends towards its connatural end naturally; and this movement is due to a certain conformity of the thing with its end.[150]

Without the theological virtues, there is no knowledge of God because there is no conformity to God.

150. ST I-II.62.3.

143

The last statement in this quote is telling. In explaining how the theological virtues act similarly to the intellectual and moral virtues in directing the human creature to her end, Thomas uses an analogy between a connatural and supernatural end. Just as desire moves one toward its connatural end naturally, so it moves one to its supernatural end. This is the telling phrase: "a thing is moved and tends toward its connatural end naturally." Just as it is with a connatural end, so it is with a supernatural end. By analogy we can also say, "a thing is moved and tends toward its supernatural end, connaturally." This helps us understand what Thomas means when he sets forth the position that through divine illumination the intellect receives the articles of faith which are the subject matter of faith. 'Divine illumination' is not some mystical, otherworldly reality; it is a participation in what is always already present in the world, just as the intellect itself only is because of the 'natural light' that makes its activity possible. Both are transcendental in the sense that they are the conditions for the possibility of knowing, which also always requires at the same time the will's desiring. But they are not transcendental in any sense of a reflexive posture that assumes an ego distinct from its immersion in the world and its desires. They are transcendental only while they are at the same time participatory in the desires that move the will and thus the intellect, which are desires for what is good and true. To be moved by them is to participate in the goodness of God's creation; it is to be moved by truth to what should be loved. The more one loves, the more one knows. The more one knows, the more one loves.

If we ask Aquinas whether the proposition 'God exists' is the same as, radically different from, or given new significance from the perspective of faith, I think his answer would be yes. It is 'the same as' in that the 'idea' we have of God lets us know that what God is cannot be known positively in terms of the intellect's composing and dividing that usually constitutes truth in the intellect — except inasmuch as the intellect negatively composes and divides so that it denies to God composition, imperfection, lack, finitude, mutability, and plurality. Yet faith as thinking with assent is radically different from the thinking with assent that all people potentially share by nature, by living together in a common creation, and who rightly reason that God is not these things, for faith takes up something new with respect to this proposition; something that must be there even to be able to negate. It takes up an assent that begins to recognize God as the fullness of these 'things' such that they are no longer 'things.' We can make this inference across incommensurables, but when we do it will require a different kind of knowledge — one where faith and reason are not set in opposition. And this is 'radically different' even though it is also grounded in an 'idea' of God which recognizes that we are speaking of the same thing — and this everyone calls God.

Faith is a theological virtue. As such, it is distinct from, but always related to, intellectual and moral virtues, which are natural human powers. As Aquinas puts it, virtues are habits that are differentiated based on the "formal difference of their objects." Because God is the object of the theological virtues, they differ from the moral and intellectual virtues, whose objects are "something comprehensible to human reason." God cannot be comprehended by human reason; therefore faith cannot be only a moral or intellectual virtue. However, this does not require that faith be incommensurable with the intellectual virtues. After all, many philosophers who did not possess the theological virtue of faith still spoke and wrote well about God, even if it is not true knowledge. As previously mentioned, in his *Disputed Questions on Truth*, Aquinas recognizes that Aristotle understands well his subject matter when he teaches in *Metaphysics* X that the Divine Intellect is that which measures and cannot be measured.[151] Of course, Aristotle did not know the fullness of what he taught. He did not recognize that the Triune God was the measure, nor who the Divine Intellect was. Yet that is why Aquinas could be so impressed with Aristotle's knowledge of divine things and still say that the milkmaid who knows Jesus knows more than Aristotle. Aristotle, along with select other philosophers, represented the best that a natural theology could produce. Natural theology was not something just anybody could know by consulting his or her immanent rational faculties; it was the result of intellectual labor by the best philosophers. But without the perfection of the theological virtues, and the teaching of sacred doctrine, true knowledge of God is not possible.

For Aquinas, as for Augustine, God is Triune and this can only be given in sacred doctrine; therefore the first aspect of faith is not finally true reasoning about God. Yet acknowledging God as Triune is not some act of faith separate from reason; the second aspect of faith entails the intellect acknowledging its "highest and most authoritative object." Faith represents the pinnacle of the intellect's reasoning activity. God as Triune, even though this knowledge is mediated via revelation, becomes the highest ob-

---

151. *Quaestio disputata de veritate*, vol. 3, q. 1, art. 2.

ject the intellect can think or speak. Of course, this second aspect, along with the third aspect where the will moves the intellect to God as the highest good, reorders the first aspect. 'That God is' now becomes 'that God is Triune,' who is our First Truth and highest good. Even the language of the first aspect is assumed in the second. We cannot say 'God is Triune' without saying 'God is. . . .' But if the philosopher closes off the proposition 'God is' from 'God is Triune,' or treats the former as a category larger than the latter, then this first potential aspect of faith closes itself off from a true reasonable ordering. Even if it is open to the second and third aspects of faith, the first aspect could only ever be considered an imperfect virtue, for it only says something about God's creation without saying what can be said about God. Because creation cannot be understood outside Christology, faith and reason find their best articulation by thinking through the logic of the incarnation, which entails the doctrine of the Trinity.

While Karl Barth was moving Protestant theology away from the sterile natural theology of neo-Protestantism, Henri de Lubac and Hans Urs von Balthasar were performing a similar task in challenging the role of 'nature' in neoscholasticism. This did not cause them to abandon the project of natural theology altogether, but to incorporate Barth's criticisms and read 'nature' through an 'analogia entis' that was primarily understood through the incarnation. (This seems quite similar to Barth's 'analogia fidei.') This was a great gain for both Protestant and Catholic theology in the twentieth century. It is a gain that we should not lose. It can be lost if we cling to a faith that eschews philosophy and loses the ability to speak of goodness or truth. It can also be lost if we return to a neoscholasticism that draws on a metaphysical objectivism to recover goodness and truth but loses their connection to Christology for a supposed universal reason that allows us to make claims, or have conversation, beyond dogmatic theology. In a world of the demise of truth and goodness we are easily tempted to take one of these two routes, to retreat to a faith that does not know metaphysics or to assert a metaphysics that neglects the historical mediation of faith. But both options should be eschewed. Instead, we should continue the conversation among Barth, Balthasar, and de Lubac in order to avoid repeating the ills that sorely afflicted modern theology. Barth recognized the dangers a natural theology can produce politically. De Lubac recognized the same with respect to a doctrine of pure nature. These are lessons we should not forget. Balthasar did not always see the political significance of his theology, but he showed how philosophy and a kind of 'natural' theology had a key role to play in the divine drama. The conversation between them should help us avoid any Protestant pull toward fideism or post-Tridentine Catholic pull toward a natural rationalism.

We need not choose between Barth and Turner. By bringing them into conversation with others of modern theology's discontents, and especially Victor Preller, we find a range of responses as to how we relate faith and reason in order to speak faithfully of the Triune God. If we move too far in the direction of a neoscholastic rationalism, then we could be left with a negative theology, in which reason as nature tells us everything we need, especially when it comes to politics, economics, and ethics and the supernatural gets cordoned off into some realm apart from nature. If we move too far in the direction of a Barthianism that refuses to acknowledge its metaphysics, or fails to move from humanity to divinity, then we will lose the importance of the divine names and turn God into an ineffable sublime. We will be tempted to think of God as other than the God who first gives his name to Moses, a name that the dynamic movement of Greek metaphysics needed even if it did not fully possess. But if we think through the logic of the incarnation, then we will see how the 'ways' to God from philosophy or humanity will find their completion in the 'way' Christ is. To think through the logic of the incarnation requires metaphysics.

CHAPTER 3

Theology: The Divine Name

How shall we speak of God so that we avoid the modern errors of fideism and rationalism? How shall we do this so that we do not assume God is an ineffable sublime about whom nothing or everything can be said, or a mythological creature about whom we must use a univocal account of language if we are to speak truthfully? This chapter addresses these questions, as well as the second modern ill — Feuerbach's projectionism. How can we recognize the truth in Feuerbach's contextualization of our speech about God and at the same time refuse to limit language to its context, which the so-called 'end of metaphysics' tempts us to do? We already began to develop a response to this question by noting Aquinas's 'modus significandi'/'res significata' distinction and its similarity to Barth's response to Brunner that the 'how' of language does not determine its 'what.' The relationship between this understanding of language and metaphysics will be developed in Chapter Four. This chapter asks questions that the 'end of metaphysics' disciplines us not to ask, questions about God, truth, goodness, and being. To ask these questions is to acknowledge a role for metaphysics in theology.

Why should theologians acknowledge a role for metaphysics? As Tarski stated, it is often nothing but a philosophical invective, a sign of muddleheaded thinking that lacks precision and/or verification. Of course 'metaphysics' does lack precision and verification; it does not attempt, like logical positivism or classical foundationalism, to posit a complete system not needing any supplementation from outside. This is why theologians should not only acknowledge but celebrate the return of metaphysics after the collapse of logical positivism and classical foundationalism. This collapse puts an end to what William Desmond calls a system of 'postulatory finitism,' which "has the effect of closing thought off from thinking the signs of transcendence as other than immanence."[1] This finitism was no discovery but an invention, a program that walked away from questions of truth, goodness, and beauty. With the return of metaphysics these questions surface once again. They can, and should, be asked without appealing to sacred doctrine, but they should never exclude it.

Metaphysics, then, is less a totalizing whole within which everything can be asked and answered and more a 'way' that opens language up, pointing beyond itself to something profound, something mysterious. Christian theologians who operate dialectically find metaphysics a grave temptation that can only be negated. Those who do theology analogically find sacred doctrine necessary to complete and correct metaphysics much as grace perfects and corrects nature. Metaphysics pursued well opens a way that leads into sacred doctrine. The tradition of the divine names and Aquinas's five ways trace these ways into the Way that makes the ways themselves possible. In fact, the tradition of the divine names and Aquinas's five ways work against a negative theology precisely because we can only negate when we first receive God's name as a 'perfection' that then allows us to remove all that is imperfect from our language about God. If we did not have this original affirmation, our language would be about nothing but ourselves. We would be reduced to silence or to doing nothing more that speaking about creation even in its negation.

1. Negative Theology?

For Barth, Aquinas embodies the error that culminates in Feuerbach; he speaks of God via an 'analogia entis' that provides a natural measure of God that is other than God's self-disclosure. He subordinates theology to metaphysics. Victor Preller disagrees; he reads Aquinas as doing something similar to what Barth himself did. Aquinas's work is thoroughly theological, requiring dogmatics to complete philosophical claims. Milbank and Pickstock also read Aquinas against any "Tridentine absurdities" that

---

1. Desmond, "Neither Servility nor Sovereignty: Between Metaphysics and Politics," in *Theology and the Political: The New Debate*, ed. Creston Davis, John Milbank, and Slavoj Žižek (Durham, N.C.: Duke University Press, 2005), p. 158.

would allow for a two-source theory of truth, cordoning off philosophy from theology. They read him, as did de Lubac, through Augustine where faith's illumination discloses nature; yet de Lubac still holds forth more of a place for Vatican I's two-source theory of truth. Denys Turner does not read Thomas in terms of Augustine's doctrine of illumination. He defends the Vatican I reading of Aquinas where nature (reason) and faith are different, albeit related, sources. Sorting through the differences and commonalties among these different readings of Thomas is exceedingly complex, but one of the key pieces is the role of God's perfections and their relation to negative theology. Can reason reach these perfections? If not, can it only negate? Or does reason assume, and possibly first receive divine perfections, in order to be about its proper task, removing those terms that do not express God's perfections?

John Paul II's *Fides et Ratio* presents the Catholic Church's position on the relationship between both faith and reason and theology and philosophy. Reason has much more than a negative role; it can conceive of God when it works in harmony with faith. Much like Leo XIII's *Aeterni Patris,* which inaugurated a renewed interest in Thomas Aquinas as a philosopher, John Paul II gives a privileged place to Aquinas because of the care with which he related theology and philosophy.[2] "A particular place is reserved for Thomas," states John Paul II, because of the "harmony" he produced between faith and reason.[3] Nevertheless, this harmony allows philosophy a "necessary autonomy."[4] By conceding that faith and reason occupy "autonomous" spheres, John Paul II restates Vatican I's two-source

---

2. John Paul II sets *Fides et Ratio* within the context of Leo XIII's *Aeterni Patris.* "Despite the fact that more than a hundred years have passed since the appearance of Leo XIII's Encyclical *Aeterni Patris,* a work frequently cited in this Encyclical, even so we think it imperative to insist more clearly on the close link between faith and philosophy." That seems to be a subtle qualification or nuance to *Aeterni Patris,* which did not always maintain that "close link" well. John Paul II then goes on to emphasize the "importance of philosophical reflection both in explaining culture and in moderating personal and social morality," and its contribution to theology. Then he states, "For these reasons we have judged it both appropriate and necessary to underline the importance of philosophy for the understanding of faith, as well as the limits philosophy faces when it forgets or denies the truths of Revelation." *Restoring Faith in Reason: A New Translation of the Encyclical Letter Faith and Reason of John Paul II Together with a Commentary and Discussion,* ed. Laurence Paul Hemming and Susan Frank Parsons (London: SCM, 2002), pp. 162-63.

3. *Restoring Faith in Reason,* p. 71.

4. *Restoring Faith in Reason,* p. 75.

theory of truth. He sees this as consistent with how Thomas Aquinas related these two spheres, for although they are independent they work together in harmony. But this changed at the end of the Middle Ages when this autonomy produced a "dangerous discord."[5] Then reason sets itself in opposition to faith, and polices against it.

John Paul II does not address whether that discord could have developed if it were not for the gradual autonomy of philosophy from theology in the later Middle Ages. He assumes philosophy had this autonomous status during that time, and that it posed no problem to faith. Problems arise when the harmonious relationship between them gets lost. At the end of the Middle Ages and into early modernity, the difference became opposition. Thus like every theologian in this conversation, John Paul II recognizes that the Christian theological tradition set in motion the conflict between faith and reason in the later Middle Ages, a conflict which characterizes modernity and makes fideism and positivism problematic tendencies. All these theologians except Barth look to the work of Aquinas in order to avoid the error of fideism that arises when faith and reason are assumed to conflict with each other. As John Paul II puts it, St. Thomas "is an authentic exemplar for those who seek truth . . . because he radically protected the particularity of Revelation, without at the same time diminishing the proper course of reason."[6]

John Paul II extols the "proper course of reason" throughout *Fides et Ratio*. Like Denys Turner, he concedes philosophy its autonomy and prizes it sufficiently that he states, "Philosophy will be the place where human culture and Christian faith come together, and will provide the place of agreement between believers and non-believers."[7] This is an argument one could not imagine Barth making. Yet for John Paul II, reason must be connected with Wisdom; this "sapiential task" of philosophy requires that it opens itself to theology which the limits of a modernist pure reason do not permit.[8]

Henri de Lubac's theology can easily be read as an earlier exemplification of the proper ordering between faith and reason, theology and philosophy, which John Paul II sets forth. De Lubac understood himself as do-

5. *Restoring Faith in Reason*, p. 75.
6. *Restoring Faith in Reason*, p. 127.
7. *Restoring Faith in Reason*, p. 129.
8. *Restoring Faith in Reason*, p. 133.

ing primarily 'natural theology.' His *Discovery of God* was an effort to show how philosophy should be open to theology for philosophy's own sake without philosophy requiring submission to the authoritative dogmas of the church. Criticized for avoiding explicit mention of Christian dogma in this book, he responded that just because it may not have been explicitly mentioned did not mean it was absent. How was it present? It was present in that philosophy must first be led by a 'via eminentia' before it can begin its task of negation. The proper course of reason in de Lubac and John Paul II is not that reason first does its work and once it comes upon its inevitable limitations, faith steps in to complete it. Instead, the excess that is our analogical participation in God's perfections comes first. It makes reason possible because it can only work from the excess of truth and goodness that is unavoidable in everyday life.

For de Lubac, we can conceive of God, and these conceptions "truly signify God," yet how they do this is directly related to their inadequacy. He writes, "Our concepts have the power to signify God truly — and yet strictly speaking we cannot seize God in any one of them; or rather that is how they truly signify him."[9] In other words, God always exceeds our concepts and thus no single concept suffices. Rational conceptuality works within the context of the 'more' that is given to us in revelation (to Moses and in Jesus). God speaks first and we are then summoned to ask, "What is your name?" This is the first theological question and is always the basis upon which it works. De Lubac explains this by drawing upon Aquinas's three ways of speaking about God in question thirteen of the prima pars: "In the dialectic of the three ways *(affirmatio, seu positio; negatio, seu remotio; eminentia, seu transcendentia),* the via eminentiae does not, in the last analysis, follow on the via negationis; it demands, inspires and guides it. Although it comes last, the via eminentiae is covertly the first. . . . The affirmation is, at bottom, mind itself."[10] The mind participates in a way that exceeds its conceptuality and yet makes that conceptuality possible. This means negative theology is always derivative from something excessive.

For de Lubac, like Milbank and Pickstock, but unlike Turner, the Augustinian interpretation of Aquinas works against the dominance of a negative theology. The mind's inevitable participation in God's perfections works backwards in allowing us to conceive by reason what cannot be

---

9. De Lubac, *The Discovery of God* (Grand Rapids: Eerdmans, 2002), p. 128.
10. De Lubac, *Discovery of God,* pp. 122, 124. ST I.13.1.

known. Because our knowledge always assumes the 'more' of God's perfections, the 'via eminentiae' is the foundation for our knowledge of God. The mystical and philosophical do not contradict each other. De Lubac writes, "St. Thomas merges the two points of view [mystical and philosophical]. . . . The 'desire to see God' which he regards as natural to us, is certainly, at bottom mystical in character. . . . Nevertheless St. Thomas tries to establish its reality in a purely rational manner, starting from the effects which the intelligence desires to know in their Cause so as to know them fully."[11] Reason assumes a mystical participation in God's perfections for it to do its work, even in a "purely rational manner." Balthasar develops this theme as essential to the "truth of God." He writes, "Important for our purposes is the fundamental proposition that, undergirding every conscious intellectual endeavor (to 'prove the existence of God,' for example), is the basic fact that man 'posits' or 'positively affirms' God." This affirmation and way of eminence "remains superior to all subsequent negations."[12] Once we see this "fundamental proposition," we can make sense of something often overlooked in Thomas's discussion of the 'quinque viae.' In the prologue to question three of the prima pars, Thomas not only states that we know God in a confused and general manner, and that we do this primarily through negation, but he suggests this negation occurs by "denying of Him whatever is opposed to the idea of Him — viz., composition, motion, and the like." Here Thomas explicitly states that we can negate only because we already have an "idea" of God. His five ways do not begin outside dogmatic theology, they operate within it; for where does this "idea" of God originate if not, as he has already told us, from sacred doctrine? If we did not know God's name, I AM, we would not know what to negate. Aquinas affirms this when he discusses the divine names and draws on Exodus 3. This revelation is the excess, given in the bush that burns without being consumed, that makes theology possible. As it makes speech of God possible for Moses, so this kind of illumination makes possible all speaking well of God. It is why theology always begins in the way of eminence even while this eminence requires ordinary signs.

De Lubac and Balthasar begin with the 'eminentia, seu transcendentia'; it leads to the 'remotio' which then makes possible a rational

11. De Lubac, *Discovery of God*, p. 150.
12. Hans Urs von Balthasar, *Theo-Logic: II: The Truth of God*, trans. Adrian Walker (San Francisco: Ignatius, 2004), p. 96.

'affirmatio.' Turner seems to follow a different order; 'remotio' rather than 'eminentia' provides the rational conceptuality which human creatures can at best produce. This is why he finds God "in human language," not within "its characteristic rationality," but rather "in the disordered collapse of speech into paradox, oxymoron and the negation of the negation."[13] This "theological rhetoric," which begins with negation rather than perfection, seems to leave less room for theology's confidence in speaking about God. But this is ambiguous in Turner. He also recognizes that for Thomas, as for Dionysius, the apophatic "consists in the excessus of the 'cataphatic.'"[14]

Milbank and Pickstock's Augustinian Thomism makes two important claims about faith and reason that avoid privileging negative theology. First, "reason and faith in Aquinas represent only different degrees of intensity of participation in the divine light of illumination and different measures of absolute vision." If we read this statement in light of something like Exodus 3 it loses any abstract metaphysical feel and makes good sense of Scripture. To see a bush requires an illumination that comes from outside us. To see a bush revealing God to us requires a much more intense illumination. Reason and faith then are less different intellectual activities than the same intellectual activity, varying in intensity. Since all such activity is a "participation" in the "divine light of illumination," reason and faith differ only in the "intensity of that participation." Second, they nevertheless recognize difference in the two activities because reason presupposes faith yet faith requires "discursive argumentation" for its own intelligibility. Therefore they also state, "And, furthermore, that reason itself requires faith because it already presupposes the operation of grace, while, inversely, faith still demands discursive argumentation and is only higher than reason because it enjoys a deeper participation in the divine reason which is direct intuition or pure intellectual vision." The result of this is an acknowledgment that for Aquinas there can be on the one hand no "philosophical approach to God independent of theology," and on the other no "confinement to biblical revelation independent of the Greek legacy of

13. Turner, *Faith, Reason, and the Existence of God* (Cambridge: Cambridge University Press, 2004), p. 106. I do not see how the statement here fits with Turner's later claim, sympathetic to Pseudo-Denys, that he has a "'grammar' of talk about God. . . . For even if we do not have a proper 'concept' of God . . . we have a use for the name 'God,' a use which is governed by determinable rules of correct and incorrect speech" (p. 158).

14. Turner, *Faith, Reason, and the Existence of God,* p. 188.

metaphysical reflection."[15] The first error would lead to neoscholastic rationalism; the second toward fideism.

Turner finds this position unconvincing. He sees in it an Augustinianism more akin to that of Henry of Ghent than Aquinas, for it does not allow for a sufficient account of reason alone. Their 'Augustinianism,' he states, "goes far beyond any defended by Thomas, who says nothing at all, anywhere at all, about the human intellect's participation in the divine self-understanding involving any kind of experience of its actuality, not even of a 'pre-ontological' kind."[16] This reference to a "pre-ontological" experience of the human intellect's participation in the divine is the key to Turner's criticism of Milbank and Pickstock, yet this does appear to be a misreading of their position. Milbank and Pickstock explicitly state that "faith demands discursive argumentation." They do not suggest that faith or reason is a pure participation of the human intellect in the divine mind without discursive argument.

Milbank and Pickstock develop their argument on the basis of the ordering in the *Summa* of God's (so-called) 'attributes,' taking seriously that being is presented first through negation, but this negation is quickly supplemented by perfection. Perfection is the second 'attribute' (or 'name') Aquinas mentions after identifying God as 'being' and 'simple.' Simplicity functions primarily as negation; God has no composition — no form/matter, no body/soul. Because this negative 'attribute' is so quickly qualified by 'perfection,' Milbank and Pickstock can properly speak of the "primacy of perfection" in Aquinas.[17] Here they follow a similar transcendental argument we already witnessed in de Lubac and Balthasar. God's perfection is not a matter of an "empirical observation" in nature; rather, the imperfect only makes sense against the tacit background of the perfect.

15. Milbank and Pickstock, *Truth in Aquinas* (London: Routledge, 2000), p. xiii. Milbank does not always honor the importance of the first revelation of God's name to Moses and sometimes seems to assume that Greek metaphysics suffices without its prior confirmation in that revelation. This revelation also qualifies, but does not displace, that metaphysics.

16. Turner, *Faith, Reason, and the Existence of God*, p. 95.

17. This claim seems warranted based on what Thomas writes about perfection in the prologue to question three of the prima pars. Thomas writes, "Primo ergo inquiratur de simplicitate ipsius, per quam removetur ab eo compositio. Et quia simplicia in rebus corporalibus sunt imperfecta et partes, secundo inquieretur de perfectione ipsius." (First therefore we inquire of simplicity itself, through which is removed from God composition. And because simplicity in the corporeal body is imperfect and in parts, second we inquire of perfection itself.)

Pickstock and Milbank state, "Here, indeed, it *might* seem that we only know the most perfect (or absolute good) 'to be' because we respond to a certain pre-ontological insistence on the ideal (Plato's Sun of the Good beyond Being which itself discloses Being)."[18] This suggests the possibility of a pre-ontological, a priori illumination as necessary for our knowledge, which is how Turner reads them and asks the question, What would such a 'pre-ontological illumination' be? Are they arguing that even before being itself is present to us, our mind is illumined by an ideal beyond being? It is this appeal to the pre-ontological that troubles Turner, and given the lack of clarity as to what 'pre-ontological illumination' is, Turner's concern seems warranted. But note their qualification through the use of the word 'might.'

They do not endorse this version of a Platonic "pre-ontological insistence on the ideal" unqualifiedly. They continue, "Nonetheless, it suggests equally that, for Aquinas, the guiding apprehension of perfection is *not* after all of a pre-ontological formal possibility (as it soon became for Duns Scotus) but rather is a dim and remote perception of a plenitude of infinite actuality. The insistence of the ideal is, after all, as much ontological as pre-ontological."[19] Had Milbank and Pickstock been more attentive to the biblical tradition of the divine names Aquinas draws on, they could have presented their point in biblical as well as Platonic sources, for what is this "infinite actuality," except God's name: I AM? The "ideal," or apprehended perfection, in, through, and by which all things appear is not a transcendental a priori in the Kantian sense. It is not a formal epistemological category that comes before the ontic and ontological. They conclude, "Therefore Aquinas does not really have recourse to an a priori vision of the Good in the sense of a Kantian epistemological reflection on the structures of finite understanding, but to a Platonic and Augustinian ontological recollection of something real and eternal."[20] What exactly does this mean?

Their position suggests that the human intellect "recollects" the infinite actuality from which it originates and that all knowing and being only makes sense against the backdrop of this perfection, which is nothing other than God's being. In other words, Christian theology affirms that

18. Milbank and Pickstock, *Truth in Aquinas*, p. 29.

19. Milbank and Pickstock, *Truth in Aquinas*, p. 29. The argument is not easy to follow here, but it seems to be rejecting something like Avicenna's essence that has 'esse' only accidentally and thus must be prior to 'esse.'

20. Milbank and Pickstock, *Truth in Aquinas*, p. 29.

God is the fullness of being, lacking nothing and independent of creation. God has no "real relations" with creation. Nevertheless, God shares 'being' with creatures, who are only as they participate in the being God is. They do not have an 'essence' that exists prior to the act of being ('esse'). Even though essence and existence are distinct, they only emerge from God's creative plenitude as pure act. This is because, as Dionysius (and the Bible) affirms, God's being is to communicate itself. The creation of beings that are not God, does not take away from God's being or render those things divine. Scripture and metaphysics reinforce each other. This fits Aquinas's discussion of God's perfection, where he notes that God as 'ipsum esse per se subsistens' contains the perfection of all things within God's being.[21] This also fits Milbank's understanding of the "ontological impossibilities" Christian theology demands.

Milbank sets forth three ontologies of the impossible: "The impossibility that anything should exist outside of God, who is replete Being" (impossibility of Creation); the impossibility of sin where creatures "discover an illusory 'of themselves' wherewith to reject the absolute in the name of something lesser" (impossibility of Fall); and the "impossibility of redemption for a fault which, since it cuts finite being off from (infinite) reality, would appear to be without redress, even by that reality" (impossibility of Redemption).[22] These three ontologies of the impossible, like Barth's understanding of the relationship between covenant and creation, work backwards. Milbank writes, "We now only glimpse the impossibility of Creation through the impossibility of the Fall, and both through the impossibility of the Redemption, even though Creation does not entail Fall, nor Fall, Redemption."[23] Here we find Milbank answering the question why there is something rather than nothing. The answer is 'gift.' The gift of Christ to redeem us is the plenitude that allows us to 'glimpse' the Fall and thereby Creation. This answer assumes that love is as basic to our existence as reason, which is something Balthasar endeavored to show. We do not understand reason well if it remains unrelated to love. We can only know what we love and love what we know. Love is the perfection against which Creation and reason can appear.

---

21. ST I.4: "Cum ergo deus sit prima causa effective rerum, oportet onmium rerum perfectiones praeexistere in deo secundum eminentiorem modum."

22. Milbank, *Being Reconciled* (London: Routledge, 2003), p. 63.

23. Milbank, *Being Reconciled*, p. 63.

John Paul II states this well. "The truth Revelation allows us to know is neither the mature fruit nor the highest reach of the reflections of human reason. On the contrary, it is the expression, together with its particular characteristics, of a totally free gift: it stirs up and disturbs ideas and requires that it be accepted as a declaration of love."[24] Only on the basis of an ontology of love can gift be understood. Because love, and not pure reason, is the basic structure of being, the failure of human reason to achieve its infinite desires is not negative but positive. Thus we do not need to negate reason in order to believe, but rather supplement and intensify it. We receive knowledge as a gift. To forget the necessity of gift, or to bracket it out as philosophically problematic, is equivalent to forgetting that our very being only comes through the laborious gift of another. Of course, gift's necessity does not entail reception. I can reject the gift of being. Gift, another name for the Holy Spirit, is the fullness of being, the perfection that surrounds us with an inevitable desire for truth, goodness, and beauty. It illumines our lives.

Do either Milbank or Pickstock then assume that this 'illumination' is a direct participation of the human intellect in the divine without the use of natural human powers? They both seem consistently to deny this position. In *Theology and Social Theory*, Milbank writes,

> The distinction between 'revealed' and 'natural' knowledge is really located by Aquinas in a much more fundamental framework of the participation of all human rationality in divine reason. (So all knowledge implies faith in God for Aquinas.) Revelation increases this participation through means that do not violate the normal workings of analogy and participation: the inner illumination of the mind is strengthened, new outer signs are provided in history. In one sense, even within theological understanding, natural principles go on being 'more certain' than supernatural ones. But in another sense, the light of revelation strengthens our grasp of natural principles and of what is implied within them.[25]

As Pickstock and Milbank argue in *Truth in Aquinas*, so Milbank argues here that revelation cannot be set against natural knowledge; it "intensifies" it and thus makes it even more certain.

24. *Restoring Faith in Reason*, p. 29.
25. John Milbank, *Theology and Social Theory* (London: Blackwell, 1990), p. 248.

Has he moved away from this position? He repeats it in *Being Reconciled*:

> Reason orientated only to beatitude supposedly within our grasp dispenses with hope, only to land up as without hope, and as best resigned to this condition. Likewise if such a reason is taken as hermeneutically decisive, it must downgrade the promptings, urgings, and longings of the *body*. The supernatural in us may be intelligence as such, intelligence thinking through us, but is also always conjoined with sensation, as Aquinas taught. Therefore intelligence begins as a bodily exercise, accompanied by desire that reaches into the unknown. Only by an exercise of an artificial abstraction can we prise reason apart from desire, which reaches beyond our capacity. This prised-apart 'pure reason' is also a totally individualistic reason, whether on the level of the single person or of collective humanity.[26]

The key difference between Milbank and Turner has less to do with 'natural' or revealed theology, and more with whether 'natural' theology should primarily be advanced in terms of being or in terms of the perfections of being. Milbank finds that Scotus distances being from its perfections. But this "totally obliterates the 'phenomenological' dimension implicit in Aquinas (and in Anselm, following Augustine), which assumes that to grasp a perfection is to see the infinite shining through the finite and calling the finite above itself."[27] For this reason Milbank dismisses any firm distinction between faith and reason, where reason alone can prove the existence of God, as "Tridentine absurdities."

If reason always assumes the prior excess of faith, does Scripture do anything more than make explicit what is always already implicit in every act of knowing? Does sacred doctrine do something more than this? The Thomistic renewal among modern theology's discontents matters because of how it addresses this question. Thomas addresses it in the secunda secundae when he examines Augustine's definition of faith as "to think with assent."[28] If faith is to think with assent ('assensione cogitare') then faith cannot be set in opposition to reason, for the activity of thinking ('cogitare') is an activity of the intellect. But what does it mean 'to think'

---

26. Milbank, *Being Reconciled*, p. 121.
27. Milbank, *Being Reconciled*, p. 77.
28. ST II-II.2.1.

('cogitare')? Is there a thinking which is something other than assenting? Aquinas would say yes. Following Augustine, he speaks of three uses of 'to think.' The first is to think 'communiter,' or in a general way, which is "pro qualibet actuali consideratione intellectus" (by any actual consideration of the intellect). Here to think is simply the activity of the intellect. 'Cogitare' is what the intellect does. This, of course, is not yet faith, but faith is not to be had without the intellect's activity of thinking. We begin with this "general way" of thinking and then proceed to thinking "magis proprie consideratio" (more properly considered). Here thinking is a certain 'inquisitione' or inquiry, which is the intellect's activity before it reaches perfection "per certitudinem visionis." This 'cogitare,' because it is not a perfection, is not an activity of God, but of creatures. This is why Augustine does not call the Son the 'Thought' of God, but the 'Word.' 'Cogitare' is the intellect's deliberating either "circa intentiones universalis" (concerning universal intentions, concepts, or notions) which belong to the intellectual part of the soul or "circa intentiones particulares" (concerning particular intentions, concepts, or notions) which belong to the sensitive part of the soul. To think, 'communiter' as the bare faculty of thinking, is not faith, for here thinking with assent is inevitable; one cannot avoid it.

We can apply this way of thinking to what Thomas assumed was an inevitable aspect of all thought when it comes to God. In the second question of the prima secundae Thomas replies to the objection that knowledge of God would be "per se notum" (self-evident) because it is naturally in us by saying, "cognoscere deum esse in aliquo communi, sub quadam confusione, est nobis naturaliter insertum, inquantum scilicet deus est hominis beatitudo, homo enim naturaliter desiderat beatitudinem, et quod naturaliter desideratur ab honime, naturaliter congnoscitur ab eodem"[29] (to know God exists in a general way under a certain confusion is naturally inserted in us, inasmuch as God is man's beatitude, for man naturally desires beatitude, and what is naturally desired by man is naturally known by him). Similar to the distinction in the secunda secundae between thinking "in a general way" and thinking "properly" considered, Thomas distinguishes a natural knowledge of God in a confused and general way from knowledge of God "simpliciter." The latter only happens through faith; the former is, like the activity of thinking itself, a necessary form of assent to the creature's being. It is a necessary feature of reason,

29. ST I-II.2.1.

but it is not faith and it is not knowledge of God properly considered. At most it is knowledge of God 'communiter'; for proper knowledge of God we need faith. This cannot be had apart from sacred doctrine.

This helps us make sense of the prologue to question three in the prima pars. Thomas begins his questions on God's 'attributes' by saying, "Cognito de aliquo an sit, inquiriendum restat quomodo sit, ut sciatur de eo quid sit" (knowledge of whether anything is, continues inquiring in what way it is, so that it knows of it what it is). Here again we are 'thinking' of God not from the perspective of a perfected vision, but through the intellect's activity of inquiry. However, when it comes to God, this inquiry cannot reach its end: "sed quia de deo scire non possumus quid sit, sed quid non sit, non possumus considerare de deo quomodo sit, sed potius quomodo non sit" (because we are not able to know of God what he is, but what he is not, we are not able to consider of God how he is but more how he is not). Notice that Thomas does not starkly juxtapose our ability to consider what God is from what God is not. The "potius" in the above sentence is significant. Thomas does not say that we will *only* consider what God is not, but we will consider "more" what God is not within the context of the intellect as inquiring. This explains the odd expression he uses when he discusses how we can "remove" from God everything that is not fitting. He writes, "potest autem ostendi de deo quomodo non sit, removendo ab eo ea quae ei non convenient. . . ." (we are able to show, however, how God is not by removing from him what is not fitting to him). Of course, as already noted, Thomas assumes an 'idea' of God, of what is 'fitting' to God, before he can make any negations.

This inevitably raises the question, from where does this more that allows us to negate come? It comes from the call to follow a 'via,' which is what the inquiring intellect seeks. This call assumes a tacit perfection that starts the intellect inquiring in the first place. It produces desire for the good and the true. Sacred doctrine and the incarnation give flesh to that way and help bring the inquiry to its fulfillment. But what the incarnation gives us is not a proposition. It gives us a way, a way of inquiring after God. Thomas's theology is a meditation upon the significance of John 14:6: "I am the way, the truth, and the life." The logic of his investigation follows this 'way' before it can arrive at truth. This 'way' draws us into itself; it leads us. All the other 'ways' that the intellect and will follow in their desire for the true and good assume this 'way' as their origin and goal. This is not something we can naturally know, although we naturally pursue it. Nor is it something we can naturally attain, even though we inevitably attempt to do so and fail. But the inadequacy of philosophical reflections on the true and the good, and the constant program to diminish them, point to some such reality. Our desire for beatitude, for goodness, truth, and beauty, even in the perverse forms they take, unsettles us and lead us on a way that, if we are truthful, should cause us to refuse to settle for any idol of our own making, for reducing God to our own projection. That is an unreasonable position. The alternative is to receive knowledge of God in our active inquiry, a knowledge we can make a contribution to, but only in and through faith. Jesus is the way into God because he invites us into this way. His humanity is the sign, the means to move from humanity to divinity; for he bears the divine name. But if we did not know the divine name, we would not know Jesus bears it.

2. The Divine Name(s)

Aquinas's five ways assume a journey that requires the rest of the *Summa* for its intelligibility. They are not sufficient in themselves any more than are the so-called 'attributes' Thomas first uses to speak of God in the prima pars. We are told this explicitly. First, Aquinas tells us that he can only show us some ways for God's existence; they are not necessary reasons. Our situation is like that of the disciples standing before Jesus in John 14: frightened because we do not know the way, but knowing we desire happiness. We are moved toward it; we want to go where he is going without understanding what this means. But like them, we also do know the Way even as he stands before us. Our dilemma is that we do not know that we know it because we cannot recognize that in seeing the creature Jesus we also see the Father.

All our truthful speech of God is possible because we already participate in that 'way,' for we were created in and through it and thus have a natural desire for it, but we do not naturally recognize it. We recognize its naturalness only in retrospect, after we receive the gift of faith.[30] For Thomas, only because Jesus is the way and the destination can we finally

---

30. Here I think that the putative difference between Aquinas and a Reformed doctrine of total depravity on the noetic effects of sin is much overstated. Both have the same consequence: without the revelation of the divine name(s), we do not know God.

find our way. He told us this in the prologue to question two in the prima pars, and he makes it more explicit when, after he has told us "what God is not" in questions three through eleven and how God is known by us in question twelve, he then helps us make sense of all these questions by speaking of God's "names" in question thirteen.[31]

Questions three through eleven teach us primarily that God is not a creature. Because all knowledge in Aquinas comes through the "causal relationship of creation," these questions show the limits to philosophy and any 'natural reason.'[32] If all we had in the prima pars were the first eleven questions, it would raise the question, addressed in question twelve, how could creatures know God at all? We would have to settle for an apophatic theology. This possibility Aquinas emphatically rejects in favor of the tradition of the divine names in question thirteen. Only after it can we read questions three through twelve well.

Aquinas begins his discussion on our knowledge of God with the claim that no created intellect can see God, for, as Dionysius teaches in the *Divine Names*, "Neither is there sense, nor image, nor opinion, nor reason, nor knowledge of Him."[33] The beginning point for the discussion both of our knowledge of God, and how we name God, is this tradition of the divine names, which are given in Scripture.[34] Aquinas did not offer us a natural theology that sought to demonstrate God's putative 'attributes' from reason alone; instead, we know God's name from Scripture, and the

31. This is Thomas's own explanation to these questions in the *Summa* in the prologue to question three.

32. Rudi te Velde argues, against Sokolowski, that "one cannot think of God apart from the causal relationship of creation." For this reason, he disagrees with Sokolowski that Aquinas, like Anselm, thinks of God primarily in terms of "the distinction" between God and creation. Rudi A. te Velde, *Aquinas on God* (London: Ashgate, 2006), p. 91 n. 24.

33. ST I.12.1 obj. 1.

34. Kevin Hart thinks Aquinas misreads Dionysius as giving us a positive theology. He states, "Even the Divine Names, which is usually taken as the source of pseudo-Dionysius's positive theology, begins and ends by stating that negative theology is to be preferred to positive theology." *The Trespass of the Sign: Deconstruction, Theology and Philosophy* (New York: Fordham University Press, 2000), p. 199. I don't see how this is the best way to read the prayer that begins *The Divine Names* when Dionysius prays, "Let the divine law of the writings now determine us from the beginning of our inquiry." We will see below how Dionysius assumes a positive knowledge of God's name akin to Augustine and Aquinas. Pseudo-Dionysius, *The Divine Names and the Mystical Theology*, trans. John D. Jones (Milwaukee: Marquette University Press, 1999), p. 107.

question is how we make sense of this in light of the fact that we can only name God from creatures.[35] He never asks 'how can we speak of God' as if this were somehow a legitimate question. His question is like Anselm's — given that we do speak of God by faith, how can we do so?

If the divine names give neither sense, image, opinion, reason, nor knowledge of God, then the logical conclusion is that they remind us primarily that God is unknowable. Aquinas rejects this conclusion. God is "supremely knowable" because God is pure act. God has no potentiality that awaits actualizing so that we can then know who God is. God is not hidden, waiting to develop God's character so that we will then know God. Nor does God withdraw in revealing God's self such that our language about God must only be dialectical. God gives himself in superabundance that only blinds because of its excess; for this reason our language about God must be analogical. As pure act, God is the most knowable of all beings, but this does not mean that we naturally know God. If we do not know God, however, this is not because God hides from us; it is because of the "excess of the intelligible object above the intellect." God is that splendor of luminosity whose presence blinds.

But isn't this just avoiding the question? God is the most knowable of all beings, for God is being itself, but God is not knowable by us? For Aquinas, this does not avoid the question, but shifts the burden of proof. God always gives us all that we need for knowledge of him; our vocation is to receive the gifts we need to see it. For this reason, Aquinas argues that to deny a vision of God to a created intellect is against both faith and reason. It violates faith because God is our ultimate beatitude. The happiness that draws us toward it is something other than our own projection. It violates reason because "there exists in every man a natural desire to know the cause of any effect which he sees; and thence arises wonder in men." If to see God could not be attained by a created intellect, then this desire would be "void."[36] Reason is born out of desire, not as lack but as wonder.

Reason produces in us a desire for God. This is a 'natural' desire that cannot be naturally attained. For it to be satisfied we need an Image of God in the created intellect.[37] This is necessary because we know the cor-

---

35. Janet Martin Soskice's essay "Naming God: A Study in Faith and Reason," in *Reason and the Reasons of Faith,* ed. Paul Griffiths and Reinhard Hütter (London: T&T Clark, 2005), points this out brilliantly.

36. ST I.12.1 resp.

37. ST I.12.2.

poreal eye cannot see God based on the Aristotelian principle which states that "act is proportional to the nature which possesses it."[38] If we were left with this Aristotelian principle, we would either be required to do natural theology and offer a proof for God's existence based on natural reason alone, which is always the temptation of a too rigorous adoption of Aristotelianism in theology, or deny God can be known altogether. Neither possibility suffices.[39] Thomas rejects the Aristotelian temptation by taking up the objection that "a created intellect can see the divine essence by its own natural powers" and rejects this possibility.[40] He states, "It is impossible for any created intellect to see the essence of God by its own natural power. For knowledge is regulated according as the thing known is in the knower. But the thing known is in the knower according to the mode of the knower. Hence the knowledge of every knower is ruled according to its own nature."[41] Given that knowledge of God is to be the measure and not the measured, this nicely states the 'problem' of the knowledge of God. The "mode of being," God's being, "is above the nature of the knower." His conclusion, however, is not that knowledge of God is a problem, but that it is only a problem when we confine ourselves to nature alone. God provides something more. "Therefore the created intellect cannot see the essence of God unless God by His grace united Himself to the created intellect as an object made intelligible to it." This is why theologians should not be surprised that philosophers constantly seek to develop a natural proof for the existence of God, but always fail in the attempt to do so. When they seek this, they remain trapped within Aristotle's principle and refuse to receive that which goes beyond philosophy without contradicting or negating it. In fact, this gift makes the natural desire intrinsic to the philosophic quest intelligible. Only when grace illumines nature is it possible to know God. God does this by uniting God's self with the created intellect.

How does God unite with the "created intellect"? This occurs through "the illumination of the intellect" where "some supernatural disposition should be added to the intellect in order that it may be raised up to such a great and sublime height." This is a "created light" that makes the

38. ST I.12.3 resp.

39. Against any modern account of evidentialism Thomas does state, "a person can have a probable opinion that a proposition is demonstrable, although he himself does not know it as demonstrated." ST I.12.7 resp.

40. ST I.12.4 obj. 1.

41. ST I.12.4 resp.

creature "deiform."[42] We should not, however, think of this notion of illumination as only a reference to the believer; it is also a Christological reference. Throughout these questions in the *Summa*, Aquinas draws implicitly on the Gospel of John where Jesus is both the "I am" and the "true Light." This language of image, union, and created light will be used to explain Christology in the tertia pars. Christ is the "created light of glory" that makes unity between God and the created intellect possible. In the tertia pars Aquinas asks, "whether Christ had the knowledge which the blessed or comprehensors have?"[43] This would be the beatific vision. It would seem that Christ would not possess this, for such a vision is "a participation of Divine light" (Ps. 35:10). But Christ has much more than this, for he has "the Godhead itself substantially abiding in Him."[44] But since this created light is what makes possible knowledge of God, and since Christ is not only the destination, but his humanity is also the only way to that knowledge, he possesses this vision as its cause in others.

> What is in potentiality is reduced to act by what is in act; for that whereby things are heated must itself be hot. Now man is in potentiality to the knowledge of the blessed, which consists in the vision of God; and is ordained to it as to an end; since the rational creature is capable of that blessed knowledge inasmuch as he is made in the image of God. Now men are brought to this end of beatitude by the humanity of Christ according to Heb. 2:10. For it became Him for Whom are all things, and by Whom are all things, Who had brought many children unto glory to perfect the author of their salvation by His passion. And hence it was necessary that the beatific vision of God should belong to Christ pre-eminently, since the cause ought always to be more efficacious that the effect.[45]

Notice that Christ's *humanity* is the cause of our completion in beatitude. But how can this be if humanity itself does not have the means to fulfill its end? Thomas addresses this by raising and answering three objections against Christ possessing the beatific vision in his humanity. This discussion in the tertia pars illumines how we attain knowledge of God as

42. ST I.12.5 resp.
43. ST III.9.2.
44. ST III.9.2 resp.
45. ST III.9.2 resp.

laid out in the twelfth question of the prima pars.[46] The objections are: First, Christ "had not a participated light, but He had the Godhead substantially." Second, Christ was "blessed through being united to God in person." Third, the human creature has a "double knowledge — one by nature, one above nature." The beatific vision then is above nature in the blessed, but in Christ it was even a "higher supernatural knowledge." His reply to each of these objections helps us understand how illumination works in question twelve of the prima pars.

His first reply draws on the doctrine of the hypostatic union to emphasize that it is Christ's soul, "which is a part of human nature," that received a "light perfected from the Divine Nature," and thus "is perfected with the beatific knowledge whereby it sees God in essence."[47] In the second reply he emphasizes that the hypostatic union is not only an "uncreated beatitude" but also a "created beatitude." In the latter Christ's "soul was established in the last end of human nature."[48] The third reply gives evidence of the overlapping between nature and grace in Aquinas's work. He writes,

> The beatific vision and knowledge are to some extent above the nature of the rational soul, inasmuch as it cannot reach it of its own strength; but in another way it is in accordance with its nature, inasmuch as it is capable of it by nature, having been made to the likeness of God, as stated above. But the uncreated knowledge is in every way above the nature of the human soul.[49]

Aquinas presents two forms of knowledge in Christ. There is the created knowledge, which is the beatific vision of Christ's soul, part of his human nature that illumines all other wayfarers. There is also the uncreated knowledge, which is Christ's immediate vision of God's essence; something he can only mediate to us through his created knowledge. It illumines us.

---

46. That Thomas is explicitly linking ST I.12 and ST III.9-10 can be seen in the prologue to III.10 where he states, "But again, because much has been said in the First Part (Q. 12) of the beatific knowledge, which consists in the vision of God, we shall speak here only of such things as belong properly to the soul of Christ."

47. ST III.9.2 rep. obj. 1.

48. ST III.9.2 rep. obj. 2.

49. ST III.9.2 rep. obj. 3.

This helps us make sense of Aquinas's eighth article in question twelve of the prima pars, "Whether those who see the Essence of God see all in God?" He responds, "Therefore no created intellect in seeing God can know all that God does or can do, for this would be to comprehend His power; but of what God does or can do any intellect can know the more, the more perfectly it sees God."[50] How do we see "more perfectly"? We do so through participation in Christ. We need the argument he lays out in the tertia pars to make sense of what he says here in the prima pars.

This should also help explain how the natural knowledge of God works for Thomas, including the role for the five ways. He raises the question, "Whether God can be known in this life by natural reason," and answers,

> Our natural knowledge begins from sense. Hence our natural knowledge can go so far as it can be led by sensible things. But our minds cannot be led by sense so far as to see the essence of God; because the sensible effects of God do not equal the power of God as their cause. Hence from the knowledge of sensible things the whole power of God cannot be known; nor therefore can His essence be seen. But because they are His effects and depend on their cause, we can be led from them so far as to know of God whether He exists, and to know of Him what must necessarily belong to Him, as the first cause of all things, exceeding all things caused by Him.[51]

Here we find how the five ways function, for they are all ways that also begin from sense. They show the limits to philosophy or natural theology. "We can be led from them" only so far. We can only be led *from them* to know God because God exceeds them, and in that excess makes them possible. This is a significant form of knowledge, for it places us in a position to receive something that is more than natural in order to complete what is natural.

Thomas explains this "something more" in the final article of question twelve in the prima pars when he states, "We have a more perfect knowledge of God by grace than by natural reason." But this more perfect knowledge does not operate independently of natural reason; it "strengthens" it by an "infusion of gratuitous light" such that the two things natural

50. ST I.12.8 resp.
51. ST I.12.8 resp.

reason produces — "images derived from sensible objects" and abstracting "intelligible conceptions" from them — gain something more. These images are not only our own projections but they are also "divinely formed." (This is explained in question fifteen with Thomas's account of the Divine Ideas.) These two things are related to the two kinds of nouns we use, concrete and abstract.[52] They are all our natural reason could produce and neither is adequate to name God, but through the illumination of grace, we understand something more; we recognize the possibility of something that transcends both of them. The "infusion of gratuitous light" comes from the causal power of Christ's hypostatic union. It gives creatures the faith to 'see' what exceeds sight. This vision is not against reason; it is a "kind of knowledge." Thomas concludes, "Faith is a kind of knowledge inasmuch as the intellect is determined by faith to some knowable object."[53]

We are now in a position to see how Aquinas's Christology warrants speaking of God. He takes this up in question thirteen of the prima pars when he returns once again to the tradition of the divine names. Thomas summarizes what we have learned so far. Speaking of God can only begin with what is natural to us. In this sense, Aquinas recognizes a kind of projection. He states, "Because we know and name God from creatures, the names we attribute to God signify what belongs to material creatures, of which the knowledge is natural to us." This produces a dilemma for us because we use abstract nouns to signify simplicity and concrete nouns to signify substance and perfection. We have no "abstract concretes" or "con-

<hr />

52. The logic underlying Aquinas's position here reflects the 'pre-Kantian tradition' which, as Robert Brandom states, "took it for granted that the proper order of semantic explanation begins with a doctrine of concepts or terms, divided into singular and general, whose meaningfulness can be grasped independently of and prior to the meaningfulness of judgments." Brandom, *Articulating Reasons: An Introduction to Inferentialism* (Cambridge, Mass.: Harvard University Press, 2000), p. 124. Brandom notes that Kant rejects this and makes judgment more fundamental than the prior ordering of terms. He writes, "One of [Kant's] cardinal innovations is the claim that the fundamental unit of awareness of cognition, the minimum graspable is the judgment." Frege follows Kant here when he makes his claim, "only in the context of a proposition does a name have any meaning." *Articulating Reasons*, p. 125. Would this post-Kantian 'cardinal innovation,' one which Wittgenstein takes up, fundamentally alter Aquinas's theo-logic? If so, it could strengthen his position since these two sets of terms cannot adequately name God outside the judgments that are necessary by us. Such judgments have already been made by the church in its active reception of dogma, and continue to be made in their ongoing development.

53. ST I.13.12 rep. obj. 3.

crete abstracts" which would be necessary to name God well. We have no adequate language for God.

Aquinas then begins his discussion on the tradition of God's names by citing John Damascene's claim that names cannot be predicated of God substantially. He takes a surprising turn in this question, for, given what he said up to this point, we would think he would agree with Damascene — our language does not predicate names of God substantially. To understand why he rejects this opinion, how it does not contradict all he said up to this point, and why we can not only predicate affirmative names of God, but even speak of God literally, four features of his argument must be kept in mind. First, Aquinas negotiates between univocal and equivocal predication in favor of analogical predication. Second, he does this without it becoming something of a 'shell game' because of the distinction between 'modus significandi' and 'res significata.' Third, this distinction contributes to a threefold use of signifying: negation, affirmation, and excellence. Fourth, when we intend to speak of God, we intend to restate and remember the name given to us, and this name is also given to Jesus. If we fail to realize that the culmination of Aquinas's first thirteen questions in the *Summa* stands in this tradition of the divine names, we will miss the two key transcendental conditions for speaking of God. God gave God's name to Moses. Jesus claimed this name for himself.

2a. Divine Names between Univocal and Equivocal Predication

What do divine names signify for Thomas? When Aquinas asks whether the names 'wise' and 'good' are predicated of God substantially, he begins his response by rejecting two opinions, the first attributed to Moses Maimonides and the second to Alan of Lille. For Maimonides affirmative names "express some remotion from God"; they do not "express anything that exists positively in Him." Here language only signifies by equivocation, which would be similar to remotion. When we speak of God, we only say what God is not. All we have is a negative theology and thus the divine names would signify nothing but a negation of our language as it is used for God. For Alan of Lille, however, affirmative names "signify His relationship towards creatures." This would be a univocal form of predication; it recognizes affirmative names for God, but it understands them as causally connected with names we use for creatures. The first does not distinguish affirmative from negative predication. The second assumes that when we name God we do so by a simple relation between God and us.

Aquinas rejects both opinions for three reasons. "First because in neither of them can a reason be assigned why some names more than others are applied to God." Why should we call God 'wise' rather than 'red'? If our speaking of God does no more than tell us what we cannot say, then to say God is good and wise is to say the same thing as God is not composite or God is not red, which is to say the same thing that God is not a creature. It does no more than this. Likewise, a direct causal relation between God and us cannot help us name God, for God causes all things. If the affirmative names of God name that causal relation, then every creaturely medium equally names God as well as any other because there is nothing God does not directly cause. The second reason he rejects both opinions is "because it would follow that all names applied to God would be said of Him by way of being taken in a secondary sense." This would be similar to the term 'healthy' and 'medicine.' We can call medicine 'health' in a secondary sense, but this would be misleading if we truly intended to speak of medicine. We can speak of God through negation and causal relation, but this gives us no primary names for God; we could not truly intend to speak of God. This relates to the most important reason for rejecting negation and causation as the primary means by which we speak of God — "because this is against the intention of those who speak of God. For in saying that God lives, they assuredly mean more than to say that He is the cause of our life, or that He differs from inanimate bodies." Here we have the heart of the matter, and it is a simple argument. When we intend to speak of God, we intend to speak of God — not creation. We do this and we understand that we do it, even if we might have a difficult time explaining how language accomplishes its goal.

It is interesting to note how modern the arguments are that Aquinas rejects in rejecting the positions of Moses Maimonides and Alan of Lille. He examines the two forms of signification that characterize contemporary theology. Equivocal predication is similar to Kant's critique of reason where we cannot say anything meaningful of God because such language would have to name a noumenal reality for which we know a priori that our way of knowing gives no access. God becomes that unpresentable sublime and all names have the same status before it. Theology becomes everything and nothing at the same time. Univocal predication is similar to Feuerbach's projectionist signification. What we say about God can be said only because of what it says about us. Aquinas recognizes both possibilities; he does not dismiss them outright but absorbs them within a richer account of language that does not begin, as both these accounts do, with a narrow dogmatic a priori as to what language can and cannot accomplish. He does this because he recognizes that when we intend to speak of God we intend to speak of God. Our desire can be satisfied, albeit never completed.

The most satisfying response Aquinas gives is that our language always does more than any simple univocal predication would assume. This is related to his third form of signification, the 'via eminentiae.' For this reason he concludes with a "different doctrine" from Maimonides and Alan of Lille, stating that "these names signify the divine substance, and are predicated substantially of God, although they fall short of a full representation of Him." How does this make sense? How can these names be both substantially predicated of God and at the same time fail as a "full representation"? This is only possible because of the 'via eminentiae.' "Hence every creature represents Him and is like Him so far as it possesses some perfection; yet it represents Him not as something of the same species or genus, but as the excelling principle of whose form the effects fall short, although they derive some kind of likeness thereto, even as the forms of inferior bodies represent the power of the sun." Does this not help us make sense of the way of perfection in Aquinas's five ways? This desire for the better is a desire for God. The divine name satisfies the desire, not by closing it off into an immanent completion, but by allowing us to recognize and make sense of the natural desire we have for a perfection we can never achieve on our own. We do not name God from our desire, but name our desire from God.

Aquinas returns to this relationship between univocal predication and the 'via eminentiae' in question thirteen, article five. He states, "Univocal predication is impossible between God and creatures." His argument takes up the name 'wise' discussed earlier in article one. What does it mean to call God wise? This signifies a quality in a human person, but "when we apply it to God, we do not mean to signify anything distinct from his essence or power, or existence." This means our use of God-language has a twofold aspect. We must understand how it applies to creatures and how it does not. "Thus also this term wise applied to man in some degree circumscribes and comprehends the thing signified; whereas this is not the case when it is applied to God; but it leaves the thing signified as incomprehended and as exceeding the signification of the name."[54] If the signification exceeds the name and means that God is "incomprehended," how does this not lead to equivocation? It would seem to place theology in the role Kant established for it. For this reason, as soon as he denies univocal predication he immediately rejects equivocal as well and instead states that "these names are said of God and creatures in an analogous sense."

2b. Divine Names: Modus Significandi/Res Significata

Aquinas's discussion of the divine names can be very confusing. The names we use of God are used in the same way that we use them of creatures; we have no peculiar, private language to speak about God. But even though we use them in the same way, they do not signify the same thing. This requires Aquinas to distinguish the way of signifying from the thing signified. When we say "Aristotle is wise" and "God is wise" our mode of signifying is the same. We have a subject, a verb, and a predicate; in Wittgenstein's terms — the surface grammar is identical. This mode of signifying assumes timefulness; time inevitably lapses from the "A" to the final "e" in the locution "Aristotle is wise." I have no other way to signify things. Our mode of signifying assumes composition. I put a subject and predicate together assuming they are not merely synonyms. Every mode of signification is a creaturely reality, produced by creatures. And yet — even though the mode of signifying is the same for these two statements, they do not signify the same thing; the depth grammar differs. When we say, "Aristotle is wise and God is wise," they cannot both be brought under the same extension: "x is wise." Some relationship between 'wisdom' exists between the predication in both statements, but to predicate wise of anyone assumes degrees that always assume something more. How do I know that he is wiser than Ajax? Aristotle's wisdom appears against the backdrop of a tacit 'more' that allows comparisons of better to be made. If it were not for that 'more,' we would not know Aristotle is wiser than Ajax. We must know the more to be able to use the term 'wise' well. Without it judgment would be impossible and then rational activity would cease. This 'more' is more knowable than the statement "Aristotle is wise." God is the perfection of wisdom.

This distinction between the mode of signifying and the thing signi-

54. ST I.13.5.

fied is what allows affirmative predication of God. Aquinas defends this in question twelve against Dionysius, who stated, "Negations about God are true; but affirmations are vague." Aquinas states, "True affirmative propositions can be formed about God. To prove this we must know that in every true affirmative proposition the predicate and the subject signify in some way the same thing in reality and different things in idea." This is another way of putting the 'modus significandi'/'res significata' distinction and Aquinas applies it directly to speaking about God, "God, however, as considered in Himself, is altogether one and simple, yet our intellect knows Him by different conceptions because it cannot see Him as He is in Himself. Nevertheless, although it understands Him under different conceptions, it knows that one and the same simple object corresponds to its conceptions. Therefore, the plurality of predicate and subject represents the plurality of idea; and the intellect represents the unity by composition."[55] If someone interprets Dionysius as implying that language cannot speak of the 'res' because of the limitation of the 'modus,' then such a person has misunderstood how language works and placed it in an unnecessary straitjacket.

Aquinas explains how theological language works by noting how we 'take' the same term to be 'referring' in different ways.[56] Not all language does the same thing; in fact, the same language in different contexts has different uses. All affirmative propositions imply composition. But this by no means requires that the thing signified by such propositions has composition. We can compose statements about simplicity that make perfectly good sense. Language need not have a strict one to one correspondence. Here is where Aquinas and Wittgenstein meaningfully interact.

Aquinas's distinction between the mode of signifying and the thing signified bears a family resemblance to Wittgenstein's distinction between surface and depth grammar. Too much of modern theology, influenced by the nominalist and designative linguistic turn, works solely with a surface grammar. It fails to see the expressivist character of language. We are not trapped within language. Therefore we need not look at its structure in order to discover meaning or truth. What we do with language, how we take it up, exceeds the mere structure language gives us. Language signifies in the same way Christ's humanity does.

55. ST I.13.12.
56. ST I.13.12 rep. obj. 3.

This is why the influence of nominalism on modern theology makes it so difficult to speak well of God. It loses this insight and produces that designative tradition that is trapped within language, always trying to determine precisely how terms refer, usually by thinking about thinking. Epistemology becomes the gatekeeper for how we can supposedly use language. Wittgenstein offers a more 'expressivist' account of language's referential power, for part of his genius was to remind us again and again that words do not do the same thing. This simple truth is one Aquinas likewise saw. Humans use language; language does not use humans. We can intend and take up language to refer — even using the same term, such as 'wise' or 'good,' for a variety of intentions. This is why the names of God are not to be placed in three categories — negations or affirmations or excellences. Each name can be, and must be, used to do all of this. They can even do it such that the thing signified remains the same and is the more excellent way, negated and affirmed simultaneously.[57]

2c. Divine Names: Negation, Affirmation, Via Eminentiae

The distinction between the mode of signifying and the thing signified helps us understand how names can be excellences, affirmations, and/or negations. If all language were univocal signification it could only be affirmation and not an excellence. If all language were equivocal signification it could only be negation. But if we distinguish how we signify from what is signified, then it is possible that we both affirm and negate the how in order to express a more excellent way that *literally* names the 'res.'

Aquinas explains how a term can function as a creaturely mode of signification that must be negated in order to speak well of God, and also be an affirmation — even a "literal" name of God. He explains this by responding to Dionysius' claim that we can only name God from God's

---

57. Note how Thomas brings all three forms of signification together simultaneously in order to argue for substantial predication. "Now from the divine effects we cannot know the divine nature in itself, so as to know what it is; but only by way of eminence, and by way of causality and of negation as stated above. Thus the name God signifies the divine nature, for this name was imposed to signify something existing above all things, the principle of all things and removed from all things; for those who name God intend to signify all this." ST I.13.8 rep. obj 2.

58. ST I.13.2.

creaturely processions and not from God's essence. Aquinas agrees.[58] This would seem to lead logically to the claim that no name can be applied literally to God, because we only know the names from the procession of creatures. Thus, names can only be applied metaphorically, but Thomas rejects such a conclusion. Beginning with the affirmation that we can only name God from God's processions, and that "all such names imply some kind of corporeal condition; for their meaning is bound up with time and composition and like corporeal conditions," Aquinas's conclusion that we can speak literally and substantially of God comes as a surprise.[59] How does this work? He answers, "Our knowledge of God is derived from the perfections which flow from Him to creatures, which perfections are in God in a more eminent way than in creatures." Our intellect apprehends these perfections in creatures and "signifies them by names." *What* is signified applies most properly to God; as for the *mode* of signification, "they do not properly and strictly apply to God; for their mode of signification applies to creatures."[60] We use the mode of signifying that is possible from creaturely processions. This mode can be negated when it refers solely to creatures. God is not wise in a univocal manner, as Aristotle is wise. For this would make Aristotle's wisdom the measure of God's, and that cannot be speaking well of God. However, we must also affirm that Aristotle's wisdom is analogous to God's; otherwise we would have equivocation and would be saying nothing meaningful at all. Finally wisdom is most properly applied to God, for God is the perfection, simplicity, and unity such that God makes Aristotle's wisdom possible and not vice versa.

The pattern for this way of speaking about God is the way Thomas already noted in the prologue to question two of the prima pars and then developed in the tertia pars. Jesus Christ is the 'way' or 'logic' of our speaking of God, for he is the Procession who takes on creatureliness without confusing it with divinity in the concretion of his one Person. Thomas's account of how we can speak of God fits seamlessly with his discussion of composition in the divine and human natures in the incarnation.

2d. Divine Names: Christ Is the Via Eminentiae

Thomas offers three main proper names for God. It is interesting to note

58. ST I.13.12.
60. ST I.13.13.

how each of these proper names fits with remotion, affirmation, and excellence. The first name he discusses is 'He Who Is.' This is "the most proper name of God."[61] He raises an objection against such a proper name based on the use of signification set forth by Alan of Lille and his own admission that we can only signify God through creatures — "every divine name seems to imply some relation to creatures, for God is known to us only through creatures." This means that we cannot speak of 'Being' as God's proper name, for it applies not so much to God but to the relation between God and creation. Thomas's reply to this objection is intriguing: "It is not necessary that all the divine names should import relation to creatures, but it suffices that they be imposed from some perfections flowing from God to creatures. Among these the first is existence, from which comes this name, HE WHO IS."[62] Here we find an explicit reference between the first 'attribute' of God Thomas discusses in the prima pars and Exodus 3. Metaphysics and Scripture come together. Faith and reason mutually support each other in this reply. What we receive through faith — the divine name in Exodus 3 — is also supported by reason. Scripture and metaphysics work in harmony.

Aquinas cites three reasons as to why God's name is He Who Is. In so doing, he shows how the revelation of the divine name in Exodus 3 renders intelligible the discussion of God's 'attributes' in the prima pars.

---

61. ST I.13.11. I will avoid discussion of Gilson's 'metaphysics of exodus' here, for I don't think we should choose between God's 'being' and 'goodness' once we recognize the convertibility of the transcendentals. Nor do I think the Hebrew of Exodus 3:14 invalidates the tradition of the divine names. I find compelling Gilson's statement that Exodus 3:14 teaches us "once and for all that the proper name of God is Being," and that this has important implications for how we speak of God. If this meant Being comes prior to goodness, and is intended to qualify Dionysius' claim that God is self-diffusive goodness, then it seems to me a mistaken distinction. To view the good as Platonic and the source of being, or as Aristotelian and the desire of being, does not seem to require that we privilege goodness or love above being or vice versa. At his best, Thomas held these together as, Rudi te Velde explains in *Participation and Substantiality in Aquinas* (Leiden: Brill, 1995). Being first falls under the intellect, and the good is what the will desires. Only when we divide these from each other do we need to choose between them. To think we must side with Bonaventure or Thomas on this is unnecessary. See Fergus Kerr, *After Aquinas: Versions of Thomism* (Oxford: Blackwell, 2002), pp. 81-82; Robert Barron, *The Priority of Christ* (Grand Rapids: Brazos, 2007), pp. 235-45. John Milbank finds Balthasar siding with Bonaventure against Thomism in his *The Suspended Middle: Henri de Lubac and the Debate Concerning the Supernatural* (Grand Rapids: Eerdmans, 2005), p. 74.

62. ST I.13.11 rep. obj. 3.

First, because of its signification. For it does not signify some form, but being itself. Hence since the being of God is His very essence (which can be said of no other being), it is clear that among other names this one most properly names God; for everything is named according to its essence. Secondly, because of its universality. . . . Now by any other name some mode of substance is expressed determinately, whereas this name HE WHO IS determines no mode of being, but is related indeterminately to all; and that is why it names the *infinite ocean of substance.* . . . Thirdly, from its consignification, for it signifies being *in the present;* and this above all properly applies to God, *whose being knows not past or future,* as Augustine says.[63]

Here Thomas makes allusion to the names of God that came before in the prima pars: being, simplicity, perfection, limitlessness (eternity), immutability, and unity. Being is God's name, and this is given to us. But faith seeks reason, and we find in a creaturely medium such as language good reasons as to why God's proper name is He Who Is.

Along with 'He Who Is,' Thomas also suggests that 'God' and the tetragrammaton (YHWH) are proper names.[64] Once again we see how his threefold form of signification assists us in understanding the divine names. 'He Who Is' as the infinite ocean of being is the cause of all being. This warrants affirmative propositions, for all being participates in this Being. As the "object intended by the name," the term 'God,' which in some contexts would not be a proper name, is proper because when we intend this term to refer to He Who Is we follow the way of excellence. 'God' refers most excellently to God. The tetragrammaton is most proper because this, of all God's proper names, is the one that is incommunicable. It is the name that cannot be named and thus functions through remotion.

These names are necessary for two reasons. First, they allow us to speak well of God. We know God's name and can now speak substantially and literally as long as we keep in mind all the qualifications that are required by the modus significandi'/'res significata' distinction and the threefold form of signification through negation, affirmation, and excellence. Second, this name allows us to identify Jesus as the bearer of the name. Here we find Aquinas more biblical than Barth, who stated that we must not form a preconception of God before looking to Jesus and therefore did not

63. ST I.13.11 (Pegis).
64. ST I.13.11 rep. obj. 1.

always keep faith with the Old Testament tradition of the divine name. To understand who Jesus is we must have the 'preconception' of God that the revelation to Moses gives. If we do not have it, then we will not know that Jesus has the name. His "I am" statements would be lost on us. Then we will fail to see the beauty of the logic of the incarnation where we recognize how the One Who Is, the impassible, immutable, and simple One can be passible, mutable, and composite without ceasing to be the One Who Is. The incarnation will lose its power and possibly become mythology where we not only confess, as we must, that Jesus is God, but we will wrongly conclude humanity is divinity. Metaphysics helps us avoid this.

3. The Loss of the Divine Names and Speaking Well of God

Language such as divine immutability, impassibility, and 'actus purus' basically disappeared in the twentieth century; the theologians who defend them today are a distinct minority. Those who would recognize them as arising from this biblical tradition of the divine name are even fewer. Such a loss makes it more difficult to speak well of God, for it loses the 'way' or logic of speaking of God that Jesus is. As already noted several times throughout this work, Luther's theology of the cross began a trend in theology that emptied God of these divine names. Dennis Ngien recognized that Luther went "beyond" Chalcedonian Christology. His doctrine of justification led to a hyper-Alexandrian rethinking of Christology where the "mutual attribution of the two natures" in Christ lead to an assertion of "passibility in God's very being."[65] Ngien suggests that this "alters our definition of what constitutes divinity" such that it "ceases to be Platonic."[66] He does not explicitly accuse the tradition of the divine names as a false "Platonic" importation into the biblical witness, but he assumes it, and he assumes Luther corrects this mistaken view of God. This is a mistaken assumption; it is the mistake of the 'hellenization' thesis.

65. Dennis Ngien, "Chalcedonian Christology and Beyond: Luther's Understanding of the Communication Idiomatum," *Heythrop Journal* 45 (2004): 59, 65. Whether this common interpretation of Luther is adequate is not something I will engage in at this point but leave to Luther scholars. Suffice it to say that his 1540 disputation on the divinity and humanity of Christ explicitly affirmed God's impassibility in a way identical to Cyril of Alexandria. Nonetheless, he does use infelicitous expressions in his account of how the two natures relate.
66. Ngien, "Chalcedonian Christology and Beyond," p. 65.

The list of contemporary theologians who follow Luther in altering the names of God based on God's possibility is long. But Ngien makes an important point when he correlates Luther's 'communicatio idiomatum,' where each nature is directly attributed to the other, with a new way of speaking about God. For all Christian theological language finds its warrant, or lack thereof, in how we speak of God in how we speak of Christ's two natures in his single Person. The human nature of Christ is the 'modus significandi' (the way of signifying) by which we can speak of God in temporal, historical, finite terms. This 'modus significandi' represents all human speech. It is therefore composite, finite, limited, imperfect, mutable, and passible. However, prior to the dominance of contextual theology and its reliance upon Feuerbach's projectionist account of theological language, theologians assumed this 'modus significandi' could name, even literally, the 'res significata' — the 'thing' signified, who is God. This is because of the hypostatic union that unites these two natures. As goes impassibility, so goes the ability for language to name something other than a mere human creature. For what is at stake in the doctrine of impassibility is nothing less than the possibility that we can speak of God in such a way that this speech is something other than speaking about ourselves. The losses of the doctrine of impassibility, the tradition of the divine names, and a theological language that is other than projectionist, explicitly or implicitly, go hand in hand.

The doctrine of impassibility finds few defenders among theologians today. I find Thomas Weinandy convincing when he cites A. M. Fairbairn's 1893 statement: "Theology has no falser idea than that of the impassibility of God," and then offers the following comment, "This severe judgment . . . is now shared to a greater or lesser degree, by many, if not most, contemporary theologians. Since the latter part of the nineteenth century there has been a growing consensus that the traditional claim, held to be axiomatic since the Fathers of the church, of God's impassibility is no longer defensible."[67] Weinandy states the situation of contemporary theology well, but he doesn't offer us much of an explanation as to why this sea change in theological language took place. It is puzzling how such a commonly shared theological language disappeared so quickly and thoroughly in the twentieth century. Why did this happen? Weinandy suggests one reason is the way twentieth-century theologians addressed the problem of evil and

---

67. Weinandy, *Does God Suffer?* (Notre Dame, Ind.: University of Notre Dame Press, 2000), p. 1.

protest atheism. It was assumed that the suffering of the modern era was so overwhelming that our theology must take it into account. It had to be relevant to it. A common response to protest atheism, as one sees in Moltmann, is that if God does not suffer with us, then God cannot love. Suffering and love become identified. This is an odd argument, peculiar to late modernity, where it is somehow considered comforting to think of God as suffering as we do. This tacitly plays into the projectionist theories of language assumed in much of modern theology, based as they are on a univocity of the concept of being. Our love requires suffering so God's must as well; otherwise we cannot adequately address the problem of evil. The 'res significata' is reduced to the 'modus significandi.'

This is a peculiar argument; unfortunately, twentieth-century Westerners hold no market on suffering. Earlier generations witnessed horrible suffering as well, but they did not think it called into question the tradition of the divine names. They did not think the 'identity' of God should be changed to be 'relevant' to their unique times. Julian of Norwich witnessed the Black Plague, but never thought it required us to rethink the doctrine of God. Did she fail to witness to God as loving? Did the Cappadocians, Augustine, Dionysius, Anselm, Aquinas, and others mislead us by the language they used about God? Did they know nothing of human suffering such that they presented God as something other than love even though Aquinas gave Love as one of the proper names of the Holy Spirit? Only by privileging the uniqueness of late modernity, does the assumption that our suffering is so unique we must discard traditional language about God make sense. But this says more about the posture of late modernity than it does about the reasonableness of our language about God.

Weinandy rightly names the problem of evil as one of the reasons for the sea change that occurred in speaking of God in the twentieth century, but it alone cannot account for this sea change. Other factors contributed to this loss of language. They are the dominance of Harnack's hellenization thesis on twentieth-century theology; the mistaken assumption that language such as simplicity, immutability, and impassibility primarily represent metaphysical attributes known by reason alone; the philosophical assumption that we are at the end of metaphysics and thus the end of those attributes as well; finally, all of this history and philosophy adversely influenced biblical scholarship so that the tradition of the divine names as an interpretation of Exodus 3 got lost and became something other than sacred teaching.

3a. The Hellenization Thesis

Adolph von Harnack sought to identify the true essence of Christianity. In so doing, he found orthodox doctrine and sacramental practice to be a fall from the purity of Christianity into Greek philosophy. This occurred in the second century through the identification of Christ with Greek philosophy's 'logos' thereby giving a "metaphysical significance to an historical fact."[68] Unlike Aquinas's argument for the divine names, Harnack divided Scripture and metaphysics and therefore divided faith and reason as well. He found the identification between Christ and a metaphysical logos to be "inadmissible" because it "did not lead with any certainty to the God whom Jesus Christ proclaimed."[69] Harnack's hellenization thesis can best be understood as an intensification of Protestantism's principle of 'sola fide.' This is the origin of much of the fideism rampant in liberal Protestantism today. It eschews metaphysical reason altogether. Once historical studies assumed Harnack's theological assumptions, it turned its attention to the Bible in an effort to rid putatively static Greek thought from dynamic Hebrew thinking. But as Robert Wilken has argued, this hellenization thesis "has outlived its usefulness" and it is time to "bid a fond farewell to the ideas of Adolph von Harnack" and the hold they have had on historical theology for over a century. Any careful reading of the sources, as Wilken provides, demonstrates that at most the "spirit of early Christian thought" was a "Christianization of Hellenism" rather than any hellenizing of Christianity.[70]

Harnack's hellenization thesis would not have been so persuasive if a transition had not occurred in the doctrine of God, beginning perhaps

68. Harnack, *What Is Christianity?* trans. Thomas Bailey Sanders (Gloucester, Mass.: Peter Smith, 1978), p. 204.

69. He writes, "The proposition that the Logos had appeared among men had an intoxicating effect, but the enthusiasm and transport which it produced in the soul did not lead with any certainty to the God whom Jesus Christ proclaimed." Harnack, *What Is Christianity?* p. 205. This was originally Gnosticism (acute Hellenism), but this identification with the Logos and Christ nevertheless prevailed especially in "Greek Catholicism."

70. Robert Louis Wilken, *The Spirit of Early Christianity* (New Haven: Yale University Press, 2003), p. xvi. Wilken's work shows how mistaken Harnack's thesis was. He persuasively demonstrates that early Christian thought represents more "the Christianization of Hellenism" than the "hellenization of Christianity." I will seek to show the significance of this below in arguing that what became God's so-called metaphysical attributes were much more an articulation of the divine name.

with Suarez and culminating in Locke, where the tradition of the divine names, known primarily through the revelation of Holy Scripture and set forth as a judgment about its intrinsic logic, became a tradition of divine attributes known primarily through natural reason. This made it appear as though these 'attributes' had more to do with a natural or metaphysical reason over and against sacred doctrine.

John Locke argued that although Scripture provides no adequate proof of God's existence because of its contingent nature, natural religion (reason) more readily provides such evidence.

> And we ought to magnify his Goodness, that he hath spread before all the World, such legible Characters of his Works and Providence, and given all Mankind so sufficient a light of Reason, that they to whom this written Word never came, could not (whenever they set themselves to search) either doubt of the Being of a GOD, or of the Obedience due to Him. Since then the Precepts of Natural Religion are plain, and very intelligible to all Mankind, and seldom come to be controverted; and other revealed Truths, which are conveyed to us by Books and Languages, are liable to the common and natural obscurities and difficulties incident to Words, methinks it would become us to be more careful and diligent in observing the former, and less magisterial and positive and imperious, in imposing our own sense and interpretations of the latter.[71]

Locke looks to natural reason for a proof of God's existence, and thinks that the traditional language of God can be discovered by natural reason alone because it offers something more than the contingent signs of faith. Thus the knowledge of God's 'attributes' becomes known through reason alone, reason without faith.

Janet Soskice finds this to be a marked divergence from the theological tradition of the divine names. She writes,

> When Aquinas dealt with such predicates as 'eternal,' 'One,' and 'simple,' he stood in a tradition of reflections de nominibus dei going back to Denys the Areopagite and beyond — a theological and mystical as well as a philosophical tradition. Locke's confidence that not only God's existence but also God's qualities could be spelled out apart

71. Cited in Long, *John Wesley's Moral Theology* (Nashville: Abingdon, 2004), p. 85.

from revelation and through rational reflection alone is new, or rather was new in Descartes, whom Locke follows here. Appellations that had been distinctively theology became with Descartes the terminology of rational analysis and metaphysics alone. With Descartes the 'Divine Names' have become the 'classical attributes.'[72]

Once the divine names become metaphysical attributes known by reason apart from sacred teaching, then we lose the connection between these attributes and their context in the biblical narrative. Faith and reason become sundered. We therefore think that because we can find these 'attributes' in Aristotle and Plato rather than in Moses, we become more faithful tellers of the biblical narrative by rejecting them. Ironically, through this rejection we actually begin to speak about God more in terms of Aristotle's *Categories* or Plato's *Timaeus* and lose the most important aspect of the doctrine of 'sola scriptura,' which is that if we are to recognize the divine nature in Jesus we must know God's name, which is given to us in the Old Testament. The Old Testament is necessary to understand the New. The divine name given to us in Exodus 3:14 is the Name that Jesus also bears and thus we can worship him without fear of violating the commandments revealed to Moses. If we lose the name, of which the Impassible One is a logical extension, then we will lose the ability to recognize in Jesus a way of signifying that leads us to something which is more than finite, temporal, and composite.

3b. The End of Metaphysics

Once the tradition of the divine names was transformed into metaphysical attributes, then God as Simple, Perfect, Infinite, Eternal, Impassible, and Unchangeable became subject to the same fate as metaphysics itself. The modern era proclaimed the end of metaphysics. If the 'attributes' of God depended upon a pure metaphysical reason, then with the end of metaphysics, those attributes would likewise come to an end, and this is what we see taking place in much of contemporary theology. It radically shifts, almost in a discontinuity with Christians who came before us, how we speak of God. However, in this post-secular age, the pronouncement of the

72. Soskice, "Naming God," in Griffiths and Hütter, eds. *Reason and the Reasons of Faith*, p. 247.

end of metaphysics rings more hollow than previously; we are beginning to recognize the pronouncement was premature.

Kant's antinomies of pure reason supposedly rendered metaphysics meaningless.[73] Science then sought to limit knowledge to observation and evidence. The linguistic turn in philosophy claimed to reduce all metaphysical questions to linguistic ones and thus supposedly rendered those questions meaningless as well. This philosophical tradition culminated in logical positivism, which claimed both metaphysics and theology were arational enterprises that had no significant meaning because they could not pass the verificationist test. Much of the American pragmatist school also supposedly eschewed metaphysics. Thus most of the powerful philosophical and scientific discourses of the nineteenth and early twentieth centuries claimed we were at the end of metaphysics. If metaphysics is a natural use of reason distinct from faith, and it gives us access to God's nature, then the end of metaphysics would have brought with it the end of speaking of God through those traditional attributes. But this is not what metaphysics was prior to Suarez.[74]

If 'metaphysics' has come to an end, it is a particular kind of metaphysics built on a classical foundationalism that assumed an unwarranted doctrine of the transcendental 'I.' What came to an end was not metaphysics, but an unwarranted metaphysical use of language based on this transcendental 'I.' Wittgenstein helped uncover the true problems with this metaphysical use, but it is a mistake to think his work contributes to the end of metaphysics altogether. As long as people continue to assume and act as if truth, goodness, and beauty matter (to do otherwise is impossible), and as long as some ask questions about God and being (to do otherwise is possible), metaphysics has not yet come to an end.

73. Alvin Plantinga offers a convincing argument against accepting Kant's antinomies in his *Warranted Christian Belief* (Oxford: Oxford University Press, 1999), pp. 21-30.

74. See Jean Luc Marion's "Metaphysics and Phenomenology: A Summary for Theologians," in *The Postmodern God,* ed. Graham Ward (London: Blackwell, 1997), pp. 279-96. Marion defines metaphysics since Suarez as "the system of philosophy from Suarez to Kant as a single science concerned both with what is universal in 'common being' *(l'etant commun)* and in 'essence' (or essences)" (p. 281).

3c. Historical-Critical Readings of the Divine Name

The profound modern philosophical influence on biblical interpretation falsely misled Bible scholars to reject the tradition of the divine names as Greek metaphysics (even though one seldom finds these scholars spending much time engaging Greek metaphysics). The assumption was that the Greek of the Septuagint or the Latin of the Vulgate (and other local Latin versions of the Old Testament) misled the church fathers and theologians to find in the divine name Greek metaphysical attributes. Gerhard von Rad is well-known for making just this claim. The revelation of God's name, he writes,

> has from the very beginning keenly attracted the interest of theologians, because they believed that here at last was a reference giving a comprehensive and fundamental account of the nature of the revelation of Jahweh, and reducing it, so to speak, to a final axiomatic formula (Ex. 3:14) but caution has to be exercised at this point; for nothing is farther from what is being envisaged in this etymology of the name of Jahweh than a definition of his nature in the sense of a philosophy (LXX ἐγώ εἰμι ὁ ὤν) — a suggestion for example of his absoluteness, aseity, etc. Such a thing would be altogether out of keeping with the Old Testament. The whole narrative context leads right away to the expectation that Jahweh then intends to impart something — but this is not what he is, but what he will show himself to be to Israel.[75]

Once again we see a false distinction between Scripture and metaphysics and thus faith and reason.

Von Rad imagines that traditional Christian language of God must be redefined because the Hebrew *'ehyeh 'asher 'ehyeh* cannot be adequately rendered by the Greek ἐγώ εἰμι ὁ ὤν. (Von Rad doesn't mention the Latin *ego sum qui sum,* but he would find it as objectionable as the Greek.) The Greek misleads us to imagine we had "a definition of his nature in the sense of a philosophy" and thus we came up with terms such as absolute-

---

75. Von Rad, *The Theology of the Old Testament* (Edinburgh: Oliver & Boyd, 1962), p. 180. This claim continues to have power in comtemporary theology, especially among some Barthians. It results in theologians questioning the divine names tradition. See for instance Neil MacDonald's *Metaphysics and the God of Israel* (Grand Rapids: Baker Academic, 2007), p. 53.

ness and aseity, which are other ways of speaking of God's perfection, simplicity, and impassibility. Of course, von Rad never cites any evidence that this is what the theologians were doing. He doesn't quote passages in Augustine or Aquinas where they refer to Greek sources in order to explain Exodus 3:14. He simply assumes the tradition does this, and claims instead to be giving us the true meaning of the biblical text read apart from its corrupt history of metaphysical interpretation.

Ironically, it is von Rad and his heirs who read the Scripture with a metaphysical use of a transcendental 'I'; for they claim to know its true meaning by standing over and against it, reading it neutrally, without standing in any tradition of interpretation. Thus they fail to recognize the traditioned interpretation within which they stand — the hellenization thesis, the proclaimed end of metaphysics, and the modern tradition of the divine names translated into metaphysical attributes. They fail to see how these philosophical movements influenced their biblical interpretation. All these must be assumed before von Rad's argument makes sense. It only emerged when it did because of these formative causes.

The above four intellectual shifts caused a reevaluation not only of the doctrine of divine impassibility, but also of how we speak of God. This reevaluation has been a mistake, and my suspicion is that it had more to do with the influence of the hellenization thesis and the presumed end of metaphysics than any 'pure' reading of the Bible. Playing the Greek (and Latin) off the Hebrew in Exodus 3 has less to do with what the historical-critical method can truly deliver and more to do with the modern theological and philosophical assumptions that undergird it. This produced a drastic shift in language about God; the tradition of the divine names was no longer viewed as a reasoned judgment from Scripture that was also witnessed to by reason. Instead these names became 'attributes' known by natural reason alone through a metaphysical objectivism, which are either to be affirmed or rejected on that basis. This misreads what the church fathers were doing; they were using reason (or philosophy) to show the limits of reason (and philosophy) in order to open us up for the reception of something that was more than reason — the sacred wisdom revealed in Scripture.

Robert Barron explains this quite well. He traces how Anselm's so-called 'ontological proof' for the existence of God is misread as offering this kind of metaphysical seizure of God's name, which is akin to what Adam and Eve attempted to do. In contrast to this faulty reading of

Anselm, Barron reads it in the tradition of the giving of the divine name. Anselm's desire to find that one argument to demonstrate God does not work because his mind grasps it, but because like Moses, God gives him "the Name." In fact, it is the same name. What Anselm receives as a gift, God is that than which nothing greater can be conceived, is the same gift Moses receives, "I am who I am."[76] Barron notes that Aquinas's insistence that God's essence is God's existence and all that this implies is a further explication of this name. It is also the name which Jesus will bear.[77]

One of the more interesting discussions of the divine names tradition comes from the work of the evangelical theologian Carl Henry.[78] Henry found arguments such as von Rad's, based on the Hebrew alone, unconvincing. He would be surprised to find himself an ally of Wittgenstein on these matters, but his take on them is similar. Henry writes, "Happily many scholars are moving beyond the Semantic hypnosis that reduced 'biblical understanding' to an analysis of word-structures and the derivation of their elements from root-originals. . . . It is contextual use more than etymological origin that determines the sense of meaning of concepts and words."[79] On this basis Henry does not overstate the significance of the divine name *'ehyeh 'asher 'ehyeh* against the *ego sum qui sum* as often happens in evangelical theology with its commitment to the modern notion of the 'original' language. Henry nevertheless could not escape

76. Anselm's ontological argument was certainly not entirely new. Augustine used a similar name for God as the basis for how we must treat Scripture in *On Christian Doctrine* when he stated as a principle of biblical interpretation that a sign is either to be used or enjoyed. Only the sign 'Deus' finally signifies something to be enjoyed. "For God although nothing worthy may be spoken of Him has accepted the tribute of the human voice and wished us to take joy in praising Him with our words. In this way he is called *Deus*. Although He is not recognized in the noise of these two syllables, all those who know the Latin language, when this sound reaches their ears, are moved to think of a certain most excellent immortal nature. For when the one God of gods is thought of, even by those who recognize, invoke and worship other gods either in Heaven or on earth, He is thought of in such a way that the thought seeks to attain something than which there is nothing better or more sublime." *On Christian Doctrine*, trans. D. W. Robertson Jr. (New York: Macmillan, 1958), p. 11.

77. Robert Barron, *The Priority of Christ: Toward a Postliberal Catholicism* (Grand Rapids: Brazos, 2007), pp. 210-15. Barron's work in this excellent volume is the kind of theological progress we should hope for from the conversation between Barth and Balthasar, and among postliberals, communio Catholics, and Radical Orthodox 'sensibilities.'

78. See his sixth thesis, "God Names Himself," developed in chapters 12 through 16 of *God, Revelation, and Authority, Volume II: God Who Speaks and Shows* (Waco: Word, 1976).

79. Henry, *God, Revelation, and Authority*, p. 212.

the hellenization thesis.[80] He challenges the English translation "I am the One who is" as a Greek metaphysical importation. He states, "There is indeed no basis in this text for any philosophy of static divine Being, and one can only deplore the speculative identification of YAHWEH with *ens realissimum* ('most real being'). Surely no abstract notion of *ontos on* is here in view."[81] Who is Henry critiquing here? He cites the Benedictine scholar Paul Heinisch who interpreted Exodus 3:14 as setting forth the theological position that God's "existence is from Himself, that His origin is not from some other being. Philosophically expressed . . . He *is* being."[82] Henry suggests that this traditional language that states God's essence is God's existence is a "philosophy of static divine Being," which is unwarranted by God's giving this name in Exodus 3:14. This is a traditional liberal Protestant argument that fails to understand the profound biblical and metaphysical achievement of the traditional language.

When an evangelical theologian like Henry questions traditional Christian language about God as a Greek importation, we realize how far the currents of the hellenization thesis run and how often evangelical theology is a species of liberal Protestantism.[83] This could be a lingering influence on Henry of his doctoral advisor, Edgar Sheffield Brightman, who not only challenged God's impassibility, but also every other traditional name as well, including infinity, perfection, and unity. Brightman accepted Harnack's hellenization thesis with little critical reflection. Language about God, for him, was a "problem" that required unpalatable antinomies. He wrote,

> There is, then, some truth in Harnack's idea that the hellenization of Christianity through the influence of philosophy on theology was a secularization. It meant that the interests of the divine dignity overawed and crowded out the interest of human suffering. Traditional orthodox theism, with its attributes of omnipotence and the rest, seems

80. His training at Boston University with Edgar Brightman would have been greatly influenced by the hellenization thesis.

81. Henry, *God, Revelation, and Authority,* p. 213.

82. Henry, *God, Revelation, and Authority,* p. 213 n. 3.

83. Clark Pinnock is a very different kind of evangelical theologian than Carl Henry, but he too challenges the tradition of the divine names, finding in the early church a move from history to metaphysics in the interpretation of Exodus 3:14. See his *Most Moved Mover* (Grand Rapids: Baker Academic, 2001), p. 116.

to be more closely allied with the supposed demands of pure form or of an *ens perfectissimum* than with the data of rational experience or the logic of rational necessity. . . . Human suffering requires a God who can act for the relief of suffering; divine dignity demands a God who is *actus purus*, actuality without potentiality of anything more. Human suffering requires a God who can love; divine dignity requires a God who is impassible and for whom, therefore, love is divested of significant content for the human sufferer. Human suffering seeks a God who can answer prayer; divine dignity, as expounded by Saint Thomas, holds that God's will admits of no variation or change any more than his knowledge.[84]

Brightman assumes, and partially affirms, the tradition of metaphysical attributes, but he does so by imposing upon them a false alternative between metaphysical dignity and historical application. Thus he wrongly interprets 'actus purus' and impassibility as producing an aloof, static deity who must now be supplemented with suffering and potentiality. Henry's rejection of the name "I Am the One Who Is" runs close to his teacher's acceptance of Harnack's thesis, which does indeed make for an odd alliance, the ultra-liberal Brightman and the conservative Henry, but it is one we see repeated again and again in contemporary theology when it comes to speaking of God.

Henry does challenge Harnack's thesis more so than Brightman. He writes, "If, however, the Old Testament provides no basis for a speculative doctrine of Being, neither does it provide a basis for turning YAHWEH into an antimetaphysical symbol, and for denying that God in his self-revelation communicates some truth about his inmost nature."[85] Contra von Rad, the divine name of Exodus 3:14 does suggest "the eternity of the divine Being, the God who is faithful from generation to generation as the One who is." How does this differ from the tradition of the divine names that Henry rejected?

I fear that one of the reasons modern theologians were led away from the traditional language of the divine names is due to a basic misun-

84. Brightman, *The Problem of God* (New York: Abingdon, 1930), pp. 173-74. There is a similarity to Brightman's theology here and that of process theology, openness theism, and Moltmann's work. For a discussion and debate on this see D. Stephen Long and George Kalantzis, eds., *The Sovereignty of God Debate* (Eugene, Ore.: Cascade, 2008).

85. Henry, *God, Revelation, and Authority,* p. 213.

derstanding of what theology does. Many critique this tradition because these names do not explicitly appear in the biblical text as names of God. Besides the question whether or not "Being" is a proper name for God, where do we find warrant for Simplicity, Perfection, Limitlessness, Unchangeableness, Impassibility, or Oneness? Of course, biblical support for each of these names can readily be found. The book of Hebrews tells us "Jesus Christ is the same yesterday and today and for ever" (Heb. 1:8). Some already suspect the book of Hebrews for its 'platonizing' tendencies, but if the Scriptures have to be purged of Platonism for the sake of the Scriptures, then we have a self-defeating argument. But passages that offer a counter-witness are also present. Those who oppose impassibility will often cite Jonah 3:10, "When God saw what they did, how they turned from their evil way, God repented of the evil which he had said he would do to them; and he did not do it." How do we make sense of God's impassibility with such a passage? Quite easily, for would we do away with God's simplicity and make God composite because Scripture tells us that God walked with Adam and Eve in the garden, or that God closed the doors on Noah's ark? Both actions normally assume bodiliness, but the doctrine of simplicity rejects the claim God has a body, which of course would be to turn God into a graven image and violate the heart of the revelation to Moses. It would embody that fideism Fleischacker warns against when reading Scripture. Reason must constantly explicate this requirement of faith without in turn making God into an ineffable sublime. For instance, the doctrine of God's simplicity is both reasonable and biblical, for we are commanded not to turn God into a creature, into an idol of our own making.

Of course, once impassibility is called into question, so is simplicity. Then we will need to think of God as a composite body in some sense; for if God is 'passible' then God must be like us, a composite being capable of reception of something and thus filled with a potentiality that can receive *passus*. Clark Pinnock suggests such a possibility in his open theism:

> There is an issue that has not been raised yet in the discussion around the open view of God. If he is with us in the world, if we are to take biblical metaphors seriously, is God in some way embodied? Critics will be quick to say that, although there are expressions of this idea in the Bible, they are not to be taken literally. But I do not believe that the idea is as foreign to the Bible's view of God as we have assumed. In tra-

dition, God is thought to function primarily as a disembodied spirit but this is scarcely a biblical idea. For example, Israel is called to hear God's word and gaze on his glory and beauty. Human beings are said to be embodied creatures created in the image of God. Is there perhaps something in God that corresponds with embodiment? Having a body is certainly not a negative thing because it makes it possible for us to be agents. Perhaps God's agency would be easier to envisage if he were in some way corporeal.[86]

Pinnock follows through with the logic of God's passibility in a way that Moltmann, whom he credits with moving theology in this direction, does not. But there is a consistent logic to Pinnock's position, for once we posit passibility, we must posit bodiliness and deny simplicity. The two go together. But here of course Pinnock has simply defined God as a creature, and not done so via the logic of the incarnation. For here humanity is divinity. His literal biblicist picture may be an effort to free us from a kind of Calvinist fundamentalism on God's sovereignty, which is admirable. But in the process it forgets the first two commandments and loses the tradition of the divine names.

4. Augustine, Dionysius, and Aquinas on the Divine Names

Much of the confusion over the names of God on both the theological left and the theological right arises from a misunderstanding of the relationship between theology and Scripture. As David Yeago notes, "One of the consequences of the Western Church's two centuries of fumbling with the implications of the historical-critical method is a loss of any sense of the connection between the classical doctrines of the Church and the text of Scripture." We fail to see how doctrines emerge "as analyses of the logic of scriptural discourse, formal descriptions of the apprehension of God *in* the texts, which then serve as guides to a faithful and attentive reading *of* the texts."[87] I think this is clear when we examine those passages in their writing where the church fathers use the names of God.

86. Pinnock, *Most Moved Mover*, p. 34.
87. Yeago, "The New Testament and the Nicene Dogma: A Contribution to the Recovery of Theological Exegesis," in *The Theological Interpretation of Scripture*, ed. Stephen E. Fowl (Oxford: Blackwell, 1997), p. 87.

Von Rad is right to note a correlation between the tradition of the divine names that identifies God with being and the tradition that also calls God 'Absolute,' (an alternative for Perfection). Many theologians did interpret Exodus 3 to mean that God's literal or proper name is 'Being.' They also thought that this correlated to other names. Thus in *On True Religion*, Augustine writes, "Eternity is ever the same. It never 'was' in the sense that it is now, and it never 'will be' in the sense that it is not yet. Wherefore, eternity alone could have said to the human mind, 'I am what I am.' And of eternity alone could it be truly said: 'He who is hath sent me' (Ex. 3:14)."[88] Eternity becomes a name for God based on the name given in Exodus 3.

In *Faith and the Creed*, following closely the logic of the New Testament, Augustine also attributes "the name" to Jesus.

> According to his nature as only-begotten Son of God, it cannot be said of him that he was, or that he will be, but only that he is. What was is not now, and what will be is not yet. But he is unchangeable without variation or temporal condition. I think there is no other reason for the name by which he proclaimed himself to his servant Moses. For when he asked by whom he should say he had been sent if the people to whom he was sent should scorn him, he received the answer, "I Am who I Am" and it was added: "Say to the children of Israel, He who is hath sent me unto you."[89]

The name does not come from an Aristotelian account of substance, although Augustine did see similarities between it and how the Platonists taught him to speak of God. In the *Confessions* he admits that as long as he was trapped within Aristotle's categories, he could not yet speak well of God. "I thought that everything that existed could be reduced to these ten categories, and I therefore attempted to understand you, my God, in all your wonderful immutable simplicity, in these same terms, as though you too were substance and greatness and beauty were your attributes in the same way that a body has attributes by which it is defined. But your greatness and beauty are your own self: whereas a body is not great or beautiful

---

88. Augustine, "Of True Religion," in *Augustine: Earlier Writings*, ed. J. H. S. Burnaby (Philadelphia: Westminster, 1953), p. 275.

89. Augustine, "Faith and the Creed," in *The Fathers of the Church: A New Translation* (Washington: Catholic University of America Press, 1985), p. 357.

simply because it is a body."[90] The name 'Simplicity' functions here to critique any improper Aristotelian metaphysics. Augustine assumes God's essence is God's existence, and this means God does not have 'attributes' in an Aristotelian sense. How then can the tradition of the divine names be so easily discounted as underwriting some Aristotelian doctrine of substance?

Janet Soskice states that Aquinas's use of the so-called 'metaphysical attributes' is indebted to Dionysius's *Divine Names*. Dionysius can be easily dismissed as offering us an apophatic theology where we are reduced to silence before a God who is "beyond beingly being." But as Soskice rightly notes, Dionysius's *Divine Names* emerges from a theological, mystical, and philosophical tradition. He does not separate faith and reason, nor think it necessary to critique reason in order to make room for faith. But consistent with Anselm, Aquinas, and Wittgenstein, Dionysius used philosophy in order to show its limits so that the theologians can stand in a position to receive the gift of knowledge that faith is.

Dionysius begins his work by following Paul in 1 Corinthians 2:4, "And my speech and my message were not in plausible words of wisdom, but in demonstration of the Spirit and of power, that your faith might not rest in the wisdom of men but in the power of God." Dionysius only quotes the first part of this verse and then states, "We are to make known the truth of what is said about God not by trusting the persuasive logoi of human wisdom but by bringing forth the power of the Spirit which moves the theologians." This is a form of "unknowing" because it is a knowing not grounded in our 'logoi,' that is, our rational and intellectual powers and activities, but in an 'ekstasis,' a getting caught up in the movement of the Spirit that makes theology itself possible. But notice what it means to be caught up in the "Spirit which moves the theologians": "In general then, one must neither dare to say — nor clearly to conceive — anything about the hidden divinity beyond being contrary to what has been divinely manifested to us in the sacred writings."[91] Our ascent toward God is not, then, a grasping in the darkness through our own intellectual powers. It is instead a fasting or purgation of our own conceptuality, which is itself a rational activity. It is "knowledge beyond being," which has the consequence of receiving the divine name, but this reception is an active passivity.[92]

---

90. Augustine, *Confessions* (New York: Penguin, 1984), p. 88.

91. Pseudo-Dionysius, *The Divine Names and the Mystical Theology*, p. 107.

92. Pseudo-Dionysius, *The Divine Names*, p. 108.

"Once we refuse such [logos, intellect, and being] in our ascent, to the extent that the ray of the godhead freely gives of itself, we are drawn inward toward greater splendors by a temperance and piety for what is divine." The Divine gives itself to us, "then what is divine uncovers itself." It uncovers itself by separating its own " non-measuredness, as uncontained, from what is measured."[93]

Our ascent is the intellectual activity which Aquinas calls 'remotio.' But as de Lubac noted, such an activity is only possible because of an 'eminentia' that renders the 'remotio' intelligible. This 'eminentia' cannot fully name the 'res' it takes up and which takes it up. Yet it allows us to know both what God is not, and therefore also acknowledge the more who God is. The latter is the reception of the gift of the divine name. This reception emerges from an unknowing, which is a conceptual askesis where we refuse to identify God as a creature, even as 'being' itself. The first name Dionysius offers us is 'Monad and Unity,' a name that derives from God's "simplicity and partlessness." The second name is 'Trinity,' which is the "three person manifestation of the fecundity beyond being." Third is 'Cause of Beings,' which results from the divine goodness. Fourth is 'Wise and Beautiful.' Aquinas's own development of the divine names tradition in the prima pars of the *Summa* takes up these names Dionysius gives us, expands them, and synthesizes them with the work of St. Augustine. Aquinas begins with God's unity and simplicity because this is the necessary conceptual askesis to receive God as Triune. God's unity is central to the doctrine of the Trinity. In fact, if we do not insist on God's simplicity, we will fail to receive the doctrine of the Trinity well; we will wrongly think that Trinity signifies some quantity and think the three persons are more like three individuals or the members of a committee working in harmony. Dionysius concludes with the name God gives us in the sacred writings: "It is differenced in a unified way: being given to all beings . . . one Be-ing (hen on)."[94]

Aquinas stands in this tradition. We are wayfarers drawn by 'beatitude' to follow a way we do not yet know. We are summoned by the Wise and Beautiful, and this is an inescapable feature of being. Those who attend with great earnestness to this way can discover some knowledge of God. But human nature alone, including human reason, cannot achieve this end; it only is a necessary means. For this reason Aquinas states in the

93. Pseudo-Dionysius, *The Divine Names*, p. 108.
94. Pseudo-Dionysius, *The Divine Names*, p. 126.

first article of the *Summa* that something beyond philosophy is necessary "because man is directed to God as an end that surpasses the grasp of his reason." But this does not lead to any fideism; it only establishes a problem. We are directed to an end, which exceeds our grasp, but we must first know the end before we can "direct [our] intentions and actions to the end." This end is present in all our actions, but it is not present or known as it should be, and thus our actions and intentions are not what they should be. It is possible that some will know the truth about God, but only "a few, and that after a long time, and with the admixture of many errors."[95] This is no ringing endorsement of a natural theology. Instead, it suggests that our way toward beatitude (our 'natural desire' for it) sets us in a direction that a few profound intellects glimpse, but they can only glimpse. To see as they should will require a "science" more than sciences "that proceed from principles known by the natural light of the intellect."[96]

The science that allows us to see more than by the "natural light of the intellect" is sacred doctrine. It includes "all things which have been divinely revealed."[97] Revelation here, however, is not propositional knowledge but a 'form' of divine light that then illumines all other sciences by looking at them through the aspect of divinity.[98] It is more a 'way' than a 'what.'

For Thomas this science is possible because of a theological understanding of signification. "The author of Holy Scripture is God, in Whose power it is to signify His meaning, not by words only (as man can also do), but also by things themselves." This gives a twofold form of signification between the historical or literal and the spiritual. Every science has the first form of signification where a word represents a thing. But in the science of sacred doctrine, "the things signified by the words have themselves also a signification." Aquinas presents a complex account of signification, even more complex than that of Aristotle in his *De Interpretatione*, because Aquinas recognizes not only a semantic triangle, but also a figurative interpretation that is established upon and presupposes the first form of literal

---

95. ST I.1 resp.

96. ST I.2 resp.

97. ST I.1.3 resp.

98. "Sacred doctrine, being one, extends to things which belong to the different philosophical sciences, because it considers in each the same formal aspect, namely, so far as they can be known through the divine light. Hence, although among the philosophical sciences some are speculative and others practical, nevertheless, sacred doctrine includes both; as God, by one and the same science, knows both Himself and His works" (ST I.1.4 resp.).

signification ("qui super litteralem fundatur, et eum supponit"). His Christology makes this rich double signification possible. This is clear when he explains the threefold sense of the spiritual signification. All three senses are indebted to Scripture and to Dionysius and based on the statement, "Now this spiritual sense has a threefold division. For as the Apostle says (Hebrews X.I) the Old Law is a figure of the New Law, and Dionysius says the New Law itself is a figure of future glory."[99] The figuration of the Old Law in the New Law is the allegorical sense. But this figuration itself has a double aspect. If it is figured in what Christ has already done it is the moral sense. If it is figured in what "relates to eternal glory" it is the anagogical sense. Therefore a single word in Scripture can have multiple senses. This only makes sense because the word, like all historical signs, participates in a Christic reality that gives it a depth such that every word can now be 'figured' in the form (or mode of union) which Christ is. This is the logic of the incarnation.

The logic of the incarnation is not a necessary 'grammar' or 'logic.' It cannot be presented in terms of a logic that requires things to be either analytic or synthetic. For on the one hand, the logic of the incarnation assumes a union of two 'natures,' neither of which contains the other within it. It might then appear that they are synthetic, not analytic. But on the other hand, the logic of the incarnation assumes that all of creation only makes sense inasmuch as it is already 'contained' in the Second Person of the Trinity. There is nothing outside of this which conditions creation. Creation is *ex nihilo*. This would appear to make the relationship between God and creation analytic, not synthetic. Yet neither of these logics adequately expresses the incarnation. Its logic cannot fit well within the philosophical tradition from Hume through Kant through logical positivism and its collapse that assumed this analytic/synthetic distinction as necessary for something to be meaningful. If one of these is necessary for a proposition to be meaningful, then the confession that Jesus is the incarnation of God could only be meaningless. But why should theologians assume that this is the only logic we have in order to make something meaningful?

The incarnation offers a different 'logic' based on the 'grammar of faith, where these two natures cannot be compared on the same plane of 'being,' because being is not a category larger than God. The two natures are noncompetitive and non-contrastive. The incarnation is unique, but

99. ST I.1.10 resp.

not private. That is to say, the logic of the incarnation can be expressed in ordinary human language; it already contains all that is necessary to speak well of God incarnate. We do not need to create some obscure language in order to speak of the incarnation. Ordinary language already does all that it needs to do. It can achieve its purpose. For instance, the two natures cannot compete because they do not occupy the same 'logical space.' This is what the divine names tradition insures: God is not a creature who competes with Christ's humanity for some space or time. The divinity and humanity of Christ are not competing 'substances.' Thus while it might appear paradoxical to us for divinity and humanity to be joined in a 'hypostatic union,' this says more about our limited understanding of both natures than it does the incarnation.

5. Thomas's Five Ways and the Way of Jesus

Because humanity and divinity can be 'hypostatically united,' we must be able to move from knowledge of humanity to divinity without violating the reason by which God created all that is not God. Because humanity and divinity remain distinct in their natures even in the hypostatic union, we must not assume that knowledge of humanity is knowledge of divinity. Jesus is God and therefore can be worshiped, but humanity is not divinity. This logic of the incarnation provides the basis for how best to interpret what Aquinas does throughout the *Summa*. It illumines how we should think about the 'five ways' or his so-called 'proofs for the existence of God.'

Aquinas told us in the prologue to his discussion of God in the first thirteen questions of the prima pars that in order to "teach the knowledge of God" we must attend to Christ "who as man, is our way to God."[100] In the prologue to question two in the prima pars he explains the basic structure of his *Summa*, the 'principalis intentio' (principal intention) of sacred

---

100. See Joseph Incandela's "An Augustinian Reading of Aquinas and Wittgenstein" for the importance of this prologue as well as the tertia pars as both relate to the five ways. *Grammar and Grace: Reformulations of Aquinas and Wittgenstein*, ed. Jeffrey Stout and Robert MacSwain (London: SCM, 2004), pp. 31-32. See also Robert Barron, *The Priority of Christ: Toward a Postliberal Catholicism* (Grand Rapids: Brazos, 2007), p. 217, where he distances Thomas from neoscholastic misreadings and states, "Despite the distortions of the neoscholastics and the caricatures presented by the moderns, authentic Thomism is conditioned through and through by the person of Jesus Christ."

doctrine is knowledge of God, not only as God is in God's self, but also as God is the "principium rerum et finis earum" (the beginning and end of things), especially of rational creatures. For this reason, the *Summa* is laid out in three parts. The first part treats God. The second part treats the movement of rational creatures to God and the third part treats Christ who as 'homo' is our way of intending God. Thomas writes that this third part is "de christo, qui, secundum quod homo, via est nobis tendendi in deum" (of Christ who as man is the way of our tending to God). This expression should not be lost when reading through the first part of the *Summa*. The 'via,' which Christ is in our tending to God, frames the discussion of the five 'viae' which follow upon this prologue.

The five 'viae' of the prima pars point to, and depend upon, the one 'via' who is Christ. We can speak of both the five ways and the one way without explicitly speaking of each at the same time, but ultimately, they cannot be separated. For instance, the argument for God based on degrees of perfection tacitly assumes the excess that Jesus himself is, who as truly 'homo' is also truly God. This provides warrant for using creaturely means such as language to speak of that which always exceeds speech — God. Or to put it another way, the hypostatic union makes possible a participation in God's simplicity by that which is composite (i.e., creature). Only this could truly account for perfection. Likewise, if we don't recall the discussion of the prima pars when we read through the Christological questions in the tertia pars, they will lose their poignancy. The Christological developments in the tertia pars render intelligible the articles on God's 'attributes' in the prima pars, and the language Thomas develops to speak of God in the prima pars points to the climax of our tending toward God, which comes to us in Christ, who is the 'way' to God.

This theme is central to the *Summa*. He picks it up again in the prologue to the tertia pars.

> Forasmuch as our Savior the Lord Jesus Christ in order to save His people from their sins (Matt. i.21), as the angel announced, showed unto us in His own Person the way of truth *(viam veritatis nobis in seipso demonstravit)*, whereby we may attain to the bliss of eternal life by rising again, it is necessary, in order to complete the last end of human life, and the virtues and vices, there should follow the consideration of the Savior of all, and of the benefits bestowed by Him on the human race.

In the tertia pars, we receive the answer that clarifies both the ways Thomas laid out as demonstrations for God in the prima pars and the virtues and vices that lead to, and away from, God in the secunda pars. In other words, the five ways depend upon the way of truth that Jesus is.

The relationship between the five ways and Jesus as the way can also be seen in Thomas's commentary on the Gospel of John, particularly chapter 14. This chapter begins with Jesus consoling his disciples that even though he is going away from them, they need not fear because his Father's house has "many rooms." Thomas describes these many rooms as the "various participants in the knowledge and enjoyment of God."[101] This implies degrees of happiness and Thomas raises the question if this is proper in glory. He makes a twofold distinction in response to this question: an absolute and a qualified perfection.

> I answer that a thing can be perfect in two ways: absolutely and in a qualified sense. The absolute perfection of happiness is found only in God, for only he knows and loves himself to the extent that he is knowable and lovable (since he knows and loves infinitely his own infinite truth and goodness). From this point of view, the supreme good itself, which is the object and cause of happiness, cannot be greater or less. This is because there is only one supreme good, which is God. But in a qualified sense, that is, considering certain conditions of time, of nature and of grace, one person can be happier than another depending on the possession of this good and the capacity of each. The greater the capacity a person has for this good, the more he shares in it, I mean he participates in it more the better disposed and prepared he is to enjoy it.[102]

This account of the degrees of happiness bears a great similarity to the five ways in the prima pars of the *Summa*.[103]

---

101. Aquinas, *Commentary on John*, trans. James A. Weishipel (Albany: Magi, 1980), p. 330.

102. Aquinas, *Commentary on John*, p. 330.

103. With his five ways, Thomas responds to two objections to God's existence that have a striking resemblance to contemporary arguments for atheism: the existence of evil and an immanent, naturalistic account of all things. I noted earlier that Philip Quinn sets forth two "defeater" arguments for theism: the problem of evil and the projectionist account of God language one finds in Feuerbach, Freud, and Durkheim. For Quinn, an "intellectually sophisticated adult theist in our culture" will know these two arguments against theism and need to provide counterarguments in order to hold a rational faith. Note how similar are

The five ways that lead to God depend upon motion, the nature of the efficient cause, possibility and necessity, degrees of perfection, and governance of the world. What do these have to do with the way Jesus is? Aquinas's commentary on John gives insight into this question. Jesus is the way to the "many rooms" that are in the Father's house. They are our participation in the *knowledge* of God. In fact, "this place is God himself . . . in whom, is the abundance of all perfections." Jesus prepares a way for us into the knowledge of God, into God's infinite perfections. Jesus does this, as Thomas puts it in the commentary, "in five ways." The Lord's departure "makes room for faith, shows them the way" (secundo demonstrando eis viam ad locum eundi), and he effects the way "by his prayers for them," "by attracting them to what is above," and "by sending them the Holy Spirit."[104] Jesus makes knowledge of God possible in five ways: his absence after the exaltation, his presence as a sign, his ongoing priestly activity, his aesthetic attraction, and his agency in sending the Spirit. As tempting as it is, I am not correlating the 'quinque modis' of Thomas's commentary directly with the 'quinque viae' of the *Summa* (although such might be possible). But there is at least a family resemblance between them. When we examine the central biblical reference for Jesus as the way (John 14), it cannot be a mere coincidence that we find such family resemblances between the *Summa* and the commentary on John 14.

Jesus is the way that draws creatures toward their true end, which is the glory of the Father. For Thomas all of 'nature' is interpreted within this sign, and thus we expect to find a witness to the way of Jesus by the very movement, efficient causality, the becoming necessary of what was only possible, the desire for the perfect, and the ability to pursue intelligently the end in which we live, move, and have our being. The five ways of the prima pars may appear as natural, independent 'proofs' for the existence of God, but if so it is at most because they are the presupposition for following the way noted in the tertia pars and the commentary on John. They are not ends in themselves. We can find evidence that philosophers outside the church possessed some knowledge of these ways, but they are only finally

Aquinas's two objections to God's existence. First, "If, therefore, God existed there would be no evil discoverable; but there is evil in the world, therefore God does not exist." Second, "For all natural things can be reduced to one principle, which is nature, and all voluntary things can be reduced to one principle, which is human reason, or will." The first objection reads like Hume, the second like Feuerbach. The five ways are responses to these two objections.

104. Aquinas, *Commentary on John*, p. 333.

intelligible because of the way of Jesus. They are what we would expect if Jesus is who the church proclaims him to be. Because creation occurs in and through him, it bears a created desire to move toward that perfection of being, which is God, which Jesus shows us and to which he draws us. Creation is always Christologically significant.

Because of the hypostatic union, we have in Jesus the way and the destination (truth and life) united. For Thomas, Jesus is the 'way' in his humanity. He is the 'truth' and the 'life' in his divinity. He comments on John 14:6 by stating, "The way, as has been said, is Christ himself . . . because this way is not separated from its destination but united to it, he adds, and the truth, and the life. So Christ is at once both the way and the destination. He is the way by reason of his human nature, and the destination because of his divinity."[105] Thomas then explains truth in terms of our words and Christ as the Word:

> Now truth is the conforming of a thing to the intellect, and this results when the intellect conceives the thing as it is. Therefore, the truth of our intellect belongs to our word (since it is not measured by things, but things are true in the measure that they are similar to the Word); the Word of God is truth itself. And because no one can know the truth unless he adheres to the truth, it is necessary that anyone who desires to know the truth adheres to this Word.[106]

Truth and Christology are indissolubly linked, for the Father can only be known "by his Word, which is his Son."[107] Thomas then gives us an explicit account of this truth that relates language, knowledge of God, and Christology:

> And just like one of us who wants to be known by others by revealing to them the words in his heart, clothes those words with letters or sounds, so God, wanting to be known by us, takes his Word, conceived from eternity, and clothes it with flesh in time. . . . Therefore, the Father is known in the Son as in his Word and proper image. Now since every

---

105. Aquinas, *Commentary on John*, p. 336.

106. Aquinas, *Commentary on John*, pp. 337-38. Thomas admonishes his reader, "Therefore, cling to Christ if you wish to be secure, for you cannot get off the road because he is the way."

107. Aquinas, *Commentary on John*, p. 339.

created word is some likeness of that Word, and some likeness, though imperfect, of the divinity is found in every thing, either as an image or a trace, it follows that what God is cannot be known perfectly through any creature or by any thought or concept of a created intellect. It is the Word alone, the only-begotten Word, which is a perfect word and the perfect image of the Father, that knows and comprehends the Father.[108]

The likeness (similitude) that we are to God is deficient to provide adequate knowledge of God.[109] It expresses an imperfect desire for something more than creation itself. The incarnation offers that more. It provides the basis for what we can naturally know about God, for it offers the 'way' toward which all other ways implicitly and explicitly point. It primarily allows us to use language of God so that our intellect intends and forms an idea of God that is not false, even though we can only name God from imperfect creatures. That we can only name God from creatures means that all our ideas of God imply composition. Thus they will border on idolatry; they will appear to be nothing other than statements about creatures, and thus they will be false.

Thomas readily admits that all our language about God comes to us through creatures, but he develops this basic premise such that he can admit the 'natural' character of our language about God without conceding the all too modern assumption that this inevitably means that our language about God is nothing but projection. He can do this because he knows that our mode of signifying is not univocal to what is signified. If it were, all that we could say of God would come by way of remotion; we could only speak of God by always removing or placing under erasure everything that is said. Then we would be postmodern. But the tradition of the divine names would not allow for this, for it gives us a true knowledge of God, and not just equivocal statements. It even gives us proper names.

In the tertia pars Aquinas draws on the divine names to help us understand the incarnation. He asks "whether it was fitting that God should become Incarnate." He begins with the important objection against its fittingness because God should remain — given his immutable and impassible nature — as he always was, "without flesh." Thomas replies to this objection, stating that "the mystery of the Incarnation was not completed

108. Aquinas, *Commentary on John*, pp. 339-40.
109. For a helpful discussion of the twofold likeness of creation to God and its 'deficiency' see Rudi te Velde, *Participation and Substantiality in Thomas Aquinas*, pp. 95-117.

through God being changed in any way from the state in which He had been from eternity, but through His having united Himself to the creature in a new way. But it is fitting that a creature which by nature is mutable, should not always be in one way."[110] Here we find a different understanding of the interaction between divinity and humanity than we saw with Lutheranism. Divinity does not 'become' humanity in the sense that God exchanges natures. Instead, God 'becomes' Jesus who is both divine and human in one Person without losing the distinction between divinity and humanity. This creates a 'new way,' but it is not a 'way' that could ever undo the revelation to Moses that God is not and cannot be 'creature.' The language of impassibility and immutability not only remain intact; they are shown to be essential to understand the mystery of the incarnation. If God were in God's nature mutable and passible, then the incarnation would be superfluous, at most an expression of what God already is and in no sense a 'new way.' Properly understood, in the incarnation God remains God and thus unchanged. Creatures remain creatures and thus subject to change. What surprises us in the incarnation is not that God becomes something other. We can readily find such myths from antiquity to modernity. What surprises us is God makes a way for our deification by becoming other without changing the sameness of God's being or making us other than creatures. The result is that we are changed, not God.

In the second question of the tertia pars Aquinas rehearses the various 'grammars' by which theologians sought to express the unity of the human and divine in Jesus. Following Chalcedon closely, he rejects speaking of the unity of the two natures by collapsing them into one or by dividing the natures into two persons or hypostases. But he also rejects uniting them through 'habitation,' where the divine is merely clothed in human flesh; through 'affection,' where the unity is primarily a moral unity of will; through 'operation,' where the human flesh is the instrument of the divine; through a dignity of honor, where all the honor given to the Son of God is also given to the Son of Man; and through an equivocation, where there is merely a 'communication of names.' These five possibilities: habitation, affection, operation, dignity of honor, and equivocation, fail to express the incarnation well. They all share a common error of failing to acknowledge the profound unity Jesus is in his two natures. For Aquinas, the union between the two natures is one of 'hypostasis'; it is not of 'essence' or 'nature,'

110. ST III.1.

nor is it merely accidental. What does this 'hypostatic union' signify? It means the agency of the one Person, the earthly creature Jesus of Nazareth, is in his human nature the same agency as that of his divine 'nature' and this union perfects humanity. This is why Thomas argues the incarnation occurred at the proper moment in history, neither at its beginning nor its end; for "imperfection precedes perfection in time" in making things perfect, while "perfection precedes imperfection" in terms of efficient causality. Here is a reference to two of the five ways, perfection and causality, and both are related to the incarnation.[111] The incarnation occurs in the middle of time so that it can perfect the imperfect which temporally precedes it and at the same time be the perfect efficient cause of all that proceeds from it, even that which is imperfect. We would not know the latter without the former. As we have already noted, Christ as the wisdom of God is the exemplar cause for creation. Thus he is its origin, its 'way,' and its 'destination.'

The purpose of creation is for it to be made perfect in Christ. This desire for perfection is central to the five ways. We see this in the very first objection to God's existence in question two of the prima pars. Because God is infinite goodness, evil should not exist. Thomas never suggests that the way out of this 'problem of evil' is to make God less than infinite goodness. Instead, following Augustine, the only possible 'reason' for evil is that God might make it good.[112] All five ways assume this basic movement. We are not only moved by ourselves, but are also moved by something outside of us. This makes us creatures with potentiality. God as 'actus purus' is not moved toward something, for God is the something toward which all things move. Likewise, God is the first efficient cause of all that is unless we posit an infinite regress of cause and effect. With such an infinite regress, we would not be able to make sense of the temporal 'order' we inhabit. Such a temporal order recognizes that there is something rather than nothing. Why is this so? Nothing sensible and finite necessarily exists or it would not have potentiality. Since things do exist, but not out of necessity, why is there not nothing? Perhaps necessarily existent being makes this possible? But for what reason? The fourth and fifth ways explain the reason for motion, causality, and possibility. Things bear within them a 'gradation' of goodness.

111. ST III.1.6 resp.

112. ST I.2.3 obj. 1 and reply. We must be careful in positing a 'reason' for evil. As Augustine noted in his better moments, evil has no 'reason.' It is absurd.

We could not recognize the good, the true, the noble, the beautiful if we did not assume a 'maximum' against which such appear, a way of 'perfection.' Aquinas states, "Therefore there must also be something which is to all beings the cause of their being, goodness, and every other perfection; and this we call God."[113] God is the good and true that everyone tacitly acknowledges by their practical consensus and action. Far from denying the fall and our sinfulness, this tacit knowledge, which is made manifest after the incarnation, exacerbates our situation. Christ's perfection shows us our imperfection. Theological virtues expose the vices for they can be nothing but privations. Without the former we would not even be baffled by evil.

When Thomas begins his discussion of Christology in the tertia pars, this 'way of perfection' guides his reflections. Once again he draws on Dionysius; this time to explain why God's reasons for the 'when' and 'where' of the incarnation must be good and fitting.

> To each thing, that is befitting which belongs to it by reason of its very nature; thus to reason befits man, since this belongs to him because he is of a rational nature. But the very nature of God is goodness, as is clear from Dionysius (Div. Nom. i). Hence what belongs to the essence of goodness befits God. But it belongs to the essence of goodness to communicate itself in the highest manner to the creature, and this is brought about chiefly by his so joining created nature to Himself that one Person is made up of these three — the Word, a soul and flesh, as Augustine says (De Trin. xiii).[114]

Theology comes as a gift communicating God's goodness to creatures for their own perfection, showing them their imperfection. The ability to speak of God is, of course, a human ability. But it is an ability made possible by the gift of creation, the giving of the divine name and Jesus' bearing the name for our sake.

6. The Five Ways among Modern Theology's Discontents

This discussion on negative theology, the divine name, and the five ways should help us critically assess the differences among modern theology's

113. ST I.2.3 resp. (Pegis).
114. ST III.1.1 resp.

discontents as to how we might relate faith and reason and speak of God in such a way that it moves us beyond some of the limitations found in the modern bifurcation between faith and reason and its twin problems of fideism and rationalism. The five ways offers a focused interpretive lens to address for this assessment.

De Lubac, John Paul II, and Denys Turner defend Vatican I's reading of Thomas Aquinas. They urge theologians to take more seriously the role of reason set forth at Vatican I, especially as it makes room for philosophy based on an 'autonomous' use of reason.[115] Turner, like John Paul II and Vatican I, puts forth his argument, however, not in terms of a pure reason, but on the theological proposition that "Christians should think, as a matter of faith, that the existence of God is rationally demonstrable, as a dogmatic decree of the first Vatican Council says."[116]

Turner defends the Vatican I decree "that there is a twofold order of knowledge, distinct not only as regards its source, but also as regards its object." The sources are found in the different levels of "natural reason" and "divine faith."[117] Turner faults Barthianism, Radical Orthodoxy, and the nouvelle théologie for failing to recognize this important distinction. He characterizes the difference between his position and theirs in terms of two propositions. The first is held by Vatican I, Denys Turner, and perhaps Henri de Lubac and John Paul II, although how Vatican I is interpreted is itself subject to conflicting interpretations. Fergus Kerr, Victor Preller, Barthians, and Thomists like Hauerwas and Radical Orthodoxy would hold the second. Here are the two propositions:

1. There are reasons of faith for maintaining that the existence of God must be demonstrable by reason alone.
2. The existence of God is knowable with certainty by reason but only within and as presupposing the context of faith.

What is the difference between these two propositions? The first suggests that a domain called "reason alone" exists that faith generates but which does not then presuppose the context of faith.[118] The second sug-

115. See *Restoring Faith to Reason*, p. 87.
116. Turner, *Faith, Reason, and the Existence of God*, p. ix.
117. Turner, *Faith, Reason, and the Existence of God*, p. 3.
118. The status of this "reason alone" in Turner's argument is ambiguous, which

gests that reason proceeds only within a larger context of faith; reason is not identical to faith but it works within a context of faith. Is this a distinction without a difference? The significance of the difference can be seen in the political import of both propositions. Both would deny fideism. Neither collapses reason into faith or faith into reason, divides them into to discrete entities, nor seeks to correlate them. The difference is that the first finds a natural alliance between religion and political liberalism as we saw with Fleischacker. It allows for a reason that is public outside of the church's teachings on faith, which then could easily be rendered private. The second makes an alliance between religion and political liberalism much more difficult, for it denies this independent public realm and the public/private distinction.

Turner critiques the reformulated Thomism in the nouvelle théologie, Radical Orthodoxy, and the Barthian Thomists for precisely this reason. With regard to the latter, he writes that Barthians "do not need a Thomas Aquinas reconfigured by Catholics in Barth's image."[119] This neglects, however, the fact that Protestants might think it useful for Catholics to reformulate Thomism through Barth's critique of modern theology in order to avoid reading him in terms of a problematic late medieval 'analogia entis' that continues a Tridentine form of Christianity incapable of receiving anything from Protestantism because it is a priori dismissed as fideistic. In one sense, this is what the nouvelle théologie accomplished. But Turner is no more convinced that Catholics need a Barthian Thomas than Protestants a Thomistic Barth.[120]

The difference between faith and reason in Turner and de Lubac and that in Milbank, Hauerwas, and Barth can also be seen in the much more positive role for Thomas's five ways as philosophical proofs for God's exis-

---

makes it all the more interesting. He clearly rejects interpreting it in terms of Kant's pure reason yet he says explicitly that "reasons of faith" should lead Christians to the conviction "that the existence of God must be demonstrable by reason alone." Turner, *Faith, Reason, and the Existence of God*, p. 14.

119. Turner, *Faith, Reason, and the Existence of God*, p. xii.

120. The dogma Turner defends from Vatican I seems to be a direct descendant of the Council of Trent that distanced itself from the Protestants' emphasis on total depravity by insisting that although "all men have lost innocence in the prevarication of Adam" and that neither Gentiles "by the force of nature" nor Jews "by the very letter of the law of Moses" had the power to liberate themselves, still "though free will, weakened as it was in its power and downward bent, was by no means extinguished in them." *Creeds of the Church*, ed. John H. Leith (Atlanta: John Knox, 1982), p. 408.

tence. But for de Lubac, Thomas's five ways begin people on a journey to God; they cannot finally attain the goal. He finds them persuasive as rational starting points. This makes it all the more curious why Turner distances his position from the nouvelle théologie; for at least in de Lubac's case compelling starting points in reason for God's existence are always open to any person who is open to them. De Lubac writes, "Movement, contingency, exemplarity, causality, finality, moral obligation: the eternal categories are the starting-points open to man; they are always to hand and always resist his critique."[121] Perhaps de Lubac differs from Turner in that these ways are nothing but starting points that send us in a certain direction. They are not finally proofs based on reason alone. Reason never stands alone in de Lubac — it is always on pilgrimage; it is always en route, on a 'way.' He writes, "The ways which reason adopts on its journey to God are proofs, and these proofs, in turn, are ways."[122] This entails that although these proofs are rationally known by nature, they are not naturally recognizable to us in our nature. "All men know God 'naturally,' but they do not always recognize him."[123] The problem is not, then, lack of a natural proof based on reason, but the lack of 'taste' for the proof; the problem is aesthetic. De Lubac concludes, "So, in the matter of God, whatever certain people may be tempted to think, it is never the proof which is lacking. What is lacking is taste for God."[124] This taste cannot be developed without a 'sign.'[125] The signs that produce a proper taste for God are given in faith through God's revelation in Christ. Reason works best within that context, which is what concerns Turner about de Lubac's theology. Reason has its place only within the context of faith. But it is *reason* that has this place. But this is what raises problems for Turner's interpretation of Aquinas. Is it possible for reason ever to work outside the context of faith given Thomas's Christocentrism?

Turner does not think Aquinas's five ways succeed as rational proofs, but he thinks faith makes the attempt necessary. Barth also thinks Aquinas attempts and fails to prove God through the five ways, but he thinks any such attempt is an effort to measure God by something other than God's self-disclosure. Preller, de Lubac, Kerr, Milbank, Pickstock, and Hauerwas

121. De Lubac, *Discovery of God*, p. 60.
122. De Lubac, *Discovery of God*, p. 74.
123. De Lubac, *Discovery of God*, p. 75.
124. De Lubac, *Discovery of God*, p. 83.
125. De Lubac, *Discovery of God*, p. 88.

do not see the five ways as an attempt to prove God "by reason alone" even if for "reasons of faith." Preller states, "The proofs . . . are tangential to Aquinas's doctrine and even dangerous."[126] They assume a univocity of terms that potentially makes them ontotheological.[127] The five ways don't work because "we cannot derive from them any 'first cause' or God who is not univocally tied into the causal chain or system of perfection of which he is supposedly the intelligible explanation."[128] This univocity makes the demonstrations dangerous, underwriting ontotheology.

Preller's critique of Thomas's five ways appears to be the exact opposite of Turner's position, but such a conclusion would be mistakenly drawn. For when Preller explains what the five ways do, his explanation bears a striking resemblance to what Turner thinks reason alone accomplishes in speaking about God. Preller writes, "To postulate a final context in which the world would be intelligible, one must, ironically, postulate that which remains most opaque and unintelligible from the context of the world itself."[129] The failure to speak well of God through the five ways becomes a compelling reason for speaking well of God.

Fergus Kerr has a slightly less appreciative sense of Thomas's five ways. Following Leo Elders, Kerr traces the genealogy of the five ways and states that they are "all unoriginal, handed down from ancient philosophy."[130] So Thomas is rehearsing common philosophical arguments for the existence of God without putting a great deal of stock in them; in fact they need to be supplemented by sacred doctrine or they can actually mislead. For Thomas shows that they could be arguments for a deity who is "spatially extended and corporeal (1.3.1)." Here Aquinas agrees with Kant's original use of the term 'ontotheology.' But, notes Kerr, "This possibility shows how little Thomas thinks the five ways have achieved."[131] Kerr does not state that the philosophical arguments accomplish nothing; instead, they achieve "little." They could be shared by idolatrous and non-idolatrous conceptions of God. However, Kerr does not see the philoso-

---

126. Preller, *The Divine Science and the Science of God: A Reformulation of Thomas Aquinas* (Princeton: Princeton University Press, 1967), p. 107.

127. Preller doesn't use the term, but certainly uses the concept; see Preller, *Divine Science and the Science of God,* p. 135.

128. Preller, *Divine Science and the Science of God,* p. 135.

129. Preller, *Divine Science and the Science of God,* p. 135.

130. Fergus Kerr, *After Aquinas: Versions of Thomism* (Oxford: Blackwell, 2002), p. 70.

131. Kerr, *After Aquinas,* p. 76.

phers' argument as based on any pure reason or pure philosophy; instead, these philosophers are "implicitly theologians (Aristotle explicitly so)."[132] The difference between Kerr and Turner is the extent to which the proofs are based on 'reason alone.' For Kerr the arguments move to another key when placed within the harmonious context of faith; they are transposed.

Hauerwas also does not see the five ways as rational proofs based on a natural theology alone. He reminds us that the five ways were put forth at a time when few people denied the existence of God. So Thomas's "little coda" — 'and this everyone understands to be God' — that concludes each way was simply an attempt to connect what everyone already knew and believed "in the ordinary world."[133] Milbank and Pickstock's reading of the five ways resembles Hauerwas's. For them, Aquinas's 'demonstrations' "offer weakly probable modes of argument and very attenuated 'showings.'"[134] Exactly what they mean by 'showings' is unclear. Their understanding of what Aquinas is doing with the five ways could be similar to what Wittgenstein did in the *Tractatus* (although Mibank remains critical of Wittgenstein's influence in theology); Wittgenstein, as Pears notes, was doing a kind of negative theology. It is not so much what the five ways say as what they don't say but only show. Perhaps, then, rather than predicating of God what he is, they show us what cannot be said. If that is the case, we are left with the question whether all these readings of Thomas finally differ. Turner insists they do. His claim differs from the others, because they assume "the existence of God is knowable with certainty by reason but only within and as presupposing the context of faith." He assumes "reasons of faith" require a demonstration of God "by reason alone."[135]

What should we expect from reason in speaking about God? Should we expect, and seek to set forth, a rational proof for God's existence outside the domain of faith? Is such a domain possible? These are Christological questions. If, as Scripture sets forth, Jesus is the One "through whom are all things and through whom we exist" (1 Cor. 8:6), then he is the precondition for what reason, especially metaphysics, might accomplish. This is why the 'analogia entis' matters. As Rudi te Velde puts it, the

132. Kerr, *After Aquinas*, p. 65.

133. Hauerwas, *With the Grain of the Universe: The Church's Witness and Natural Theology* (Grand Rapids: Brazos, 2001), pp. 26-27. Hauerwas draws on George Hendry's *Theology of Nature* (Philadelphia: Westminster, 1980) for this position.

134. Milbank and Pickstock, *Truth in Aquinas* (London: Routledge, 2001), p. 28.

135. Turner, *Faith, Reason and the Existence of God*, p. 16.

'analogia entis' is "metaphysical continuity-in-difference."[136] Analogy assumes the "effect is somehow differently the same as its cause."[137] This has political implications. We need not privilege difference over sameness as modern liberalism does, nor sameness over difference as fascism does. We can move beyond this unpalatable either/or.[138]

For Thomas, reason follows the way of the effect back to, and from, its cause.[139] But following where effects lead is less of an epistemological endeavor and more an ontological one. Te Velde gives us a key to interpreting the five ways; they are not 'epistemological' arguments about how we can know God. They are about 'intelligibility,' in particular "the intelligibility of being (ens et verum convertuntur)."[140] In other words "the question as to whether God exists is first and foremost a matter of finding an access (via) to the intelligibility of God."[141] For Thomas, Jesus is that access. Following him is equivalent to following the effect to its cause. Anyone who pursues the latter will inevitably find its perfect completion in him and its imperfect similitude in themselves, for they were created into his image.

Because of the metaphysical basis for analogy, te Velde finds Aquinas's use of analogy vastly different from Wittgenstein's.[142] He assumes Wittgenstein's work only criticizes metaphysics. If this is true, then little rapprochement between Aquinas and Wittgenstein would be possible. This would cause a division, if not a chasm, between those theologians discontent with modernity who draw on Wittgenstein, such as postliberals, Kerr, Preller, and Hauerwas and those who seek to recover metaphysics, such as Milbank, Pickstock, the nouvelle théologie, and important theologians such as te Velde and Turner. But, as I hope to show in the next chapter, this is an unnecessary chasm, for it is a misunderstanding of Wittgenstein. Wittgenstein does not bring metaphysics to an end; he cri-

---

136. Te Velde, *Aquinas on God*, p. 96.

137. Te Velde, *Aquinas on God*, p. 102.

138. See D. Stephen Long, *The Goodness of God* (Grand Rapids: Brazos, 2001), pp. 120-27.

139. This is the reason te Velde finds the "negative reading" of Thomas unpersuasive. It "tends to overemphasize the radical distinction between God and the world at the cost of their relationship as cause and effect." *Aquinas on God*, p. 74. It is also why he disagrees with Sokolowski's reading; see p. 91 n. 24.

140. Te Velde, *Aquinas on God*, p. 28. For his discussion of the five ways, see pp. 37-65.

141. Te Velde, *Aquinas on God*, pp. 38-39.

142. Te Velde, *Aquinas on God*, p. 109 n. 37.

tiques its improper uses and opens up the possibility for a kind of meta-physics that recognizes the limits of philosophy so that faith and reason no longer police one another.

CHAPTER 4

Language

If ontotheology and the 'analogia entis' are temptations to subordinate theology to metaphysics, or to divorce them from each other, then the proper response is not to eschew metaphysics, but to recognize its legitimate role in theology. This chapter seeks the remedy for these third and fourth modern ills in an unlikely alliance between Wittgenstein and Aquinas. The alliance is unlikely because many find in Wittgenstein's philosophy a critique of metaphysics, even another pronouncement of its end. If so, it would hold forth little promise in bringing together theology and a metaphysical philosophy after they were placed in a dangerous discord in the later Middle Ages. This discord remains in modernity and gives rise to some of its key philosophical moves. In providing a philosophical therapy to those moves, I will argue, Wittgenstein proves helpful for the recovery of metaphysics and its reconciliation with theology. Likewise, Wittgenstein's critique of inappropriate metaphysical uses of human agency resonates well with Aquinas's understanding as to how speaking of God works. As some have argued, we may be able to read Aquinas better after Wittgenstein.

Joseph Incandela wittingly suggests that Aquinas and Wittgenstein "show up at the same parties these days" because of the "good taste of their hosts who know enough to invite guests to their gatherings who have much in common and are capable of meaningful interaction."[1] Augustine is the mediator for this meaningful interaction. Incandela traces four com-

---

1. Jeffrey Stout and Robert MacSwain, eds., *Grammar and Grace: A Reformulation of Aquinas and Wittgenstein* (London: SCM, 2004), p. 45.

ponents of a "medieval Augustinian moral inquiry" that show the similarity between Aquinas and Wittgenstein. These components are similar to virtue epistemology where knowledge is not a collection of propositions based primarily on justified beliefs; instead knowledge is the cultivation of the virtue of wisdom, which always entails a relationship between the intellectual and moral virtues.[2]

The first component of the medieval Augustinian tradition is to receive "the authority of the teacher," which entails at the same time a second component, "the transformation of the student." Because knowledge is not a collection of facts but the cultivation of wisdom, students must be transformed morally and intellectually to pursue truth and goodness. A third component is that the emphasis on practical wisdom shifts the character of "rational justification." It is not a procedure or a principle from which certainty emerges; instead, rational justification is at best discovered. As Alasdair MacIntyre states, rational justification is retrospective.[3] Finally, the cultivation of wisdom is noncompetitive. Its purpose is never to dominate, but to discover truth, which will produce peace, joy, and rest.

How does this Augustinian tradition of moral inquiry bring Aquinas and Wittgenstein into "meaningful interaction"? It helps us recognize the limits of philosophy, especially as a methodism seeking epistemic justification, and then be able to stop doing it when we need to and begin to do something more productive, even something like theology. Rather than accepting that the limits of philosophy, even the limits of epistemology, constitute the limits of knowledge, we seek the 'more' that transforms us and then places philosophy in its proper light. Practical wisdom teaches us the difference between legitimate and illegitimate philosophical questions. Certain philosophical quests seek answers to questions for which no questions can legitimately be raised, especially when it comes to epistemology. Both the quest for certainty and the quest for the a priori limits of what we know we cannot know trap us in unnecessary muddles that do not cultivate wisdom but abstract intellectual solutions to problems that do not exist. For Wittgenstein the task of philosophy is to be able finally not to do it, to be able to walk away from some questions not because they raise pro-

---

2. See Linda Zagzebski's *Virtues of the Mind* (Cambridge: Cambridge University Press, 2002).

3. Stout and McSwain, eds., *Grammar and Grace*, p. 45. Incandela uses MacIntyre to set forth this medieval Augustinianism.

found universal questions of human existence that are difficult to answer, but because they are unintelligible, like trying to answer the question how to construct a circle two inches by three inches in diameter.

For a teacher to show students the proper sense of questions is itself an exercise in practical wisdom and peacemaking. We do not need to answer some questions, or take on some supposed difficulties, because they are illusory. What we need is a 'therapy' to see how we are trapped within them, and how we might escape them like a "fly out of a bottle" without ceasing to be involved in those activities that are necessary for our being human. For of course some questions must be addressed: "Am I my brother or my sister's keeper?" "Will you make graven images before me?" "Why is there something rather than nothing?" But others are really nonsensical: "How can we speak of God when we know all our speech is contextual and primarily about ourselves?" Wittgenstein's philosophy does not help us escape the true questions that make us human. It does not evade metaphysics, but shows us how modern epistemology trapped us within an improper metaphysical use of the 'I.'

1. Metaphysics versus Metaphysical Use

Some answers to questions emerge only because the questions themselves are constructed out of pure air. Wittgenstein challenged this kind of 'metaphysical' *use* of language, asking what kind of subject we would have to be to use language for such purposes. He showed how this use led to a philosophy that generated problems that did not exist in everyday life. One first had to be trained into the problems before they could become such, and part of the disease of philosophy was that it clung to the production of these problems thinking they needed to be solved. Wittgenstein reestablished proper limits to philosophy by teaching us to ask whether language could be used in everyday life to question what the philosophers sought to question. He taught us to ask transcendental questions such as, "Where would I have to stand to ask that?" That Wittgenstein brings us back to our everyday use of language does not mean that we now stand in that rather tired tradition of overcoming metaphysics; it means just the opposite. This is why he gives us an account of language that still allows us to do theology without either assuming that it must be acceptable solely to a modern, foundationalist logic or that it must be nonsense. Wittgenstein wrote,

When philosophers use a word — 'knowledge', 'being', 'object', 'I', 'proposition', 'name' — and try to grasp the essence of the thing, one must always ask oneself: is the word ever actually used in this way in the language-game which is its original home? — What *we* do is to bring words back from their metaphysical to their everyday use.[4]

In this quote he does not reject 'essences' or questions of being, object, the 'I', etc. He refers to the "essence of the thing," which is something metaphysics pursues. But then he asks if the search for them assumes some standpoint no philosopher could inhabit. He questions, as we shall see, whether we can think of philosophy as some second- or third-order discourse that abstracts from how we actually live in the world and seeks to give the limits to it.

To use language metaphysically is to stand outside the everyday use of theological language by people of faith and know a priori that their use of the term 'God' has no real reference because we 'know' the real by peering behind our language and finding the essence of the real to be nothing. Then we 'know' our task is to take what they think they are doing when they say 'God,' and make it meaningful, or make it something other than what it is, by placing it within its proper (modern) epistemological limits.

Paul Holmer was one of the important early voices in bringing Wittgenstein's philosophy in conversation with theology. He taught at Yale and could be considered an early forerunner of postliberal theology. However, Paul DeHart finds Holmer outside the realm of the more sober theological reflections stemming from Hans Frei, differing from Frei in that for Holmer the "'fideist' title came close to the mark."[5] Holmer, like D. Z. Phillips, exemplifies Frei's type-5 theology, a theology that only allows for self-description and doesn't provide an adequate space for an external critique of the language of faith even from an ad hoc correlation. Frei typologizes theologies based on their use of first-, second-, and third-order discourses. He writes,

There are first-order theological statements of belief and confession. There are second-order statements examining or reflecting on these

4. Wittgenstein, *Philosophical Investigations,* trans. G. E. M. Anscombe (New York: Macmillan, 1968), p. 116.

5. DeHart, *The Trial of the Witnesses: The Rise and Decline of Postliberal Theology* (London: Blackwell, 2006), p. 31.

first-order statements in the context of the discourse itself — that is, within a Christian context. And then there are third-order statements that clarify or show us why or how it is the case that statements within a religious context are not the same as apparently similar or identical statements made outside the religious context.[6]

This allows Frei to place various theologies in a typology based on their use of internal (first- and second-order) versus external (third-order) discourses. DeHart finds this the element of Frei's work that makes it salvageable for contemporary theology. It shows the inevitability of correlation.[7] But this is convincing only if we could identify these various discourses. What kinds of language are first-, second-, or third-order? Lindbeck offers a similar distinction between first- and second-order discourses in his account of doctrine. What Holmer offers is a more consistent application of Wittgenstein that calls into question this language of internal/external or various orders altogether. To place his work in a typology based on those distinctions is to overlook what Wittgenstein showed him. I will critique Holmer not for failing to offer an adequate correlation between internal or external discourses, but for failing to see that he need not eschew metaphysics given Wittgenstein's philosophy.

Wittgenstein challenged the language of internal and external or first- and second-order discourses because of how language and the world necessarily interact. After telling us how strange it is that we should be able to "do anything with the language we have" given what some philosophers tell us it can and cannot do, he goes on to state, "One might think: if philosophy speaks of the use of the word 'philosophy' there must be a second-order philosophy. But it is not so; it is rather, like the case of orthography, which deals with the word 'orthography' among others without then being second order."[8] A presumed second-order discourse assumes we somehow transcend our first language and now critically reflect upon it from some privileged standpoint outside of it. How is this possible? What use of language allows for clear demarcations between these orders? Do we have different grammars for these levels? If so then we are less in language than it is in us.

6. Hans W. Frei, *Types of Christian Theology* (New Haven: Yale University Press, 1992), p. 48.

7. DeHart offers a convincing case that this typology represents a synthesis between Troeltsch and Barth, both mediated through H. Richard Niebuhr, in Frei's work.

8. Wittgenstein, *Philosophical Investigations*, p. 121.

Like the grammar of any language, theology provides the rules that believers internalize so that they can worship and speak of God well. Holmer found "merit" in Wittgenstein's enigmatic phrase, "theology as grammar."[9] Speakers of a language do not always recognize the rules of grammar by which they speak even though they must use those rules in order to speak well. Theology is like that. It makes explicit what is implicit in the practice of worship. This means that theology is not some second-order activity that abstracts from the believer's everyday use of speaking of God in order to normalize and systematize that use, which gives theology and the theologian entirely too much power. Theology is not 'critical reflection' on some praxis — liturgical or ethical — that seeks to make it more reasonable than it already is. Theology is like rules of grammar that faithful believers have already internalized such that they can worship God well without creating problems for themselves; problems that never existed until the theologians, like the philosophers, created them. Theology as grammar "must be absorbed" by the believer, and when it is, "the hearer is supposed to become Godly."[10]

Holmer draws on Wittgenstein's 'theology as grammar' in order to develop a consistent logic to Christianity synchronically and diachronically. If we know how to worship the Triune God, if we know how to go on in a consistent way, then of course we have a logical continuity across time and space as to who God is. Otherwise we would simply have a series of disconnected fragments. To assume this is possible is as foolish as to assume that somehow the people who came before us ate, slept, communicated, and reproduced in ways incommensurable with ours. How we must live in this world shows consistent logics in our languages and practices, even if they are never completely translatable. The logic that lets us know how to go on prevents Christianity from being pure construction, nonsense, or just free play. It allows for Christianity to have both its own logic and at the same time a logic that anyone who uses language could understand. Holmer states, "For just as grammar of a language is not quite an invention, nor do we simply make up our logical rules, so we do not design theology just to suit ourselves, nor do we invent it as we would a pleasant saying."[11]

9. Paul Holmer, *The Grammar of Faith* (San Francisco: Harper & Row, 1978), p. 17.
10. Holmer, *The Grammar of Faith*, p. 19.
11. Holmer, *The Grammar of Faith*, p. 20.

Holmer shows the logic to the grammar of faith both negatively and positively. Negatively, we do not possess a single logic that dominates all our thinking; nor is such a foundational logic present in all of our practices.[12] Wittgenstein searched for such a logic in his *Tractatus*. It was the failure of this search that made him see that language did not need this kind of 'metaphysical' supplement in order for it to achieve its purposes. Like Wittgenstein, Holmer brings theological language back from its metaphysical to its everyday use. This should not be confused, as I fear it is even by Holmer, with a rejection of metaphysics altogether. Wittgenstein does not admonish us to eschew metaphysics. He admonishes us to avoid thinking that philosophy should be concerned with finding the 'essence' of being, language, knowledge, etc., by abstracting from the everyday use through some putative 'metaphysical *use*' that claims to have levels above levels or internal and external forms of reference. He critiques a 'meta' that is 'beyond' without being 'in the midst of.'[13]

How do we *use* language metaphysically? When we assume a position outside language, culture, or even being itself that allows us to reflect back on these and offer the definitive conditions for their proper use. This would be nonsense, for it is self-contradiction. We use language to tell us what language cannot do. In opposition to such a metaphysical use, Holmer seeks to use language in the only way we can use it, as we do in everyday life. Everyday use does not set limits on what questions can be reasonably asked a priori. It does not assume we know those limits a priori and must be confined to their proper, albeit limited, sense. That assumes a 'metaphysical use' which only a philosopher could claim to possess. Sometimes those who claim to be most practical and pragmatic are in fact most committed to such a metaphysical use; this is true of Rorty's pragmatism, which is really a metaphysical *use* of language indebted to nominalism.

But Holmer not only gives us a negative development of the logic intrinsic to the grammar of faith; he also provides a positive development, the flipside of the negative one. Theology is more than a reactive discipline within a contested field of power. Theology does not need something else for it to be meaningful. Holmer writes, "There is something terribly wrong with thinking that every linguistic assertion needs explaining and unpack-

---

12. He writes, "Rationality is polymorphic, and we have to learn a greater rather than a lesser sophistication about the use of such a term." Holmer, *The Grammar of Faith*, p. 74.

13. This twofold understanding of metaphysics comes from William Desmond.

ing, as if it were incomplete and partial until placed in a mutually enriching and artificial context of theological or metaphysical discourse."[14] The positive development of the grammar of faith is that the church's language of God is adequate just as it is. If we know how to worship, if we know how to be disciples, then theological language always already achieves its purpose. Only theologians or philosophers find it meaningless until they make it refer to something other than what it already is. But this move is always a subtle capitulation to atheism, for it assumes that how we speak of God doesn't work. It will only work if we can situate it from a level above it.

Holmer shows how attempts to make Christianity meaningful by means of terms such as 'meaning,' 'mythology,' 'symbol,' and 'history' are simply continuations of that metaphysical use of terms from which Wittgenstein's work frees us.[15] This leads him to set forth an interesting theology where we do not simply speak 'about' God, but 'of' God. Theology does not make the term 'God' meaningful. Instead, Holmer asks "that attention be paid to the actual workings of the speech-forms. When they are put to work in their appropriate contexts, then the meanings simply occur." If theologians think their task is to make speaking about God meaningful because without the theologians' help the term 'God' loses its meaning, then the game is up before theologians ever begin. All they can accomplish is to prove correct those who find the term 'God' meaningless. But a reasonable theology never seeks to do this; it doesn't give 'meaning' to our language. To

---

14. Holmer, *The Grammar of Faith*, p. 43.

15. Holmer, *The Grammar of Faith*, p. 47. Like Frei after him, Holmer finds Bultmann's theology unreasonable because of the metaphysics Bultmann must assume to do what he does. Holmer notes of the biblical authors, "But they did not know they were mythological and Bultmann does, and thereby hangs the interesting and dubious tale" (p. 57). Holmer makes the same criticism of Tillich for thinking that speaking of God will be meaningful again if when we use the term 'God' we recognize that we are referring to being. Holmer notes, "It is surely very strange to have to say that you are referring to something when you talk about God, Jesus, and the Holy Spirit" (p. 91). He is also insightful as to the silly use of the term 'symbolic' in much of theology. "That dogma causes us to think that meanings are kinds of events, objects, persons or things lying behind language, and for which language is to stand. Then all of language, verbal and written, is a symbolic activity. But this is a piece of metaphysics, not a matter of common sense or scientific description" (p. 118). Holmer sees this "metaphysical view of language" infecting nearly all the new calls in the modern era for a 'new theology' that can somehow give 'meaning' to the old Christian doctrines. "Thus my inclination is to view the current theological desires for new theological and conceptual systems as largely a consequence of a mistaken view of language" (p. 126).

assume otherwise is to assume a metaphysical use of the concept 'God' that denies our everyday use of this concept, and peers behind it to the 'real' that can identify why those who use the term fail to understand its meaning. It assumes moral or intellectual failure on the part of those who say "Amen!" when they hear, "The word of the Lord," or "The body of Christ." As Holmer puts it, "For having the concept 'God' is also to have a certain set of functions in one's life. If one knows how to use the word *God* in prayer and worship, then one has the concept." This is where the logic and grammar of faith is found. One does not think, but look in order to see it.

Joe R. Jones develops well Holmer's insights.[16] Like Holmer, he draws on Wittgenstein to present the logic of the Christian faith, especially Wittgenstein's distinction between a surface grammar and a depth grammar. He uses this distinction analogous to the medieval use of the formal/material distinction and Turner's extension/intension distinction of meaning. Surface grammar "pertains to the ordinary grammar of the rules of putting different types of words together into intelligible sentences." The depth grammar is "the actual use of the sentences in living speech."[17] This is a fruitful distinction, for it helps us avoid a metaphysical use of language that abstracts from its everyday use by examining the essence of the grammatical form at the expense of how we actually use the language. This is not to deny that every language does have a formal essence as is found in the surface grammar. For instance, if I violate the surface grammar of the previous sentence I could get something like this: "pertains grammar. the former sentences to the words ordinary of The rules of types putting different of together intelligible into." This violation of the surface grammar prohibits meaning. The sentence now becomes nonsensical. The grammatical form is necessary to convey meaning; however, this could tempt us to think that meaning resides only with this form. Once we assume this, then we are tempted to begin a quest that abstracts some essence from the sentence without attending to how the sentence is actually used in everyday life. This was a consistent theme in 'postliberal' thought from Holmer through Frei and Lindbeck. We do not translate language into a proposition which can then be given a truth function in order to have meaning. If

16. Jones explains this term by stating, "I propose there is something called Christian language that can be spoken and used in most of the natural languages." *A Grammar of Christian Faith: Systematic Explorations in Christian Life and Doctrine* (Lanham, Md.: Rowman & Littlefield, 2002), p. 4.

17. Jones, *A Grammar of Christian Faith*, p. 6.

we do that, then we get form without content, the general without the particular. We can give each part of the sentence a logical symbolic form, turn verbs into assertion signs, place it all into an equation and get the logical form of the sentence. From there we can develop truth tables that will allow us to know under what conditions the sentence could be meaningful — even though we would never need to know the material content of the sentence. Wittgenstein's philosophical therapy seeks to heal us from such a truth-conditional theory of meaning and "craving for generality." We cannot discover truth by attending solely to the essence of the surface grammar. Its usefulness is to help us express the depth grammar, which is discovered not only in the logical form of the sentence, but how that logical form can be used — its content, or meaning.

But Jones, like Holmer, turns this Wittgensteinian critique of a metaphysical use of language into a critique of metaphysics itself, and this is unnecessary. This is where 'postliberalism' fails to follow through consistently on the grammar of language. It cannot work without truth. Language itself opens up toward metaphysical transcendentals such that we need not be overly concerned about internal discourses. The act of communication renders them impossible. As we will see, Wittgenstein teaches us that language does not make truth; truth makes possible language even when it can only do so in and through language.

Jones jettisons the tradition of the divine names by wrongly understanding them as metaphysical attributes that somehow lose the biblical grammar. He wants to keep closer to the biblical grammar than he thinks the Christian tradition has done. Here we might be trapped within a language that does not open up to something that exceeds it. For instance, he follows much of modern theology in rejecting God's immutability and impassibility. He speaks of "the grammar of God's becoming" as the only "realistic" Christian speech that can refer to the incarnation. He writes, "This grammar is explicit if we are realistic about God's having an interactive triune life with the world, even to the point of becoming incarnate in a human life."[18] To make sense of this he distinguishes God's 'actuality' from God's 'essence,' and argues that the former changes and suffers while the latter does not.[19] "In actuality God can change, become, be responsive to,

18. Jones, *A Grammar of Christian Faith*, p. 202.
19. Jones writes, "While God's essence is itself immutable and does not change, God's actuality can change, become, can live." *A Grammar of Christian Faith*, p. 207.

be affected by, suffer with, and be in real relation to that which is other than God."[20] This not only shows the influence of Moltmann's work on Jones's theology, but it also shows his rejection of the theological tradition of the divine names, particularly as Aquinas develops it.

Aquinas teaches that no 'real relation' exists between God and creation. For Aquinas, such a 'real relation' would turn creation into a fourth hypostasis of the Trinity or turn God into a creature. It would deny the Triune nature of God and turn God into a quaternity. Christians do not worship creation. Aquinas's language makes explicit what all Christians do in worship. Jones never intends to give the creation this status. He rejects a process metaphysics that would make God necessarily dependent upon creation. But he nevertheless calls into question the longstanding Catholic tradition, taught by Augustine, Anselm, and Aquinas, that God's essence is God's existence.

Jones, like Holmer, finds this tradition too 'metaphysical.' Holmer referred to Aquinas's 'theism' and charged that it "made all of learning appear to depend in subtle ways upon something metaphysical."[21] He thinks the linguistic turn avoids this metaphysics, but his use of metaphysics is confined to metaphysics 1, 2, or possibly a critique of metaphysics 5. He fails to see the close relationship between the tradition of the divine names, an adequate account of the 'grammar of faith,' and metaphysics 3 and 4.

Jones applies Wittgenstein's linguistic therapy to theology, as did Holmer before him, and suggests that the tradition of the divine names prevents us from seeing clearly the depth grammar of the faith. If Jones is correct, then we should reject that language. To speak well the depth grammar that Christ is Lord is more important than speaking a surface grammar of God's immutability and impassibility, which is what everyone once called 'God.' But the 'surface grammar' that teaches us first to recognize God's essence is God's existence, that God has no real relations with creation, and that God is simple, perfect, immutable, infinite, eternal, and a unity is what allows us to speak well the depth grammar that Jesus Christ is Lord and that God is Triune. Once we lose the former, we will lose the ability to speak well of God, for we will lose the sheer gratuity of the incarnation and its 'logic,' as well as the reason found in creation and the impor-

20. Jones, *A Grammar of Christian Faith*, p. 208.
21. Holmer, *The Grammar of Faith*, p. 160.

tance of the Creator/creature distinction. If God is in God's own being what humanity is — mutable and passible — the incarnation is unnecessary, a decorative symbol at best. It is not a new creation. Because of the depth grammar, the 'res,' we are led to the surface grammar, to this 'mode' of signifying God. We have not transcended the former when we use the latter.

The surface grammar of the 'metaphysical' tradition of Aquinas has an everyday and not a metaphysical use. It does not ask us to abstract from the event of the incarnation and our use of the concept God in Christian worship in order to stand outside of it and ask what the objective metaphysical conditions are by which God can become human. Instead, it makes explicit what we implicitly do when we give Jesus the 'name' and worship him as God, finding him to be the visible face of the invisible God. The divine names tradition assumes that God is not an object in the world over which we can have control by affecting God in any kind of necessary relation. This is metaphysics. It is the inevitable opening of a sign that exceeds its context (metaphysics 3), or the beyond that interrupts immanence "in the middle" (metaphysics 4). Inasmuch as the adoption of the linguistic turn in theology fails to recognize the need for this metaphysics, fails to see how in this sense theology needs philosophy even as it exceeds it, it will fail to speak well of God.

Matthew Levering develops this understanding of metaphysics to show how speaking well of the Triune God "requires that theologians reject the alleged opposition between scriptural and metaphysical modes of reflection without conflating the two modes."[22] They have related but distinct starting points. Both emerge from the tradition of the divine names beginning with Exodus 3, but "metaphysical inquiries" begin with "creaturely realities" and "inquire into what it would mean to be 'not a creature.'"[23] If we did not have the irruption of the divine name we would not know God is not a creature, and we might not realize that language has this ability to speak about something other than its own context. We would make God a being, and not the One Who Is.

Scripture and metaphysics are not in opposition but mutually reinforcing. One begins with creation to speak of that which is not creature

22. Matthew Levering, *Scripture and Metaphysics: Aquinas and the Renewal of Trinitarian Theology* (Oxford: Blackwell, 2004), p. 2.
23. Levering, *Scripture and Metaphysics*, p. 7.

(Aquinas). The other begins with the One who is not creature to learn to speak of creation (Anselm). We do not only use creation to refer to God, but assuming God is that 'more' which is to be discovered in the 'via eminentiae,' we can also learn to speak of *creation* by referring to that which it is not, the simple, infinite, impassible, immutable, perfect, eternal Triune God who has no needs creation satisfies or exploits; who does not need any real relation with creation because God is always already complete through the subsistent relations that constitute God's very unity. The first commandment given to Moses requires that we do metaphysics.

If the Yale school confuses Wittgenstein's therapy for overcoming a metaphysical use of language with overcoming metaphysics itself, this is a serious weakness. This may be a temptation Wittgenstein poses to us if we read him as a pragmatist more concerned with action than contemplation. As Levering also notes, once we begin to ask what use is the Holy Trinity, we tend to divide Scripture and metaphysics, wrongly thinking that the proper answer will be action rather than contemplation. We are then tempted to turn knowledge and speech of God into an instrumental value that is good for something rather than the intrinsic good that makes all other things good. Metaphysics helps us avoid this temptation.

Theology is similar to metaphysics. That should not be denied. If, as Holmer and the theological tradition have always argued, God is not an object in the world, then the concept 'God' requires 'metaphysics,' and theologians should not shy away from it. But a metaphysical *use* of language claims to give the human subject a reference point outside of language that sets limits to what language can do. This is why only those philosophers and theologians who think they have a metaphysical use of language could proclaim an end to metaphysics.

Jones argues that the metaphysical tradition of theism improperly sets forth the grammar of faith. It is part of the "platonic problem" whereby "the unchangeable (the essence) is more real than the changeable." He writes, "This grammatical development in the church's discourse makes it difficult, if not impossible, to talk consistently about God acting in creation, history, becoming incarnate, being affected by the world — matters that seem important to the biblical witness."[24] But this misses something essential to the biblical witness; it is precisely this metaphysical language that allows us to speak well of *God* acting in creation and history and becoming

24. Jones, *A Grammar of Christian Faith,* p. 206.

incarnate without ceasing to be who God is. Because we receive the gift of the divine name, we can also set forth an adequate metaphysics of creation. For Aquinas, contra Avicenna, creation is not a preexisting essence that receives existence as an accident. Essence and existence are really distinct, but God creates without a prior essence to which he gives existence. God in God's self is not really distinct in essence and existence because God is simple. For this reason God is 'pure act,' which obviously cannot be some kind of static aloof being waiting to be moved by creation.

2. The Linguistic Overturn of Metaphysics

Christian theology has a stake in asking metaphysical questions and should not encourage any tradition of philosophy that finds reason's maturity in walking away from them. To walk away from such questions altogether is to confuse a critique of an improper metaphysical use of language with the language of metaphysics itself. The latter is necessary for Christian theology. Must it then reject analytic philosophy and the linguistic turn if it is to recover the necessary task of metaphysics? David Hart seems to think so. He finds promise in continental philosophy for theology, but analytic is at most something theologians need to overcome. He states that "modern continental philosophy is very much the misbegotten child of theology, indeed a kind of secularized theology. . . ."[25] But this is a reason for theological engagement with it. Continental philosophy needs theology in order to overcome its "internal struggle against itself." The consanguinity between them allows theology to be a resource to bring peace to philosophy's turmoil. "Theology," he states, "is always already involved in the Continental tradition — its longings and nostalgias, its rebellions and haunting memories, its interminable flight from the Christian rationality that gave it life." But for Hart no such "natural kinship" can be found be-

25. Hart, *The Beauty of the Infinite: The Aesthetics of Christian Truth* (Grand Rapids: Eerdmans, 2003), p. 30. Hart finds the similarities between modern continental philosophy and theology in that philosophy's "governing themes everywhere declare its filiation — ontology is concerned with the being of beings, phenomenology with truth as manifestation and the unity of knowledge and being, hermeneutics with interpretation and the transmission of texts; the questions of transcendence and immanence, the moral law, the transcendentals, the meaning of being, substance and event, time and eternity, freedom and fate, and the logic of history remain the essential matters of Continental thought."

tween theology and analytic philosophy. He writes, "There are theologians who believe theology has something to learn from and contribute to the analytic tradition of philosophy (here I reserve judgment), but even if this is so the encounter would be a purely apologetic enterprise; there is no natural kinship."[26]

R. R. Reno and Fergus Kerr are two theologians who find much more than a "purely apologetic enterprise" in theology's engagement with the analytic tradition. For Reno, theologians have been too preoccupied with continental philosophy, especially in its deconstructive mode. Analytic philosophy can help theology recover its 'foundations.' He writes, "analytic philosophy is unequivocally and fundamentally a force for the strengthening of truth, not its weakening."[27]

Likewise, Fergus Kerr finds the dismissal of analytic philosophy among contemporary theologians shortsighted. He writes, "Analytic philosophy — unbelievably — is regularly dismissed as nothing but 'talk about talk', or deplored as reluctant or even impotent to discuss the Big Questions (evil, death, the meaning of life, etc.). Worse still, in the judgment of many Christian theologians, and Catholics especially, it is, in John Haldane's words, 'something to be avoided as a serious threat to one's grasp of God, goodness and truth.'"[28] Kerr seeks to rectify this mistaken view of analytical philosophy, encouraging theologians to spend as much time with Frege, Russell, Wittgenstein, Quine, Davidson, and "their followers" as they do with Nietzsche, Heidegger, Levinas, Derrida, "and their kin."

Whether we find analytic philosophy productive or unproductive in theology depends, in part, on theology and metaphysics' relationship to the linguistic turn. The linguistic turn treats metaphysical questions as problems of language; sometimes this causes philosophers to think they can simply walk away from metaphysics. Other times it causes them to present a version of metaphysics that is so policed it can no longer ask substantive questions. But the linguistic turn, like analytic philosophy, is not some monolith one is simply for or against. Charles Taylor identifies two important traditions of the linguistic turn. The first is the 'designative' and

26. Hart, *The Beauty of the Infinite*, p. 30.
27. R. R. Reno, "Theology's Continental Captivity," *First Things* 162 (April 2006): 33.
28. Fergus Kerr, "Aquinas and Analytic Philosophy: Natural Allies?" *Modern Theology* 20:1 (January 2004): 123.

the second the 'expressivist.'[29] The first traps the pursuit of wisdom within language and confines it to immanence where language and its relation to truth are reduced to pointing. The second recognizes that metaphysics cannot be done by abstracting from language, but by turning to it. The first is found in the nominalist turn that undergirds some analytic philosophy, especially its 'verificationist' strands. The second is found in an 'expressivist' tradition that can also be found in analytic philosophy. The first inevitably turns theology over to the deliverances of secular reason; the second can help theologians recognize the truth of theology.

The designative tradition runs from Hobbes through Locke and Condillac. Taylor also finds a significant residue of this tradition in Quine, Davidson, and Rorty. Here language primarily designates objects in the world; language places us outside the objects, trying to represent them to ourselves as best we can. Taylor states, "Like all naturalistic theories, these theories are framed as theories elaborated by an observer about an object observed but not participated in."[30] It assumes a use of language based on quantitative judgments that are non-subject dependent. Such a philosophy of language, emerging from nominalism, contributes to a mechanistic universe and leaves it disenchanted. This also produces a politics characterized by the two dominant modern notions of equality and direct access. In contrast, premodern societies were 'vertical,' where politics was a participation within Ideas to which no one had direct access, but each person's or group's access was mediated through others. Taylor explains the different form of access found in modern political arrangements: "The principle of a modern horizontal society is radically different. Each of us is equidistant from the center; we are immediate to the whole. We have moved from a hierarchical order of personalized links to an impersonal egalitarian one; from a vertical world of mediated access to horizontal, direct access societies."[31] This has a correlate in a designative understanding of language.

The designative tradition also remains committed to the primacy of epistemology. Charles Taylor notes that the Davidson-Rorty approach leaves us trapped in an unnecessary epistemological muddle, for this trajectory of the linguistic turn represents a 'designative-instrumental' un-

29. Charles Taylor, *Human Agency and Language: Philosophical Papers 1* (Cambridge: Cambridge University Press, 2004), p. 255.

30. Taylor, *Human Agency and Language*, p. 255.

31. Taylor, *Modern Social Imaginaries* (Durham, N.C.: Duke University Press, 2004), p. 158.

derstanding of linguistic meaning that assumes a mediational epistemology. Language functions by 'pointing'; this refers to that, which is a legacy of nominalism.

For Taylor, the designative theory arises from medieval nominalism. It "rejected the discourse-thought model of the real. It denied that there are real essences of things, or universals. True, we think in general terms. But this is not because the world exists in general terms as it were; on the contrary, everything that is is a particular. The universal is not a feature of the world, but an effect of our language. We apply words to classes of objects, which we thus gather into units; that is what makes general terms."[32] Language, then, only has an instrumental role in that it refers to 'objects' primarily as particulars. Language does not express 'reality' so much as it collects and points to it. The result is a scientific approach to language that dissolves it of any mystery and culminates in an effort to "illuminate meaning by tracing the correlations between words and things — or, in more contemporary guise, between sentences and their truth conditions."[33] We find ourselves confronted with a sharp internal/external divide that must be correlated.

Taylor identifies the Davidson-Rorty approach as 'neo-designative':

> This theory can be called 'neo-designative' because it attempts to give an account of meaning in terms of the truth-conditions of sentences. These truth conditions are observable states of affairs in the world; hence once again we have the basic *démarche* of a theory which tries to explain the meaning of language in terms of the relation of linguistic elements to extra-linguistic reality.[34]

Taylor invites us to give up altogether any attempt to "explain language in terms of something else." Once this is done, we can abandon a mediational epistemology and recognize the mystery that always surrounds language. Then truth does not look for the conditions by which language refers to reality; instead truth is manifest through music, art, facial expressions, liturgy, etc. Sentences are much too limiting to be the primary vehicles bearing the weight of truth.

---

32. Taylor, *Human Agency and Language*, p. 218. For how Taylor traces this to nominalism see p. 224. Given this description of nominalism, it is easy to see how it understands meaning primarily as extensional.

33. Taylor, *Human Agency and Language*, p. 221.

34. Taylor, *Human Agency and Language*, p. 243.

Taylor contrasts the designative-instrumental tradition with the 'expressive-constitutive' emerging from Herder, Hamann, and Humboldt, a tradition that draws on a more Augustinian understanding of language.

> So the paradigm and model of our deploying signs is God's creation. But now God's creation is to be understood expressively. His creatures manifest his logos in embodying it; and they manifest the logos as fully as it can be manifest in the creaturely medium. There can be no more fundamental designative relation, precisely because everything is a sign. This notion is nonsense on a designative view. For words can only have designative meaning if there is something else, other than words or signs, which they designate. The notion that everything is a sign only makes sense on an expressive view.[35]

The expressive-constitutive theory 'manifests' meaning without assuming that such manifestation relies on something more basic such as pointing or designating reality. But in so doing it also assumes a certain mystery to language that the designative seeks to demystify by rendering language more transparent, often through the constraints of the principle of verification.[36]

Taylor places Wittgenstein in the expressive-constitutive tradition. This makes sense, for Wittgenstein argues that language is useful, but that its usefulness is not what makes it true. If we think that the usefulness of language is the condition for truth, then we will miss his most important contribution to language and truth and place him in the tradition of the linguistic turn emanating from Hobbes, Locke, and Condillac. That would be unfortunate, because Wittgenstein explicitly avoids such an instrumentalizing of language as the basis for truth. He states, "Then do you want to say that 'being true' means: being usable (or useful) — No, not that; but that it can't be said of the series of natural numbers — any more than of our language — that it is true, but: that it is usable, and above all, is used."[37] Language is not what is true in Wittgenstein; it is useful. But language is useful because it expresses truth. It does this unproblematically,

35. Taylor, *Human Agency and Language*, p. 223.

36. Taylor's designative/expressive bears a strong family resemblance to Albert Borgmann's apodictic/deictic in his *Technology and the Character of Our Communities* (Chicago: University of Chicago Press, 1987).

37. *Remarks on the Foundation of Mathematics*, I, para. 405, quoted in David Pears, *The False Prison*, vol. II (Oxford: Clarendon Press, 1988), p. 451.

but it does it in such a way that we cannot peer behind it to some universal, extra-linguistic criterion called 'truth.' This might suggest an idiosyncratic interpretation of Wittgenstein, who also wrote, "the tendency of all men who ever tried to write or talk Ethics or Religion was to run against the boundaries of language."[38] Isn't language a boundary against which religion and ethics falter? Isn't this what puts an end to metaphysics?

David Pears begins his two-volume treatment of Wittgenstein with the argument that Wittgenstein's work, like Kant's, is 'critical' in that it recognizes "the human intellect is a limited instrument and philosophy's task is to turn its back on itself and make it discover its own limitation and then mark them in a self-abasing but salutary way."[39] This critical task of philosophy is accomplished by self-criticism because "there is no higher discipline set above philosophy" for Wittgenstein.[40] Pears could be interpreted as suggesting that in showing us the limits of philosophy Wittgenstein shows us the limits of what can be reasonably thought. If this is the proper interpretation (and I don't think it is), then it raises the question why we need Wittgenstein's work at all; why would Kant's critical task not fit the bill?

Is the proper interpretation of Pears's and Wittgenstein's work that the limits of philosophy are the limits of language and these limits are the limits of reason? Do we then know these limits? If so, they will also be assumed to be the limits for any pursuit of wisdom. Then the heart of theology, which is as Turner notes that we can make inferences across logical incommensurables, is a priori ruled out. Does Wittgenstein's philosophy allow for such inferences? The *Tractatus* seems to rule them out. Wittgenstein states, "The limits of my language mean the limits of my world" (5.6), and "We cannot think what we cannot think: so what we cannot think we cannot say either" (5.61). Does this rule out theology? I can speak the word 'God,' but Wittgenstein's point here is not the obvious one that I can speak about things that do not exist. I can speak of unicorns, the bald King of France, and the victorious Chicago Cubs. Wittgenstein's argument is against solipsism; it suggests how inappropriate it is for the solipsist to say,

---

38. From Wittgenstein's *Lectures on Ethics*, cited in Scott Davis's "Wittgenstein and the Recovery of Virtue," in *Grammar and Grace*, p. 175.

39. Pears, *The False Prison: A Study of the Development of Wittgenstein's Philosophy*, vol. I (Oxford: Clarendon, 1987), p. 3.

40. Pears, *The False Prison*, vol. I, p. 3. This claim marks a crucial distinction between Wittgenstein and Aquinas on the consequences of the limits of philosophy.

"The world has this in it, and this, but not that" (5.61). In other words, if language sets the limits of my world, then I don't have an ego that exists outside it which determines the limits. I am fully ensconced in the world just as language itself is.[41] My ego does not limit the world. This does not rule out metaphysics and theology, rendering them unintelligible non-sense about which we cannot say anything reasonable. Such an interpretation would make Wittgenstein Kant, where God becomes at best a sublimity beyond representation about which nothing reasonable can be said. But recall Wittgenstein's comment in the *Philosophical Remarks:* "Time and again the attempt is made to use language to limit the world and set it in relief — but it can't be done."[42]

3. Conflicting Interpretations of Wittgenstein

Does language limit what can reasonably be said? Or does it open up the possibility of showing more than what can be designated (metaphysics 3)? Two conflicting interpretations of Wittgenstein can lead in either of these directions. This is why the designative tradition as well as the expressive one can claim Wittgenstein as an ally (as we shall see in the next chapter on truth where the deflationists claim him for their strongly designative project). The designative would interpret him through the statement in his preface to *Tractatus:* "What can be said at all can be said clearly, and what we cannot talk about we must pass over in silence." The expressive would interpret him through his letter to Ludwig Ficker, "My work consists of two parts: the one presented here plus all that I have *not* written. And it is precisely this second part that is the important one. My book draws limits to the sphere of the ethical from the inside as it were, and I am convinced that this is the ONLY rigorous way of drawing those limits."[43] If what is most important is what we cannot say, what we must pass over in silence, then how would we know what the most important sphere of ethics, let alone religion, is? This would be simply another version of a Kantian "policing of the sublime." But Pears notes that in the *Tractatus* "the possibility of saying

41. I am indebted to Pears, *The False Prison*, vol. I, p. 164, in part for this interpretation.
42. Pears, *The False Prison*, vol. I, p. 175.
43. James Klagge, ed. *Wittgenstein: Biography and Philosophy* (Cambridge: Cambridge University Press, 2001), p. 86.

some things in factual discourse depends on the actuality of other things which cannot be said."[44] This assumes a kind of transcendental argument that recognizes language always shows more than it designates.

There is a key difference here between reading Wittgenstein as setting forth a verification principle and reading him as challenging any claim for a private language. The former would rule out the meaningfulness of theology and lead to something like the failed logical positivists who wrongly saw Wittgenstein as an ally. The latter not only gives space for theology, it shows how it is always already meaningful — 'theology as grammar.' The difference between the 'verificationist' and 'contra private language' interpretations is the difference between representation and public accessibility. Representation assumes language does one thing and seeks to tailor all epistemic justification to that single thing. Language designates a reality outside language. We have a strong internal/external distinction. Public accessibility assumes language has a variety of uses which can only be communally situated, and learning those uses is itself diverse forms of epistemic justification. The former assumes a bad kind of rationalism where everything is reduced and verified by a single method. The latter assumes the pursuit of wisdom where no single method can be had. Wittgenstein's work assumes the latter. As Pears notes, "Learning is possible only if there is a standard of success which the pupil can apply to what he does in order to improve his performance. . . . When Wittgenstein's position is set out like this, it can be seen to survive the objection that it relies on the questionable assumption that meaning extends no further than actual verifiability."[45]

Charles Travis helps explain this by referring to Wittgenstein's "public access principle." He writes, "Any fact relevant to fixing W's semantics must be a fact which an indefinite number of judges could grasp and properly appreciate."[46] Public accessibility is neither objectivity nor a transcendental a priori. It rejects any claim that language is private and therefore radically incommensurable with other so-called fideistic private languages. But it does not then assume complete translatability. The public accessibility principle does not say any individual or community could

---

44. Pears, *The False Prison*, vol. I, p. 143.

45. Pears, *The False Prison*, vol. II, p. 344.

46. Travis, *The Uses of Sense: Wittgenstein's Philosophy of Language* (Oxford: Oxford University Press, 1989), pp. 75-77.

grasp and appreciate Wittgenstein's semantics; instead "reasonable judges" give meaning its publicity. Reasonable judges do not have some private language of expertise upon which they draw; they are reasonable judges because of what they can do with our everyday language. Wittgenstein states, "When I talk about language (words, sentences, etc.) I must speak the language of every day. Is this language somehow too coarse and material for what we want to say? *Then how is another to be constructed* — And how strange that we should be able to do anything at all with the one we have?"[47] It is on this basis that he rejects the language of first- and second-order discourses.

Reasonable judges use everyday language to express meaning, which could not be expressed without the language even when the meaning must exceed the literal signification of the terms employed. Take, for instance, the statement, "God is eternal." Such a statement cannot bear its truth if we are confined to the designative sense. The sentence has a beginning in space and time, which its truth does not. We cannot verify this statement by pointing to, or indicating, its object. Nevertheless, we know what it is saying even when what it says exceeds how we say it. If we are confined to the immanence of the grammatical form, we will lose the 'res' it signifies. The fact that what it says exceeds the means by which it says it poses no problem for its everyday use. It only poses a problem for philosophers, as we saw with Derrida's 'deconstruction' of the divine name when he stated that the 'I am' could only be "the admission of a mortal."[48] Derrida makes God's speech in time an impossibility. But this assumes a univocity between God's speech and ours that would either require the reduction of God to a mortal or the loss of speech that could adequately express God. It assumes the designative tradition with its metaphysical and methodological nominalism. Methodological nominalism and a designative-instrumentalist view of language cannot give an account of how we can reasonably speak of God, and so it renders such speech arational. But that denies what most of us can recognize, believers or nonbelievers — if God is, then God is eternal, even though we have no idea how to formulate the relationship between eternity and time (as David Burrell reminds us). But that does not mean we are speaking nonsense.

47. Wittgenstein, *Philosophical Investigations,* p. 120. See also Travis, *The Uses of Sense,* p. 337.

48. Hart, *Trespass of the Sign* (New York: Fordham University Press, 2000), p. 287.

Thomas's 'modus significandi'/'res significata' distinction expresses this mystery. He recognizes that we cannot stand outside our mode of signifying and create some second-order discourse that gives us a critical distance upon it in order to point to the thing signified. No such second-order discourse is possible. Instead, reasonable judges show us the meaning of language through and in language, not by standing outside it and getting an objective position against it or distance over it. They, too, only function within a community.

In no sense does this suggest that a standard of success is simply what a community decides, for that would be another version of solipsism or semantic skepticism. Pears distances Wittgenstein from this kind of fideism. "The appeal to the community is not final, because factual language, whether spoken by a solitary person or by millions, has to preserve the constancy required if yesterday's predictions are to come true today."[49] Essential for meaning is the virtue of constancy. This is the heart of the argument against any private language. Standards of success for using language well cannot be solipsistic.[50] This is what allows us to obey or disobey a rule. If there is such a thing, then something like a private language is finally without meaning. There are always "agreements in judgments" that cannot be arbitrary. They will be based in a form of life which is not simply a voluntarism — by an individual or a community — but has "stabilizing resources."[51]

Pears finds Wittgenstein "following two parallel lines of investigation." The first refuses to concede a space for the 'ego' outside the world which can function as a "private world or microcosm" in order to secure meaning. This would be true of the ego of an individual or a community. The second is "a critique of attempts to use sense-data as the limiting baseline of such a world."[52] The first would be a form of Cartesianism (and Pears would add Platonism) and the second empiricism. Both produce a

---

49. Pears, *The False Prison*, vol. II, p. 369.

50. Wittgenstein shows this in sec. 258, p. 92 of the *Investigations* where he correlates the sign "S" for a particular sensation and then suggests keeping a diary every time one has this sensation. He writes, "Can I point to the sensation? Not in the ordinary sense. But I speak, or write the sign down, and at the same time I concentrate my attention on the sensation — and so as it were, point to it inwardly. — But what is this ceremony for? For that is all it seems to be!"

51. Pears, *The False Prison*, vol. II, p. 369.

52. Pears, *The False Prison*, vol. II, p. 235.

'private language' that cannot be reasonably defended. Pears argues, "When he [the solipsist] tried to set himself up in a private world based on his ego, he would lose the discriminating references to individuals on which his theory depended; and when he tried to set himself up in a private world limited by the line of his own mental sense-data, he would lose the capacity to register their different types, and so he could not preserve his own identity in complete detachment from everything in the physical world."[53] Solipsism presumes a mind-world problem that cannot be remedied, because it is not a problem that actually exists. Only when we seek a kind of certainty based on the secure place of the ego separate from the world can such a problem arise. But only this ego could possibly know the limits of language the way the verificationist principle claims to know them.

4. Aquinas's Higher Discipline

Aquinas and Wittgenstein share a commitment against both Cartesianism and empiricism for the embodied character of all human knowing. We are within the 'world' and never set apart from it in some secure place of private meaning. Language shows us this, and it is both the promise and problem for speaking well about God. But language does not trap us inside it; that is the problem from which Wittgenstein frees us. In fact, as Pears recognizes, language is for Wittgenstein "a late arrival on a busy scene of long-established activities."[54] Nothing in Wittgenstein would prohibit Denys Turner's point that the incarnation shows us that logical inference works across incommensurables, even if we can only explain how language does not rule this out and not how language makes it possible. Aquinas's understanding of language makes more sense after Wittgenstein. As Incandela notes, "For these reasons we can read Aquinas more correctly after Wittgenstein."[55] But there is an important difference between them. Although Aquinas and Wittgenstein both recognized that an essential part of the philosophical task is to show its limitations and how signs normally exceed themselves, Aquinas, unlike Wittgenstein, thought there was a discipline higher than philosophy — sacred doctrine.

53. Pears, *The False Prison,* vol. II, p. 235.
54. Pears, *The False Prison,* vol. I, p. 55.
55. *Grammar and Grace,* p. 45.

Theologians must be careful in drawing upon a philosophy of language to express the unique logic of the incarnation; we should not place it within a philosophy that a priori states that language cannot speak of God because God is not an object in the world. If language primarily 'designates,' then the incarnation will make no sense. Charles Taylor's analysis of the linguistic turns is helpful here. With the expressivist linguistic turn, language actually constitutes the things it expresses. Articulation and identification go together.[56] A Marian theology will help us make sense of this; it requires a place for human participation and contribution even in the incarnation. The Word expresses itself by giving itself over into human hands. This can never be private. Balthasar recognized this important relationship between publicity, language, truth, and the incarnation when he wrote,

> In itself the thing of transcendent beauty, the miracle of Being (revealing itself in all existing things), is a 'holy mystery made manifest': of its own essence (as the Good) it tends toward public manifestation, simply by being always public, open to all; in this sense it is the true.[57]

Because language is never private, Charles Taylor notes, it "serves to place some matter out in the open between interlocutors . . . to put things in public space."[58] The constitutive dimension of language "provides the medium through which some of our most important concerns, the characteristically human concerns, can impinge on us at all." This makes possible judgments and standards. If language primarily designates, the only judgment is the adequacy of representation. The best we can then do is to find coherence among the representations. This could never make sense of the logic of the incarnation, for its 'grammar' consistently denies that God can be *designated* by Jesus' flesh alone. This would be to confuse and mix the two natures.

Although the constitutive dimension "puts things in public space," it does not do so in terms of an independent criterion, but only in a particular language. The language we use matters in the constitution of theology, politics, and morality. This requires a politics that is subject-dependent. Taylor points out that "people of very different cultural vocabularies have quite

---

56. Taylor states that "coming to articulate our sense of some matter is inseparable from coming to identify its features." Taylor, *Human Agency and Language*, p. 256.

57. Balthasar, *Theo-Drama II: Dramatis Personae: Man in God*, trans. Graham Harrison (San Francisco: Ignatius, 1990), p. 32.

58. Taylor, *Human Agency and Language*, p. 259.

different kinds of feelings, aspirations, sensibilities, experience different moral and other demands, and so on."[59] This means that judgments will be based on "qualitative contrasts" that are subject-dependent. A qualitative contrast assumes we must make judgments in which who the subject is matters. This would contrast with Rawls's notion of the original position where the distribution of political goods is independent of the subject.

Qualitative contrasts became problematic after the epistemological turn in the seventeenth century, which sought to produce morality along lines similar to the model used in the natural sciences. It ruled out qualitative contrasts for two reasons. First, for qualitative judgments, who the subject is matters and we were now supposed to be equal individuals each of whom, based on their individual dignity, had an immediate access to goods, including knowledge. Second, morality based on qualitative contrast requires inter-subjective judgment. But after the epistemological turn, subjects became individuals who could be placed within a formal equivalency. This supposedly made possible a universal and neutral objective quantification that would adjudicate among competing positions without making any qualitative contrasts. Instead we could have independent criteria for making judgments. All cultures, all persons, all societies, all 'religions,' all forms of life were to be treated equally and assessed by criteria that were independent of these forms of life. Such an understanding of judgment can only make sense in terms of the designative tradition of the linguistic turn. It inevitably leads to the direct, equal access society; it is the basis for political liberalism.

An expressive-constitutive philosophy of language falls on hard times in modernity, for it assumes a politics, morality, and ontology in opposition to much of that which modernity developed. The expressivist tradition assumed a universe based on 'Ideas,' in which creatures participated at various levels. This participation had to be mediated, and thus it bore a necessary hierarchy that often (although not necessarily, I would argue) tended toward patriarchy. Taylor notes, "As a peasant, one was linked to a lord who in turn held from the king. One was a member of a municipal corporation which had a standing in the kingdom or exercised some function in a Parliament with its recognized status and so on."[60] Although such a politics holds little promise for us today, it also recognized a depth to lan-

59. Taylor, *Human Agency and Language*, p. 269.
60. Taylor, *Modern Social Imaginaries*, p. 159.

guage, which was thrown out with this politics. Language participated in a hierarchical richness that assumed a mysterious, supernatural liturgical reality that was mediated in and through the church. The designative flattens this reality. The expressivist-constitutive linguistic turn assumes a realist metaphysics, just as the designative turn assumes a nominalist one.

The linguistic turn does not put an end to metaphysics, but poses a stark question — which turn? Which metaphysics? Adopting one of these linguistic turns brings with it different accounts of truth and politics. Because Christianity is not mythological and the distinction between creature and Creator is never to be violated, the logic of the incarnation cannot be well expressed if we think of language in terms of designation. Jesus is God, but divinity is not humanity. This expresses the great truth and mystery of the Christian faith. We can use language to express it, but we cannot point to what it designates. Chalcedon teaches this and it is reasonable if we think of language as 'expressive-constitutive,' but not if we think of it as designative. This will mean that truth is not simple representation, but a way that expresses more than a surface, empirical reality can allow. We will not abandon 'correspondence' or realism, but the task, as Wittgenstein understood, will be "realism without empiricism."[61] Empiricism is a great temptation. It seems practical, concrete, and material. It is bound up with verificationist theories of meaning that seem to allow us to determine whether we are actually saying anything at all. But, as Fergus Kerr notes, "If we cannot mean what we say unless we have a way of verifying it, the constraints upon what we assert as true or false may drive us to remain within the limits of empiricism and, in religion, silence us altogether."[62]

In the designative tradition, the linguistic turn polices what language can do such that it renders theology meaningless. The linguistic turn in the expressivist tradition does not have the same effect. It can help us understand the truth of theological language. For instance, John P. O'Callaghan finds common cause with the modern 'linguistic turn' in what it seeks to overcome. Attributing knowledge of things to internal, mental representations produced an intractable problem of "epistemological skepticism and anti-realism." The 'linguistic turn' overcomes this problem because it challenges the assumption of "the privacy of the inner mediating objects of

---

61. Wittgenstein wrote, "Not empiricism and yet realism in philosophy, that is the hardest thing." Quoted in Kerr, *Theology after Wittgenstein* (Oxford: Blackwell, 1986), p. 131.
62. Kerr, *Theology after Wittgenstein*, p. 130.

mental attention." It does so by recognizing that all such objects are "social and public."[63] The latter has the advantage of 'meaning holism,' which recognizes that a word has meaning only in the context of a larger whole, which is socially and publicly constructed (an advantage we owe to Kant and Frege). Meaning holism challenges logical positivism, which could not escape the modern epistemological problem of mental representationalism. However, O'Callaghan rightly asks, what is finally gained by transferring "a private artifact in an individual mind, like an idea" to a "public artifact in a social mind, like a word?"[64] O'Callaghan thinks this simply replaces the problem of epistemological skepticism with semantic skepticism. If we have no public access to the 'idea' in the privacy of the mind, then the turn to language raises the question whether we have a public access to a 'word' that has been socially constructed? Have we merely broadened the notion of 'mind' from that of an individual to that of a collective?

The problem of epistemological and semantic skepticism is a problem of the tendency toward fideism.[65] To assume that all language functions in an identical way, one which would require an inner translation into some kind of 'mentalese,' is the fideism that affirms the dogmatic character of the tradition of 'mental representationalism.' The philosopher or theologian who affirms this must 'know' how the 'cryptographer' in the mind works. Semantic skepticism does not have this dogmatic problem. It need not construct a language no one speaks ('mentalese') in order to solve the problem of reference. However, the problem of reference does not disappear, for we still have to account for how it is that we translate from one language to another. That we do this is relatively uncontroversial. Yet how we can translate, and exactly what we do when we do it, is a controversial matter.

Theology assumes translation across specific languages because most Christians assume and confess that the God we identify and worship is the same God across differences in language and culture synchronically and diachronically.[66] As long as we confess this, we cannot be fideists. It is only

63. John P. O'Callaghan, *Thomist Realism and the Linguistic Turn* (Notre Dame, Ind.: University of Notre Dame Press, 2003), pp. 8-9.
64. O'Callaghan, *Thomist Realism and the Linguistic Turn*, p. 9.
65. Fideism always assumes a private language that cannot be made public. Since this is impossible, it is tempted toward violence to prevent its inevitable publicity and accountability.
66. I recognize that some contextual theologians claim their account of God cannot be translated outside their culture. I am unconvinced and think this shows the tendency to-

if we claim an impermeable membrane to our culture and its language that fideism could arise. But this works against the logic of Christian faith. In fact, I do not need to speak or know some 'original' language to know that I worship and can identify the same Triune God as Paul, Athanasius, Julian of Norwich, Aquinas, and other Christians who speak diverse languages in various cultures. If this is true, then it assumes 'translation' across languages. For Aquinas this is possible because language works neither like the 'Platonism' of the early Russell nor like the empiricism of the logical positivists. Every word cannot be made to refer to some object, whether that object be an 'idea' internal to the subject, or an idea or thing external. This is not how language functions when we speak of God.

Aquinas drew on Aristotle's 'semantic triangle' in his *On Interpretation* in order to explain this:

> Words spoken are symbols or signs of affections or impressions of the soul; written words are the signs of words spoken. As writing, so also is speech not the same for all races of men. But the mental affections (παθήματα τῆς ψυχῆς) themselves, of which these words are primarily signs, are the same for the whole of mankind, as are also the objects of which those affections are representations or likenesses, images, copies.[67]

Cooke's translation easily lends itself to Putnam's concern about the 'cryptographic model' of language when he translates 'passions of the soul' as mental affections. This suggests that words are signs of things that vary across cultures in terms of writing and speaking, but they are universal in the 'mental affection' to which they refer. Thus although the words 'God,' 'Gott,' 'Dieu,' 'Dios,' 'Allah,' etc. obviously differ, they have the same 'mental' reference that insures translatability because it is not subject to the contingency of speech and writing. But is this Aristotle or Aquinas's position? Do the passions of the soul insure meaning across conventional uses of language because of some identical idea in the mind? What are 'passions of the soul'?

O'Callaghan explains this well. He notes that for Aquinas, "the *passio*

---

ward fideism in modern theology as well as an unwillingness toward accountability to other Christians.

67. Aristotle, *On Interpretation*, trans. Harold P. Cooke (Cambridge, Mass.: Loeb Classical Library, 1983), p. 115.

animae is not an intermediate object brought to mind or thrown up before the mind between *word* and *res,* but rather the manner by which the use of the *word* brings to mind the *res.*"[68] It is similar to the 'modus significandi.' This is based on a twofold distinction of signification. First is the "relation of a word to a res signified." Second is the "relation of a word to a means by which the word is related to a res signified."[69] The modern linguistic turn, especially in the designative tradition, only focuses attention on the first form of signification. It assumes the 'passions of the soul' are just 'ideas,' as with Locke or Hobbes. This inevitably underwrites a nominalist metaphysics where such 'ideas' are nothing but conventions in our heads to help us remember a vast multitude of particulars we could not otherwise remember.

But with Aquinas's second form of signification we see that the passions of the soul are not just 'ideas' in the mind — they are a class of beings that are general in that they are both in the thing and in the mind such that we participate in them. They are not contained in us. They are the divine ideas by which God creates, and whose primary exemplar is the Word made flesh. They are that which allows for a 'mode of signifying' because the agent participates, is informed by, and becomes conformed to the 'res' through the 'passiones animae.' For O'Callaghan, the Thomistic-Aristotelian tradition is not about mental representationalism. Instead, it "holds that words express what we understand of things. Words attach to reality because our cognitive faculties attach to reality in some way." Therefore "understanding is a kind of becoming identical with the [thing] being understood."[70] This is possible because of the importance of form. Words then are not mental ideas expressed materially. Nor do they primarily register sense data. They are not placeholders for a vast multitude of particulars. They both "express" and "attach." This offers an alternative to methodological nominalism.

5. Methodological Nominalism

Methodological nominalism treats being, truth, and goodness as distractions that must be cut down to size to fit our language. It offers us only

---

68. O'Callaghan, *Thomist Realism and the Linguistic Turn,* p. 25.
69. O'Callaghan, *Thomist Realism and the Linguistic Turn,* p. 22.
70. O'Callaghan, *Thomist Realism and the Linguistic Turn,* p. 3.

three options for assessing the truth of what can and cannot be known: empiricism, science, or language use. It brackets out arguments that assume beauty, truth, and the good can illumine our language just as much as language illumines them. However, philosophy has never been able to pursue language usage without assuming these transcendentals. They cannot be successfully bracketed out. Methodological nominalism does not work without a willful act of forgetting.

Nominalism is a metaphysics that states essences or universals are not entities through which God creates, sustains, and redeems the world; instead everything God does is particular. All universals or essences are mere names that help us negotiate among the various particulars. An individual cannot remember every particular human creature or chair or animal that God creates, so she uses 'names' like 'human creature,' 'chair,' or 'animal' to help recognize the particular object before her. These objects are all individual bits of data that she inputs into her memory, which cannot hold all the data, so she produces 'names' to encompass the data. These names are like placeholders; they have no existence other than their logical existence in my mind, and they have no function other than their usefulness in helping individuals construct and negotiate their own reality. They are logical concepts, not ontological. But since these logical constructions are nothing but logical constructions, we must always be willing to abandon them for better ones.[71] We also must constantly simplify, do away with the richness of language and the relations it names, which circle around the data in order to present the data itself. And of course this does not apply only to persons, chairs, and animals; it also applies to goodness, truth, beauty, and even 'Person' or 'hypostasis.' This is the reason nominalist theologians struggle in sustaining the truth of the Christian doctrine of the Trinity and Christ's two natures.[72]

Nominalist metaphysics held sway over much of English thought in

---

71. Michael Gillespie traces the radical innovations Ockham introduces into Scholastic theology with his "rejection of realism." "The rejection of realism undermines syllogistic logic. If all things are radically individual, then universals are merely names (nomina), verbal tools created by finite human beings for the purpose of dealing with the vast array of radically individual things. Logic thus becomes a logic of names or signs rather than a logic that expresses the real relations among things." *Nihilism Before Nietzsche* (Chicago: University of Chicago Press, 1995), p. 18.

72. See Gillespie, *Nihilism Before Nietzsche*, p. 24. Gillespie writes, "Ockham was able to sustain this doctrine only by contradicting his own theory of universals."

the fourteenth century.[73] Did it produce habits of thought that shaped not only theology but also English speaking philosophy? Its influence on two seminal English philosophers, Hobbes and Locke, is unmistakable and noncontroversial. What might be controversial is the extent to which these habits of thought continue to shape some within the tradition of analytical philosophy. For Hobbes, four principles constitute knowledge. First, "we have such and such conceptions." These conceptions are "motions in some internal substance of the head," which emerge from objects exterior to us. Second, "we have thus and thus named the things whereof they are conceptions." Third, "we have joined those names in such a manner as to make true propositions." Finally, "we have joined those propositions in such a manner as they be concluding."[74] Names identify particular conceptions. Language allows us to combine these particulars into universals and make judgments. But this is where language misleads us. Hobbes states, "The universality of one name to many things, hath been the cause that men think that the things themselves are universal." They "deceive themselves by taking the universal or general appellation, for the thing it signifieth."[75] But the universal is no thing; it is a mere name.

Hobbes uses this account of language to explain and critique the notions of both the true and the good. Truth is a function of propositions (what we would today call statements), which must have an accurate formal logic supported by evidence grounded in experience.[76] Truth qua truth does not exist as an entity; it only exists in the relation between a particular statement and the experienced reality to which it refers. Likewise no such thing as the good exists. The good is simply goodness, a relation to us, as it pleases or displeases.[77] Hobbes's nominalist method lies behind his metaphysics and his political philosophy.

73. Gillespie, *Nihilism Before Nietzsche*, p. 24.

74. Hobbes, *Human Nature and De Corpore Politico* (Oxford: Oxford University Press, 1994), p. 41.

75. Hobbes, *Human Nature and De Corpore Politico*, p. 36.

76. Hobbes, *Human Nature and De Corpore Politico*, p. 38. Hobbes argues that this "invention of names" allows men to exceed beasts, but it also makes possible "error."

77. Hobbes, *Human Nature and De Corpore Politico*, p. 44. "Every man, for his own part, calleth that which pleaseth, and is delightful to himself GOOD; and that EVIL which displeaseth him; insomuch that while every man differeth from other in constitution they differ also one from another concerning the common distinction of good and evil. Nor is there any such thing as ἀγαθός ἁπλῶς, that is to say simply good. For even the goodness which we attribute to God Almighty, is his goodness to us. And as we call good and evil the

Locke continued these nominalist habits of thought. Language begins with individual articulate sounds. These are then fashioned into words that "stand as marks for the Ideas within [one's] own Mind." These ideas are the consequence of sense-impressions from objects external to one's mind. They stand in for the object when it is no longer present; words name those ideas. But this is insufficient "for a perfection of knowledge." For if every particular sensation was marked by a particular idea characterized by its own word then "the multiplication of Words would have perplexed their Use." The "remedy" for this "inconvenience" is that "language had yet a far-ther improvement in the use of general terms, whereby one word was made to mark a multitude of particular existences."[78]

Hobbes and Locke certainly made a 'linguistic turn' in philosophy; they did not suggest that all metaphysical questions could be reduced to questions of language. But they inaugurated a tradition of trying to put an end to metaphysics by being attentive to language. Kant acknowledged Locke thought he could resolve metaphysical dilemmas by turning to com-mon experience. His own critique of metaphysics assumed Locke's project failed:

> In more recent times, it has seemed as if an end might be put to all these controversies and the claims of metaphysics receive final judgment, through a certain physiology of the human understanding — that of the celebrated Locke. But it has turned out quite otherwise. For however the attempt be made to cast doubt upon the pretensions of the supposed Queen (metaphysics) by tracing her lineages to vulgar origins in com-mon experience, this genealogy has, as a matter of fact, fictitiously been invented, and she has still continued to uphold her claims.[79]

Locke's turn to common experience was based on how our use of words misleads us, so I think it proper to see in Locke the origins of the modern linguistic turn especially as heralded by the early Rorty.

---

things that please and displease; so call we goodness and badness, the qualities or power whereby they do it. And the signs of that goodness are called by the Latins in one word PULCHRITUDO, and the signs of evil TURPITUDO; to which we have no words precisely answerable."

78. Locke, *An Essay Concerning Human Understanding* (Oxford: Oxford University Press, 1979), p. 402.

79. Kant, *Critique of Pure Reason*, trans. Norman Kemp Smith (New York: St. Martin's Press, 1965), p. 8.

Hobbes and Locke share in common three basic moves with the modern linguistic turn. First, universal or general terms like 'true,' 'good,' and 'beautiful' are wrongly construed as metaphysical entities because our language betrays us. Second, meaning requires a careful and precise analysis of words and their complexes. We must begin with atomic inputs. This does not prohibit positing abstract entities, but such 'entities' lack existence. They can only be logical concepts whose meaning depends on our use of them. Here 'true' and 'good' lack intensional meaning. They are primarily extensional, designating all the particular true or good things that the 'general term' stands in for. Third, meaning is composed of two elements: the object and its ability to be perceived by us as well as our ability to name objects, associate them into complexes, and abstract from them to form generalities for our own use.

Does this nominalist method define analytic philosophy? We must first acknowledge that 'analytic' philosophy doesn't actually exist. It is a tradition of thought that calls into question whether the very distinction between analytic and synthetic, so central to both Hume and Kant, is sound. Quine and many others in this tradition deny this distinction; it is a "dogma of empiricism" that we can do without.[80] This not only qualifies but dismantles Ayer's logical positivism with its principle of verification because it required things to fit either an analytic or synthetic logic. For Ayer, "a sentence had literal meaning if and only if the proposition it expressed was either analytic or empirically verifiable."[81]

Much as whether such a thing as 'analytic' exists, any cursory reading of the 'analytic' tradition finds it to be a tradition of debate and disagreement such that one can hardly be for or against it. Analytic philosophers, and others close to them, do not have a common approach to language, truth, theories of meaning, metaphysics, or God. Yet it does seem reasonable to suggest that what constitutes the tradition of analytic philosophy is attentiveness to language as an effort to resolve or dissolve metaphysical disputes.

For theology to think it has a stake in deciding for or against analytic or for or against continental philosophy would be shortsighted. Any call to hitch theology to either analytic or continental philosophy a priori misun-

---

80. See Quine, "Two Dogmas of Empiricism," in *From a Logical Point of View* (New York: Harper Torchbooks, 1961), pp. 20-47.

81. A. J. Ayer, *Language, Truth, and Logic* (New York: Dover, 1952), p. 5.

derstands the relationship between faith and reason. No philosophy can be used without 'conversion.' Every genuine philosophy inevitably seeks the truth of what is and therefore can provide a nature possible of theological perfection. Both analytic and continental philosophy can provide an opening to theology and both are incomplete and inadequate as they are; both are in need of theological supplementation. Both can point in the direction of theological truth; neither can affirm what theology must — truth is less a proposition carried by statements (or some other linguistic vehicles) and more a Person. Some analytic philosophy, however, does pose a challenge to an adequate theological metaphysic when it putatively eschews metaphysics and walks away from key questions of being, truth, and goodness. The designative linguistic smuggles into philosophy a normative and 'anorexic' metaphysic that cannot do justice to the truth of the gift of being.[82] This may be why David Hart finds little rapprochement between theology and analytic philosophy.

Hart never explains why he asserts there is no consanguinity between analytic philosophy and theology, but he overlooks the fact that much of analytic philosophy is also the 'misbegotten child' of Scholastic theology, especially its careful attention to language.[83] This seems to worry Hart, for after this assertion he immediately enters into a criticism of 'Yale school' theology. Narrative, he argues, is used as a "shelter against critique and against the ontological and epistemological questions that theology must address (inas-

82. William Desmond finds the antecedents of analytic philosophy in the Aristotelian tradition with its emphasis "that to be is to be intelligible; and to be intelligible is to be determinate." Although he affirms in part this quest for unity, he also recognizes that the "univocal ideal of intelligibility" leads to a reduction of the metaphysical quest, especially in some analytical philosophy. He writes, "Any good Aristotelian will remind you that the determination of unity is amenable to a more comprehensive articulation than we find in the anorexic self-starvation of the positivistic mind and some of its analytic descendents." William Desmond, *Being and the Between* (New York: State University of New York Press, 1995), p. 17.

83. Frege's work cannot be understood without recognizing that it recovers the significance of logic from medieval theology. As Michael Dummett noted, Frege is the first philosopher after Descartes to begin philosophy with logic rather than epistemology. Logic presumes a realism whereby the mind and the world are not a priori divided. It does not lend itself well to a mental representationalism that inevitably separates the 'internal' representation from the external thing and concludes in skepticism. Frege's philosophy did not assume this. Dummett, "Frege," *Encyclopedia of Philosophy,* ed. Paul Edwards (New York: Collier, 1967), p. 225.

much as it is a discourse concerning the Logos)." Hart finds narrative theology, and the analytic tradition, too trapped in language, too committed to narrative and incapable of developing an adequate aesthetics, ontology, and epistemology that would allow us to move beyond language.[84]

Hart does not dismiss the importance of language for theology; he makes something of a linguistic turn when he writes, "Christian rhetoric can be undertaken only from within Christian doctrine." But he does not want theology confined to language; it must also *"speak out of its story in a way that is not 'narrative' only, in a simple sense, and in a way that can find resonances and correspondences in the language and 'experience' of those who are not Christian."* Hart confesses that this assumes "the possibility of a consummation of all reason in a vision and a wisdom that cannot be reached without language, but is as much *theoria* as discourse."[85] This requires metaphysics 3 or 4 as necessary for the theological task. For Hart, analytic philosophy lacks substantive engagement with beauty and truth beyond language. It has little or no place for contemplation. Some analytic philosophers certainly do this. They treat metaphysics as if it were only metaphysics 1 or 2. But as I have shown above, others like Wittgenstein provide precisely what Hart recognizes theological truth requires.

If I read Hart's concerns accurately, I want to be both against and for him. I want to be against him in his assuming some sharp distinction between analytic and continental philosophy that privileges the latter as a theological conversation partner but sees the former only in need of conversion. I want to be for him in that the difficulty with some narrative theologians and analytic philosophers is related to their reception of the linguistic turn; the problem is not the linguistic turn per se but the methodological nominalism that comes along with it. But if this is correct, then the problem with analytic philosophy is not philosophical but theological or metaphysical. It is its consanguinity with theology that makes some analytic philosophy problematic.

Fergus Kerr, drawing on Michael Dummett, states that the key difference between the continental and the analytic philosophical tradition is that the latter, unlike the former, "took the 'linguistic turn.'"[86] Of course, atten-

---

84. Hart, *The Beauty of the Infinite*, p. 31. He states, "The Christian story is the true story of being."

85. Hart, *The Beauty of the Infinite*, p. 31.

86. Kerr, "Aquinas and Analytic Philosophy," p. 127. If attentiveness to language characterizes analytic philosophy, then the question is which account of this attention provides

tion to language is an ancient philosophical theme. One finds it in Plato's *Cratylus,* Aristotle's *De Interpretatione,* Augustine's *On Christian Doctrine,* and in Aquinas's *Summa.* It was a central preoccupation in Scholastic theology and logic. As Gilles Emery stated, "From its beginning scholasticism is characterized by a remarkable progress in analyzing language."[87] This would not have happened without the recovery of Aristotle in the Middle Ages. Analytic philosophy is best understood as a continuation of this analysis of language, which maintains connections, albeit not often recognized, to medieval metaphysics. However, much of analytic philosophy, especially in the designative tradition, believed that attention to language would dissolve metaphysical questions altogether. The linguistic turn became an alternative to metaphysics. It supposedly put an end to it, but as argued above, it does not put an end to metaphysics but ends metaphysics in nominalism alone.

Does the linguistic turn require this nominalist metaphysics? Rorty states that it requires at least methodological nominalism. "It is probably true that no one who was not a methodological nominalist would be a linguistic philosopher."[88] Rorty seems agnostic regarding whether concepts and subsistent universals exist. But only one method can successfully be used to determine their existence: "The fact is that our only knowledge of these entities is gained by inspection of linguistic usage."[89] He seems to conflate these two claims: the linguistic turn requires methodological nominalism and entities such as concepts and subsistent universals can only be known through linguistic usage. These two claims are not necessarily linked together. Because essential Christian doctrines like the Trinity

---

for such a characterization? Any answer to this question is exceedingly complex. Some possible answers to this question are:

1. mental representationalism (Locke, Hobbes)
2. innatism (Chomsky, Fodor)
3. Platonic realism (the early Russell, Frege, Peirce)
4. nominalism (later Russell, Pragmatists)
5. designative and neo-designative (Davidson, Quine)
6. meaning holism (Frege, Wittgenstein, Dewey, Putnam)
7. expressivism (Taylor)

These answers are not necessarily exclusive of each other. Nor do they exclude continental philosophy. Heidegger and Derrida are also attentive to language.

87. Gilles Emery, O.P., *Trinity in Aquinas* (Ypsilanti: Sapientia, 2003), p. 32.

88. Richard Rorty, ed., *The Linguistic Turn: Essays in Philosophical Method* (Chicago: University of Chicago Press, 1967), p. 11.

89. Rorty, *The Linguistic Turn,* p. 10.

and Christ's two natures entail the kinds of realities Rorty links with methodological nominalism, Christian theologians cannot be indifferent to his claims. We can agree that concepts and subsistent universals are only known through linguistic usage, but we cannot begin with methodological nominalism, for it already takes a position on the question of concepts and subsistent universals. It denies or brackets out their reality in order to show how language itself can illumine why we should not ask the question if such entities exist. Methodological nominalism is not neutral toward this question; it assumes nothing fruitful can occur by asking it. It walks away from it. Thus the game is rigged in advance, which is not an adequate way to pursue wisdom.

Notice, for example, Rorty's claim for the 'methodological revolution' linguistic philosophers bring to philosophy. It avoids the limitations of Kant's critique of metaphysics, which failed to see that in setting the limits to what we could know it already claimed to exceed those limits. Linguistic philosophy avoids this mistake by setting the limits not anthropologically, but as A. J. Ayer noted, "from the rule which determines the literal significance of language."[90] By turning to language, Ayer and others posed a question to all theologians and metaphysicians. Rorty puts it this way: "Tell us what counts for or against what you are saying and we shall listen; otherwise, we have a right to ignore you."[91] Is this not the temptation among some analytic philosophers who limit a priori what can count as a truth claim so that it can be managed? They often do this with epistemology by asking the question Pilate posed to Jesus: "What is truth?" In other words, if you cannot verify the 'what' that constitutes truth, then your claim to truth can be ignored. The result is that 'what' becomes the only permissible truth claim. But this question can also be put another way, a way that takes the power of adjudicating verification away from the philosophers. We theologians can say to them, tell us what counts as a proper method for determining the rule that lets language use adjudicate what questions can be asked. If you insist that we must be methodological nominalists then we will ignore you. Why should we be so limited a priori? How is such a limitation not mere dogmatism?

Nominalism has significant consequences for how we render intelli-

90. Rorty, *The Linguistic Turn*, p. 5. I don't see how this makes any advance over Kantian apriorism.

91. Rorty, *The Linguistic Turn*, p. 5.

gible the good and the true. They primarily become 'properties' or semantic features of particular linguistic constructions or statements about the beliefs of individuals. It is no surprise that, as occurred with Hobbes, the good is now necessarily related to an individual's preferences and the true depends upon linguistic utterances such as sentences. Philosophical theories of the good in this tradition logically lead to theories such as utilitarianism, rational choice, or Bayesian decision theory; all theories that assume the normativity of marginal utility. It is also used for a theory of truth. As Donald Davidson puts it, "Decision theory, and the commonsense ideas that stand behind it, help make a case for the view that beliefs are best understood in their role of rationalizing choices or preferences. Here we are considering only one kind of belief, the belief that a sentence is true. Yet even in this case, it would be better if we could go behind the belief to a preference which might show itself in choice."[92] We should not be surprised that the modern linguistic turn finds common cause with a rationality based on marginal utility.

For Rorty, methodological nominalism separates contemporary philosophy from the preceding philosophical tradition. It resituates metaphysical and theological questions within the context of a methodological nominalism, which now provides the only context within which a proper answer might be given. Rorty attributes this methodology to Wittgenstein, citing the same claim I quoted above to distinguish between metaphysics and a metaphysical use: "When philosophers use a word — 'knowledge,' 'being,' 'object,' 'I,' 'proposition,' 'name' — and try to grasp the essence of the thing, one must always ask oneself: is the word ever actually used in this way in the language-game which is its original home? What we do is to bring words back from their metaphysical to their everyday use."[93] Rorty finds Wittgenstein's work at home in methodological nominalism.

---

92. Davidson, *Inquiries into Truth and Interpretation* (Oxford: Oxford University Press, 1984), pp. 147-48. See also a more developed account of marginal utility as important for a theory of truth in his "The Structure and Content of Truth," *Journal of Philosophy* 87:6 (June 1990): 326-28. Marginal utility as rational choice appears to be the common basis for Davidson's so-called principle of charity. In "The Structure and Content of Truth," he states, "The possibility of understanding the speech or actions of an agent depends on the existence of a fundamentally rational pattern, a pattern that must, in general outline, be shared by all rational creatures. We have no choice but to project our own logic on to the language and beliefs of another," *Inquiries into Truth and Interpretation*, p. 320.

93. Rorty, *The Linguistic Turn*, p. 13.

Is Rorty correct about Wittgenstein? Does he support methodological nominalism? I have tried to argue against this interpretation of Wittgenstein. In the *Tractatus*, Wittgenstein did affirm Occam's razor. He wrote, "If a sign is useless, it is meaningless. That is the point of Occam's maxim. (If everything behaves as if a sign had meaning, then it does have meaning.)"[94] This statement in the *Tractatus* is similar to the heart of Wittgenstein's project — meaning is in its use. What is meant by 'use'? Is it similar to verification? If so, then Rorty is correct and we have little space for theological knowledge within the linguistic turn. The knowledge of God has a certain uselessness to it, which is to say, it is good in itself. If by 'use' we mean "what is it used *for*" — then a proper response would be "for no other thing." Knowledge of God is intrinsically good. It is not a means to any other good. But if by 'use' we do not signify a 'means' to something, then it is still possible to do theology after Wittgenstein. Knowledge of God is, in Kierkegaard's language, self-incriminating. One cannot know it without it being "of use" in one's life such that life is encumbered by this knowledge. One cannot truly know God without that knowledge producing faith in terms of 'credere in Deum.' But if we ask "what is it used *for*?" then we treat our language about God as an instrument to designate something else. This always assumes atheism even when we speak voluminously of God.

Rorty takes Wittgenstein's question and turns it into an all-encompassing philosophical method where "the view that all the questions which philosophers have asked about concepts, subsistent universals, or 'natures' which (a) cannot be answered by empirical inquiry concerning the behaviour or properties of particulars subsumed under such concepts, universals, or natures, and which (b) can be answered in *some* way, can be answered by answering questions about the use of linguistic expressions, and in no other way."[95] What cannot be answered by empirical appeals or science can only look to language.

Much of contemporary analytic philosophy treats both the ancients and Scholastics as if they had a simple representationalist theory of language that posits two key components: the mind and the thing, or object, outside of the mind. Too often, this is what is taken to be the basic understanding of knowledge in 'Western metaphysics,' and becomes the object

---

94. Wittgenstein, *Tractatus Logico-Philosophicus,* trans. D. F. Pears and B. F. McGuiness (London: Routledge, 1999), 3.328.

95. Rorty, *The Linguistic Turn,* p. 11.

of philosophical critique, supposedly leading to an end of metaphysics. Putnam calls this the 'cryptographer' model of language and attributes it to Aristotle.[96] Rorty accuses the ancients, particularly Plato, of thinking of 'mind' as a mirror whose purpose is to reflect adequately things or objects outside the subject (metaphysics 5). Language, it was assumed, was merely a conduit between these two, and true knowledge emerged when the mind merely 'mirrored' the objects in the world.[97] This is too simplistic. In the *Cratylus* Plato does argue against the position of Hermogenes, who states that names are mere conventions. For Hermogenes names are not natural to particular things, but are used "only because of the rules and usage." Socrates contests this interpretation, for he fears it will lead to solipsism both in our use of language and in our account of truth. Socrates questions Hermogenes, "Is the being or essence of each of them [names] something private for each person? . . . or do you believe that things have some fixed being or essence of their own?" Socrates argues that they do have a kind of natural fixity, otherwise truth would be arbitrary — "if what each person believes to be true is true for him no one can truly be wiser than anyone else."[98] But for Socrates the natural correctness of names is similar to the natural use of tools. Words function naturally in the same way that tools do. Drilling cannot be done with a loom; weaving cannot be done with a drill.[99] The similarity here between Plato and Wittgenstein is intriguing, despite the common interpretation that Wittgenstein is an anti-Platonic thinker. That may have more to do with what is meant by 'Platonism' in contemporary philosophy than with any careful comparison of them. Words have specific natural usages that cannot be made merely anything one wants. Thus for Plato, not all words do the same thing.[100]

96. Putnam, *Representation and Reality* (Cambridge, Mass.: MIT Press, 1992).

97. Richard Rorty's *Philosophy and the Mirror of Nature* (Princeton: Princeton University Press, 1979) offers a compelling criticism of this model of knowledge as mental representation based on the mind as mirror. He convincingly argues for an end to epistemology. But Rorty too easily assumes this simple structure in most of ancient philosophy, especially Plato. And he does so without textual evidence. For a much more complex account of the ancients and Scholastics see Robert Miner's *Truth in the Making* (London: Routledge, 2004) and John P. O'Callaghan's *Thomist Realism and the Linguistic Turn*.

98. Plato, *Cratylus*, in *Plato: Complete Works*, ed. John M. Cooper (Indianapolis: Hackett, 1977), pp. 103-4.

99. Socrates teases out the insight, "So a name is also a sort of tool." *Plato: Complete Works*, p. 106.

100. *Plato: Complete Works*, p. 119. Plato nevertheless has a projectionist understand-

Despite this multiple use of words, and despite Socrates' claim that "using names" is a "sort of action," the heart of Plato's argument is found in Socrates' claim, "the correctness of every name we analyzed was intended to consist in expressing the nature of one of the things that are."[101] Who knows exactly what Plato means by this, but it can easily lend itself to an interpretation similar to that which Putnam and Rorty critique and which the early Bertrand Russell endorses. His linguistic turn embodies the caricature that often goes by the name 'Platonism' in analytic philosophy. The early Russell sought to give the meaning of every word through a symbolic mathematics.[102] Each word indicates some extralinguistic reality that can be referenced through a quantificational or functional analysis.

Few philosophers still hold forth this kind of caricatured Platonic realism, although many continue to attribute it to Plato and the 'Western' philosophical and theological tradition. Nominalism is often embraced to avoid this caricatured 'Platonism.' Analytic philosophy is not of one piece, not all such philosophers embrace the nominalistic method, but as Rorty stated, it does seem to be the dominant method used, and it is related to a particular view of the linguistic turn. Does this mean Hart is correct? Theology's task in engaging analytic philosophy is primarily conversion?

Kerr finds theology, especially Thomism, and analytic philosophy, "natural allies." Both help us see how "a picture held us captive." Language tempts us to see the world in terms of its own structure, where subjects represent objects through mental events. We wrongly imagine that analyzing this structure into its most primitive elements will give us the securest form of knowledge of the world. This tempts us to a building-block theory of meaning and a correspondence theory of truth that cannot avoid redundancy and therefore finds expression in deflationary accounts of truth. Attention to language can help us overcome our captivity. This common move finds general agreement between theologians and some analytic philosophers, especially those committed to holism or narrative, which is a salutary consequence of a linguistic turn. But perhaps a picture still holds us captive?

Could it be that *the* picture that holds us captive is that a single pic-

---

ing of god-language. For instance, Plato denies that we have any access to the names for the gods or that the gods use. When it comes to the gods, all that we know is the names creatures give them.

101. *Plato: Complete Works*, p. 139.

102. Bertrand Russell, *Principles of Mathematics* (New York: Norton, 1996), p. 42.

ture holds us captive? In other words, the linguistic turn is content to free us from our captivity to intractable metaphysical problems by drawing our attention to language and overcoming epistemological foundationalism. This is salutary but insufficient, for this very attention to language tempts us to be held captive by another picture, which is that by attention to language we can simply walk away from metaphysical and theological questions and they will disappear. We have escaped one bottle only to find ourselves trapped unnecessarily in another. All this does is push these inevitable questions to the margins of the intellectual life, and the academy. Perhaps we should call this 'the linguistic overturn,' where it is assumed that metaphysical questions are *only* problems of language and that all "intellectually sophistical adults" in our culture know that such questions should not be asked. In this 'overturn,' being, and its transcendental predicates such as goodness, truth, and beauty, are *reduced* to problems of language and thus only to be answered by disciplines like the empirical sciences, sociology, or psychology. Philosophers seek to serve these disciplines and thus are tempted to walk away from these problems without illuminating them for us because this linguistic (over)turn supposedly removes the questions we ask about them. Philosophy becomes a useless endeavor with no positive role to play other than telling us what questions we can no longer ask. This is not philosophical inquiry; it is a philosophical program. Moreover, some analytic philosophers think by reducing these metaphysical problems to linguistic ones and walking away from them, they have somehow kept themselves pure from the metaphysical problems. They have not. What they have done is adopt one metaphysical solution — the nominalist one — and falsely assumed that it would somehow 'eliminate' metaphysics (to quote Ayer).

In minimalist and deflationist theories of truth, 'truth' is not illumined, but simply avoided as a linguistic redundancy we can do without in analytic philosophy. But redundancy theories of truth are not the only theories present in analytical philosophy; they are one position among contending positions. No one should dismiss the linguistic turn because it leads to deflationism. The problem is not the linguistic turn per se; in fact I think linguistic philosophers overstate the disjunction between the modern linguistic turn and the preceding philosophical tradition, which also recognized language's role in illuminating questions of God, being, truth, goodness, and beauty. The difficulty with the modern linguistic turn is not that attention to language illumines metaphysical questions; Aquinas recognized that much. The difficulty is that the modern linguistic turn is a metaphysical stance on those questions. It follows the late Scholastics in denying the existence of subsistent universals; it turns this into an a priori method that seeks to police reason from faith. It uses a philosophical method to restrict faith to an arational domain. Aquinas and Wittgenstein undo this policing. They show us the limits of philosophy not in order to deconstruct it, but to redeem it and make a place for it within the gift we receive in sacred doctrine. Philosophy has its own integrity when it does not exceed its proper limits and seek to police the questions asked. The limits Wittgenstein placed on philosophy for the sake of a life worth living is similar to the limits Aquinas put on philosophy for the sake of the Christian life as a way of following Jesus into the truth of God.

If postliberal (Protestant) theology is tempted to eschew metaphysics for biblical narrative, Roman Catholic (neoscholastic) theology is often tempted to divide metaphysics from theology and make the former the foundation for the latter. Both will give us an inadequate account of language and truth in light of the doctrine of the incarnation. In his natures, Jesus is human and divine where each maintains its distinctiveness. Divinity is not changed into humanity or vice versa. Neither is either confused with the other. We must use language that maintains this difference, which is what the divine names provide. But Jesus is not primarily 'two natures'; he is a Person who bears the name. In his Person, which is who he is in his agency, the two natures are neither divided nor contrasted according to function. As the holy fathers taught, "The distinctiveness of each nature is not nullified by the union. Instead, the 'properties' of each nature are conserved and both natures concur in one 'person' and in one *hypostasis*."[103] Jesus is not the nuclear fusion of two natures that antedate him. He is the Person in whom, and through whom, we see both 'natures' — creaturely existence and divinity.

Both Thomas Aquinas and Hans Frei, using very different language, express well this logic of the incarnation. This is because they both recognize how the hypostatic union allows us to speak of Jesus' human and divine natures through a unified Person who has a single agency presented throughout the Gospels, including the continuity of identity to which the Apostles bear witness pre- and post-Easter. Hans Frei set forth the thesis

103. The Chalcedonian Definition, in *Creeds of the Church*, 3d ed., ed. John H. Leith (Atlanta: John Knox, 1982), p. 36.

that "the development of the gospel story is such that Jesus' identity as the single, unsubstitutable human individual that he is comes to sharpest focus in the death-and-resurrection sequence taken as one unbroken sequence."[104] In other words, Jesus' identity is constant through his crucifixion and resurrection; any talk of a pre-Easter Jesus and post-Easter Christ violates the narrative continuity in the Scripture and the singular identity and agency which Jesus is. It divides the natures and loses the Person. That Jesus is the single Person is of course a surprising claim, which Frei himself recognizes: "It is indeed an astonishing thing that the cosmic, immortal redeemer figure should be not mirrored by but identified completely with a human being of particular historical identity. Quite likely it was as astounding to the original authors and little community from which they emerged as it is to any of us — if not more so."[105] With this unsubstitutable identity, Scripture already demythologizes God by presenting him through the passion, crucifixion, and resurrection of Jesus, and it is within this grammar that Scripture is best read. Jesus' agency in Scripture allows us an intention toward God. This is why the doctrine of the hypostatic union is so important both for reading Scripture and for the logic of theology. It also helps us understand how Jesus is the truth of God; he is this only because he is the 'way' ('via') and we are 'wayfarers.'

104. Hans Frei, "Theological Reflections on the Accounts of Jesus' Death and Resurrection," in *The Identity of Jesus Christ* (Eugene, Ore.: Wipf and Stock, 1977), p. 14.
105. Hans Frei, "Theological Reflections on the Accounts of Jesus' Death and Resurrection," p. 13.

CHAPTER 5

Truth

This work began by suggesting that the consequence of the modern ills affecting our speaking of God is a subordination of the political to power, where power is conceived fundamentally as self-assertion. It accomplishes this by making national identities the most important identities to which persons adhere. These identities are most often not founded upon common truths or goodness, but upon the will and its ability to enter into combinations. This too, of course, is a metaphysical claim and one that may not stand up to critical scrutiny. Perhaps this is why metaphysics comes to a supposed end? Throughout this work, the argument assumes that metaphysics and politics go together. Once we no longer ask the questions of the transcendentals — "What is good?" "What is truth?" "What is to be?" — then we will get an impoverished politics. The argument also assumes truth is associated with the specificities of the Christian life and teaching, especially as it comes as a gift in Christ. These two assumptions do and should make people nervous.

If politics needs metaphysics and metaphysics needs the specificities of Christian doctrine, then isn't the logical conclusion some kind of theocracy where theology subordinates politics to itself? If so, then we would lose the significant gains of modernity, where liberal democracy, at its best, invites people of diverse faiths, and even of no faith, to live together in tolerance and peace. I unequivocally affirm this sentiment; in fact, like many moderns, I live it every day within my local neighborhood with gratitude and without question. But I'm not convinced that liberal democracy truly supports or sustains this way of life because it often asks people of faith to subordinate the truth of their convictions to a different understanding of truth — the truth that power alone can bind people together. It converts us to this way of life and seems willing to use violence against any who will not convert. Is there no alternative? It should come as no surprise to anyone that Christians, Muslims, and Jews who hold to the specificities of their faith find themselves ill at ease in such an overarching metaphysics. How can we recognize this without lending support to those powerful forces among all three faiths that seek to subordinate politics to 'truth' by claiming and exercising the instruments of state power, thereby reaffirming the consequence of the modern ills that truth is subordinated to power? How can we bring together truth, faith, and reason without disastrous political consequences?

Truth is perhaps the most pressing political matter for theology. The political and ecclesial question before us is how to subordinate power to truth and goodness without unwittingly using truth and goodness as mere forms of self-assertion. Rowan Williams recognizes well the problem we face. He writes,

> To the extent that popular liberal and pluralist thought assumes with blithe unawareness a basic model of meaningful action in terms of assertion, it assumes a final social unintelligibility, and ultimate inability to make sense of each other's actions (which involves understanding so as to query and reexpress) — and thus raises the specter of the purest fascism, an uncriticizable exercise of social power in the name of a supposed corporate assertion.[1]

A politics incapable of giving reasons, and reasons that we presume are true, will only be able to create social bonds through the assertion of will. Eventually, such a politics may catch up with us; it may become what it claims to be. It raises the "specter of the purest fascism." How can politics be established upon truth and not the mere assertion of will? How can we establish truth as something other than the mere assertion of will, which raises the specter of pure fascism in the first place? A simple but important response is to remind people of faith that state power is not the only form of politics. The church as a transnational community, founded upon sameness, offers a politics that need not fear truth and goodness.

---

1. Rowan Williams, "Introduction," in *Theology and the Political: The New Debate*, ed. Creston Davis, John Milbank, and Slavoj Žižek (Durham, N.C.: Duke University Press, 2005), p. 2.

1. The Politics of Truth

Assertion of will most often constitutes the modern political subject. It supposedly relativizes all claims to truth and goodness because they are assumed too dangerous a foundation for political and social bonds. Yet this moral dogma that constitutes a modern political subject also entails, in that very constitution, that we uncritically obey this dogma. To recognize a different kind of politics is to be freed from this form of obedience. Many modern and postmodern persons find obedience to the church difficult not because they have assessed the truth of its claims and find it wanting, but because they accept this moral dogma which makes truth itself suspect. We know before we even make truth claims that they will be dismissed as covert power plays. The game is rigged in advance. What is surprising is that the clergy rig the game more so than others. They do so by uncritically accepting this very modern moral dogma and allowing it to police theological truth.

R. R. Reno identifies this kind of moralism by citing an editorial published by a Protestant pastor. It is a common but by no means convincing or well thought-out argument that the cause of violence in our world is due to religious people who claim to know the truth. Citing that pastor's argument, Reno wrote,

> Universal claims on behalf of faith (the minister was scrupulous to include in this camp claims about salvation in Christ alone) lead to hatred, bigotry, and oppression. Dogmatism and the dogmatic personality are at the root of our problems. The way toward peace and cooperation, he concluded, requires us to realize that our religious faith is culturally conditioned and relative to our unique personal needs.[2]

The irony of this all too common critique of religious truth is that it is based on a moral dogma that assumes dogmatic truth inevitably leads to violence, yet the moral dogma that yields this conclusion is somehow immune from the adverse effects dogmatic claims to truth necessarily produce. I have tried to argue elsewhere that this analysis of violence gets the cause of violence in modernity exactly backwards.[3] Although religious

2. R. R. Reno, "Theology's Continental Captivity," *First Things* (April 2006).
3. See *The Goodness of God: Theology, Church and Social Order* (Grand Rapids: Brazos, 2000), pp. 283-92.

people have without a doubt perpetrated violence in the name of God, this is seldom the reason for warfare since the Enlightenment. It assumed that the privatization of religious convictions would lead to a common, public moral discourse that could produce the conditions for peace because it would be free from any theological dogma.[4] After the Enlightenment, religion is at most a subtext in the causes that lead to war. People now war in the name of nations, whether to defend existing national boundaries or to liberate people for the creation of new ones. To be political is to have a national identity with clear, specifiable borders. Sometimes people invoke 'God' for the sake of these wars for democracy and liberation that defend or create these borders. Oddly, these themes do not seem to lead to the same kind of moral outrage that Reno noted by the Protestant preacher above. Seldom do we hear people cry out against democracy or the democratic nation-state because of the violence perpetrated in its name.

Reno rightly critiques such a facile analysis of the cause of violence and contends that for Christian theologians to begin to counter this all too common analysis, we will need to recover a robust account of truth. There can be no sustainable Christianity without the recognition that "Christian faith is dogmatic and its claims to truth red-blooded."

Reno then questions how contemporary Christianity finds itself in such a fix, where Christians, especially the clergy, readily abandon the truth of their faith convictions to serve the moral good of the zeitgeist. Drawing upon the work of the Catholic theologian Thomas Guarino, Reno suggests that one answer is Christian theologians' "captivity to continental philosophy," especially their fixity upon non-foundationalism and the so-called end of metaphysics. This captivity prevents us from setting

---

4. See Kant's "What Is Enlightenment?" as one source for this moral dogma. He asks, "Which restriction is an obstacle to enlightenment, and which is not an obstacle but a promoter of it?" Then he answers, "The public use of one's reason must always be free, and it alone can bring about enlightenment among men. . . . By public use of one's reason I understand the use which a person makes of it as a scholar before the reading public. Private use I call that which one may make of it in a particular civil post which is entrusted to him. . . . Here argument is certainly not allowed — one must obey." *Foundation of the Metaphysics of Morals and What Is Enlightenment?* ed. Lewis Beck (New York: Macmillan Publishing Company, 1987), p. 87. Given this starting point in modern political theory, it is no surprise that the two influential attempts to develop Kant's insights for contemporary politics by Habermas and Rawls consistently flounder on the question as to how to include the possible truth of religious convictions in their public reasoning.

forth our "red-blooded" truth claims.[5] Reno encourages theologians to overcome their captivity to continental philosophy and begin to make common cause with analytic philosophy because it can provide a much-needed foundation in truth.

R. R. Reno, Thomas Guarino, and David Hart, as well as many of modern theology's discontents, identify a common problem — theology loses its commitment to truth and allows that commitment to be policed by other dogmatic moral and political claims. Hart develops a 'theological aesthetics of truth' in conversation with continental philosophy and finds analytic philosophy unhelpful. Reno identifies the problem as theology's captivity to continental philosophy and advises theologians to look to analytic philosophy. Guarino does not advocate for or against continental or analytic philosophy, but following John Paul II, he suggests we need a 'range' of metaphysical options that will provide a foundation for the truth of Christianity. This foundation will not be a classic foundationalism, but a reasonable support for faith that does not displace it.

Although I find wise counsel in Reno, Hart, and Guarino's diagnosis and their respective remedies, both need to be supplemented by something more than acknowledging the loss of truth and calling for a recovery of it with the appropriate philosophical foundation. If this is all we have, then we might find ourselves tempted to return to neoscholasticism and its understanding of nature, thinking we have resolved the difficulty before us.

The so-called end of metaphysics subordinates the truth of theology to ethics and politics. Therefore, we cannot adequately address this loss if we fail to provide an analysis that recognizes the links among politics, metaphysics, truth, and theology. While on some points I find analytic philosophers helpful, some of the continental philosophers Reno worries about the most offer us an interesting analysis of the relationship among these various 'disciplines,' which theology can use in its necessary task of recovering truth.

Several years before Reno expressed his concern that theology had become captive to continental philosophy, Paul Griffiths found in some of its proponents a natural desire for God, or as he put it, "instances of pagan yearning for Christian gold."[6] Griffiths recognized that Catholics "might

---

5. R. R. Reno, "Theology's Continental Captivity."

6. Paul Griffiths, "Christ and Critical Theory," *First Things* (August/September 2004). I am indebted to Hans Madueme for directing my attention to this important essay.

embrace" some of the criticisms Lyotard, Žižek, Eagleton, and Badiou bring to bear on academic culture. For instance, although Alain Badiou insists there is no God, he nevertheless finds in St. Paul's conversion an example of the kind of 'philosophy' necessary to overcome the prevailing 'ethical ideology' that always subordinates truth to a liberal politics ruled by the language of rights and diversity. For Badiou the language of 'rights' requires that our political bonds are grounded in evil because we must first be victims who need protection before we can be political agents. 'Diversity,' 'the other,' and 'inclusivity' merely repeat what already is. This language only tells us what we already know; we live in a world with people different from us. But in modernity this emphasis must always be viewed as a potential threat, and so it is emphasized. Then rights can be granted to protect us from it. As an alternative to this Badiou seeks a politics grounded in the priority of goodness and truth where the modern political problem is not recognizing the other, but "recognizing the same."[7] For this we need a strong account of truth and a fidelity to an event that will not fit into the prevailing ethical ideology.

Badiou recovers Plato because Plato offers this strong account of truth:

> The second thing that interests me is Plato's conviction that philosophy doesn't add up to very much without the category of truth. This is my antimodern or anticontemporary aspect, for this category is suspected, criticized, that is, denied, by most contemporary trends. I would even say that philosophy means little without the idea that there can be eternal truths. . . . Of course, this idea is present in the whole of classical metaphysics, but in Plato, it remains somewhat questioning and fragmentary. . . . This suits me as a philosopher, this rhythm, in which we place ourselves under the sign of the question of truth even as we recognize that it can never be the object of a self-sufficient or complete demonstration.[8]

Badiou is, of course, a false friend to theology. He *uses* the language of grace, truth, and metaphysics because he recognizes that this language stands in opposition to liberal, modern political and economic arrangements, but he

---

7. Badiou, *Ethics: An Essay on the Understanding of Evil*, trans. Peter Hallward (London: Verso, 2001), pp. 25-27.

8. Badiou, *Ethics*, p. 120.

seems more interested in standing in opposition to these arrangements than he is recovering grace, truth, and metaphysics.[9] Nevertheless he gives us insight into the relationship among politics, metaphysics, and truth. He notes that the reason we do not have adequate accounts of goodness and truth is not because we lack proper metaphysical foundations, but because modern politics and ethics polices against them. Our emphasis on 'difference' results in a sameness that polices against common truths.

> Respect for difference, of course! But on condition that the different be parliamentary-democratic, pro free-market economies, in favor of freedom of opinion, feminism, the environment. . . . That is to say: I respect differences, but only, of course, in so far as that which differs also respects, just as I do, the said differences.[10]

Badiou identifies the modern problem where truth (and goodness) are always subordinated to a politics grounded in evil and makes us question if recovering metaphysics can accomplish much without at the same time challenging the modern political and economic arrangements that police 'truth' in the first place.

Any recovery of 'truth' must do much more than reassert the importance of metaphysics. It must face the question whether modern political and economic arrangements are key reasons why truth gets subordinated to politics and why proclaiming the 'end of metaphysics' gained such a hearing in modernity and much of postmodernity. In discussing politics, we are not moving away from metaphysics, for politics is the working out of metaphysical principles. This is why Hauerwas's work remains as important for its critique of these political arrangements as for his recovery of 'metaphysics.' These two are inextricably related.

Guarino recognizes that Hauerwas has a place for the kind of metaphysics that is necessary as the foundation for Christian doctrine, but he questions whether Hauerwas follows through with his insight. Guarino writes,

> But while Hauerwas is convinced that a metaphysical approach properly subordinating philosophy to faith is entirely legitimate, he does

---

9. His account of Paul is similar to nineteenth-century neo-Protestant thought where grace is opposed to law because the former is universal and the latter particular.
10. Badiou, *Ethics*, p. 24.

not see, perhaps because of an overweening Barthianism married to his fondness for contemporary nonfoundationalist thought, that some *prima philosophia* is, in fact, necessary if theology is not to fall into fideistic assertion, lacking the further intelligibility provided by the philosophical order.[11]

Guarino does not call for a classical foundationalism, nor for theology to subordinate itself to, find itself rendered intelligible by, or correlated to, philosophy. He does not call for metaphysics 5, but only for the kind of metaphysics that recognizes the full-blooded truth claims Christian doctrine inevitably must make.

2. The Truth of Politics

Guarino's criticism of Hauerwas bears much truth, but not, I think, because he is so fond of nonfoundationalism for its own sake. If anything, Hauerwas is more concerned with the political implications of metaphysics than metaphysics itself. Guarino's critique overlooks how closely Hauerwas (intentionally or unintentionally) relates questions of metaphysics and questions of politics. This is something that many who call for a 'first philosophy' fail to acknowledge. Although their call is important, we must also recognize that political and economic forms of life carry assumed 'metaphysics.' This is Wittgenstein's contribution. Forms of life always assume an answer to the question, "What is?" If we do not recognize these associations, we could easily find ourselves doing mere 'ideology' or advocating a metaphysical use of language that neglects its historical and communal mediations.

When Hauerwas argues that the church is political, this is a tacit metaphysical claim. He writes, "Christian discourse is not a set of beliefs aimed at making our lives more coherent; rather it is a set of constitutive skills to rightly see the world."[12] The church offers those skills, but they are not skills that create a world; they help us "rightly see it." They are practices that allow us to see the truth of God's creation. His critique of 'liberal de-

11. Thomas Guarino, *Foundations of Systematic Theology* (London: T&T Clark, 2005), p. 305.

12. Hauerwas, *Dispatches from the Front* (Durham, N.C.: Duke University Press, 1994), p. 7.

mocracy' is that it prevents us from seeing this *truth* in that it forges our bonds in such a way that we must always subordinate truth to power. To critique democracy because it polices truth is to engage in metaphysics, unless we think of metaphysics in terms of a caricatured metaphysical objectivism that appeals to some utterly transcendent realm, which bears no relationship to, or critique of, ordinary life. I think it safe to say that Hauerwas finds liberal democracy and certain forms of capitalism assuming a bad metaphysics. We cannot have Christian truth and affirm them at the same time. They do not let us raise questions of faith, truth, or goodness. They fail to see that the truth of Christianity must be politically (but not nationally) embodied so that we can see what is really there. This requires an understanding of politics where it does not designate one thing — the modern nation-state. The term 'politics' expresses much more than this. It has a richness to it grounded in the plurivocity of God's creation. Hauerwas's work assumes not only a metaphysical realism, it assumes a Christological realism as the necessary metaphysics for a philosophical account of truth.[13]

In his *Democracy and Tradition,* Jeffrey Stout offers one of the best critiques of the Hauerwasian position, which assumes modern liberal democracies police theological truth by positioning themselves as neutral procedural institutions immune from any tradition of the good or true. Stout readily concedes democracy is not a neutral procedure; it is a 'tradition,' which in its North American version possesses the virtues of "piety, hope, and love or generosity." 'Pragmatism' best expresses this tradition. Thus, Stout states, "pragmatism is democratic traditionalism."[14] With these claims Stout makes an intriguing assault on two different philosophical and theological camps. Against philosophers such as Rawls who see in democracy a tradition-neutral proceduralism that prohibits religious traditions from usurping the necessarily neutral public square, Stout sides with liberalism's critics such as MacIntyre, Hauerwas, and Milbank. But against MacIntyre, Hauerwas, and Milbank, who find the liberal democratic tradition of rights to eclipse a tradition of virtues, Stout sides with a *tradition* of pragmatism. He refuses to concede MacIntyre and Hauerwas's

13. It bears similarities to Andrew Moore, *Realism and the Christian Faith: God, Grammar, and Meaning* (Cambridge: Cambridge University Press, 2003), which will be discussed below.

14. Jeffrey Stout, *Democracy and Tradition* (Princeton: Princeton University Press, 2004), p. 13.

analysis of liberalism as necessarily eclipsing virtue. The liberal version of democracy found in pragmatism, particularly in Whitman's *Democratic Vistas*, offers a virtue tradition immune to MacIntyre or Hauerwas's criticism. Thus, as Stout himself puts it, he charts an "acceptable path between the liberalism of Rawls and Rorty, on the one hand, and the traditionalism of MacIntyre and Hauerwas on the other."[15]

Has Stout successfully charted this path? To do so he must position liberalism as a tradition with virtues so that it cannot fall prey to MacIntyre's critique, which is very similar to Badiou's: liberalism inevitably ends in nihilism where a formal and fictive right triumphs over substantive goods such as truth. It tries to create social bonds not based on something good and true, but on an evil to be avoided, which may be why it is so prone to violent reaction. To make his argument Stout marginalizes the influence of Rousseau, Kant, or Mill as the architects of modern democracies, which is where pragmatism enters into the argument. Emerson, Whitman, and Dewey are the true fashioners of democracy as a tradition, and the latter is as indebted to a version of Hegelianism that emphasizes tradition as are MacIntyre and Hauerwas, although they do not always come clean on this inheritance. Stout does not argue from a putatively neutral, universal standpoint. He too stands in a tradition and defends its virtues against contending traditions. In so doing, he opens politics more broadly to persons with theological convictions than either Rawls or Rorty can do. As he puts it, "I am trying to articulate a form of pluralism, one that citizens with strong religious commitments can accept and that welcomes their full participation in public life without fudging on its own premises."[16]

If Stout is successful, then the truth of theology would not be subordinated to an overarching political discourse. Persons of faith could enter into (national) politics without the assumption that faith is so dangerous that it must be made private before such persons can be granted access to politics. Those of us with theological convictions welcome the invitation, but an ambiguity in the sentence quoted above creates a reluctance to accept it uncritically. What is the antecedent for the 'its'? Is Stout telling us that he welcomes theological convictions in his democratic tradition as long as they do not entail "fudging" on the premises of "public life" within

15. Stout, *Democracy and Tradition*, p. 296.
16. Stout, *Democracy and Tradition*, p. 296.

that tradition? Or is Stout telling us that he welcomes theological convictions without asking persons to "fudge" on those convictions? I assume he thinks he can have both. But I'm not convinced he has yet shown us how to do so, and for that reason the question as to how political liberalism can entertain the truth of theological convictions remains open. How does it not subordinate truth to power and demand the end of any theology or metaphysics that assumes truth is more basic than the will to power? I think the reason he cannot yet do so is because of his equivocation on truth. Pragmatism's non-realism, as well as epistemic and deflationary accounts of truth in the analytic tradition, cannot provide the kind of metaphysics the Christian tradition requires. They do not negate it; they walk away from it finding its questions either not worth our time or too dangerous to ask.

Stout argues that "pragmatism is democratic traditionalism," yet he also distances himself from certain aspects of this pragmatist tradition, especially in its development of truth. He states, "My most obvious departure from Dewey is my claim that truth is not an essentially relative concept." He seeks a non-relative, non-metaphysical account of truth that does not a priori exclude theological claims. This is essential to his defense of political liberalism. If a conception of truth relativizes convictions a priori, then they will be subordinated to power and have no more political status than Rawls and Rorty permit them. But if truth does not relativize theological convictions, Stout's project also faces difficulty. For to assume the 'truth' of a theological claim, especially an infallible truth such as Roman Catholicism purports to possess, the inerrancy of evangelicals, or the perfection of the Wesleyan tradition, could lead to a diminution of the social virtue of 'generosity,' which Stout identifies as a core virtue of the democratic tradition. If you think you have infallible, inerrant truth, or a perfect good, how can you be open to others who do not share your truth or good?

For Stout, liberalism's core virtue is its openness to diverse understandings of truth and goodness. Does this, as Badiou and MacIntyre suggest, become a singular identity that polices others while supposedly 'respecting' their difference? Can liberal democracy have a place for people who claim to know or embody 'the truth'? If it cannot, what could it possibly mean by diversity? For Stout, it is important that no such truth claim can finally be determined. Such a claim can only be honored (and here Badiou's open-ended Platonist truth agrees with Stout) if the truth remains open, if it is grounded in a fallibilism that allows for the virtue of generosity the tradition of liberalism produces.[17] So for instance when it comes to doctrinal differences Stout notes that "no one knows how to resolve such differences of doctrine" and to think otherwise does damage to the virtues of the pragmatist tradition. Yet this is inaccurate. Nearly every church does have a way to resolve these differences internally and they regularly do so. They also have mechanisms to resolve them ecumenically, as the Joint Declaration among Lutherans and Catholics may yet demonstrate. The question is if Stout's insistence on the irresolution of dogma is descriptive or normative? Do liberal democracy's virtues depend not only upon the irresolution of doctrinal differences but also upon their production?[18]

For Stout then, on the one hand, the truth of theological convictions cannot a priori be ruled out if democracy is to be generous and have a place for people of faith. On the other hand, democracy must relativize theological convictions if people of faith are to be generous to others in liberal democracy. Negotiating between these two positions leads to some of the most difficult and promising aspects of his proposal, which produce both difficulties and promises. The promise lies in Stout's resistance to an "aggressive postmodernity" that subordinates truth to power, a subordination pragmatism itself could support. Here he would seem to side with Reno and Guarino. Stout recognizes the peculiar problem of truth in our contemporary context and follows the analytic tradition in his analysis. He distinguishes "adjudication, justification, and truth" as "distinct concepts" and argues that they require "separate explications." The difficulties are Stout's separate explication; for once these terms are given independent explications, then we lose the interrelationship between politics, epistemology, and metaphysics.[19] Stout then thinks he can have politics without

17. Truth as a transcendental would also be open-ended, but it would not entail fallibilism. We can never possess the fullness of truth; this would be to possess God. But this does not mean we could not know truth without reservation.

18. Anthony Marx suggests that the modern nation state requires doctrinal differences for its own development. It could not arise from a "catholic homogeneity." See Marx, *Faith in Nation: Exclusionary Origins of Nationalism* (Oxford: Oxford University Press, 2005).

19. I fear this is a common problem in the analytic tradition. It divides up truth, epistemology, and metaphysics into discrete units of analysis without attending to how they influence each other. It loses any 'holistic' approach to the world we actually live in where such things inevitably relate to each other.

metaphysics. Once this occurs, the political significance of the separate explications easily gets lost under a putatively metaphysically neutral or
post-metaphysical analysis. We fail to see that the analysis of the terms
then requires a priori that certain theological positions that assume infallible, inerrant, and perfect truth(s) must be rejected before their claims to
truth are even heard.

What is truth in Stout? He distinguishes justified belief (an
epistemological claim) from truth. Justified belief is contextual, and allows
for us charitably to read those with whom we disagree. Stout writes, "If being justified in believing something is a contextual affair and if differences
in upbringing and life experience are relevant contextual factors, then perhaps our religious opponents are justified in believing what they believe."[20] This could lead to relativism with respect to truth. If truth were
justified belief it would lead to this. But Stout knows this would alienate
people of faith from democratic traditions, for it would require them to
subordinate doctrinal truth claims to something that would relativize
them. As David Novak rightly argues, neither Jews not Christians can accept any account of truth that so relativizes their convictions. "Relativism,"
he notes, is "dangerous" to any profound ecumenical dialogue, for it "denies" what both Jews and Christians affirm — "some things are true all the
time everywhere for everyone." Novak writes,

> Indeed, these claims, like "God elects Israel" or "God is incarnate in Je-
> sus," are what Judaism and Christianity are all about. In fact, Judaism
> requires Jews to die as martyrs rather than exchange Judaism for any-
> thing else, even something as similar to Judaism as Christianity. Chris-
> tianity makes a similar claim on Christians. Martyrs are willing to die
> for what they believe to be the highest truth one could possibly know
> in this world, because without a commitment to the existence of truth,
> one cannot affirm the truth of God.[21]

Can Stout find a place in the democratic tradition for such a theological metaphysics of truth? He tries to "combine a contextualist account of
justification with a nonrelativist account of moral truth," but he seeks to

---

20. Stout, *Democracy and Tradition*, pp. 33-34.
21. David Novak, "What to Seek and What to Avoid in Jewish-Christian Dialogue," in
Christianity in Jewish Terms, ed. Tikva Frymer-Kensky, David Novak, Peter Ochs, David
Sandmel, Michael Singer (Boulder: Westview, 2000), p. 4.

do this without metaphysics.[22] The democratic tradition as pragmatism assumes it has come to an end. Nevertheless, Stout seeks to undo common oppositions with respect to metaphysics, justification, ethics, and politics. That common opposition assumes certain 'packages' that one chooses. The first package would be "metaphysically realist with respect to truth, anticontextual with respect to justification, and cosmopolitan with respect to rights and obligations." The second is the mirror side of this: "metaphysically antirealist with respect to truth, contextualist with respect to justification, and parochial with respect to rights and obligations."[23] By showing us how we do not need to accept either one of these packages, Stout makes possible a 'metaphysical realism' that would allow for the kind of robust truth Christian theology requires. But he cannot finally accept this. His pragmatist tradition requires "ethics without metaphysics." Thus truth remains epistemic and free from any realism. "I am happy to say that truth is absolute if this is understood strictly as a remark about how the term 'true' behaves in our language. But I still hold that defining truth as correspondence has no explanatory value."[24]

Stout cannot find anything substantive in the equivalence schema of realist theories of truth. This would appear to be the case for both Tarski's convention 'T' as well as Alston's 'alethic realism.'[25] The latter makes two claims:

1. The REALIST CONCEPTION OF TRUTH is the right way to think of truth in the sense of 'true' in which it applies to beliefs, statements and propositions.
2. Truth is important. It is often a matter of considerable import whether a particular bearer of truth value is true or false.[26]

22. Stout, *Democracy and Tradition*, p. 239.
23. Stout, *Democracy and Tradition*, p. 247.
24. Stout, *Democracy and Tradition*, p. 248.
25. The difference between these two is that Tarski's convention 'T' is only extensional and defines truth for formalized, artificial languages. It can only address 'material equivalences.' Alston seeks a more intensional account of truth that fits with our ordinary use of the term. See William P. Alston, *A Realist Conception of Truth* (Ithaca: Cornell University Press, 1996), p. 31. Stout, like Tarski, seems to be able only to think of truth in terms of an extensional analysis.
26. Alston, *A Realist Conception of Truth*, p. 1.

Like Stout, Alston distinguishes epistemic 'requirements' from the metaphysics of truth. He also denies we must choose one of the 'packages' Stout identifies. Yet Alston questions the kind of minimalist, redundancy, or deflationary theory that appears in Stout. He notes that some find deflationary accounts persuasive for ontological reasons. "Considerations of ontological economy dictate that if we can get along without committing ourselves to a property of truth we should do so."[27] This is an interesting criticism, and it would seem to suggest a tighter connection between metaphysical realism and a realist conception of truth than either Alston or Stout claim.[28] In other words, a nominalist commitment to metaphysical simplicity drives the concern to find a minimalist theory of truth. Alston recognizes that some philosophers follow the redundancy tradition because it requires the least ontological commitment. How different this is from Christian theologians who must affirm the reality of 'beings' such as subsistent relations if they are to make sense of the worship of Jesus as God. We cannot abide by the ontological simplicity nominalist metaphysics entails if we are to make sense of what we do in worship each Lord's Day. However, nominalist metaphysics does lead more readily to a cosmopolitanism in rights and obligations because they can be given such a generic, formal understanding that they stand separate from ontological commitments to truth and goodness. This is the problem Stout identifies and seeks to move us beyond.

Stout recognizes that the key political issue before us is truth and metaphysics. But he finds metaphysically realist accounts unpersuasive.

> If the notion of correspondence is going to capture the absoluteness of truth, 'reality' will have to mean something like the world as it is in itself — a metaphysical conception if there ever was one. But this conception seems ill-equipped to become involved in a relationship of correspondence that could explain substantively what property one attributes to a proposition by calling it true. To be the sort of thing to

27. Alston, *A Realist Conception of Truth*, pp. 49-50.
28. Alston states, "alethic realism has no bearing on disputes between metaphysical realism and antirealism, but there are qualifications to be made." *A Realist Conception of Truth*, p. 79. Although he himself would be a 'metaphysical realist,' his alethic realism could just as easily be affirmed by "the nominalist about properties or the atheist" (p. 81). I confess I do not see how this works if his second premise of alethic realism bears significance. Alston seems to acknowledge this on p. 84.

which a proposition could correspond, reality has to be divided up into units that bear some resemblance to propositions. Specifying what these units are appears to involve placing reality under a description. But how can one do this without losing one's theoretical grip on the independence of the world?[29]

This is a common critique of realist theories of truth. They assume that reality must be independent of our descriptions, but we can only speak of reality under a description. It is also a reductive account of correspondence truth theories that assumes something like Wittgenstein's *Tractatus* defines what 'correspondence' means.

Milbank and Pickstock give a much more nuanced and interesting account of a correspondence theory of truth that is something more than matching units of reality with propositions. They present a threefold account of truth in Aquinas. First, "truth in God and in the world is, on the one hand, an ideal although actual reality, because it expresses desire for the good; and, on the other hand, it is real because it is convertible with being." Second, this does not make truth only abstract, for it is also a "property of all finite modes of being insofar as they participate in God." Third, "truth is in the human intellect" for Aquinas because it assumes "divine illumination" (following Augustine) and it "receives forms as species from individual material substances" (following Aristotle).[30] Here truth cannot be explained in terms of either side of the 'packages' Stout identifies. Yet truth is still a property related to what is, even as that will be the work of the human intellect illumined by God and participating in God's being via the material reality creation is. This is obviously not ontological simplicity. Nor does it reduce truth to how sentences function. What does it actually give that a redundancy theory would not provide with greater simplicity and less metaphysical obfuscation? A brief answer is that it takes into account that people want to know not how truth is used but if something like their belief in God is true and why the good and the true seem to be necessary features of being and not just of sentences, statements, and locutions.

Stout's critique raises this important question: if our grip on reality comes under a description, then how can we maintain the independence of reality of Milbank and Pickstock's richly contoured metaphysics of truth or

29. Stout, *Democracy and Tradition*, p. 249.

30. John Milbank and Catherine Pickstock, *Truth in Aquinas* (London: Routledge, 2001), pp. 10-11.

Alston's alethic realism? How do we account for the 'reality' side of the equivalence scheme when it is always presented to us in language? Alston recognizes this critique and thinks it confuses perception and judgment. For this critique to work, to perceive is to judge; that is, every act of perception already brings something under a description, which is a judgment. For Alston, this ignores "the presentation or givenness of something to one's awareness," which is something other than my subjective judgment. He recognizes, "facts are not simply given to us," but he suggests that along with the aspect of judgment in perception, there is "still an *element* of normal perceptual cognition that is different from any deployment of concepts or acts of judgment."[31] Exactly what that element is Alston has a difficult time saying (for obvious reasons). However, he shows the difference by asking us what a visual presentation of an object adds that mere thinking about it lacks.

Stout recognizes his own position could lead to the kind of subjective idealism Alston finds unconvincing. He acknowledges a relationship between this anemic 'metaphysics' and politics. He notes that some readers will argue "democratic culture needs something more solid to depend on for the justification of its commitments" than the "ethical life of a people." This appears to "leave ethical discourse without something sufficiently determinate or independent of us to be true *of*, or be *about*."[32] He does not want to collapse truth into justification. In fact, he thinks this is the problem of postmoderns who inevitably reduce truth not just to coherence of beliefs, but take the next logical step and reduce it to power.[33] Here I find myself in agreement with Stout, as would, I believe, Alston, Milbank, and Pickstock. Yet to avoid this Stout finally adopts Horwich's minimalism, preferring to call it "moderate pragmatism," and draws on Arthur Fine and Scott Soames's development of the minimalist theory of truth.[34]

In his book *Truth*, Horwich states that many philosophers and others find agreement in two "points about truth," which are "each proposition specifies its own condition for being true (e.g., the proposition that snow is white is true if and only if snow is white), and second that the underlying nature of truth is a mystery." He then claims, "The general thrust of this book is to turn one of these sentiments against the other. I want to

31. Alston, *A Realist Conception of Truth*, p. 93.
32. Stout, *Democracy and Tradition*, p. 246.
33. Stout, *Democracy and Tradition*, p. 250.
34. Stout, *Democracy and Tradition*, p. 252.

show that truth is entirely captured by the initial triviality, so that in fact nothing could be more mundane and less puzzling than the concept of truth." The whole point of minimalism is, like democratic pragmatism, to avoid any mysterious or metaphysical claims about what truth is.[35] By siding with this minimalist theory of truth, Stout tacitly agrees with the postmodernists more so than does Milbank.

As we noted in metaphysics 2, some postmodernists find metaphysics to be a totalizing discourse that needs to be deconstructed for the sake of emancipation (which seems to make postmodernity nothing but the logical extension of modernity). Stout does not deny this understanding of metaphysics, but he finds postmoderns too preoccupied with the putative ill effects of metaphysics. He states,

> But what if ordinary truth-talk has been innocent of metaphysics all along? Then disclosing the incoherence of metaphysics might deflate the pretensions of a few metaphysically obsessed professors, yet it hardly promises to uncover a nasty secret about the civilization of a whole. The pragmatic remedy is to drop the identification of truth with power, cut out the narcissism that goes with it, and recover the democratic instinct that fueled the critical project in the first place.[36]

Would that it were this easy. How is this anything more than an assertion? Ordinary language about truth is anti-metaphysical because it is not a property, it does not attach to reality, and it is primarily a matter of language. Stout's analysis assumes the conclusion — truth has nothing to do with metaphysics. It then sidesteps the postmodern critique — nor is it about power. So what is truth? The pragmatist tradition has neither helped us understand it nor moved us beyond the postmodern 'disclosure' that claims to truth are disguised assertions of power. If anything, it intensifies such suspicions.

Stout "rejects any form of pragmatism that proposes, immodestly and unwisely, to reduce truth to some form of coherence, acceptance, or utility."[37] He seeks a non-metaphysical and non-relative truth, but when he tells us what this non-relative truth is, it seems to be neither non-relative nor substantially true. He states, "What we have agreed to do, in effect, is to treat truth in practice as something that cannot be settled simply by communal agree-

35. Horwich, *Truth*, 2d ed. (Oxford: Clarendon, 1998), p. vii.
36. Stout, *Democracy and Tradition*, p. 256.
37. Stout, *Democracy and Tradition*, p. 251.

ment. It is this underlying social agreement on the use of certain words in the process of self-criticism that gives the term 'true' its non-relative sense."[38] Does this suggest something more than the assertion of a communal agreement that we will not treat truth as mere communal agreement? Is that the best the democratic, pragmatist tradition can give us? How is truth here not just a metaphysical regulative ideal that assumes no one has access to the real-in-itself, which we know infallibly? If so, then the real violation of the communal agreement will be to make substantive truth claims. Stout needs more than this if his defense of liberalism as democratic pragmatism is going to do something other than 'police' theological convictions. His important project needs to give us a more significant, and a better metaphysical, treatment of truth than this one if it is to do more than merely stand in the tradition of the redundancy theory which claims to eschew metaphysics all the while drawing upon it. It will need to acknowledge the relationship between some account of metaphysics and political and economic forms of life.

3. Truth as Inevitably Metaphysical

Deflationists argue that 'true' in our language misleads us; we misunderstand it because we see it as a metaphysical entity based on the faulty notion of correspondence. Thus disquotationalism, prosential, and performative theory all argue the true is not a property and there is nothing that it sets forth which cannot be set forth without it. The sentences where we use 'true' will not change their meaning if we do not use the term. This may be the conclusion of an inevitable trajectory once we begin with Tarski's notion of a formally correct theory of truth that eschews metaphysics a priori and seeks to develop truth only extensionally through the semantic notion of satisfaction. Once we discover that Tarski simply assumed the true and worked with it, and that his 'Convention T' ('snow is white' is true if and only if snow is white) can work when the truth predicate is eliminated, then the question inevitably rises, why do we need to continue to use the term 'true' at all? We will then have to interpret it as redundant or as a matter of 'force' (Strawson's performative theory). Or we can develop the 'weak thesis' of Ramsey, where 'true' has more of a pragmatic function. Or 'true' becomes necessary not as a property, and cer-

---

38. Stout, *Democracy and Tradition*, p. 277.

tainly not as a transcendental predicate of being, but in that it allows, as Quine suggests, 'semantic ascent.' It allows us to generalize, to point away from the sufficiency of any natural language to a metalanguage, It allows us to move from the sentence to the world through generalization. But if 'true' only has the status of this 'generalizing device,' then it seems to do little more than repeat the nominalist impulse in Hobbes and Locke. Can philosophy consistently limit itself to such an account of truth? Despite their efforts to render truth unmysterious as in Horwich's minimalism, or 'cut it down to size' as with Austin, philosophers inevitably bear witness that truth is still something more. Its mystery cannot be so easily avoided.

Deflationist theories of truth, whether they be disquotational, prosentential, or performative, prove theological critics of analytic philosophy correct. They render superfluous the language of truth; it becomes talk about talk; it is nothing but a generalizing device that can be replaced by a proform, rendered redundant by disquotation, or understood as primarily a matter of force. Are these theories compelling accounts of how the words 'is true' function in English sentences or are they the logical result of a methodological nominalism? Do they only work because they limit what questions we get to ask in the first place? Have these philosophers actually been attentive to how language works or are they implementing a program that limits language to what they find verifiable? In fact, these theories of truth, when they do not claim too much as the prosentential theory does, point to something more than semantic ascent alone. We see this with Tarski and Austin. Frege recognized it when he stated, "Truth is obviously something so primitive and simple that it is not possible to reduce it to anything still simpler. . . . What, in the first place, distinguishes it from all other predicates is that predicating it is always included in predicating anything whatever."[39] Truth is the condition in which we live; it is not a tool we use. It conditions speech; speech does not condition it.

Many philosophers in the analytic tradition acknowledge that the methodological nominalism Rorty advocates for the linguistic turn must be exceeded. Truth always breaks the bounds of language from within it. Take for example the status of concepts or subsistent universals in Tarski. His semantic theory does not eliminate metaphysical questions such as, "What is truth?" but seeks to clarify their meaning. He rejects the claim that it is metaphysical or ametaphysical. It is a (putative) neutral concept

---

39. Michael Beaney, ed., *The Frege Reader* (Oxford: Blackwell, 1997), p. 228.

that nevertheless requires more than this if we are to speak of beauty or God. He says, "Thus, we may accept the semantic conception of truth without giving up any epistemological attitude we may have had; we may remain naïve realists, critical realists, or idealists, empiricists or metaphysicians — whatever we were before. The semantic conception is completely neutral toward all these issues."[40] However, that Tarski began with Aristotle's definition of truth, and that he argued for something like a correspondence between a sentence and reality or states of affairs, led critics to accuse him of a naïve realism (F. Gonseth) and of being metaphysical (Nagel). To the first objection Tarski states that a sentence such as "snow is white" "implies nothing regarding the conditions under which" it would be true. It only implies that someone "asserting or negating" that snow is white must also "be ready to assert or reject the correlated sentence: the sentence 'snow is white' is true."[41] To the second argument Tarski suggests that the term 'metaphysics' is more a "professional philosophical invective" than a precise argument. The term 'metaphysics' can mean "a general theory of objects (ontology)," or the opposite of empiricism.[42] He does not reject the latter meaning and suggests there are needs that the semantic conception of truth satisfies that are not pragmatic. They are more like 'aesthetic' or "perhaps religious" needs.[43]

How does the semantic conception of truth meet quasi-aesthetic or religious needs? To explain this he appeals to an aesthetic argument. "I do not think that a scientific result which gives us a better understanding of the world and makes it more harmonious in our eyes should be held in lower esteem than, say, an invention which reduces the cost of paving roads or improves household plumbing." But how can the semantic theory of truth speak of 'harmony'? Thomas Aquinas, with his notion of truth as 'convenientia,' would be able to help Tarski say what appears as a gesture beyond his semantic conception of truth. Creation desires harmony because of the end it serves. Truth and beauty are convertible. But such a gesture is impermissible within methodological nominalism where truth is primarily a useful generalizing device.

Austin acknowledges that the term 'true' is an extraordinary term

40. Tarski, "The Semantic Conception of Truth," *Philosophy and Phenomenological Research* 4 (1944): 352.

41. Tarski, "The Semantic Conception of Truth," p. 361.

42. Tarski, "The Semantic Conception of Truth," p. 365.

43. Tarski, "The Semantic Conception of Truth," p. 370.

that cannot be rendered "logically superfluous" by correlating it to how ordinary terms work, like 'red' or 'growls.'[44] And in an opaque and undeveloped footnote he suggests that the transcendental predicates of being "*unum, verum, bonum* . . . deserve their celebrity. There is something odd about each of them." But acknowledging their oddness does not make room in Austin for another question of truth beyond what a conventional use of language posits. Instead he states, "Theoretical theology is a form of onomatolatry."[45] To analyze 'true' as something other than how it functions within sentences is to turn the name into an idol. While Tarski remains agnostic about metaphysical questions, Austin finds them species of 'onomatolatry.' He walks away from these transcendental predicates of being, finding something more manageable for philosophy.

As we saw with Stout, the tradition of pragmatism is an effort to bring metaphysics to an end. In so doing, many pragmatists equate the truth with what works, or with what is made. It too reduces the true to the useful and eschews mystery in favor of some kind of verification. James establishes the debate on the question of truth between 'pragmatists' and 'intellectualists' and asks us to choose between them. He begins his account of truth by setting forth a "dictionary definition" both sides could accept: truth is "a property of certain of our ideas. It means their 'agreement' as falsity means their 'disagreement' with reality."[46] But what divides these two schools of thought is the question, what constitutes agreement or disagreement with reality? He attributes to the intellectualists the understanding that for agreement "a true idea must copy its reality."[47] But he finds this unsatisfactory; the "great assumption" for the intellectualists is "that truth means essentially an inert static relation."[48] But who are these intellectualists? James does not name names, but his argument tars idealists, Platonists, Thomists, and others with this brush.[49]

---

44. J. L. Austin, "Truth," in *Truth*, ed. G. Pitcher (Upper Saddle River, N.J.: Prentice Hall, 1964), p. 26.

45. Austin, "Truth," p. 26.

46. James, "Pragmatism's Conception of Truth," in *Pragmatism and the Meaning of Truth* (Cambridge, Mass.: Harvard University Press, 1978), p. 96.

47. James, *Pragmatism and the Meaning of Truth*, p. 96.

48. James, *Pragmatism and the Meaning of Truth*, p. 96.

49. "Some idealists seem to say that they [our ideas] are true whenever they are what God means that we ought to think about the object. Others hold the copy-view all through, and the Absolute's eternal way of thinking." *Pragmatism and the Meaning of Truth*, p. 96.

He posits his pragmatic notion of truth as verification against this intellectualist tradition. Pragmatism asks the question, "Grant an idea or belief to be true, what concrete difference will its being true make in anyone's actual life?" The answer is, "True ideas are those we can assimilate, validate, corroborate, and verify. False ideas are those we cannot." This leads to his thesis, "Truth *happens* to an idea. It *becomes* true, is *made* true by events. Its verity *is* in fact an event, a process: the process namely of its verifying itself, its *veri-fication*. Its validity is the process of its valid-*ation*." Yet the supposed novelty of truth as verification in pragmatism misleads William James. This is not an understanding of truth that should force us to choose between pragmatism on the one hand and metaphysics on the other. It should not cause us to think that its realization in technology makes the world flat. We can acknowledge that we contribute to truth, which is something we see around us every day, without thinking that the true is what we construct. In fact, Nicholas of Cusa makes a similar claim, merging an 'idealist' claim of truth with the notion of truth as making, which Robert Miner calls "image-making."[50] In fact, Cusa is the first to use the term 'verification' to explain truth. But he does so within a conception of divine ideas where the true as made cannot be separated from its telos as such an idea and its connection to what is. Cusa never requires an either/or such as James's either-pragmatism-or-intellectualism. Otherwise we would not know to what purpose something is to be made or have an adequate account of harmony, which are questions James's pragmatism cannot ask. His notion of 'what works' appears to be self-evident, measured by something called 'reality,' but he cannot give us the resources to understand that reality outside of 'what works.'

Pragmatist theories of truth can replace 'is true' with 'what works,' but they cannot dispense with the true as correspondence to reality altogether. Thus they imply but cannot explicitly ask, "Works for what?" They recognize that the true requires a human contribution; it is made and therefore will be associated with language. Yet their notion of this contribution cannot avoid modern technological reductions of the true to the efficient, to its cash value.[51] A correlation theory of truth recognizes that it

50. Robert Miner, *Truth in the Making* (London: Routledge, 2004), p. 23. As Miner puts it, for Cusa, "Image-making is not inferior to the contemplation of originals. It is the closest approximation to the divine art."

51. Cardinal Joseph Ratzinger found in Vico's similar understanding of truth the un-

points to something other than sentences even while it only does so through sentences. It has a space for the true as 'extraordinary'; truth is not logically superfluous. But truth can only be correlated to an immanent 'historical event' because of its demonstrative character. It has to have a 'this' that can point and designate some object, this cat on that mat.[52] Tarski gestures toward a theory of truth that makes more modest claims for what our attention to language produces.

Davidson developed Tarski's work for natural and not just artificial languages.[53] Unlike Stout, he brings together a theory of meaning and a theory of truth. As Richard Kirkham puts it, "Davidson's idea can be seen as a fulfillment of the old adage that the meaning of a sentence consists in its truth conditions." This would seem to point in the direction of an "intensionalist" rather than an "extensionalist theory of truth."[54] But Davidson's early coherence theory would not allow for us to provide the meaning of truth. In a coherence theory of truth all that can justify a belief is another belief, where a belief is a sentence that is held to be true. We cannot give a meaning for true beyond extensionality. That is to say, rather than using the intensionalist analysis "truth means that . . . ," Davidson finds Mates's problem convincing and develops Tarski's extensionalist analysis, "S is true iff p."[55] Thus we cannot give the meaning of 'true,' and

---

doing of the premodern metaphysical world and the dominance of the modern technological one. We moved from 'verum est ens' (being is truth) to 'verum quia factum' (truth is the made). He finds this transition deeply problematic. If the true is only the made, as it seems to be in pragmatism, then such an account of truth will not be able to express adequately the logic of the incarnation. However, this should not cause us to think that we can do away with the human contribution to truth, as Aquinas and Cusa taught. In fact, this too is found in the logic of the incarnation with Mary's yes. Ratzinger, *Introduction to Christianity* (San Francisco: Ignatius, 2000), p. 59.

52. Austin states, "A statement is said to be true when the historic state of affairs to which it is correlated by the demonstrative conventions (the one to which it 'refers') is of a type with which the sentences used in making it is correlated by the descriptive conventions." "Truth," p. 22.

53. See Richard Kirkham, *Theories of Truth: A Critical Introduction* (Cambridge, Mass., MIT Press, 1995), p. 223.

54. Kirkham nicely sets forth the distinction: "The extensional project is the project of correctly filling in the blank in X is true = _____," whereas intension offers "the informational content of the expression as distinct from the set of objects denoted by the expression." *Theories of Truth*, p. 8.

55. Ernest Lepore, ed., *Truth and Interpretation: Perspectives on the Philosophy of Donald Davidson* (Oxford: Blackwell, 1989), p. 7. Mates's problem critiques Frege's intensionalism

should not seek to do so. We can only classify the conditions under which specific statements can use the term 'is true.' Rorty finds this convincing and fitting with his own pragmatism. He states, "The greatest of my many intellectual debts to Donald Davidson is my realization that nobody should ever try to specify the nature of truth." This has theological consequences. Rorty claims that following Davidson, "truth, like the God of orthodox monotheism," is "tiresomely ineffable."[56] Because God and truth are "tiresomely ineffable" all we can finally do is walk away from them. We cannot give them 'meaning'; the most we can do is list those relations between sentences and their conditions that will allow us to use the term 'true' such that it can be verifiable. True has an extensionalist, but not an intensionalist, meaning. If this is the case, then as Kirkham rightly notes, we are limited in the questions we can ask. He writes, "If we conceive of the *definition* of 'truth' as a statement of the necessary and sufficient conditions for something being true, then, of course, an extensional theory of truth does provide a definition of truth." But what it does not ask is, "What is the meaning of 'true,' 'truth' and 'is true'?"[57] An extensionalist theory of truth will not work for theology, not only because 'Deus non est genere,' but also because, as Reno notes, truth has a full-blooded and embodied character that makes it more than a generalizing device.

4. Must We Be Fallibilists?

Pragmatism not only cannot answer the question, "What is truth?" but it also admonishes us not to ask this question, at least in Rorty's case. For others, if we ask it, we should ask for something accessible, not something that exceeds its verification. Has Stout moved us beyond this? He recognizes that an anti-metaphysical account of truth could be "inherently antitheological" as it is in Rorty, and seeks to offer an argument against

---

where "whoever believes D believes D." In other words, D can be explained in terms of an "intensional isomorphism." Mates argues that no synonym for D holds in all cases and therefore intensionalism is incoherent. Jerrold Katz defends a form of intensionalism that does not assume Frege's "criteria for inference by substitution into opaque context." See Lepore, *Truth and Interpretation: Perspectives on the Philosophy of Donald Davidson*, p. 60.

56. Rorty, "Introduction" to *Truth and Progress: Philosophical Papers*, vol. 3 (Oxford: Oxford University Press), p. 3.

57. Kirkham, *Theories of Truth*, p. 22.

this.[58] He nevertheless follows Rorty and advocates his "cautionary theory of truth," which is fallibilist.[59]

Fallibilism seems to make sense. Because of this, it is a much more serious threat to Christian doctrine and practice than the hermeneutics of suspicion. The hermeneutics of suspicion assumes that every claim to truth is a disguised power play that needs to be unmasked for the interest it serves. This has become so widespread among educated Westerners that it is boring and predictable. In fact, as the philosopher William Desmond states, "The hermeneutics of suspicion is vulgar. It shows traces of a ressentiment that would expose as questionable every hiddenness of greatness."[60] Nearly every second-year undergraduate student learns this vulgarity when they are taught that claims to truth or goodness are to be met not with genuine inquiry, but with a dogmatic attachment to the obvious — "that may be your truth but it is not mine." Of course, no one could actually live the hermeneutics of suspicion in everyday life. It would be impossible because it is a scholars' trick. If the hermeneutics of suspicion were simply an adolescent oddity, it would be no more of a problem than dyeing your hair blue to cheer on a favorite basketball team. Unfortunately, it remains present into adulthood. Bernard Williams recognizes this in his *Truth and Truthfulness*. A passion for truth motivates the more superficial suspicion against it, but this does not work reflexively on those who then use that suspicion against others, nor refuse to accept the consequences if their hermeneutics would be right. As Williams notes, "The hard-pressed chairman of an English department once confessed to me that, faced with a group of faculty accusing him of being an agent of the hegemonic power structure, he would have liked to say, 'You're right, and you're fired.'"[61] If everything really were intelligible through a hermeneutics of suspicion, this would be the proper response, but that hermeneutics always trades on something more noble than itself in order to pull off its shell game before the unsuspecting.

58. Stout, *Democracy and Tradition*, p. 256.

59. Stout writes, "A fourth use [of true] is the one Rorty calls the *cautionary* use, as in the sentence, 'We may be justified nowadays in believing P, but P might not be true.'" Stout, *Democracy and Tradition*, pp. 249, 257.

60. William Desmond, *Being and the Between* (Albany: State University of New York Press, 1995), p. 22.

61. Williams, *Truth and Truthfulness* (Princeton: Princeton University Press, 2004), p. 8.

Fallibilism is much more noble and serious an undertaking than the hermeneutics of suspicion. It suggests that we hold all our truth convictions tentatively. It asks us to be open to revision based on future experimentation or evidence that might prove them to be wrong or at least revisable.[62] If we do not hold them with this kind of openness, then we will get stuck in a dogmatism not subject to revision. Fallibilism does not ask us to choose between the truth or falsity of something, but to recognize that every claim to truth always comes with an admixture of error, so that we can revise when or if the future errors are pointed out. It asks us not to think any claim we have is infallible. It would appear to have biblical support. Paul tells us we "see through a glass darkly." Nevertheless, despite its initial plausibility, I find fallibilism difficult to affirm for three reasons. First, I do not see how it can be affirmed without by the very act of affirming it, violating it. Second, and related to this first point, fallibilism tacitly assumes a truth known sufficiently without error in the future that will be able to point out the errors of my present truth.[63] It tacitly assumes something like the 'via eminentiae' and God's perfections without being able to acknowledge them. Third and most importantly, if the incarnation is true, then it suggests that the fullness of God can be found in human form, in a human sign, without any admixture of error. Truth can be present in a sign even when it also exceeds that sign.

Let me discuss these reasons in turn. Fallibilism seems to be self-refuting. If I affirm the proposition that all knowledge comes with the admixture of error and should be open to revision, then I must assume that about fallibilism itself. How would I know that the premise of fallibilism is not the very fallible premise I currently hold that will need revision once it comes into contact with a future premise, which must be at least sufficiently infallible to call into question my presently held fallibilism? Then a second question follows. Why must the premise be future? Could fallibilism be shown to be in error by something that has already occurred

---

62. Perhaps connections could be drawn between fallibilism, liberal democracy, and a certain version of nominalism. Once everything is what it is only because God wills the particular and it could be other, we must then always be willing to concede the possibility of revision. Of course the possibility of revision itself cannot be revised within this metaphysical and political scheme.

63. Newman's development of doctrine recognized the importance of this without accepting that what we now know was in error. Fuller development does not necessarily require revision.

in time, like the incarnation, where a truth is given without the admixture of error? If I can recognize error must I not know a truth that exceeds it? If this is true, then how does fallibilism make sense? Is it not more of a program than a rational argument? Andrew Moore argues that fallibilism is "built into scientific realism," and this is a realism that must always privilege epistemology over ontology.[64] We hold that we know how we do and do not know more that we know what is. This tempts theologians to hold their convictions tentatively, because we do not know what *is*, but we do know that no one knows the conditions for how we would *know* what is.

The scientific method gave rise to fallibilism, and it works well within the limited pursuits of science, but when it is given a dogmatic status that invades theology, then science has become scientism. There is an important distinction between these two. Science is a limited pursuit that demonstrates its usefulness by its amazing accomplishments. Despite the truncated history lessons one usually gets when someone invokes Galileo's case, there is nevertheless sufficient truth in that story to keep us mindful that the church has been wrong before, probably is now, and will be in the future on many issues. We must always be open to repentance. But scientism does more than call us to repentance. It replaces metaphysics and theology and offers answers, even when those answers are that there can be no definitive answers to questions regarding the nature of truth and whether God exists. Scientism is always reductive, seeking to trap us in immanent causal laws and dogmatically demanding that every claim to truth must be like the object a scientist observes through a microscope. It must be held at a distance because the instrument between the observer and the observed will one day become more fine-tuned.

Perhaps fallibilism can be defended from the charge of self-refutation. (Merold Westphal attempts to do exactly that in his *Overcoming Ontotheology*. Although he convinces me of many things, he does not convince me of this.) This brings me back to that odd phenomenon of people who gather and respond to claims that they have heard the Word of God and partaken of Christ's body. What kind of people could do such a thing and sustain it for so many years? They must be claiming to be able to participate directly in an event whereby God is present to them in signs that obtain their goal. They 'make' God present in the world. Inasmuch as anyone can do this with a clear conscience, she or he is not yet fully con-

64. Moore, *Realism and Christian Faith*, p. 60.

verted to suspicion or fallibilism. I think this is possible only among people who at least implicitly recognize by their actions that they have received a truth, which while it is always open to further development, is also irreversible and incapable of revision. This is what the church fathers gave us at Chalcedon and is implicit in our worship when Christians gather to worship Jesus as God even though they also know from the revelation to Moses that humanity is not divinity. The Chalcedonian definition does not resolve everything. It is not a comprehensive truth of the central Christian mystery, for it can never be comprehended although it can be known. Yet the church fathers certainly thought they were giving us an ontological truth as to who Jesus was without the admixture of error. To be able to receive the words of another as Christ's words, or partake of something as simple as bread and wine as his body and blood, is tacitly to acknowledge that claim and tacitly to say no to suspicion and fallibilism.

Can the cautionary theory of truth in democratic pragmatism find a place for this? Will it allow for a robust, even metaphysical account of truth, or must it, like democratic capitalism, flatten everything into a univocal global process?[65] Stout certainly seeks to include people with theological convictions in his tradition of democratic pragmatism, but his account of truth is not yet adequate because he is so committed to the end of metaphysics. He suggests that many theologians do theology without "metaphysics in the pejorative sense" so that they, like him, do not find metaphysics (now in the pejorative sense) necessary for theology.[66] Thus consonant with such theologians he can then state, "My opposition to metaphysics is not intended to rule out a class of claims simply because they refer to something beyond or above the ontological framework assumed in the natural sciences."[67] Why then does he reject metaphysics? This would seem to open up the possibility of something like metaphysics 3 or 4, but when it comes to theologians who fit within the stricture against metaphysics, Stout offers Karl Barth as an example with a less than satisfying interpretation of Barth. It is the kind of Barthianism we have seen Milbank, Kerr, and Turner critique for its Kantianism. First, Stout affirms a reading of Barth where what makes his work palatable is that it "shatters" any direct analogy from finite things to God as the "metaphysical

65. See Thomas L. Friedman's *The World Is Flat* (New York: Picador, 2006), p. 8.
66. Stout, *Democracy and Tradition*, p. 256.
67. Stout, *Democracy and Tradition*, p. 256.

explanans." Barth takes "faith as its absolute presupposition," which will not then make strong metaphysical claims about what reason could accomplish. This is acceptable for Stout. It is also fideism. What is unacceptable is that Barth still makes God necessary as the condition for ethical discourse. "Pragmatism comes into conflict with theology in ethical theory mainly at those points where someone asserts that the truth-claiming function of ethics depends, for its objectivity, on positing a transcendent and perfect being."[68] Who did this more so than Karl Barth? Barth claimed Christian dogma is ethics. Is the Barth acceptable to pragmatism the Kantian Barth who keeps God safe in a noumenal realm and a priori knows the limits of our theological language? For pragmatism, ethics must be a larger category than theological doctrine. This is the "anthropological reduction" Karl Barth and Hans Urs von Balthasar worked against. I do not think one can make this pragmatist claim and affirm Barth.

In an interesting exchange between Rom Coles and Stanley Hauerwas, Coles questions Hauerwas's commitment to Christian orthodoxy along similar lines as those which Stout raised between theological truth claims and ethics. Orthodoxy inevitably assumes a hierarchy of truths and an institutional embodiment that militate against radical democracy. Coles states, "You have defended orthodoxy — which risks a kind of hierarchy — and I think you do so out of a sense that it is a crucial condition for engendering a people who don't fear death and who might resist the politics of empire, capitalism and the megastate (and the cultures that come with these.) Do you end up with a paradox here? Namely, that undemocratic institutions linked to orthodoxy often would be the condition of radical democracy?" Hauerwas responds, "The first thing I need to say is that I defend 'orthodoxy' because I think the hard-won wisdom of the church is true."[69] Coles points to something significant. Radical democracy claims "state and government . . . draws its legitimacy from us."[70] Coles and Hauerwas agree with this. That Hauerwas agrees with this is perplexing, for if this is the case then democracy would seem to be in contradiction to the hierarchy of truths Hauerwas affirms, for this requires a political reason that can only see the truth of politics as what we make.

---

68. Stout, *Democracy and Tradition*, p. 268.

69. Stanley Hauerwas and Rom Coles, *Christianity, Democracy, and the Radical Ordinary* (Eugene, Ore.: Cascade Press, 2007), pp. 323-24.

70. Hauerwas and Coles, *Christianity, Democracy, and the Radical Ordinary*, p. 9 n. 13.

Coles then rightly questions how Hauerwas can affirm his high church orthodoxy and radical democracy. Hauerwas's response is that orthodoxy is
not politically useful; it is true.

This has an important political significance. On the face of it Coles
would seem to be correct that a textured hierarchy works against radical
democracy. Hauerwas's claim appears to be a paradox. Democracy as self-
legitimating cannot sustain by itself the freedom he needs for its legitimation. But the problem is that Hauerwas agreed early on that democracy is
entirely self-legitimating. Here is where Guarino's critique of Hauerwas
could be illuminating. What metaphysics or first philosophy, especially
what account of truth, would allow for a proper human contribution to
democracy while avoiding the flattening it (radical or liberal) inevitably
asks of Christian claims to truth and ecclesial practices? I think Mariology
will help us answer that question. It will be a faith that offers public reasons, as Hauerwas does here, which are not mere achievements of our own
will. Orthodoxy is true because of its foundation in wisdom. It is something to be received. Therefore, we must be able to present its truth claims
not only in terms of fideistic claims, for these are no threat to liberal or
radical democracy. It can incorporate them in terms of its normal interest
group politics as one more identity it affirms. We must be able to speak
about reasons of faith. They allow for a human contribution to truth at the
same time we recognize truth is a reception. This is why a fideistic reading
of Barth will find little conflict with the flattening involved in liberal or
radical democracy.

The Barth whom Stout finds compelling, and the one he advises
Hauerwas to adopt so that he will have a more critical approach to the
church and a more substantive role for "democracy and social reform," is a
Barth who so emphasizes God's freedom that it relativizes and flattens everything, including the role of the church or any practices where God's
agency and human agency cohere. This is a decisive, perhaps *the* decisive
difference between Stout and Hauerwas. Stout writes, "From Barth's point
of view, the issue is whether the church maintains a proper recognition of
the distance between the human social practices it embodies and God's
freedom to act graciously wherever and however he sees fit."[71] God's freedom means that we can never accept any identification of God's agency
with human agency, whether it be in Scripture, preaching, the Eucharist,

---

71. Stout, *Democracy and Tradition*, p. 155.

baptism, or the lives of the saints (perhaps also in Jesus?). God's freedom to be 'other' always stands over and against such identification, calling it into question. In other words, a staunchly Reformed reading of Barth consistent with nominalism's distinction between God's absolute power and God's ordained power offers Stout his defense of a form of 'Christian orthodoxy' permissible in democracy because it will not actually ask for anything. The church cannot embody in its practices any identification of God's acts with its own. If this were true, if we were to adopt this reading of Barthian theology, then it would make it easier to fit 'Christian orthodoxy' with 'democracy,' but such a fit takes place at the expense of an adequate reading of the incarnation and its relationship to ecclesiology where the church is one of the threefold forms of the body of Christ.

Stout's reading of Barth is precisely what worries Balthasar about Barth. He could not truly affirm the church as Christ's body; he always saw this as 'laying hands on God,' and curtailing God's freedom. Balthasar puts this question to Barth:

> Does the Church — knowing as she does that she has been founded by Christ — not have the right to regard herself as true? Can she relativize herself without abrogating her obedience to her Lord? And where would such a self-relativization ever come to an end? The 'absoluteness' that the Catholic Church must claim for herself really represents her obedience, her refusal to countenance any detriment or constriction to the sovereignty of God's grace. The Church has never equated the place of her visibility with that of the elect and justified. And the certainty that she possesses depends entirely on her mission and charge. For every member of the Church, even for the infallible Pope, the essence of the Church is the *promise* of salvation and not its 'guarantee'. The Catholic knows nothing of this attempt 'to lay hands on God'.[72]

Like David Novak's refusal of relativism, Balthasar's appeal to truth here is neither 'cautionary' nor 'fallibilist.' Does this mean it lacks generosity and liberality? His recognition of the church's limitations *because* of this account of truth provides a negative answer to that question. The content and embodiment of doctrinal convictions more so than the procedural

72. Hans Urs von Balthasar, *The Theology of Karl Barth* (San Francisco: Ignatius, 1992), p. 54.

form of social bonds is what allows people to live together peaceably in neighborhoods.

5. Truth, Generosity, and Love

Stout raises a serious question to modern theology's discontents. Can their theology be generous? Does it underwrite an authoritarian structure because it claims to know the truth and identifies the church's own actions with God's? He thinks Hauerwas's insistence on "strengthening one's identification with the church at the expense of identification with the nation" for the purposes of cultivating true virtue to be disingenuous and dangerous to the virtues of the pragmatic democratic tradition. He finds nothing politically radical in such an identification. It underwrites the politics of John Paul II and William Bennett, not Dorothy Day. Stout writes, "The leading political beneficiaries of Hauerwas's revival of virtue ethics appear to have been not some latter-day Dorothy Day but Pope John Paul II and former Secretary of Education William Bennett."[73] This is an odd critique to make in the context of chastising Hauerwasians for not identifying sufficiently with the generosity of democratic pragmatism and with the nation-state. Did William Bennett have an insufficient place for identification with the nation in his account of virtue? I do not see how that could be defended even though I would strongly disagree with the shape and political use of those virtues. So Stout's argument cannot be that Hauerwas's position does not serve the nation by engaging in a broad, generous discussion about political ends, but that it does not serve the nation well because it makes room for the kinds of political ends found in John Paul II and William Bennett. It must be the content of the virtues he finds objectionable, not the social form they take. I think Stout's claim here lacks a generous interpretation of Hauerwas and John Paul II, but it is telling in that it assumes a priori certain political virtues should be ruled out in democratic societies, i.e. the virtues espoused by William Bennett and John Paul II. How then can the pragmatic tradition of democracy truly underwrite the virtues of liberality and generosity? What is the content of these virtues if they are used against others?

---

73. Stout, *Democracy and Tradition*, p. 296. I don't understand why Stout equates the politics of Bennett with that of John Paul II.

Liberality and generosity are Christian virtues (as the parable of the prodigal son should always remind us). These virtues should make place for multiple identifications that allow members of modern democracies to hold a primary membership in larger, catholic social forms that will then relativize membership in those modern democracies and create limits on participation in them. Truly generous democracies would not view those limitations as threats that must be negated for the sake of those democracies. Such democracies, formed as they are primarily by pragmatic arrangements of the distribution of power, will not then be threatened by substantive truth claims that form and limit how members in those democracies can exercise and be exercised by power. It will also allow for alternative distributions of power that create a truly complex political space. Imagine, for instance, a conciliar Catholicism where a global episcopal collegium gathers to determine if certain acts of war are just and whether Christians can participate in them. If a war were declared unjust, then Christians *voluntarily* obedient to that collegium would be recognized as having an obligation to follow the truth of that council rather than the demands of the nation. Imagine a truly democratic nation that could countenance such a possibility, even welcome it for the sake of its own democratic virtues. Of course, there would have to be reciprocity for other religions as well, and nations would need to make judgments as to what constitutes genuinely good and truthful alternative distributions of power. Persons would need to make their case in public. They would need to explain the truth of their theological and political convictions. Such a public discourse could fit well Stout's "discursive core of democratic culture": "The background of material inferential properties, the expressive resources for making norms explicit, and the practices of exchanging reasons and requests for reasons with fellow citizens are, taken together, the discursive core of democratic culture."[74] Such a revitalized democratic culture would require virtues of liberality and generosity I do not think Stout's pragmatic tradition can yet affirm. Of course, both Stout's nation and Hauerwas's church face the same critique. Where is this church? Where is this nation?

If Stout's nation would practice generosity, it will need to allow persons to serve the ends of truth that are something more than 'cautionary' and 'communal agreements.' Religious persons will always find these accounts of truth to be a challenge to their fidelity to what they have received

74. Stout, *Democracy and Tradition*, p. 196.

as a gift and to which they must be faithful. This does not imply a fideism where we cannot give an adequate account of truth. Because faith seeks understanding and grace perfects nature, our account of truth should be reasonable to those outside our faith commitments, even if they do not accept those commitments themselves. How might we think of 'truth' so that it does not lose the virtues of generosity and liberality while at the same time refusing to 'fudge' on the full-blooded dogmatic truth claims of the gospel? We do not do it by abstracting from the dogmatic truth claims to some metaphysical objectivism, or by denying it through some end of metaphysics. We do it by drawing out the truth from within these dogmatic claims.

In Christian theology, truth is first and foremost a person who gives himself to us completely and without reserve. As St. Augustine taught, it is only in the Word expressed from the Father in the Spirit that we have a fullness of truth that can constitute a 'city' on something other than the dissimulation our words inevitably convey.[75] What philosophical accounts of truth countenance this possibility? Nominalism would certainly have difficulty expressing the reasonableness of such a truth. As Michael Gillespie notes,

> Nominalism presented human beings with a Christianity freed from all pagan influences; but it was also a Christianity in which Christ played only a minor role. The doctrine of the Trinity was maintained but enormously weakened. Indeed, Ockham was able to sustain this doctrine only by contradicting his own theory of universals.[76]

Although Ockham cannot be credited or accused with the limited understanding of truth within the designative tradition of the linguistic turn, it shares his inability to make sense of the kind of universals the doctrine of the Trinity requires. It is not that such 'essence' and 'Persons' are rendered unintelligible; they cannot be adequately countenanced.

The linguistic turn overturns truth, as it does metaphysics, when it assumes the designative tradition and its nominalism. Three assumptions in some philosophies of truth repeat these nominalistic habits of thought.

---

75. Paul Griffiths, *Lying* (Grand Rapids: Brazos, 2004), and Robert Dodaro, *Christ and the Just Society in the Thought of Augustine* (Cambridge: Cambridge University Press, 2004).

76. Michael Gillespie, *Nihilism Before Nietzsche* (Chicago: University of Chicago Press, 1995), p. 24.

First, truth-bearing vehicles are primarily linguistic — sentences, statements, utterances — which can be analyzed in terms of their syntactical components and semantic value. Second, truth is primarily extensional. Third, semantic ascent and the distinction between an object and metalanguage give us what we need in order to speak well of truth. These three assumptions all assume that the human agent is alienated from the world and must find her or his way back to it. For this reason an epistemology remains central that mediates between the world and us primarily through language. This raises the question whether, for good or ill, theories of truth that assume these nominalistic habits of thoughts inevitably lead to a deflationary theory of truth. Truth becomes redundant.

A more compelling philosophical account of truth (certainly not the only one), which has a key place for the virtues of generosity and liberality, and leaves open the possibility of a robust theological and ontological rendering of truth, can be found in the work of Charles Taylor. Taylor sets his own 'meaning holism' against the 'verification holism' of Quine and Davidson.[77] He suggests that verification holism errs by continuing the epistemological tradition of finding some vehicle by which our relationship to the world must be mediated. It thinks about truth primarily through 'atomic inputs' via the linguistic turn where "the basic unit has come to be something like sentences held true, or beliefs." As Davidson states, "What distinguishes a coherence theory is simply the claim that nothing can count as a reason for holding a belief except another belief. Its partisans reject as unintelligible the request for a ground of justification of another ilk. As Rorty has put it, 'Nothing counts as justification unless by reference to what we already accept, and there is no way to get outside our beliefs and our languages so as to find some test other than coherence.' About this I am, as you see, in agreement with Rorty."[78] For Taylor, this remains 'representationalist,' for it assumes that all that can justify beliefs are

77. Taylor, unpublished manuscript, chap. 2, p. 6. Taylor defines verification holism as "supposing an atomism of the input, that is, it tells me how I have to relate a number of facts and suppositions, which can be identified (although not verified) independently of each other." Meaning holism assumes "the nature of any given element is determined by its 'meaning' (Sinn, sense), which can only be defined in placing it in a larger whole. And even worse, because the larger whole itself isn't just an aggregation of such elements." I am grateful to Charles Taylor for his permission to cite this work.

78. Davidson, "Coherence Theory of Truth and Knowledge," in LePore, ed., *Truth and Interpretation*, p. 310.

sentences that can then only be justified based on the representation of other sentences. We are told we cannot "get outside" our beliefs, which reproduces the representationalist picture. We fail to follow Wittgenstein, Heidegger, and Merleau-Ponty in acknowledging "the embedding of our explicit beliefs in our background grasp of things" and instead posit beliefs as only present in sentences.[79]

Taylor finds an alternative tradition from Kant through Witttgenstein that opposes this representationalist picture and instead draws on transcendental arguments. Kant begins this tradition by acknowledging that we have no representations, no perceptions, without an "object." For Kant we are not trapped in our representations; we only have them because of the unity of a transcendental object that we cannot reduce to a datum or a "determinate intuition." It is not a mere particular, nor just an appearance. It is the "unity of apperception" that makes the object appear to us at all.[80]

Kant was unable to bridge the gap between the tacit "unity of apperception" always present in every appearance and the appearance itself, but he set us on a tradition of holism that does not begin with atomic inputs. Wittgenstein, Heidegger, and Merleau-Ponty developed that tradition and bridged the gap. Taylor describes the difference between the latter tradition and that of Quine-Davidson as the different traditions of language already noted several times: the 'designative' and 'expressive.' Taylor finds the expressive theory more consistent with the kind of metaphysical realism we have in theologians like Augustine and Aquinas because it is only the expressive theory of language that can render intelligible 'semiological ontologies' where "everything is a sign."[81] Something like this is necessary to have the complex politics noted above.

What does meaning holism make possible that Quine-Davidson's and Rorty's verification holism denies? Rorty understands the difference well: "Taylor reads his favorite authors in the light of his conviction that 'the poet, if he is serious, is pointing to something — God, the tradition — which he believes to be there for all of us.' I read some of these same writers in the light of my conviction that seriousness can, and should, swing free

---

79. Taylor, unpublished manuscript, chap. 3, p. 1.

80. Kant, *Critique of Pure Reason*, trans. Norman Kemp Smith (New York: St. Martin's Press), pp. 137-38.

81. Taylor, "Language and Human Nature," in *Human Agency and Language* (Cambridge: Cambridge University Press), p. 223.

of any such universalistic belief."[82] Why is this freedom? If there is nothing there "for all of us," how can we possibly have a politics that would be other than the best harmony of conflicting interests? Is this reasonable? Does it not show how Rorty's verificationist holism begins with the dogma that we must be free from thinking our language actually expresses anything other than what we form ourselves, what we place in a class and represent to ourselves in ways that we can then readily verify?

Taylor's expressivist linguistic turn assists theologians thinking and speaking well of God as incarnate Word without assuming we have come to the end of metaphysics or that we possess a metaphysical objectivism. It helps us speak of a hypostasis that always is and yet becomes fully creature, even allowing a human contribution, without ceasing to be divine. Taylor's philosophy of truth helps us think through the heart of the great mystery of our faith, that Mary in giving birth to Jesus gives birth to God and therefore to truth itself. This inevitably brings truth and love, reason and will, into a unity. Wittgenstein's philosophy also helps us state this well, when it is not read in terms of designation.

6. Truth, Love, and Mary

The prosentential theory of truth, with its awkward 'thatt,' ends just as did the deflationist theory.[83] Truth has no meaning beyond what is already found in the sentence. Although the prosententialists claim to be explicating Wittgenstein by demystifying truth, I think they neglect his central teaching — to recognize philosophy's proper limits. This kind of analytic philosophy often seeks to accomplish too much. It does this when it seeks the 'what' in "What is truth?" as an independent criterion such as 'thatt,' and then seeks to demystify language, rendering its metaphysical questions harmless. If metaphysics is the questions that emerge when we recognize language is not confined by its context, then we see how the designative linguistic turn is less a reasonable limitation on truth and more a program that seeks to police these questions before they arise. Once this occurs then

---

82. Rorty, "Charles Taylor on Truth," in *Truth and Progress*, p. 84.
83. 'Thatt' is called 'proform' and functions as the antecedent for any claim to truth. 'Thatt is true' just means 'thatt' where this invented word refers to all that 'is true' refers to. It is a 'prosentence.'

the only space for theological truth is either to submit its findings to the logical mechanism philosophy constructs as that which verifies truth or accept the status of theological truth claims as fideistic. Fortunately, Wittgenstein's philosophy dethrones philosophy (not reason) from this position of privilege and discloses its limits. For that reason Wittgenstein helps theologians tell the truth. Far from accomplishing this by retreating to a fideistic space inaccessible to others, Wittgenstein accomplishes this by revealing how fideistic that search for a universal, independent criterion is. For it can only be had through a detached ego that inevitably constructs its own language which must then be the vehicle that mediates between the ego (or mind) and the world through representation. Wittgenstein's critique of the solipsistic ego in both the *Tractatus* and the *Investigations* takes away the possibility of any such ego — be that of an individual or some collective — from inhabiting a space where an independent criterion for representation could be established. He does not accomplish this by retreating into some fideistic space — that is exactly what he denies in rejecting a private language; he accomplishes this by showing how language always has a public accessibility without assuming that this equals an independent criterion. For this reason, his work can help mediate between Stout's pragmatic traditionalism where philosophy does too much and any fideistic theology where philosophy does too little.

Wittgenstein teaches us that truth is not a function of language, but language a function of truth. This is not the usual way Wittgenstein is interpreted; the prosententialists, for example, claim his work as the basis for their reduction of truth to a 'proform.' For this reason it is understandable that Wittgenstein's work raises suspicions among theologians. In his *Truth and Tolerance: Christian Belief and World Religion* Joseph Cardinal Ratzinger finds Wittgenstein's philosophy to be one of the modern variants that denies truth to religion by suggesting that the historical reality of Christ's life does not matter. Whether Christ did what Scripture said he did is irrelevant, for our faith in Christ for Wittgenstein is not a matter of truth but love.[84] For Ratzinger, Wittgenstein treats all religions as relativistic, as 'fictions' that allow us to have a worldview within which we live. They are 'games' in this trivial sense.[85]

---

84. Joseph Cardinal Ratzinger, *Truth and Tolerance: Christian Belief and World Religions*, trans. Henry Taylor (San Francisco: Ignatius Press, 2003), p. 215.
85. Ratzinger, *Truth and Tolerance*, p. 220.

Would Wittgenstein deny truth to theology? Despite his many pro-testations against uses of metaphysics, if metaphysics is understood as the adequacy of language to accomplish something more than its own context would permit, then Wittgenstein's work is no part of the 'end of metaphys-ics,' but its retrieval. His realism makes metaphysics necessary even when he worries that realism is just the flipside of idealism seeking to match lan-guage in our head to things in the world.[86] Wittgenstein teaches us not to confuse representation with realism. For this reason he offers an impor-tant qualification of the correspondence theory of truth that could mislead us to think he eschews truth altogether.

For Wittgenstein, truth is not a matter of detachment, but engage-ment, the kind of engagement that love entails and that requires judg-ments based on qualitative contrasts. Ratzinger misses this important point when he distinguishes love and truth. It is not a division Wittgen-stein made. In fact, his claim that "only love can believe the Resurrec-tion" is at the same time a claim that Jesus' grave must be empty. He wrote,

> What inclines even me to believe in Christ's Resurrection? It is though I play with the thought. — If he did not rise from the dead, then he de-composed in the grave like any other man. . . . But if I am REALLY saved, — what I need is *certainty* — not wisdom, dreams or specula-tion — and this certainty is faith. And faith is faith in what is needed by my *heart,* my *soul,* not my speculative intelligence. For it is my soul with its passions, as it were with its flesh and blood, that has to be saved, not my abstract mind. Perhaps we can say: Only *love* can believe the Resurrection. Or: It is *love* that believes the Resurrection.[87]

Sarah Coakley contrasts this approach to belief with the 'Lockean/ Humean approach,' where what matters most is "evidence carefully sur-veyed, and the degree of appropriate firmness of belief on the basis of that evidence calculated."[88] She also contrasts this with an opposing 'Barthian approach,' where the Resurrection is rendered ahistorical (which is Ratzinger's rightful concern). Wittgenstein's position could lead to this

---

86. See Kerr, *Theology After Wittgenstein* (Oxford: Blackwell, 1986), p. 133.

87. Wittgenstein, *Culture and Value,* 33e, cited in Sarah Coakley, *Powers and Submis-sions: Spirituality, Philosophy, and Gender* (Oxford, Blackwell, 2002), p. 142.

88. Coakley, *Powers and Submissions,* p. 133.

'Barthian' approach, but she disagrees that this is Wittgenstein's intention.[89] Following Putnam, she denies the claim that Wittgenstein offers us a non-realist account of religious language. Instead, he offers us an understanding of 'referring' that is something other than only pointing to evidence. This notion of 'referring' is a "family resemblance notion" where "what 'referring' is is mastering the technique of the appropriate use of a word, but such use (appropriately) *differs* in different realms of discourse."[90] She sees a similarity here with the "spiritual senses tradition" where there is a "multi-level" understanding of religious language that does not deny the importance of empirical, sense knowledge, but recognizes it is insufficient without the transformation of the senses themselves. In other words, Wittgenstein's appeal to love depends on something more akin to a 'virtue epistemology.' Love is not opposed to truth; they are both necessary virtues for knowledge. You cannot know what you do not love; you cannot love what you do not know.

Love and truth are not options. Benedict XVI's *Deus Caritas Est* makes a similar argument. We can see the invisible Father in that his love, and he himself, is made visible in the Son.[91] For us to love the Son is to be on the way to the truth of God. Perhaps the best way to understand Wittgenstein is to recognize that he too makes room in philosophy for truth as following a way and loving a 'who' more so than representing a 'what.' Wittgenstein allows for a participatory understanding of truth, much as Balthasar does when he states that our "first sin" is the anthropological reduction that thinks of truth as "thinglike," as something we can grasp. Therefore, he states "sin consists in placing the measure of truth above the measure of love."[92]

It is important to recognize that Wittgenstein never taught that truth

89. This does not represent Barth's position well. It is telling that her 'evidence' for this in Barth comes from a quote from his early work, *The Epistle to the Romans*, where he wrote, "If the Resurrection be brought within the context of history, it must share in its obscurity and error and essential questionableness." She does note that McCormack offers a "sensitive recent reevaluation of history in Barth's *Romans*." Coakley, *Powers and Submissions*, p. 134.

90. Coakley, *Powers and Submissions*, p. 144.

91. Benedict XVI, *God Is Love*, p. 21 (#17).

92. Balthasar, *Theo-Logic I: The Truth of the World*, trans. Adrian Walker (San Francisco: Ignatius, 2000), p. 264. He does not then say that love must be above truth or that we would need to side with Bonaventure against Thomas or vice versa.

is just a matter of consensus of opinion. He writes, "'The truths of logic are determined by a consensus of opinions.' Is this what I am saying? No. There is no opinion at all; it is not a question of opinion. They are determined by a consensus of action: a consensus of doing the same thing, reacting in the same way. There is a consensus but it is not a consensus of opinion. We all act the same way, walk the same way, count the same way."[93] This refers to the logic of mathematical truths; can it be applied to the logic of speaking about God? To theology? Yes when truth is understood not as a function of sentences, but of a way of life. This fits well Jesus' claim in the Gospel of John that he is the way, the truth, and the life. The order matters. It also can help us make sense of John Paul II's claim that Mary is the "suitable image of true philosophy."

If we recognize this order, then we might have a multileveled politics that would avoid the errors of Constantinianism and Christendom. The flattening of metaphysics and politics in modernity gives each individual a direct access to politics such that no one can be privileged with an account of truth or goodness that subordinates others to its power. This politics gives our lives certainty even though it renders accounts of truth and goodness at best redundant and at worst private or fideistic. No one should want to live in a politics where some fideistic account of truth and goodness gains ascendancy and rules others arbitrarily. But without an adequate account of truth and goodness how is this to be avoided? If we recognize that truth is a 'way' rather than a set of propositions attached to reality or cohering with other propositions, then we might privilege those voices that embody this way, the way found in Christ's life — forgiveness, reconciliation, hospitality to strangers — as truth because it is the divine way and is universal. Because of Christianity's dogma the virtues of liberality and generosity must be extended to all. The task of the church then is not to rule, but to make this truth present in the world. Mary is the exemplar of political and philosophical wisdom.

Thinking about truth with Mary does not ask us to choose between Wittgenstein's insight that truth is participatory and must be loved and a metaphysics based on the transcendental predicates of being such as one finds in Balthasar. They are mutually enriching and consistent with the biblical witness found in Mary and in John's Gospel. This helps us address Guarino's

---

93. David Pears, *The False Prison: A Study of the Development of Wittgenstein's Philosophy*, vol. II (Oxford: Clarendon Press, 1988), p. 46.

concerns without abandoning the reasonableness of the expressivist linguistic turn and its 'soft' historicism.

Guarino's *Foundations of Systematic Theology* makes an important and highly nuanced argument that if theologians do not have an adequate account of truth, if our appeal to doctrines is only an appeal to linguistic grammar, metaphors, or cultural contexts, then we too easily lose truth and subordinate it to power. Hermeneutics becomes nothing but politics. This, of course, is easy to do in a culture like ours, so willingly tempted to nihilism and its attendant hermeneutics of suspicion.

Guarino, however, does not simply dismiss postmodern and non-foundational philosophy; he recognizes that classical foundationalism subordinated the truth of the gospel to secular reason.[94] Nevertheless, following John Paul II's *Fides et Ratio,* Guarino thinks that recent philosophical moves that "fully historicize life and culture" lose truth and must be resisted by the recovery of metaphysics, and the necessity of a metaphysical foundation for Christian doctrine.[95] He opposes historicism. Instead of accommodating it, Christian theology needs a "prima philosophia . . . if we are to undergird philosophically the church's indefeasible claims about revelation and doctrine, if we are to speak logically and appropriately about the universality, normativity and perduring nature of Christian truth."[96] Guarino does not then advocate a neoscholastic metaphysical objectivism with its 'veritas duplex.' He notes Aquinas never had such a two-fold account of truth and is open to de Lubac's critique of Scholastic developments within Thomism, but he nevertheless argues we must recover metaphysical foundations against postmodern historicism.

James K. A. Smith appears to offer a very different reading as to how theology should appropriate 'continental' philosophy. In particular, Smith challenges whether Christians need the kind of metaphysical foundations Guarino calls for in order to have an adequate account of truth; Smith sides more with a historicism. Indeed, much like Barth, he takes a 'confessional' approach to theology, which I think Guarino might find to be a species of 'fideism.' Smith bases his claim on the truth of the dogma "there is

94. He writes, "Theology can endorse neither the kind of foundationalism demanded by historicism nor the notion that epistemic primacy may be accorded to some criterion or secular epistemological or ontological warrant other than revelation itself." *Foundations of Systematic Theology,* p. 41.

95. Guarino, *Foundations of Systematic Theology,* p. 97.

96. Guarino, *Foundations of Systematic Theology,* p. 14.

no salvation outside the church."[97] As a historical entity, the church mediates God's presence to us and thus we need to be located within its history to receive God. Therefore Christian dogma does not need to correlate itself to some reason that putatively exceeds the reason already present in the church's sacred teachings. He affirms the truth of Christian dogma without any foundation or grounding of that dogma in a metaphysical reason independent of the faith itself.

This does not mean that faith and reason can be nicely separated from each other or reduced to each other, but for Smith, faith has its reasons and those reasons do not need a foundation in some pure realm of reason. For this reason, Smith can even find a way to affirm those elements of postmodern thought many would find antithetical to the Christian faith — Lyotard's claim that we now must have an "incredulity toward metanarratives," Derrida's "there is nothing outside the text," and even Foucault's reversal of Bacon's famous statement — from "knowledge is power" to "power is knowledge." Smith finds these statements to be allies because they call into question any necessary 'correlation' between theology and some secular discourse, including philosophy. (Interestingly, Smith writes as a philosopher; Guarino as a theologian.) He does not back away from the faith's truth claims, but uses the tools of postmodernity in order to show that the historical mediation of Christian truth claims bears as much reason as do those efforts to ground theology in an a priori objectivism somehow outside of history.[98] This is what worries many theologians about current trends in continental philosophy. But Smith thinks these worries are heedless. Instead, he writes, "Scriptures give us good reasons to reject the very notion of objectivity, while at the same time affirming the reality of truth and knowledge."[99] He does not shrink from Christianity's "red-blooded truth claims." He opposes any suggestion that the truth of Christianity is only "for our unique personal needs." Nor does he find it necessary to ground those truths in 'objective,' metaphysical foundations.

Both Guarino and Smith identify the most important issue before

97. James K. A. Smith, *Who's Afraid of Postmodernism?* (Grand Rapids: Baker Academic, 2006), p. 30.

98. Smith finds this to be the problem with D. A. Carson's dismissal of the emergent tradition: "Carson simply conflates truth with objectivity." *Who's Afraid of Postmodernism?* p. 43.

99. Smith, *Who's Afraid of Postmodernism?* p. 43.

Christian theology today — how do we recover Christian claims to truth from their subordination to politics, especially when the political is understood as a field of pure power. They both offer a significant advance over Stout's inability to offer an adequate account of truth for his pragmatic democratic tradition. Having identified a common problem, their remedies differ. For Smith, the Enlightenment with its ahistorical, subject-less metaphysical foundations policed against the truth of theological claims. Once we realize those foundations are built on sand, which we can do via the tools of deconstruction, those metaphysical foundations can no longer police against the truth of the faith. For Guarino, Christian flirtation with postmodern deconstruction, its reduction of metaphysics to hermeneutics and loss of a properly informed Christian metaphysics, leads to the policing against truth claims for the faith. To recover a robust account of truth, then, we must recover metaphysical foundations.

I would like to suggest that we do not need to choose between Guarino and Smith, and for that reason we do not need to choose between analytic or continental philosophy.[100] Both can serve the ends of theological truth. Instead, as John Paul II suggests in *Fides et Ratio*, the task of recovering the proper philosophical foundations of truth can best be served by "philosophizing with Mary." Wittgenstein's recognition that only love can believe the Resurrection can make good sense of this, as does Balthasar's thinking of truth in terms of Mary's *fiat*. Both recognize the important relationship between truth and holiness. Guarino and Smith point to this relationship as well, and we can bring them together once we acknowledge the divergent uses of the term 'metaphysics' in contemporary theology and philosophy. First, what Smith critiques using deconstruction is not what Guarino defends. In fact, Smith's critique strengthens Guarino's key point. Second, the kind of metaphysics that emerges from this illuminates and is illuminated by the central mystery of our faith — the incarnation. In saying yes to the Holy Spirit, Mary gives birth to God, and therefore of course — she makes truth appear. Truth invites a human contribution. Third, because truth emerges through Mary's holiness, these two concepts — holiness and truth — must, like love and truth, be thought and performed together. "Way" also comes before truth.

---

100. Reno suggests that Guarino's argument should lead us back to analytic philosophy, but I do not find any hint of this in his work. In fact, Guarino thinks the linguistic turn is as problematic as anything in continental philosophy.

While Guarino and Smith may appear to disagree — Guarino finds nonfoundationalism the problem, Smith finds it the remedy — the disagreement is only apparent because of their different uses of the term 'metaphysics.' Smith opposes, as does Guarino, metaphysics 1, 2, and 5. Smith opposes any metaphysics that would entail an objective, ahistoricism. Guarino opposes any historicism that would deny a metaphysics where language exceeds its context. But both of them leave open the kind of metaphysics found in 3 or 4. This would be a 'meta' physics that is never a pure beyond and abstract from history, but one that is found in the midst of history in the recognition that the meaning of a sign always exceeds the sign itself. It is the kind of metaphysics toward which Wittgenstein's work points. This metaphysics is not an a priori straitjacket that then determines or limits what can be said next in some objective, deductive system. Instead, it is tacitly present in our everyday actions such that it can be shown better than it could be said. It is, at best, as William Desmond puts it, 'metaxalogical.' Metaphysics is found in the "happening of the between." Being and thought (including language) can never be reduced to each other, but nor can they be successfully distanced. There is always 'excess' that escapes our systems, our determinations, our thought. But it could not escape them completely or we would not recognize this excess. Thus the metaxalogical includes but cannot rest content with univocal, equivocal, or dialectical senses of being.[101]

Smith's work on the "logic of the incarnation" presents this kind of metaphysics. It addresses "how words can do justice to that which cannot be said."[102] He never suggests that theology can accomplish this feat without philosophy; instead he calls his project a "philosophical reflection on the possibility of theology — the possibility of speaking of God."[103] He draws upon deconstruction's critique of the metaphysics of presence in order to counter Derrida's insistence that whenever we say, "God is," we commit ontotheology. This only works, suggests Smith, when we assume a modernity that reduces "the object to the measure of the concept." Once what is present must be measured by the concept, then it forces what appears into its own limited means. Violence results. Because premoderns had a

101. See William Desmond, *Being and the Between.*

102. Smith, *Speech and Theology: Language and the Logic of Incarnation* (London: Routledge, 2002), p. x.

103. Smith, *Speech and Theology,* p. 4.

"persistent awareness of the inadequacy of concepts," Smith suggests they could speak of presence (God) without this conceptual violence.[104]

If the standard for language is that the concept must measure the object, then our two options are univocity or equivocity. One might roughly say that analytic philosophy falls prey to the former whereas the latter tempts continental philosophy. For this reason, neither can be sufficient, even though both can be helpful. However, if we correlate theology to either we are caught in an unpalatable either/or, which Smith helps diagnose:

> It would seem that either one treats all objects as present-at-hand (a positivist kataphatics) thereby denying their alterity and unwittingly engaging in violence; or, one gives up any possibility of non-violent description and thereby gives up theory (an apophatics which ends in silence).[105]

By drawing upon and critiquing phenomenology, Smith concludes that the incarnation satisfies the quest of phenomenology for a transcendence to which phenomenology never quite arrives:

> The Incarnation is precisely an immanent sign *of* trancendence — God appearing in the flesh. Thus it is a structure of both presence and absence; present in the flesh, and yet referring beyond the Incarnation — as the *signum exemplum* — retains the structural incompleteness of the sign which is constitutive of language, for to constitute the God-man as only man is to idolize the body, failing to constitute it as a manifestation of the divine. Divinity, while it cannot be reduced to this body, is nevertheless infleshed in divinity and humanity, finitude and the Infinite. This is why the God-Man is a *mediator* between divinity and humanity, finitude and the Infinite. This is also why, for Augustine, all signs function as mediator*s*: they are precisely that which both appear and at the same time maintain what they refer to in their transcendence.[106]

Smith argues from philosophy to the incarnation in order to show how it illumines and satisfies philosophical reason. Smith offers a logic and metaphysics of the incarnation where the sign Jesus is so 'saturated' with

---

104. Smith, *Speech and Theology,* p. 5.

105. Smith, *Speech and Theology,* p. 6.

106. Smith, *Speech and Theology,* p. 123. The similarity between this and Taylor's semeiology should be obvious.

excess that it signifies the fullness of God. The meaning of this sign can never abstract from history, culture, or language. In fact it is to be non-identically repeated in every history, culture, and language. But contra Derrida we would never know a priori that such iterations are inevitably violent or betrayals.

Metaphysics 3 and 4 (in contrast to 1, 2, and 5) provide the "metaphysical range" (to quote Guarino) that the incarnation illumines and in turn by which it can be illumined. Smith's nonfoundational phenomenology fits within that range. This metaphysical range helps us make sense of one of the central, and often overlooked, claims about the relationship between faith and truth in John Paul II's *Fides et Ratio*. It concludes by presenting Mary as the one who can help us make best sense of the role of philosophy in theology in their common pursuit of truth. What we cannot forget is that Mary is the 'philosophical' condition by which the incarnation is possible, even though this condition is itself always a gift. John Paul II wrote,

> Our final thought is directed towards Her whom the prayer of the Church invokes as Seat of Wisdom. Her life is truly a parable which can shed light upon all that I have said here. We can perceive a close connection between the vocation of Our Lady and what is strictly called philosophy. Even as she was called to offer up both her humanity and her feminine nature so that the Word of God might take flesh and become one of us, so also philosophy is called to carry out its rational and critical task in order to enable the fruitfulness and efficacy of theology considered as the understanding of faith. And as Mary, consenting to the message of Gabriel, lost nothing of her humanity and freedom, so too the discipline of philosophy in its accepting the superabundant truth of the Gospel loses nothing of its autonomy, but discovers that all its researches are propelled towards the highest perfection. This truth was clearly perceived by the holy monks of Christian antiquity, by whom Mary was called 'the table of intellectual faith'. In her they saw a suitable image of true philosophy and realized that they must be philosophizing with Mary.[107]

107. *Restoring Faith in Reason: A New Translation of the Encyclical Letter Faith and Reason of John Paul II Together with a Commentary and Discussion,* ed. Laurence Paul Hemming and Susan Frank Parsons (London: SCM, 2002), p. 108.

If we "philosophize with Mary," we will be in the best position of "giving birth to the Truth." Truth is not less, but it is nonetheless more, than coherence or correspondence. Truth, like every sign, is 'made,' just as Jesus, who is the Truth, is 'made' in Mary's womb. Truth is produced by holiness; it is its fruit.

To philosophize with Mary is to remember, as Balthasar stated, that the Petrine vocation to office must always be in service to the Marian vocation to holiness. In other words, the purpose of the church is to recognize and acknowledge those conditions by which we can, like Mary, say yes to God and in so doing make Jesus present in the world. Those conditions are the way of holiness that assumes the transcendentals — truth, goodness, and beauty — that are the 'nature' faith perfects and assumes, for faith assumes creation.

This is the only sense I can make of one of those 'Hauerwasianisms' that once troubled me. Hauerwas used to say, "the church makes Jesus present in the world." Such a statement could be viewed as the worst form of a bad postmodernism, a purely liberal social constructivism, or a linguistic idealism. But I think it is not any of these and in fact actually fits well with John Paul II's call for us to "philosophize with Mary." It allows us to have an account of truth that does not abstract from how we live. For what does Mary do? She says yes to God and in so doing makes Jesus present in the world such that we call her 'Theotokos.' There is an important sense then in which truth as a transcendental allows us to say (with Cusa, Vico, and William James) that the true is the made. But we must, of course, never suggest that the production of truth by the human intellect, individual or collective, is itself the true, or is the only true. Our production of truth is only true inasmuch as it participates in the Truth, who is a person, Jesus. As the church fathers said in the Chalcedonian Definition, he is "begotten of his Father before the worlds according to his Godhead; but in these last days for us men and for our salvation born [into the world] of the Virgin Mary, the Mother of God according to his manhood." In other words, we have here both 'realism' and a kind of 'constructivism.' Jesus is eternally begotten of the Father before any created signs are made. He is then the foundation upon which all things come into being (1 Cor. 8:4-6); Christian theology cannot do without this foundation. Nevertheless, Mary begets him. She makes him present in the world. The incarnation is a foundation that is at the same time made. That it is 'made' requires a historicism. That it exists prior to the made entails a metaphysical foundation.

This is why a mere metaphysical realism will not help us recover the metaphysics we need to set forth Christianity's "red-blooded truth claims." Andrew Moore develops an intriguing argument that requires a Christological metaphysical realism while at the same time acknowledging the role "culture, language, and institutions play in shaping Christianity."[108] Given the thoroughgoing idealism of movements such as the Sea of Faith Network, which cannot make sense of Christian worship, Moore acknowledges the importance of a metaphysical realism among contemporary theologians. But efforts by many theological realists to argue for a mind-independent reality based on "epistemic experience of causal relatedness to reality" do not in the end provide an adequate theological realism. Instead they still assume "that it is quite possible to draw the conclusion that our experience *conditions* reality."[109] In contrast to this, Moore offers a "transcendental argument" where he asks with Barth and Jüngel, "In what sense must God be spoken of in order that our speaking is about *God?*" This leads to his Christological realism. Those transcendental conditions are not given in creation itself, but are given in the incarnation. Moore offers a convincing argument with the one exception that he does not take sufficiently into account Mary's 'yes' as part of his transcendental argument. She is the creaturely transcendental condition for the incarnation, while it of course is the condition for her creation. Moore's Christological realism would find additional support in Balthasar's approach to truth, with the addition of the importance of philosophy because of Mary's 'yes.'

Balthasar's theological dramatics and logic developed the importance of Mariology and its relationship to truth. We conclude with his work for two reasons. First, it points in the direction of the metaphysical range that offers the robust theological account of truth we need for the sake of speaking well of God. Second, it provides a question and answer to Stout's project. The question is whether Stout's defense of the democratic tradition can find place for such a robust account of truth. Balthasar's theological explication of truth also answers Stout's concern that a theological politics should have an important place for the virtues of liberality and generosity. Balthasar provides the virtues Stout calls for, while at the same time not fudging on Christian truth claims. He does so because, like

---

108. Moore, *Realism and Christian Faith: God, Grammar, and Meaning* (Cambridge: Cambridge University Press, 2003).

109. Moore, *Realism and Christian Faith*, p. 11.

Aquinas, the pattern for thinking about truth is the pattern Jesus embodies in the Gospel of John.

Balthasar follows the divine drama closely to give us the pattern for good human action. Just as Christ's Trinitarian procession requires roles for the Father and the Spirit, so in Jesus' mission, "he makes room within himself, that is, an acting area for dramas of theological moment, involving other, created persons. . . . In this way we begin to see that, while the personal mission of Jesus is unique, it is also capable of 'imitation' by those who are called, in him, to participate in his drama."[110] This imitation is a passivity that is at the same time an activity. Jesus hands himself over in obedience beginning with the incarnation and Mary's 'yes,' concluding with his death and burial.[111] In turn, Mary and others receive him and in this passive-activity make him possible. Truth emerges as the interplay between receiving the glory of God (aesthetics) and performing that glory in our own lives (dramatics). Logic makes explicit this interplay between aesthetics and dramatics. It will always find worldly analogies in beauty, human freedom, and worldly truth and therefore make common cause with philosophy. For Balthasar, truth is an "ontological, and not merely formal or gnoseological, infrastructure of worldly being."[112] Truth is more than epistemic; it concerns what is and not simply our knowledge of it.

Philosophy, then, attends to the nature, like Mary's nature, that receives the 'supernatural.' In this reception, it is not nature that perfects the supernatural, but the supernatural that perfects the natural. In fact, nature is never pure but always ordered to this supernatural end such that saying yes to it completes its own intrinsic desires. For this reason truth is inescapable, but we can never 'master' it.

Balthasar begins the third part of his theological trilogy with the "truth of the world."[113] It is important to realize that this comes after he has discussed beauty and the good and before he discusses the truth of God. He follows Scripture well; he does not begin with truth, but with the

---

110. Hans Urs von Balthasar, *Theo-Drama: Theological Dramatic Theory,* vol. III, trans. Graham Harrison (San Francisco: Ignatius, 1990), p. 162.

111. Balthasar, *Theo-Drama,* vol. III, pp. 184-87.

112. Balthasar, *Theo-Drama,* vol. III, p. 7.

113. Balthasar states that the question this book addresses is, "What role does 'truth' play in the event of God's self-revelation through the Incarnation of the Logos and the outpouring of the Holy Spirit?" *Theo-Logic I,* p. 7. That *Theo-Logic I* was written prior to the aesthetics and dramatics is not relevant to the point at hand.

irruption of God's glory and our perception of it and then moves to divine and human action before we can even begin to discuss truth. Truth is not the first but the last word for us, even though all our words always presuppose it. Only after we have participated in this glory and followed it on the way can we discuss truth. However, we never directly begin with the truth of God, but must start with the truth of the world; thus Balthasar says, "Without philosophy, there can be no theology."[114]

Balthasar helps us understand why the philosophers' failure at cutting truth down to size is theologically significant, and why we still need philosophy. The truth of worldly being is not a thing like a sentence or a 'proform,' but a mystery. "Because truth is a transcendental property of beings, a fundamental quality and constituent structure of every being [Seinendes], which therefore shares most intimately in all the breadth and depth of being [Sein] and in all degrees and forms of existent entities [Wesen], it would indeed be strange if truth could be defined, classified, skimmed over, and finished off in a few dry propositions."[115] Like Karl Barth, for Balthasar, theology is a Christological event within which its public logic works. A theologian cannot get outside of it or subordinate it to some overarching philosophical principle. However, unlike Barth, Balthasar has little to fear from such a possibility in the first place. Because God is always the ever greater, the reduction of God to philosophy cannot be successfully accomplished; it need not be feared. It is no more possible than it would be to bring truth under control by a careful analysis of linguistic structures. Theo-logic will always find analogies in creaturely existence that are analogies of being and not just faith such as Beauty to Glory; finite to infinite freedom; the "truth of the world" to the "truth of God." This is because "the supernatural has impregnated nature so deeply that there is simply no way to reconstruct it in its pure state (natura pura)."[116] What, then, does this say about worldly truth? It is never neutral because the world is always either related positively or negatively to God.[117] Thus grace perfects or contradicts the world, but can never be indifferent to it.

Balthasar engages philosophy through the transcendentals (beauty, good, truth). He recognizes that "modern rationalism" makes us choose

114. Balthasar, *Theo-Logic I*, p. 7.

115. Balthasar, *Theo-Logic I*, p. 26.

116. Balthasar, *Theo-Logic I*, p. 12. I must confess I do not always see a sharp distinction between Barth's 'analogi fidei' and von Balthasar's 'analogia entis.'

117. Balthasar, *Theo-Logic I*, p. 11.

truth against beauty or goodness. But he finds this to be a failure in our understanding of being; for "only a permanent, living unity of the theoretical, ethical, and aesthetic attitudes can convey a true knowledge of being."[118] Surely this is why he looks to the theater before he looks to philosophy in doing theology, even though it and not the theater is necessary for theology. The transcendentals cannot be defined, for to do this would be to make them categories, which is what they become with and after Kant.[119] They can be shown. Balthasar's account of truth, then, never answers the question, "*What* is it?" In fact, when worldly truth is properly analogous to divine truth, it will always remain open to something more (as we saw with Tarski).[120] It will not assume that the question "What is truth?" can be definitively answered. This has a kind of agreement with Rorty and Davidson; truth can never be definitively specified. But that does not mean the question is "tiresomely ineffable." We know truth. We cannot avoid it because we are within it, just as we are within the second hypostasis of the Trinity. We have no access to some universal space where we can stand and get a fix on truth and exhaust it by determining what mediates it to us. We have no such solipsistic ego, isolated and alone looking down upon the world.

For Balthasar, the analogy of worldly truth to divine concerns nature, freedom, mystery, and participation. As nature truth is "always present" in all that we say and do, but never complete in our understanding. Thus it also produces a desire for more. Truth is inexhaustible. We cannot do without it, and we can never comprehend it, which does not mean we do not understand it. Truth is double-sided. It is both absolute and relative. It is absolute as the "adequation to the thing as it really is." It is also relative to human freedom, dependent upon the subject's self-determination and creativity ad extra.[121] In other words, truth is both, as the early Frege taught, something 'irreducible' and yet ever-present. Thus it is absolute. But it is also, as James taught, something produced. For Balthasar we do not have to choose between these options. There is no intellectualist/pragmatist ei-

---

118. Balthasar, *Theo-Logic I*, p. 29.

119. Balthasar, *Theo-Logic I*, p. 15.

120. "The absolutely infinite openness of truth, whose very essence is to open up at every moment to even greater truth, becomes clear to the creature out of the deepest core of the truth of its created being, out of its obedient disponibility (potentia oboedientialis) toward God's truth. Yet even, indeed, precisely this openness is not the creature's autonomous possession." Balthasar, *Theo-Logic I*, p. 53.

121. Balthasar, *Theo-Logic I*, p. 41.

ther/or. This is because Balthasar follows Aquinas in understanding truth as 'participation.' For this reason all human agents are invited to make a contribution to truth at the same time that truth makes human action possible. "The human subject enjoys here a special participation in the power of the divine intelligence positively to bring truth into being, for the archetypes present in the divine mind contain the measure of the things that God has brought into existence, the measure, then, of their truth."[122] By participating in truth, we find our being both in the Idea that makes us possible and the concrete, material existence of that Idea which we make possible by following the 'way' given to us.[123] That everyone is called to this requires virtues of public generosity and liberality.

Truth, then, has both an objective and subjective component. It is the measure of being, but this does not define it, for as such a measure it is an "infinite, unmeasureable measure" which is the "identity of thinking and being in God."[124] How could we know this if we are in it and not outside it? It is not something we know, for we do not know exactly what we are saying when we say such a thing. It is the transcendental reality of the 'more' in all our thinking and acting that requires us to speak this way. It is, as Aquinas put it, the fact that "omnia cognoscentia congoscunt implicite Deum in quolibet cognitio."[125] But this is not an "immediate knowledge of God."[126] It is a summons freely to respond to God and make manifest what is always already present in every act of knowing and being. Truth is also freedom.

Truth as freedom has an objective and subjective component as well. The objective component is that what is given to us is never simply the thing, but always in excess of it. A tree is not a mere tree, but can be much more — a place for rest, material for construction, the site for redemption. We never know the 'truth' of a tree simply by matching the name to the reality. It fits within a greater drama, and understanding its truth requires placing it within that drama. Its truth cannot finally be known until, or if, the drama is complete. This requires the freedom of the subject, a freedom

122. Balthasar, *Theo-Logic I,* p. 42.
123. "Now, through this knowledge of the ideal, in which the subject lets itself be measured by God's idea of the object, it, the subject, receives analogically a participation in the act of judgment by which God metes out truth." Balthasar, *Theo-Logic I,* p. 61.
124. Balthasar, *Theo-Logic I,* p. 41.
125. *De Veritatis,* 22.2 ad 1.
126. Balthasar, *Theo-Logic I,* p. 52.

to receive, to love, to make, to witness, and even to 'administrate' truth with God.[127]

To administrate truth with God never demystifies truth, but takes us deeper into its mystery. Truth must be 'communicated,' for it is itself a communication. Three moments constitute truth: "that which discloses itself, the ontological ground" [object]; "that which is disclosed, the appearance" [subject]; "the disclosure itself as the movement of the ground into the appearance [object and subject]."[128] This threefold mystery of truth has a correspondence to both the good and the beautiful. The good is founded upon that which communicates (ground), that which is communicated (appearance), and the communication itself (movement from ground to appearance) which is also love because the communication "has no other ground than itself."[129] Likewise we find a correspondence with beauty:

> Beauty in fact is nothing other than the immediate salience of the groundlessness of the ground with respect to and out of everything that rests upon it. It is the transparency, through the phenomenon, of the mysterious background of being. In this respect, beauty is in the first instance the immediate manifestation of the never-to-be mastered excess of manifestation contained in everything manifest, of the eternal 'ever more' implicit in the essence of every being. What arouses aesthetic pleasure is, not simply the correspondence between essence and appearance, but rather the totally incomprehensible observation that the essence really appears in the appearance (which, for all that, is not the essence), indeed, appears as an essence that is always more than itself, hence, that can never appear once and for all.[130]

Even this worldly account of truth and beauty in Balthasar assumes the doctrines of the Trinity and incarnation. Taylor's expressivist theory of language bears similarities here that a designative theory could never concede. Balthasar concludes: "Finally then [truth, goodness, beauty] show that in the end everything is comprehensible and unveiled only because it

---

127. For Balthasar, humans are "joint administrators" of God's truth. This is "man's high calling and office" which is "to bear witness to the truth." *Theo-Logic I*, p. 120.

128. Balthasar, *Theo-Logic I*, p. 217.

129. Balthasar, *Theo-Logic I*, p. 223.

130. Balthasar, *Theo-Logic I*, pp. 223-24.

is grounded in an ultimate mystery, whose mysteriousness rests, not upon a lack of clarity, but rather upon a superabundance of light."[131] This leads us back to truth as participation and on to the truth of God as well as the Spirit of truth (volumes II and III of the Theo-Logic). Good philosophy, philosophy that does not seek to close us off from the world in some tight, immanent reality, will remain open to receiving this gift, a gift that can be found in language, but never identified with it. Any democracy grounded in the good, and not in a reactive evil, will also have a generous opening to such a gift, and make space for it without forcing those who cannot receive it to do so.

Truth assumes both a gift and a contribution, both receptivity and activity at the same time. It demands a contribution by the subject, who must make some kind of public, successful performance based on a consensus of action. But how does this escape fideism? Everyone knows that the next question to ask is who decides what constitutes successful performance? Whose consensus of action counts? Isn't this still just a power move by which someone's account of successful performance asserts itself against someone else's? Especially when it comes to religion? This question tempts us either toward a "craving for generality" that wants some independent criterion free from all particular accounts of successful performance by which they can be objectively assessed or a fetishizing of the particular that walls itself off against any public accessibility. This either/or is unpersuasive because unnecessary. It requires either complete translatability or utter incommensurability.[132] As Pears notes, "If the bizarre language-game cannot be translated into ours, we shall not be able to understand it, but if it can be translated into ours, it will not raise the deep question that we wanted it to raise about its suitability for discovering an independently determined truth."[133] The desire for an independent criterion of truth arises only when we ignore the obvious — if we really needed such because of an utter incommensurability, we would not be able to recognize the need for it.

Truth always assumes participation in a first truth, which makes our production of truth, its correspondence to the truth of things, and our ca-

---

131. Balthasar, *Theo-Logic I*, p. 225.

132. See Charles Taylor's "Explanation and Practical Reasoning," in *Philosophical Arguments* (Cambridge, Mass.: Harvard University Press, 1995).

133. Pears, *The False Prison*, vol. II, p. 449.

pacity to use language possible. Without truth, we could never successfully use language even if language itself is what primarily expresses it. Like Wittgenstein, truth in Aquinas does not need to set its retrospective discovery through a form of life within a community against the assumption that the world truly stabilizes our language as it is. If the latter is not true, and truth is nothing but a product of a community's language, then there would be a so-called Wittgensteinian fideistic position. But that, of course, works against everything Wittgenstein tried to show us. Pears understands that for the later Wittgenstein, "a contribution to stability is still made by the natures of the things to which we apply our words. It is just that another contribution is made by the ways in which we find it natural to apply them, and the two contributions cannot be disentangled from one another."[134] Scott Davis notes a similar understanding in Aquinas. Truth is an act of judgment made through the agent intellect. This does not make it, as Davis notes, "arbitrary, unjustified, and irrational." Nor does our contribution to truth render the category 'nature' null and void. Instead this assumes that "human beings are animals capable of overlaying their first, animal nature with a second nature that disposes them to act not on instinct but on the basis of reasons" which are "formulated in a complex language."[135] Both Wittgenstein and Aquinas assume a nature as well as connaturality; for Wittgenstein a language game has this connatural function. It does not replace 'nature.' We still have blocks, slabs, arms, voices. But how we use them requires training. To understand this is to understand how we can have both a 'natural' and 'confessional' theology without thinking they are opposed or options between which we must chose. We never need to choose between them; it would not be possible.

Wittgenstein does not teach us that truth is a matter of relativistic language games. Nevertheless, there is a kind of 'Aristotelianism' in Wittgenstein that could easily be interpreted as similar to the rigorous Aristotelianism in nominalism, which leads to an immanence that refuses to see the excess one finds in Aquinas's 'via emenintiae.' Pears suggests this kind of Aristotelianism when he states that for Wittgenstein, "the forms revealed by logic are embedded in the one and only world of facts."[136] This

---

134. Pears, *The False Prison,* vol. I (Oxford: Clarendon Press, 1987), pp. 31-32.

135. Scott Davis, "Wittgenstein and the Recovery of Virtue," in *Grammar and Grace: Reformulations of Aquinas and Wittgenstein,* ed. Jeffrey Stout and Robert MacSwain (London: SCM, 2004), pp. 185, 187.

136. Pears, *The False Prison,* vol. I, p. 23.

could be read in one of two ways. First, it negates the possibility of divine ideas because 'forms' are *only* and *exclusively* found in the 'world of facts.' They have no excess beyond the everyday realities within which we find them. Second, it suggests that the forms are not free-floating ideas separate from existing things (caricatured Platonism), but this need not mean they are exhausted by the 'world of facts.' If it is the former, then Wittgenstein and Aquinas would have to part company. 'Forms' would only be conceptual generalizing devices we produce to keep all our facts in the proper place. If it is the latter, then they would have a similar metaphysic. Would accepting the former not be the death of theology? It would make it impossible to speak of God.

How can we speak of God if the 'forms revealed by logic' are confined to the 'world of facts'? Because God is not an object in the world, God cannot be found among the world of facts alone. Perhaps all we could then have would be a purely negative theology. But as Wittgenstein notes, "a nothing would serve just as well as a something about which nothing could be said."[137] If this is all our language can claim, then it makes Christian theology and nihilism the same. We would not be able to distinguish between them. But I don't find this to be the proper conclusion in reading Wittgenstein. He makes this statement in discussing 'pain' in the argument against a private language. To understand this argument, we must first recognize what he means by 'private.' He doesn't mean that I can't speak silently to myself, or that I cannot withhold things I am thinking from public display. Of course I can do such things. Pears explains this well. Wittgenstein expands the notion of 'private' to "what I feel has intrinsic properties which cannot be captured by any physical criteria."[138] He writes, "All that he is trying to get rid of is pain construed as something completely detached from all physical criteria. If the private language argument is valid, we could not possibly speak about any such thing, and 'what we cannot speak about we must pass over in silence.' How could it possibly be discussed in casualty stations and hospitals?"[139] Pain as an internal language, cut off from public accessibility, makes no sense in emergency rooms where people do and must speak about it in ways that allow

---

137. Pears, *The False Prison*, vol. II, p. 351; Wittgenstein, *Philosophical Investigations*, para. 304.

138. Pears, *The False Prison*, vol. II, p. 350.

139. Pears, *The False Prison*, vol. II, p. 1.

them and others to know how to go on. If not, it would have to be passed over in silence.

Is language about God similar to a private language about pain? If my speech about God is like speech about a private sensation of pain, if it is grounded in some internal experience that cannot be subject to communal judgment, then theology would be fideistic and truth could not apply to it. Then all speech about God would be thoroughly equivocal and no judgments would be possible between better and worse forms of such speech. But if that is the case, how can God be openly spoken of in church, in worship, in seminary and university classrooms? Wittgenstein's argument against a secure interior space does not rule out speaking of God; it discloses the absurdity of some theological talk that publicly claims faith is a private 'sensation' or 'experience.' When theology speaks about a feeling of absolute dependence where that feeling functions privately, or when it turns revelation into a cultic, privileged epistemology, then it will have to argue against Wittgenstein. But these are the options modern theology's discontents likewise reject. Wittgenstein restates and supports rather than refutes their positions. They all refuse to retreat to some inner secure space where faith just "knows" without any publicly accessible criteria.

What, then, are the publicly accessible criteria? Here we must return again to the distinction between a verificationist theory of meaning and the private language argument.[140] To assume that 'publicly accessible' requires a verificationist theory of meaning — as, for instance, Rorty demands in his linguistic turn — will inevitably entail a theological nominalism, with all the attendant problems that both a verificationist theory of meaning and that nominalism entail. This is a temptation for any Thomist-Wittgensteinian theological reformulation of truth and language. But the argument against private language does not entail that I can then give the conditions under which my truthful speech could be verified. As Simon Critchley notes, this fails to account for the role of the theory of verification itself.[141] Upon what does it rest? Why is it given the role of arbiter? Where would one have to stand to give it such a role? A positive response to that question will have to bring back into play that questionable

140. Pears, *The False Prison*, vol. II, pp. 348-50.
141. Critchley notes that "The verification principle is a modern version of Occam's razor." He raises the question, "If all propositions must be verified by the verification principle, then how is this principle itself verified?" Simon Critchley, *Continental Philosophy: A Very Short Introduction* (Oxford: Oxford University Press, 2001), p. 106.

ego Wittgenstein already dismantled in the *Tractatus*. But it would not rule out an argument such as Balthasar's, where "consequently, theological knowledge can exist only on the basis of faith understood as the act of holding the truth of something surpassing knowledge."[142] This could not be verified on the basis of methodological nominalism, but that does not make it private or lacking in meaning. After Wittgenstein's analysis of language, it is a reasonable conclusion because we know how to go on even after a statement like this.

Public accessibility is found in following a 'way' where truth both emerges and is produced through a "unity of life, love, and language."[143] Here again we see a striking convergence among some of modern theology's discontents. This is why Stanley Hauerwas can read Karl Barth through Wittgenstein. Truth is not about description understood as designation; instead it is about witness.[144] It expresses more than a mere description can ever accomplish. If Christian orthodoxy is reduced to truth apart from the good and the beautiful, then it will inevitably produce the very liberalism it fears. Hauerwas finds Barth to recognize this fact. "Christian orthodoxy cannot be Christian truth without living Christians. In the absence of living Christians, orthodoxy cannot help but give birth to and be opposed by mystical, liberal, existential Christianity without Christ." Neither Hauerwas nor Barth ever put this claim in terms of the transcendentals, but it clearly assumes convertibility between true and good. The good characterizes a public, successful performance of truth. This refuses fideism. Hauerwas writes, "The truth that makes Christians distinct is not a truth that is peculiar to them. It is not *their* truth but *the* truth for anyone."[145] Because it is the truth for anyone, those outside the Christian community can also make a contribution to the truth of Christianity inasmuch as both share an inevitable surface grammar of what constitutes goodness and truth if they can converse at all. Likewise their critiques of Christian performance must have a place

---

142. Balthasar, *Theo-Logic II*, p. 29.

143. Balthasar, *Theo-Logic II*, p. 278.

144. Hauerwas, *With the Grain of the Universe: The Church's Witness and Natural Theology* (Grand Rapids: Brazos, 2001), p. 146. See also pp. 173-74. Hauerwas goes on to argue that for Karl Barth, "Who and what Jesus Christ is, is something which can only be told, not a system which can be considered and described" — and thus church dogmatics and not systematic theology (p. 180). Along with telling, Balthasar would add 'enacted.'

145. Hauerwas, *With the Grain of the Universe*, p. 200.

in Christian self-description. At the level of depth grammar, significant differences emerge, but this does not exclude significant convergences at the surface grammar.

Truth is an activity, a judgment that is inextricably linked to the good, and therefore to moral transformation.[146] Incandela notes that for Aquinas "the true is the good of my mind (that is, what it seeks — its goal); and so when I am pursuing truth, I am pursuing goodness. And if *that's* the case, if we pursue goodness whenever we pursue truth, the pursuit of truth morally transforms us. . . . And so the pursuit of truth, whose source and goal is God, is an adventure in holiness and *towards* holiness."[147] This understanding of truth as an activity of judgment that cannot be distinguished from moral transformation is consistent throughout most of modern theology's discontents. We have already seen this in Balthasar; we find a similar claim in Barth. For Barth, knowledge is "the confirmation of human acquaintance with an object whereby its truth becomes a determination of the existence of the man who has this knowledge."[148] De Lubac quotes St. Bernard approvingly, "It is not argument which makes us understand these things, but sanctity."[149]

Both Milbank and Hauerwas develop a similar connection between truth and sanctity. It does not degenerate into a mere pragmatic account of truth. It does not rule out first principles, and they do not rule out the importance of human making. Milbank explains this as a kind of "'reversed Platonism,' which would preserve Plato's integration of the True, the Good, and the Beautiful, and yet grounds theory in making, the original in the copy, the cause in the effect and stable beauty in the music of transition. Such a reversal is partially brought about in the Trinitarian reworking of neo-Platonic emanation — which makes emanation integral to infinite

146. This is the heart of Preller's work and the reason he begins it with the claim that "meaning is a kind of doing." Preller writes, "'Meaning' is a kind of 'doing'. The words that we use are *significant* — our actions are meaningful — in part because they are *about* things or make *references*. . . . If it cannot be shown that God falls within the range of possible referents, it follows that we *cannot intend* a significant religious act, whatever we may think we are doing at the time." Preller, *Divine Science and the Science of God* (Princeton: Princeton University Press, 1964), pp. 6-7.

147. Joseph Incandela, "An Augustinian Reading of Aquinas and Wittgenstein," in Stout and MacSwain, eds., *Grammar and Grace*, p. 30.

148. Barth, *Church Dogmatics*, I.1, trans. G. W. Bromiley (London: T&T Clark, 1987), p. 198.

149. De Lubac, *The Discovery of God* (Grand Rapids: Eerdmans, 1996), p. 111.

perfection — by the Church Fathers."[150] It is no surprise that Milbank recognizes similarities between his reverse Platonism and Hauerwas's use of Wittgenstein:

> Hence many current proponents of an 'ethics of virtue' began by insisting on 'the agent's perspective, to distinguish intentionally informed action (although not a Cartesian intention postponed 'before' the action) from mere natural causation, which can be fully comprehended from 'outside'. However, they have quickly realized that post-Wittgensteinian considerations force one to see that if an intention is situated within an action, then it is also constituted through language, and so is in principle as comprehensible to an outside observer as to the agent herself.[151]

Milbank pushes in this post-Wittgensteinian direction to avoid conceding anything like the 'agent's perspective' as that which alone renders an action intelligible. In this he is similar to Pears's criticism of Kripke's reading of Wittgenstein where for Kripke stabilization of meaning is primarily from language use by a community.

Milbank and Hauerwas agree. Milbank sees the virtue in Wittgenstein's private language argument; Hauerwas recovers metaphysics. He cites approvingly Aquinas's statement, "Since faith rests upon infallible truth, and since the contrary of a truth can never be demonstrated, it is clear that the arguments brought against faith cannot be demonstrations, but are difficulties that can be answered." For Hauerwas, this requires a defense of first principles.[152] Drawing on MacIntyre, he states, "first principles are judgments grasped intellectually through participation in the activity in which they are embedded."[153] Hauerwas does not argue that the community provides the only stable truth; he argues instead that only 'participation' in certain activities — which would be communally established — provides access to the truth of first principles. They are not known a priori; they are discovered in the 'making' en-

---

150. Milbank, *Theology and Social Theory: Beyond Secular Reason* (Oxford: Blackwell, 1993), p. 354.

151. Milbank, *Theology and Social Theory*, p. 358. He only cites Hauerwas as the "they" here.

152. Hauerwas, *With the Grain of the Universe*, p. 209.

153. Hauerwas, *With the Grain of the Universe*, p. 209.

tailed in the exercise of certain activities. This is an argument by way of transcendental deduction.

7. What Is Truth? The Encounter between Jesus and Pilate

The conversation among Aquinas, Wittgenstein, and Balthasar helps us makes sense of Scripture's use of truth, especially in the Gospel of John; for the context within which one reads Jesus' statement, "I am the way, the truth, and the life," makes all the difference. If it is read in the designative tradition, then it will become a proposition about a reality to which the language refers, which can only be justified in terms of other beliefs. Here the reality of the risen Christ will primarily be that of a singular event and its truth resides in correlating the proper sentence to the event. Our primary means for securing truth will be epistemological, not in terms of virtue epistemology, but in terms of a search for a procedure to garner evidence so that we can justify believing Jesus is the truth. Perhaps then we will become preoccupied with the empty tomb, or tabulating as much evidence as possible in order to justify the belief through a preponderance of evidence. (One thinks of the fundamentalist method of Josh McDowell's *Evidence that Demands a Verdict* or the similar methodology, albeit with radically different results, of the Jesus Seminar.) I am not suggesting such endeavors are altogether without value; they have some merit. As Frei taught, Christianity could be empirically falsified by some archaeological discovery, such as finding the bones of Jesus of Nazareth in some tomb. But a collection of facts would not come close to the truth of what we mean when we call Jesus the way ('via') and the truth. The ordering in Jesus' statement matters: way, truth, life. Following in the way comes before discerning the truth, which culminates in life. But we cannot follow the way without a commitment to pursue truth. We cannot walk away from it. Truth both presupposes and emerges from a "form of life," as Wittgenstein would put it, or from the activity of the human intellect "composing, dividing," and forming "quidditates," or definitions of things, as Thomas presented it.[154]

In the drama between Jesus and Pilate in John's Gospel, Pilate's question on truth silences Jesus, which is its intention. It is an act of power that

---

154. Aquinas, *Quaestio disputata de veritate, Opera Omnia*, vol. 3 (Stuttgart: Frommann Holzboog, 1980), q. 1, art. 3, resp.

under the appearance of seeking wisdom truly seeks nothing more than to silence any quest for it. It is Jesus who proclaims to Pilate, "I came to testify to the truth." To which Pilate responds, "What is truth?" His question, however, is not philosophical, for it lacks any love of wisdom that would seek truth. His question has only a 'critical' task. Pilate's question does not set us forth in a pursuit of truth, for he assumes he knows the answer already — *What?* is truth. Is there any concrete, sensible reality that could be the subject of truth? He assumes not. He begins by rejecting the possibility of the logic of the incarnation. His question, then, is already a rejection of the possibility that Jesus bears witness to truth. Like so many supposed learned questions before and after him, his question does not open up an inquiry, but shuts it down. Jesus is silenced.

Careful readers of John's Gospel would know that what Jesus says before Pilate is only what he has said throughout the Gospel. It begins by equating the incarnation and truth, "And the Word became flesh and lived among us, and we have seen his glory, the glory as of a father's only son, full of grace and truth" (John 1:14). That Jesus is the fullness of truth is an essential theme in John's Gospel. Jesus establishes it in the heart of the Gospel when he tells his disciples that he will go away from them. They are fearful because they cannot follow. He reassures them with the words, "I am the way, the truth and the life. No one comes to the Father except through me." He reassures them a second time by telling them he will give them an "Advocate" who is the "Spirit of truth" (John 14:6, 16-17). Both his departure and his presence through the Spirit are linked to truth.

I am not trying to make the theological point that Jesus is the truth and that somehow settles the debate. I have avoided any tendency toward fideism in theology by way of simply asserting some dogmatic claim and then either denying that it is subject to rational accountability, or affirming that its rational accountability is only internal to the standards of the faith community whose standards are then incommensurable to all other communal standards. If Pilate's question were a truly philosophical question it would not be inappropriate. It is only inappropriate when it assumes its answer, when "*What* is truth?" is asked such that the standard for that *what* is so high that nothing finally satisfies except *what?* In fact, John the Baptist asks a similar question to Pilate's when he stands before Jesus and says, "Are you the one who is to come, or are we to wait for another?" (Matt. 11:3). This is a variation on Pilate's question, but one that assumes an answer can be given. Pilate's question, therefore, can be considered *duplicitur.*

On the one hand it is a question that establishes such a high standard for an epistemic justification of truth that no answer could possibly satisfy except to question every answer. On the other hand, it could be a question that asks for something less skeptical, a public accessibility that is not an independent criterion.

In the first case the 'what' in "What is truth?" would have to be an independent criterion, universally accessible such that it abstracts from every concrete, material reality. It would require rendering asunder love and truth. This lacks generosity, for if someone loves something and is attached to it, that person cannot have the objectivity such an account of truth demands. Reason would then require that love first be destroyed. This always assumes a detached ego whose universality must also slide into solipsism and end in skepticism. The temptation of liberal democracy is to convert us to this understanding of human agency. If this is the rational standard for truth, then Jesus' claim to be truth makes no sense a priori. Pilate must remain detached from the theological drama going on before him, abstract from it, and demand, "*What?* is truth." But the alternative to truth as an independent criterion is not fideism. Pilate's question could be asking for some public accessibility; it could be read in terms of the witness of John the Baptist. It is a generous public witness that refuses to withhold truth and at the same time refuses to use violence to secure it. It is a way that may endure violence for the sake of love in order to set forth truth; for in Jesus we see that Truth itself is generous. We need not choose between truth and love. Love demands generosity and liberality, even toward enemies.

This truth requires both an undying fidelity and love, and at the same time a generosity toward others. By its refusal to subordinate itself to 'power,' understood as willful self-assertion, it best serves the tradition of democracy. For it refuses to acquiesce to the political claim that national identities must subordinate all other political identities. Its holy indifference to national identities best offers this service. Holy indifference is not indifference toward one's neighbors, but an indifference to the claims national identities seek of us. It is not oppositional; it by no means categorically rejects these claims, for that would give them too much power over our lives. They have a limited place in God's economy, but they can never be made salvific and therefore they cannot demand the same loyalty Christ's church does, which is salvific. Its task is neither to rule, nor to be a vassal. Nor is its task to be a chaplain, but to witness to Christ as Truth by making him present in the world through worship and discipleship.

Metaphysics and politics are inextricably linked. Our politics and economics have become as 'flat' as our metaphysics. Cause and effect here cannot be easily traced. Theology as a discipline that receives something from outside human making in the process of human making cannot fit within such a flat metaphysics or politics, but it can work within it and even affirm the goodness a flat world still offers. Nevertheless, faith makes possible a reason that is other than this flattening of our existence. It is an enchanted reality with multiple levels of meaning and connections to reason that always honors reason's 'autonomous' task. Such a complex space and time is not the church's creation. It is an obvious everyday reality, like the inevitable, complex, and mysterious character of truth itself. To show that publicly is the church's politics. To gather in the name of this Truth serves the common good.

Index of Authors

Abraham, William, 13
Alan of Lille, 171-73, 178
Albert the Great, 31
Alston, William P., 274-75, 277
Anselm, 47n.47, 106n.54, 160, 164n.32, 165, 182, 188-89, 195, 225, 227
Aquinas. *See* Thomas Aquinas
Aristotle, 1, 57, 75, 134, 137-39, 141, 145, 166, 174, 177, 185, 194-95, 197, 212, 243, 251, 255, 276, 281
Athanasius, 243
Augustine, 36, 47n.47, 50n.51, 79-80, 136-37, 139-40, 145, 151, 160-61, 164n.34, 179, 182, 188, 189n.76, 194-96, 206-7, 215, 225, 251, 276, 295, 297, 307
Austin, J. L., 280, 281-82, 284n.52
Avicenna, 157n.19, 228
Ayer, A. J., 248, 252, 257

Bacon, F., 304
Badiou, Alain, 266-67, 270, 271
Baillie, John, 32n.17
Baius, M., 57
Balthasar, Hans Urs von, 3, 11-12, 39, 40, 43n.36, 45-49, 60-63, 67n.103, 68n.105, 74, 78, 80, 84-93, 98, 105-9, 111, 116-17, 146-47, 154-58, 178n.61, 189n.77, 239, 290-93, 301-2, 305, 309-16, 320-23
Barron, Robert, 68n.105, 178n.61, 188-89, 199n.100
Barth, Karl, 5, 6, 10-12, 16, 19-20, 24, 32-34, 38-39, 42-48, 54-56, 60-68, 71-79, 84-89, 92-110, 113, 115, 117, 120-21, 129n.123, 134, 137, 146-52, 158, 179-80, 189n.77, 209-10, 219n.7, 289-92, 301n.89, 303, 310, 312, 320-21
Bellarmine, R., 75
Benedict XVI. *See* Ratzinger, Joseph Cardinal
Bennett, William, 293
Bernard, 321
Boland, Vivian, 124
Bonaventure, 178n.61, 301n.92
Borgmann, Albert, 232n.36
Brandom, Robert, 170n.52
Brightman, Edgar Sheffield, 190-91
Brunner, Emil, 32-33, 34n.20, 64-65, 149
Bultmann, R., 222n.15
Burrell, David, 68n.105, 89-93, 236

Cajetan, 39, 51, 74, 76, 127
Calvin, J., 75, 103n.48
Carson, D. A., 304n.98

Index of Authors

Strawson, P. F., 279
Suarez, Francis, 39, 74, 75, 184, 186

Tanner, Kathryn, 90n.10
Tarski, A., 5, 149, 274, 279-82, 284, 313
Taylor, Charles, 20, 115n.81, 118, 123, 229-
  32, 239-41, 251n.86, 296-98, 307n.106,
  315, 316n.132
Tertullian, 109
Thomas Aquinas, 7, 10n.19, 20, 28-29,
  31, 33, 34n.20, 36, 39, 42-43, 49-80
  passim, 87-93, 98-99, 109n.63, 110-14,
  117, 119-20, 124-46, 149-84, 188-91, 195-
  216, 225-28, 233n.40, 237-38, 243-44,
  251, 257-58, 276, 281, 284n.51, 297,
  301n.92, 303, 311, 314, 317-18, 321-23
Tillich, P., 222n.15
Toletus, F., 75
Torrance, T. F., 34n.20
Travis, Charles, 235-36
Troeltsch, E., 105, 219n.7
Turner, Denys, 4, 19-20, 39n.29, 40, 52,
  68, 70-73, 89-95, 98-99, 110-23, 127-31,
  135-37, 147, 151-57, 160, 208-13, 223,
  233, 238, 289

Vanhoozer, Kevin, 54n.62
Velde, Rudi A. te, 60n.79, 117n.86,
  128n.119, 164n.32, 178n.61, 204n.109,
  212-13

Vico, G. B., 283n.51, 309
Vitoria, F. de, 28

Ward, Graham, 36
Weber, M., 115
Weinandy, Thomas, 181-82
Westphal, Merold, 5-6, 7, 50n.53, 288
Whitman, W., 270
Wilken, Robert Louis, 6-7, 183
Williams, Bernard, 286
Williams, Rowan, 262
Wittgenstein, L., 12, 20, 36, 55, 58, 91-93,
  99, 104, 111, 116, 123, 131, 133, 143,
  170n.52, 174-76, 186, 189, 195, 212-41
  passim, 250, 251n.86, 253-55, 258, 268,
  276, 297-302, 305-6, 317-23
Wolter, Allen, 54-55
Wolterstorff, Nicholas, 11n.21, 26n.4,
  39n.28, 53-54, 133n.136

Xenophanes, 41, 48, 56, 79, 91

Yeago, David, 193
Yoder, John Howard, 7

Zagzebski, Linda, 13n.26, 36n.22, 68, 71-
  73, 216n.2
Žižek, Slavoj, 24, 266

Index of Subjects

absolutism, 100-102. *See also* fundamentalism

accessibility, public, 18, 30, 235-43, 316, 318-22, 325

'admirabile commercium,' 45

aesthetics, 250, 311-16; of truth, 265

'affirmatio, seu position,' 153-55

'analogia entis,' 9-10, 12, 19, 24, 42-43, 55-81, 88, 94, 121, 150, 209, 212-15

anthropology, 36-41, 44-46, 49-50, 77-79, 91-92, 101-2

Apollinarianism, 15

apophatic theology. *See* negative theology

Aquinas. *See* Thomas Aquinas

Augustine: on Aristotle, 194-95; on beatitude, 79-80; on the divine names, 189n.76, 194-95; on faith, 136-37, 139-40; on illumination, 110; on moral inquiry, 216-17; and Thomas Aquinas, 79-80, 136-37, 145, 160-61, 196, 206-7

Baianism, 57

Balthasar, Hans Urs von, and: Barth, 11-12, 61-63, 106-8, 292; Luther, 45-46; Thomas Aquinas, 154, 314

Balthasar, Hans Urs von, views of, on:

beauty, 315; Christology, 11-12, 45-46, 109, 311-15; the Church, 292; dramatics, 310-16; the five ways, 154; grace and nature, 61-63, 146-47; negative theology, 48-49; participation, 311-14; philosophy, 11, 312, 316; the 'via eminentiae,' 154-55

Barth, Karl, and: Brunner, 32, 34n.20, 64-65, 149; de Lubac, 60-61, 63, 78-79; Feuerbach, 16, 19-20, 43-44, 46-47, 56, 102-3; fideism, 93-109; Luther, 44-46; and nominalism, 107-9, 292; and philosophy, 10-12, 75, 93, 99-103; and politics, 10-11, 42-43, 46, 78, 85, 100-102, 291-92; Stout, 289-92; Thomas Aquinas, 42-43, 64-65, 98-99, 209-10; Vatican I, 115

Barth, Karl, views of, on: absolutism, 100-102; 'analogia entis,' 10, 12, 19, 24, 55-76 passim, 94, 121, 150; anthropology, 38-39, 45, 76-78, 101-2; Catholicism, 65-68, 76-77; Christology, 11, 44-45, 63-64, 67, 76-78, 96-98, 102-3; creation, 61-63; ecclesiology, 76-77, 292; grace and nature, 61-63, 76-77; history, 96-98, 107; immanence, 47-48; knowledge of God, 85, 106; language, 32-33; metaphysics, 10, 85, 101-3; natural theology, 34, 63-66, 103-9, 146-47; the otherness of God, 77-78; neo-Protestantism, 64-65; revelation, 11, 42-43, 77-78, 94, 96-99

beatitude, 57, 84, 160, 167-68; in Augustine, 79-80; God as, 165; as natural orientation, 104, 128, 161, 163, 196-97

beauty, 281, 311-16

Brunner, Emil: Barth's response to, 32, 34n.20, 64-65, 149; on language, 32-33; on natural theology, 34n.20, 64; on Thomas Aquinas, 65

Cajetan: on Duns Scotus, 74; as Thomas Aquinas interpreter, 51, 74, 127

Calvinism, 65, 75, 101, 193

capitalism, 28-29, 269, 289, 290. *See also* economics

Cartesianism, 96, 237-38, 312

Catholicism, 62-76 passim, 85, 95, 101, 271, 294. *See also* Protestantism

'causa sui,' 5, 50. *See also* god of the philosophers; ontotheology

cautionary theory of truth. *See under* truth, theories of

Chalcedon, logic of, 4; in Barth, 11, 86; in Turner, 113

Christendom, 302

Christology and: the divine names, 179-82, 185; faith and reason, 86-89, 212-13; language, 3-4, 198-99, 225-28, 258-59; projectionism, 44-48, 91; truth, 306-13; 323-26; the 'via eminentia,' 199-207. *See also* incarnation

church: dogma of, 303-4; orthodoxy of, 289-93; and politics, 293-94, 302, 326

'cogitare,' 160-62

coherence theory of truth. *See under* truth, theories of

communal agreement, 278-79, 294

'communicatio idiomatum,' 19, 44-45, 180-81

'communiter,' 160-61

confessional theology, 84, 89, 317

consensus, 207, 302, 316

Constantinianism, 302

constructivism, 10, 309

contextualization, 15, 149. *See also* projectionism

'convenientia,' 281

correlation theory of truth. *See under* truth, theories of

correspondence theory of truth. *See under* truth, theories of

covenant, 61, 103, 158

'credere Deo,' 136-38, 145-46

'credere Deum,' 136-41, 145-46

'credere in Deum,' 136-38, 145-46, 254

'cryptographic model' of language, 242-43, 255

"dangerous discord," 12, 29, 31, 35, 83, 152, 215. *See also* faith and reason

decision theory, 253

deflationist theory of truth. *See under* truth, theories of

dehellenization. *See* hellenization, thesis of

democracy, 264, 267, 326; liberal, 101, 261-62, 269, 291, 325; and pragmatism, 269-79, 285-86, 289-94

depravity, total, 1-2, 93, 163n.30

Derrida, J., on: the divine name, 52-53, 112, 236; the incarnation, 4

desire, 74-75, 79, 163, 165-66

determination, logic of, 111-12

'deus absconditus,' 77

dialectics, 47n.47, 108-9, 118, 111, 150, 165

difference, 22, 213, 266-67, 271-72

disquotational theory of truth. *See under* truth, theories of

Christology, 306-8; designative understanding of, 17, 20, 91; everyday
use of, 55, 110, 217-26 passim, 236, 253;
expressivistic understanding of, 20,
118; and impassibility, 180-82; and the
incarnation, 3-4; and 'modus
significandi'/'res significata,' 112, 130-
35, 174-76; natural and artificial, 284;
and the theory of extension/
intension, 120-21, 123-24, 129-31, 284-
85; and truth, 279-85, 295-99, 304,
316-23
language-game, 218, 253, 316-17. See also
Wittgenstein, L.
Leo XIII: and John Paul II, 151; on
Thomas Aquinas, 69-70
Lessing's ditch, 96-97
liberalism, 213, 272, 279, 320; criticism
of, 269-70; political, 29-31, 85, 209,
240, 271, 320
liberality. See generosity
'linguistic turn,' 17, 20, 32, 228-59, 295-
98
logical positivism, 149, 186, 235, 242-43,
248
'logos asarkos,' 63-64n.94, 98, 107. See
also Christology
love, and truth: 300-302, 305, 315, 320,
325
Lubac, Henri de, and: Augustine, 79-80,
153; Barth, 60-61, 63, 78-79, 99-100;
Cajetan, 74; Duns Scotus, 74;
Feuerbach, 16, 40-42, 56; Suarez, 75;
Thomas Aquinas, 74-75, 79-80, 153-54,
209-11; Turner, 208-10; Vatican I, 113-
14, 208
Lubac, Henri de, views of, on: beatitude, 57, 79-80; Christology, 63-64;
desire, 74-75, 79, 114, 154, 210; faith
and reason, 113-14; the five ways, 209-
11; humanism, 41, 43; immanence, 47-
48, 56-61, 80; interpretation of Scrip-

ture, 27n.5, 47n.47; myth, 99-100; natural theology, 63-64, 104-5, 114, 146;
negative theology, 153; ontotheology,
51; philosophy, 79-80; politics, 10-11,
78; redundancy, 38-39, 80; the 'via
eminentiae,' 153-55; the vision of
God, 74, 79
Lutheranism, 39n.27, 44-47, 180-81, 205

MacDonald, Neil, on: Barth, 78,
129n.123; natural theology, 103n.48
Mary, 132, 239, 291, 298, 302, 305, 308-11
material. See form and object
meaning. See language
'meaning holism,' 241, 251n.86, 256, 296
metalanguage, 280, 296
metaphysical objectivism. See
objectivism
metaphysics, 4, 31-32, 149-50; and the
divine names, 185-88; end of, 185-86,
188, 215, 227, 264-65, 267; and language, 215-32, 244-57; and politics/
power, 261-89 passim, 302, 326; and
truth, 276-84, 289-91, 297-98, 302-10
metaphysics, five uses of
1: 9-10, 14-15, 225, 250, 306, 308. See
also nominalism
2: 9-10, 55, 102-3, 225, 278, 306, 308
3: 9, 31, 85, 225-26, 234, 250, 289, 308
4: 9, 85, 225-26, 250, 289, 308
5: 9-10, 14, 35, 72, 81, 218, 225, 255, 268,
306, 308. See also realism
'metaphysics of presence,' 4, 22, 306
metaxological, 306
methodism, 13, 216
Milbank, John, on: Balthasar, 60-61;
Barth, 60, 98-99, 103; de Lubac, 60;
Feuerbach, 56; Hauerwas, 321-22;
Plato, 157, 321-22; Thomas Aquinas,
155-60, 210-12; Wittgenstein, 322
Milbank, John, views of, on: Christology, 63-64, 158; the divine name,

156n.15; faith and reason, 155-56, 160; the five ways, 210-12; illumination, 116-17, 155-60, 276; natural theology, 63-64, 159-60; negative theology, 155-56; ontology, 157-58; redundancy, 39-40; verification, 123

mind-world problem, 58-59, 142-43, 238. *See also* solipsism

minimalist theory of truth. *See under* truth, theories of

'modus significandi'/'res significata,' 112, 127, 129-35, 174-76, 181-82, 236-37, 243-44

morality. *See* ethics

Moses, 41, 47, 59; receives God's name, 107, 147, 156n.15, 171, 189, 194; revelation to, 153-54, 180, 185, 192, 205, 289

mystery, 99-100, 315-16

myth, 99-100, 102

name, of God. *See* divine name(s)

narrative theology, 249-50, 256

nationalism, 24n.2

nation, nation-state, 264, 269-70, 272n.18, 293-94

natural theology, 79-81, 89, 103-9, 133, 138-47, 317; definition of, 83. *See also* 'analogia entis'; faith and reason; negative theology

'negatio, seu remotio,' 153-55, 196

negative theology, 5, 48-49, 109-12, 147, 150-63, 171, 212, 318

Nestorianism, 15, 48

Nietzsche, F., on: the end of metaphysics, 8; myth, 99; truth, 49-50

nihilism, 37, 92, 270, 303, 318

nominalism: and Barth, 64, 77-78, 107-9, 292; and language, 17, 20, 175-76, 230-31, 236, 319-20; in Rorty, 123, 221, 230-21, 251-56, 280, 319; and truth, 275, 280-81, 295-96; and Wittgenstein, 253-54, 317

nouvelle théologie, 59, 113-15, 219-20; and Barth, 77, 95; and Milbank, 77, 94, 98; in Turner, 95, 98n.30, 104. *See also* Balthasar, Hans Urs von; Kerr, Fergus; Lubac, Henri de

object. *See* form and object

objectivism, 17, 188, 269; and the 'analogia entis,' 72-73, 81; and Christology, 10, 72, 298; critique of, 304; and truth, 295

'onomatolatry,' 282

ontology, 14-15, 91, 157-59. *See also* ontotheology

ontotheology, 50-55, 81; defined, 5

participation, doctrine of, 59-60, 311-14, 316-17, 322

particularism, 13, 231. *See also* nominalism

particularity of: the incarnation, 74n.95; language, 12, 17; revelation, 152

particulars, 3, 259; and language, 224, 231, 244-48, 253-56; and generality, 92, 224, 316

'passiones animae,' 243-44

Paul, 64n.96, 139, 195, 243, 266, 267n.9, 287

perception, 131, 157, 248, 277, 297, 312

performative theory of truth. *See under* truth, theories of

phenomenology, 3, 160, 228n.25, 307-8

philosophy: analytic, 7, 118, 124, 130, 228-30, 248-51, 254-58, 265, 271-72, 298, 305, 307; continental, 228-29, 248-51, 264-65, 303-5, 307; limits of, 216-19, 233-34, 238, 258, 298-99; and Mary, 308-11; and theology, 7, 79-80, 83-84, 228-29, 248-51

Pickstock, Catherine, on: Barth, 103; the five ways, 210-12; illumination, 155-60, 276; redundancy, 39; Thomas